D1175380

Women on the
Civil War Battlefront

MODERN WAR STUDIES

Theodore A. Wilson
General Editor

Raymond A. Callahan
J. Garry Clifford
Jacob W. Kipp
Jay Luvaas
Allan R. Millett
Carol Reardon
Dennis Showalter
David R. Stone
Series Editors

Women on the Civil War Battlefront

Richard H. Hall

UNIVERSITY PRESS OF KANSAS

Boca Raton Public Library, Boca Raton, FL

© 2006 by the University Press of Kansas

All rights reserved

Published by the University Press of Kansas (Lawrence, Kansas 66045), which was organized by the Kansas Board of Regents and is operated and funded by Emporia State University, Fort Hays State University, Kansas State University, Pittsburg State University, the University of Kansas, and Wichita State University

Library of Congress Cataloging-in-Publication Data

Hall, Richard, 1930–
  Women on the Civil War battlefront / Richard H. Hall.
      p. cm. – (Modern war studies)
  Includes bibliographical references and index.
  ISBN 0-7006-1437-0 (cloth : alk. paper)
  1. United States—History—Civil War, 1861–1865—Participation, Female. 2. United States—History—Civil War, 1861–1865—Women. 3. Women soldiers—United States—History—9th century. 4. Women—United States—History—19th century. I. Title. II. Series.

  E628.H35 2006

  973.7082–dc22   2006000127

British Library Cataloguing-in-Publication Data is available.

Printed in the United States of America

10 9 8 7 6 5 4 3 2 1

The paper used in this publication meets the minimum requirements of the American National Standard for Permanence of Paper for Printed Library Materials Z39.48–1984.

CONTENTS

A photograph section follows page 107.

PREFACE AND ACKNOWLEDGMENTS

The male of the species, in his brawny egotism, has to be reminded
from time to time that he has not made history alone.

Charles S. Muir, Women: The Makers of History *(1956)*

In the past eight to ten years some very significant discoveries
have been made about women who fought disguised as men or as
occasional combatants in female garb during the Civil War. The new
information, although sometimes negative—tending to disprove stories reported earlier—has more often been positive, unearthing
important details and documentation not previously on record.
Among the battlefield heroines for whom important new information has been found are Mary Ann Clark, Lizzie Compton, Mary
Owen Jenkins, Rebecca Peterman, Marie Tepe, and Loreta Janeta
Velazquez. Women who risked their lives in other capacities, particularly those who acted as couriers and spies, scouts and saboteurs, have been included in Appendix A, Honor Roll of Civil War
Service, and Chapter 5 discusses their exploits during field duty.

The burgeoning of databases on the internet in recent years
has made possible far more historical detective work for validat-
ing stories of female soldiers in the American Civil War than
before. The new resources include online genealogy and history
databases containing unit histories and rosters, the army *Official
Records of the Union and Confederate Armies* on CD-ROM, and
powerful search engines. Also, a large number of Civil War web
sites have sprung up on the internet, often containing unit rosters, soldier letters, and other information lovingly placed there
by descendants of Civil War soldiers.

Since my previous book on this subject, *Patriots in Disguise:
Women Warriors of the Civil War* (1993), I have gained access
to a large amount of new information relating to the service of
women on field duty during the Civil War. As a result, it seemed
to be time to take stock of where we stood in regard to the

numbers of female soldiers, whether serving openly or in male disguise, and the historical documentation of their stories. Accordingly, I have reread original sources whenever possible, reinvestigated the reports, and attempted to reevaluate their credibility in light of current knowledge. During this endeavor I have functioned as an investigative reporter, constantly checking details and trying to follow the facts wherever they might lead.

The publishers of *Patriots in Disguise* chose "warriors" for the subtitle; I preferred "soldiers," which comes closest to my intended message. That is, these women trained, marched, camped, and campaigned in the field, many experiencing the violence of the battlefield exactly as soldiers have done throughout history. Not all of them were "warriors" or "heroines"; in fact, some failed miserably to disguise their gender and were unceremoniously discharged. Their intentions and their determination to serve the cause, however, were praiseworthy.

My historical "detective work" occasionally has turned up surprising results. Some cases that seemed well founded, and even had multiple sources, did not check out and must be either considered suspect or discarded entirely. Some don't quite measure up because of missing information, but they still might be true; still others are considered apocryphal (see Chapters 8 and 9). In other cases I uncovered strong confirmation or additional support, and I found quite a few new cases as well. Obviously, there are a lot of loose ends that only continued intensive research can possibly tie up. Although I have included as comprehensive a list of cases as possible, undoubtedly many others have been missed and dozens more await discovery.

Results of the Civil War regimental roster searches reported here must be interpreted cautiously and considered to be tentative findings. Many of the unit rosters are fragmentary, or "works in progress," rather than comprehensive and definitive. The search results often tend to be more meaningful when there is a positive "hit" than when no confirmation is found, though sometimes the lack of confirmation is significant as well. In any given case, the completeness and reliability of the published rosters must be taken into account.

A number of cases of female soldiers who served with known male aliases have been confirmed by records in the National Archives, yet the male names do not appear on the published rosters. After obtaining this negative finding several times, I began to suspect that expunging of records must have occurred on some occasions when soldiers were found to be female. Possibly the officers involved may have been embarrassed to admit that a woman in male disguise had fooled them.

My research also has strongly suggested that nineteenth-century news reporting on the war contained a fairly high level of garbled information. The stories often contain the wrong unit designations and wrong information about battles participated in, but are essentially accurate in other respects. These distortions have introduced errors in later books and articles about female soldiers (including some of my own writings), caused confusion about some of the stories, and complicated the search for documentation. I have tried to set the record straight on many specific points in this book.

In reexamining the historical record, I have gone back to the earliest versions of the individual stories that I was able to find, focusing on contemporary accounts from the 1860s whenever possible, and reevaluated them. On the other hand, I have accessed the very latest databases of regimental histories and rosters available to search for verification or disproof of each story. This alpha and omega approach has yielded some interesting findings.

Revolutionary War naval hero John Paul Jones is reported to have said, "I wish to have no connection with any ship that does not sail fast, for I intend to go in harm's way." The results of my new research into the stories of women who voluntarily went "in harm's way" during the Civil War are here combined with the research of others to provide a synthesis of what we now know and how we know it. Although our combined efforts have yielded a lot of new information, there is much work yet to be done.

Any author who engages in continuing historical research and builds on the collective work of others owes a debt of gratitude to the hundreds of people involved in a collegial effort to record and analyze the documentary record. Some of the most helpful, influential, and inspirational people who have contributed to this effort, actively or passively, are named here.

For early inspiration, I am indebted to Sarah Emma Edmonds, whose autobiography originally piqued my interest, and Mary Elizabeth Massey, for her truly pioneering 1966 book, *Bonnet Brigades,* subtitled on the dust jacket *American Women and the Civil War.*

I am particularly grateful to my friend and colleague C. Kay Larson for her pioneering research into the roles of women in the Civil War and for lots of practical help and support. Two other research colleagues who have been helpful and supportive are Stuart Sprague and the late Lee Middleton.

Grace Fleming of Winder, Georgia, kindly provided a draft of the information in Chapter 10 about the activities of African American women during the Civil War, based on her extensive personal research.

Fellow Civil War author Wendy King has generously provided help, advice, and specific leads on many cases.

Captain Barbara A. Wilson, USAF Ret. ("Capt. Barb"), a twentieth- and twenty-first-century female soldier, has been supportive of my work, and her web site (http://userpages.aug.com/captbarb) is a useful source of information about the historical role of women in the military.

Vicki Betts, Research Librarian, University of Texas–Tyler, maintains an online database of newspaper excerpts from the Civil War period that has been an invaluable source of information.

Richard Dobbins, Historical Data Systems online *American Civil War Research Database*, Duxbury, Massachusetts (http://www.civilwardata .com), has provided a powerful and immensely useful Civil War research tool. (For simplicity's sake, it is referred to in the text as the Civil War Database.)

Dr. Elizabeth Leonard, and DeAnne Blanton with Lauren M. Cook, have contributed two of the most important recent books about women in the Civil War; they are cited in the bibliography and frequently in the endnotes.

Librarian and fellow author Lynda L. Sudlow was very responsive to my queries related to her excellent book about Maine's contribution of women to the war effort, *A Vast Army of Women*.

Susanne Greenhagen, State University of New York–Morrisville, College of Agriculture and Technology, College Library, provided helpful postwar information about Kady C. Brownell.

Finally, the presentation of information in this book has been noticeably enhanced by my copyeditor, Martha Whitt, whose care for accuracy and attention to detail made a significant contribution.

Richard H. Hall
Brentwood, Maryland

The war for the preservation of our Union evidently did much to
advance the best interests of woman. It created a necessity for her
labor in new and untried ways. It gave her an opportunity to prove
her ability, and also to cultivate that true courage without which the
most capable person may utterly fail of success.
    Vesta M. W. Swarts, M.D., army nurse during the Civil War, in
    Mary A. Gardner Holland, Our Army Nurses *(1897)*

Women who voluntarily engaged in military activities during the
Civil War came from across the economic and social spectrum,
ranging from poor and sometimes illiterate young girls to highly
educated upper-class women. What they had in common was a
desire to participate directly in the great struggle then under way
to determine the future of the United States of America. This desire to participate, in turn, was a reflection of women's growing
independence and their struggle for equality.

   The American Civil War had its roots in the early nineteenth-
century growing pains of the fledgling country. As settlers spread
westward across the continent, remote territories were gradually
populated and new states were formed in a climate of dynamic
growth and expansion, diverse ethnic populations, differing social
and cultural values, and urban versus rural lifestyles. Members
of all the various elements sought political influence to advance
their particular viewpoint. In her pioneering book about women's
activities during the Civil War, Mary Elizabeth Massey observes,

   The thirty years preceding the Civil War were marked
   by the nation's physical growth and expansion, economic
   diversification, democratic advancement, intellectual
   progress, and tragic sectional hostility. Time-honored
   traditions, attacked from all sides by exponents of new
   ideologies, were just as determinedly defended by spokesmen
   of the *status quo....* most [women] were too busy being
   wives and mothers to participate actively in any movement

which would take them beyond home and church. Yet an ever-increasing number were becoming economically self-sufficient, better educated, and more demanding. . . . There were very few who could be classified as "strong-minded" crusaders for woman's rights and they were confined primarily to Northeastern urban areas, but the few were exceedingly noisy. Others showed signs of being restless but by no means rebellious, and the overwhelming majority were completely indifferent to the movement.[1]

Since the 1820s, a socially subversive movement in the northeastern states manifested a new activism on the part of women. No longer content to be passive ornaments or completely subservient to men, women leaders had begun speaking out for new rights: the right to agitate for social reform, the right to be accepted in occupations generally restricted to males, and the right to vote. To accomplish these goals, women began forming coalitions or associations dedicated to specific reform activities directed at perceived social ills.

In the 1830s and 1840s women's benevolent associations—like the Female Anti-Slavery Society (1835) and Female Moral Reform Society (1836) in Rochester, New York—began to embody both moral reform crusades and women's rights campaigns in interlocking fashion. The overall movement contained threads of white Anglo-Saxon Protestant values, Quakerism, and revivalism, among others. But because of deeply entrenched attitudes about gender roles, women found strong resistance to their entry into public life. As Professor Lori D. Ginzberg observes,

> On the one hand, woman's rights activists seemed genuinely surprised that most Americans did not share their indignation toward women's exclusion from the rights to become educated, hold property, travel and speak freely, and vote. Schooled in a condition of Enlightenment thinking, they experienced women's lack of rights as an inconsistency in the principles of the nation. For most Americans, however, women's role as wife precluded any claims they might make as citizens; women, they maintained, had designated their representatives when they chose their husbands. . . . Suggesting that women be given an individual vote undermined the very notion of a man's ownership of his household and his command of his dependents.[2]

Professor Ginzberg further notes that "by the 1840s, women's presence at political rallies and among campaign supporters had grown so familiar that some political parties, notably the Whigs, drew on the language of domesticity and female morality to describe their own appeal to voters."[3]

The women's movement, catalyzed by many different social threads and individual grievances, began to crystallize around three main issues: vice (i.e., immoral conduct), intemperance, and slavery. Eventually women began to think of themselves as victims of human bondage and increasingly identified themselves more strongly with black slaves. When women found themselves essentially powerless to bring about social reforms, they began campaigning for their own social and political rights. Since moral suasion alone was inadequate, political power and influence was needed to accomplish their goals.

A hardcore group of radical reformers in the Northeast tended to believe that slavery was at the center of all the nation's problems, and its abolition was viewed as being essential to moral progress. African American women in Salem, Massachusetts, were the first to organize a female abolition society in 1832. A May 1837 Convention of American Anti-Slavery Women in New York City presented a lineup of all female speakers.[4]

The landmark event for women at midcentury was the now-famous Woman's Rights Convention held at Seneca Falls, New York, in July 1848. Widely seen as a seminal event, the convention established a firm link between opposition to slavery and women's desire to be free of oppression—or, as Ginzberg expresses it, "woman's growing identification with the oppressed."[5] The resolutions passed at Seneca Falls called for equal treatment of women under the law and for women's suffrage. Although definite headway was made on several women's issues during the latter half of the century, the right to vote was not attained until 1920. The Seneca Falls conference organizers were Lucretia Mott and Elizabeth Cady Stanton. Among the 250 to 300 in attendance were about 40 men, including noted abolitionist and author Frederick Douglass.[6]

Young girls growing up in the 1840s and 1850s inevitably were exposed to this social and intellectual ferment in their own households. By the time of the Civil War, a gradually changing social order had led to countless young Northern women becoming teenagers or young adults in households whose adult females had begun to introduce many liberating influences. Often, in middle- and upper-class families, the women had some support and encouragement from adult males. As historian Nancy A. Hewitt notes, the nature of "womanhood" as being a passive and domesticated state was gradually being recast through a process of female bonding and forceful entrance into public life.[7] Through their associations women began to take the lead in tackling such social ills as poverty, crime, delinquency, and intemperance. Ministers were preaching from their pulpits that irreligion and materialism were causing these social ills, and women, typically active in church affairs, were determined to make a difference. Their female children surely were absorbing the reformist atmosphere that permeated their homes.

One of the young girls growing up at this time who later became a soldier was Sarah Emma Edmonds. She was born in 1841 and raised in New Brunswick, Canada, in a literate family and attended Anglican parish school. She perceived her father to be very oppressive toward her mother and herself, instilling in her hostility toward males and a strong desire to be independent and self-sufficient. She identified strongly with her mother. When her father tried to marry her off to a neighboring farmer, her mother helped her to escape this form of "bondage."

After fleeing home in male disguise and emigrating to the United States, Sarah Emma served as "Franklin Thompson" in the 2nd Michigan Infantry for two years. In a postwar newspaper interview Edmonds recalled her childhood in some detail, providing a rare glimpse into the psychological background of a female soldier (see Chapter 3). Her initial hostility toward men, she said, was gradually outgrown and tempered by her experiences in the army. She discovered that not all men were ogres after all, and she gained many male friends, including Damon Stewart and Albert Cowles, who came to her support after the war and helped her to obtain a pension.[8]

Women's activism in midcentury primarily was concentrated in the populous Northeast. A similar but lower-key women's movement was under way in the South, differing largely in the conflicted attitudes of educated women toward the institution of slavery. Southern women also were, if anything, even more romantically idealized than were Northern women. In the Southern ideal women ran the household and set standards for nobility and purity, and it was men's duty to protect them. Women did not participate in public affairs. Drew Gilpin Faust's definitive study of changes in women's relationship to society and politics in the South during the war provides a rich source of information and insight into this incipient revolution. As Faust observes,

> However compelling the unfolding drama in which they found themselves, southern ladies knew well that in nineteenth-century America, politics was regarded as the privilege and responsibility of men. . . . Men voted; men spoke in public; ladies appropriately remained within the sphere of home and family. Yet the secession crisis would see these prescriptions honored in the breach as much as the observance. In this moment of national upheaval, the lure of politics seemed all but irresistible.[9]

Faust provides numerous examples of women's views and attitudes during the Civil War, taken from diaries and letters, to illustrate the personal transformations brought about by the war. Although the traditionally strong boundary between private and public life was deep-seated, women became more and more involved in the political conflict going on around them in response to the upheaval in their families and personal lives. "The conflict between women's emergent patriotism and their devotion to the lives and welfare of their families became clear as southern men prepared for war."[10]

In a chapter titled "We Must Go to Work, Too," Faust discusses the increasing role of Southern women in public life due to the exigencies of warfare and the absence of able-bodied men from the home front. The new or newly expanded roles included teaching, clerical work in businesses or government agencies, labor in munitions factories, and hospital nursing.[11]

"The sphere of woman's action in our midst has been greatly enlarged since the commencement of our struggle," said the *Galveston Weekly News,* December 17, 1862, "and her true worth and beauty of character are only displayed in the hour of peril and adversity. In addition to their caring for wounded soldiers, they have engaged in manufacturing supplies for the army." The work of Mrs. J. S. Montgomery in producing cotton and wool cloth is cited. She "is busily employed with some of her Negro women in spinning and weaving, and will send garments made of this material, besides underclothes and socks, to her numerous relatives and friends in the army."

On May 13, 1864, during the fourth year of the war, the *Nashville Dispatch* noted the changed social condition of women: "Silently and imperceptibly, and also rapidly and surely...a revolution is being effected which seems destined to...produce an important and lasting change in all the relations of society." With so many men away at war, the newspaper said, women have gradually supplied the necessary workers for the labor market. "By this means new channels of business and industry have been opened to them, which have been hitherto closed." Examples mentioned included manufacturing, newspaper compositors, printers, government workers, stores, counting houses, and outdoor work such as farming.

Women also had to pitch in at home and take care of such essential chores as managing farms and laboring in the fields, as was so dramatically depicted in the movie *Cold Mountain*. In a story headlined "Women for the Times," a correspondent of the *Cleveland Herald* reported in the fall of 1863:

> It is a very common affair to see a bright-eyed young woman sitting on the reaper driving a four-horse team. But not only thus are women useful, but I have frequently seen them using the hoe. But I saw a few weeks ago in the south part of Madison, Lake County [Ohio], a spectacle which caps all the scenes in this line within my knowledge. To appearances, a rain storm was coming up, and there was one woman in the field dexterously raking up the hay with the double team, and [the] hay wagon was being driven into the field by two other women. Raker, pitcher and loader were all women.[12]

A South Carolina cavalry soldier in a postwar book described the hard conditions Southern women faced. "On one occasion a wounded soldier died, and the women, wives and widows of Confederates, had to act as pallbearers. All the men were at the front, some fighting, some wounded, some in prison, and some dead on the field. Some of these women lived on bread and water for months."[13]

The Civil War, of course, also afforded many women a unique opportunity to break out of nineteenth-century conventional molds by engaging in military service. Women performed in almost every conceivable military-related role in the American Civil War, from nurse to smuggler to spy to soldier. In addition to the soldiers in male disguise and the battlefield nurses, thousands of women enlisted as army nurses and performed yeoman service in military hospitals in major cities as well as in the field. Many experienced all the hardships and dangers of frontline service.

Early in the war women in many Southern towns and cities, due to the absence of young males away at the front, formed home guard units and trained in the use of weapons and military tactics to defend their towns if worse came to worst. The *Mobile Register & Advertiser,* Alabama, July 24, 1861, reported:

> In Choctaw County, Miss., a company of ladies has been organized for some time under the name of "Home Guards," numbering over one hundred.... The *Vicksburg Sun* tells us what they have done as follows: They have been constantly exercising on horseback and on foot with pistol, shot gun and rifle, and have attained such perfection that we doubt if there is a better drilled company in the country. Each one is almost a [Daniel] Boone with her rifle, and an Amazon in her equestrian skill.

The *Daily Chronicle & Sentinel* of Augusta, Georgia, on July 21, 1861, carried a story from the *Winchester Sentinel,* North Carolina, about a group of women seeking a supply of light weapons. "Some thirty or forty of these patriotic ladies in one of the adjoining counties have formed themselves into a company, and determined, if possible, to secure arms, and in the event of a necessity, to defend their homes and fight for the cause of liberty."

Much later in the war an all-woman home defense group was organized in the Shenandoah Valley of Virginia in December 1864. They sought official recognition from the Confederate secretary of war, but he replied that the government was not as yet prepared to accept the service of women in the field.[14] Similar units of female home-defense soldiers trained and drilled with weapons in Chickasaw County, Mississippi; Macon, Georgia; LaGrange (Troup County), Georgia; Rhea County, Tennessee; and Castroville, Texas.[15]

At least one pro-Union home guard unit was formed early in the war in the border state of Kentucky. The *Cairo City Weekly News,* Illinois, reported on July 11, 1861: "A Union Company of Kentucky Girls. —A female military company, named the Union Captivators, has been formed at Falmouth, Kentucky, and over thirty of the young ladies of the place have joined the organization. The uniform is an apron of the old-fashioned

cut, made of red, white and blue—that part covering the bosom representing the stars, and the lower part the stripes."

Although women were involved in all aspects of the Civil War, the main
focus of this book is on those women who actively participated in military
affairs, especially those who "soldiered" with the men and shared the
same hardships and dangers. Frontline nurses who were pioneering a
new field for women fit this category, as do scouts, spies, and smugglers.

According to historian Marilyn Mayer Culpepper, "Civil War nurses
were trailblazers in a field heretofore strictly reserved for men. Hospital nursing was definitely not considered a 'proper' occupation for 'gen-
teel' women at that time."[16] At the outset of the war, even the notion
of women serving as nurses was frowned upon. Author Lynda Sudlow
observes:

> The exigencies of war allowed women freedom to enter this all-
> male world [military nursing], to break the stereotypes created
> by Victorian society which confined them to domestic duties, and
> care for strangers outside their homes. Even so, the struggle for
> acceptance was extremely difficult. Arguments against female nurses
> ranged from the assumption that they would faint at the first sight
> of blood and disturb hospital wards with their hysterics, to being
> constantly in the way of doctors and unable to help with demanding
> tasks such as lifting and moving patients. Propriety and modesty were
> also factors in the public debate.[17]

This mind-set would change rapidly as the war progressed and pioneering women pitched in to establish hospital systems and to provide
resources for the establishment of the U.S. Sanitary Commission.[18] Dorothea L. Dix became Superintendent of Women Nurses in Washington,
D.C., and oversaw the appointment and assignment of army nurses.

During the war women traveled all over the country to battlefield and
camp areas as their roles in nursing and other military affairs expanded.
Women as nurses became the norm rather than the exception within a
fairly short period of time, even though their presence in field hospitals
often aroused antipathy from the surgeons. "Some of the most courageous women," writes Marilyn Mayer Culpepper, "found their true calling
in attempting to help alleviate the suffering on the battlefields. No stretch

of the imagination can possibly envision the horrors these nurses encountered"[19] (see Chapter 2).

Various women other than the female soldiers and battlefield "medics" also found their way into Civil War camps. Sometimes soldiers' wives cooked and did laundry for the regiment. But there were also officers' concubines and camp-following prostitutes; these women sometimes disguised themselves as males in army uniforms. Officers were known to have male-disguised women as "servants" while in the field, but these women generally were ringers rather than formally enlisted soldiers. It should come as no surprise that women who participated in the Civil War ranged from saints to sinners—no different from the men.

The *Nashville Dispatch*, March 12, 1863, reported under "Army Police Proceedings" that two women dressed as soldiers were arrested on board a steamship on March 7. They were found in company with a body of cavalry. Local authorities provided them with female apparel and sent them to Louisville. It is not clear whether they were real soldiers, but it seems doubtful in this case. "The Chief of Police very properly addressed a note to the officers in command of the cavalry, informing them that if these instances continued," said the report, "a severe example would be made of both women and the officers encouraging them to such a course, in accordance with an order of the Commanding General."

Nashville was one of the major cities, along with Washington, D.C., and Richmond, Virginia, that had major populations of prostitutes, typically regulated by the army and local authorities. Thomas P. Lowry, M.D., in his groundbreaking book about sexual practices during the Civil War, thoroughly documents the prostitution centers and their use by the soldiers, along with the resulting epidemic of venereal diseases.[20]

In rare cases it is possible that bona fide female soldiers were allowed to stay in service after being discovered by attaching themselves to an officer. However, there is no doubt about the probity of the large majority of female soldiers. As the noted historian Bell I. Wiley observes, "Probably the majority of women who entered the ranks in male disguise were respectable characters, motivated by patriotism or the desire to be near husbands or sweethearts. But a few were persons of easy virtue who enrolled as soldiers to further their lewd enterprises."[21]

When she was arrested in army uniform during August 1863 at Harrisburg, Pennsylvania, Ida Remington claimed to have served in the 11th New York Infantry for two years, including participation in the South Mountain and Antietam campaigns in Maryland, September 14–17, 1862, during Robert E. Lee's first northern invasion. She also told the authorities that she had been a personal servant to a captain.[22] Unfortunately for her story the 11th New York Infantry (a three-months regiment) was not at Antietam, and apparently not at South Mountain, either.

The regiment had been mustered out in New York City while the Battle of Antietam was in progress on September 16. The Order of Battle of Union troops for South Mountain does not include the 11th New York. Since the regiment was called back into emergency service for thirty days during June and July 1863, it is conceivable that Remington may have been domiciled in the regiment immediately prior to her arrest. In short, she may have been a servant to a captain in the 11th New York Infantry briefly in 1863, but her claims of real army service as a combat soldier are dubious.

Tommy, an African American girl under twenty years old, enlisted in male disguise as a body servant or valet for a captain in the 12th Rhode Island Infantry while the regiment was on duty in Lancaster, Kentucky. She served with the regiment through its campaigns and returned home to Rhode Island with the regiment when it was mustered out without her sex being discovered.[23]

At least a few cases are on record in which the officers were aware that one of their soldiers was a woman but let the soldier continue in service. A boy named Charles Norton volunteered to be servant to a Captain Reeves of Company E, 141st Pennsylvania Infantry. Charles marched with the company, cooked for the captain, and took care of his possessions. At the Battle of Chancellorsville in May 1863, Captain Mercur, who had small feet, found his boots missing. Charles was caught and confessed and during questioning was found to be female.[24]

Harriet Merrill, a resident of Watertown, New York, in the fall of 1861 enlisted at age nineteen in Company G ("Union Guards"), 59th New York Infantry. In the spring of 1862 Captain Jerome B. Taft was court-martialed for bringing her into camp as a concubine but found not guilty. During the proceedings Merrill was linked with another officer, James Miller. In any event, she was reported to have performed all the duties of a soldier, allegedly using the name "Frederick Woods" or possibly "Charles Johnson." Captain Taft reportedly knew Merrill's gender and helped her to join the regiment. She had been a prostitute before the war. No soldier by the name of Merrill appears on the regimental roster.[25]

These few borderline cases aside, many hundreds of young women enlisted as real soldiers. How widespread among the states participating in the Civil War was the phenomenon of female soldiers? Chapters 3 and 4 and the Honor Roll (Appendix A) provide rudimentary statistics showing that all of the populous Northern states, and most of the less populous ones, had female soldiers in the ranks of their volunteer regiments. Given that military records for the Southern states tend to be less complete than those of their Northern counterparts, it is interesting to see that some of the core Confederate states (especially Louisiana, North Carolina, and Virginia) also have records of female soldiers.

The results of continuing research have led me to believe that there were at least a thousand, possibly several thousand, women who served as soldiers in the American Civil War. We will never know precisely, but continued research making use of the new research tools keeps turning up additional examples. Although this is not a large absolute number and is only a tiny percentage of the 2.1 to 2.8 million soldiers estimated to have fought in both armies, it is sociologically significant for a period in American history when the role of women was carefully circumscribed and did not include doing "man's work" wearing men's clothing, much less engaging in combat warfare.[26]

The mid-nineteenth-century women's movement clearly was an important influence, at least indirectly, on the women who volunteered for Civil War service. Just as they were in the process of seeking equality and increased independence, the war broke out. Although the war had the inadvertent effect of providing new opportunities for women, the reform process otherwise ground to a halt. Social reform and politics were overwhelmed by the demons of war to which all else became subordinate.

In the concluding chapter of her book, Professor Ginzberg observes, "These reforming passions emerged in a context of religious revivals and social upheaval; they ended in war. Women reformers' optimism and faith in society's transformation largely dissipated in the enormous work of feeding, clothing, and healing Civil War soldiers."[27]

1

War on a Colossal Scale

> Many lives would change dramatically during the war as women
> temporarily divided their attention between familiar domestic tasks
> and other, less conventional work on plantations, in hospitals,
> in businesses, in schoolrooms, in offices, and even in munitions
> factories.
>   *George C. Rable, in* Civil Wars: Women and the
>   Crisis of Southern Nationalism *(1989)*

After Confederate artillery opened fire on Fort Sumter, South
Carolina, on April 12, 1861, President Abraham Lincoln called
for the states to provide soldiers to "put down the insurrection."
All over the North men left their farms, their city homes, their
jobs as clerks, tradesmen, teachers, and lawyers and rallied to
the flag. So did women. The earliest regiments to be formed, like
the 2nd Michigan Infantry, headed for Washington accompanied
by as many as thirty women who were to serve as nurses and
laundresses. After five bloody years of war, three of the women
with the 2nd Michigan received military pensions, all three having experienced action on the battlefield.[1]

Perry Mayo of Company C, 2nd Michigan Infantry, noted in his
diary for June 10, 1861:

We left Detroit on Thursday afternoon [June 6] after marching
through the city for about three hours. We were greeted with
utmost enthusiasm. The girls were stationed at the windows

waving flags and firing revolvers to cheer the men on to the great duty they had to perform.... We were nearly fed to death on the road through Ohio with pies, cakes, lemonade, and compliments. Flowers were showered on us at every station.[2]

Soldiers departing for the war from Wisconsin were given banquets and elaborate entertainment. For one banquet in Madison in July 1861, 6,000 people showed up to provide a feast and a joyful send-off for twenty companies of soldiers at Camp Randall. After supper the women were thanked for their sumptuous entertainment; then the regiments were drawn up for dress parade, and a flag was presented to each. Subsequently, other entertainments were provided, and the grand finale was a dance on the parade grounds, "in which the sturdy soldiers and the fair damsels participated in high glee." On a smaller scale the same sort of thing was being done in almost every village or town, for departing soldiers.[3]

Southern soldiers were similarly feted as they started off to war. Bell I. Wiley, in *The Life of Johnny Reb,* describes a battalion of Louisiana recruits gathering at a depot to board the train: "Fair women bestowed their floral offerings and kisses ungrudgingly" without any distinction as to society or class. The men were supplied with delicacies that they consumed as the train carried them off to war, and some took "long pulls at their heavily charged flasks." At stops along the way they were given receptions and fed various treats, sometimes obtaining kisses from pretty local girls "who adorn the right of way." Arriving in Richmond, they marched through the city to patriotic tunes, in "resplendent uniforms" and "other fine accouterments [affording] a spectacle that dazzles the eyes of Richmond's citizens."[4]

Women also accompanied the men to war in Southern regiments. The earliest Louisiana regiments that went to training camp in Pensacola, Florida, brought women along to cook, do the washing, and clean the soldiers' quarters. Camp followers also showed up early: Just before the First Battle of Bull Run in July 1861, four women dressed in male clothing were discovered in Wheat's Battalion of "Louisiana Tigers" and carted away from the front lines in a wagon. The battalion was the first unit from Louisiana to be engaged in the war and played a prominent role at First Bull Run.[5]

What turned out to be the bloodiest and most divisive war in American history thus began in a festive, almost joyful atmosphere. Leaders on both sides displayed a completely unrealistic attitude, a wrong-headed conception of the consequences of their actions, as if it were some bloodless sporting event that would be quickly decided. Fanaticism prevailed over reason and negotiation: each side considered the other to be obviously morally wrong. The mood at first was eager enthusiasm for battle; the other side would quickly be put in its place. The country's relative inexperience with war may well have been responsible for this attitude.

Until the Civil War the United States was not particularly militarily oriented, relying primarily on the mobilization of state militia to fight its relatively small wars. During the Mexican War (1846–1848), which served as a training ground for quite a few Civil War officers, the U.S. Regular Army was small but professional. Congress had set the statutory size at 10,000. When the war began, Congress authorized enlistment of 50,000 volunteers, and the size of the Regular Army also was increased somewhat. Total U.S. battle-related fatalities for the Mexican War were only about 1,700, but in a foreshadowing of the Civil War, an additional 11,000 or so succumbed to disease.[6]

At the start of 1861 the U.S. Army consisted of about 16,000 soldiers scattered across the country, stationed in company- or battalion-size units, seldom in numbers as large as the standard regimental size of about 1,000. Most were garrisoning remote western forts, deployed to protect settlers and maintain order in Indian territories, making occasional punitive raids on Indian offenders or engaging in limited battles that were little more than skirmishes. By way of comparison, army casualties at the Second Battle of Bull Run alone, on August 26–27, 1862, were 16,054. The Union ultimately, by a conservative estimate, had fielded a total of 2.1 million soldiers by the conclusion of the hostilities.[7]

The Confederate Army was more or less built from scratch, from state militia units, eager volunteers, and a relative handful of defectors from the U.S. Army ranks. The defectors, however, included a number of West Point graduates and other experienced officers. Confederate president Jefferson Davis himself was a graduate of West Point, a U.S. army veteran, a member of the U.S. Congress, and a former U.S. secretary of war. The Confederacy also began with the distinct advantage of having more and better cavalry than the Union (see Chapter 4). Its Army of Northern Virginia quickly grew to about 75,000 early in the war. Thomas L. Livermore's standard statistical reference, first published in 1900, estimates from a study of various databases that the Confederate army overall fielded about 600,000 to 1 million soldiers.

After the initial surge of patriotism with expectations on both sides for a short war, the regiments became badly depleted by losses in combat and by widespread disease due to poor sanitation in camps. Conscription laws were passed in both North and South to replenish the ranks. As the war escalated it quickly became clear that its scale was going to be unprecedented, far beyond that envisioned in the initial Union call for troops on the order of 75,000. Union secretary of war Simon Cameron, on April 15, 1861, had asked the states to contribute members of their militia "to serve as infantry or riflemen, for the period of three months, unless sooner discharged."[8]

The Confederate government adopted a draft in 1862 applicable to all white males between the ages of seventeen and fifty. The effects of conscription on Southern families were severe. Historian George C. Rable reports: "Young boys and old men, the infirm and even the recently wounded filled depleted regiments. To many women at home, it seemed that the army took the wrong men at the wrong time, leaving destitute families to fend for themselves." Underage boys were enticed to run away from home and join the army, and they were eagerly accepted by Confederate officers who badly needed "warm bodies." It is easy to see how, in this climate, young women disguised as males could make their way into the army.

The Confederate government conscription policies, although based on necessity and the harsh realities of warfare, badly alienated many Southern women. The draft put additional strain on families already trying to deal with poverty and hunger, primarily due to male breadwinners being in the army. The increasingly desperate women found themselves in a bitter struggle with a seemingly uncaring bureaucracy, arguing for the return of their husbands and sons who were needed to alleviate their sufferings. In the final analysis about 21 percent of Confederate soldiers were conscripts.[9]

In the North some individual states adopted a draft in 1862 to meet their federally mandated quotas. Then in 1863 the Congress enacted a national conscription law applicable to males between the ages of twenty and forty-five. However, draftees were permitted to hire a substitute to serve in their stead or to pay a so-called commutation fee of $300 to the government in lieu of serving in the army. Recruits were paid a cash bounty as an inducement to enlist. New legislation also increased enlistment bounties and authorized the recruiting of immigrants and African Americans into the army.

These policies soon led to the formation of opportunistic groups eager to establish profitable bounty and substitute scams which kept Union detective chief Lafayette Baker occupied for some time, and then to bloody draft riots in New York City. The practice of Federal, state, or local bounties and the purchase of substitutes to replace drafted men, notes Francis A. Lord, "permanently besmirched" the patriotic Northern recruiting program for the rest of the war. He terms them "especially vicious practices." The money-driven policies also led to the saying among the less well-to-do that the war was a "rich man's war but poor men's fight."[10]

Ultimately the draft produced very few warm bodies for the Union army ranks. In 1864 the commutations were cancelled, and the final tally showed that "four federal drafts produced only 46,000 conscripts and 118,000 substitutes (2 and 6 percent, respectively, of the 2.1 million Union troops)."[11]

When in 1861 the North and South stumbled headlong into open warfare, a large gap—more like a chasm—existed between the purely imaginary and romantic view of warfare and the shocking realities. Few, if any, leaders had any notion that the war would be a long one, or any concept of the resources that would be needed to organize and sustain a large army. Since there was no U.S. precedent for war on such a large scale, there was no national organization to provide the military uniforms, weapons, equipment, food, and other necessary supplies or the logistics for their transportation and distribution. All of a sudden tens of thousands of state soldiers who were being rushed into service had to be outfitted somehow. The task by default fell on families, churches, and other social groups. Northern women began forming ladies' aid and soldiers' aid societies to provide supplementary food, clothing, and supplies to the soldiers. Marjorie Barstow Greenbie, an early historian of women's roles in the Civil War, observes:

The fact that the first great modern war, the war that overtopped all the wars of history in geographical scope and in the men and materials involved, began as a people's movement was to have momentous consequences for civilization. The first organization of the largest national army ever assembled was accomplished by civilians who had to depend on women to meet the elementary needs of food, clothing, and comfort.... [H]ere was a war developing on a colossal scale right in the housewife's front yard. She saw the defenders of her country and of a cause...not as an army with banners, but as a collection of the various Joes and Jonathans of her own household and neighborhood. She suddenly realized that knights and heroes and warriors bold are nothing but a large crowd of men who will get into dreadful trouble, and probably die quite needlessly, if they aren't looked after better than most men can be trusted to look after themselves.[12]

Women began questioning what the government plans were for provisioning the huge volunteer army. Uniforms initially were supplied by townspeople, sometimes by the state, and typically were irregular in style and color. Aside from government-issue salted meat and hardtack, soldiers were expected to forage for their own food. Underwear, towels, and bedding had to be supplied by the soldiers' families or the soldiers' aid societies.

One of the tragic consequences of unpreparedness was the terrible waste of human life due to the diseases that swept through the army camps. Conditions were not only primitive; from the standpoint of health they were downright dangerous, a situation aggravated by the severe shortage of medical personnel of all kinds. That void would eventually be filled in part by hundreds of women who volunteered as nurses to help alleviate the enormous suffering of frontline troops. Along with the field surgeons, they labored under deplorable conditions to tend the injured, sick, and dying. Basic sanitation, in fact, was nonexistent. "Camps were pitched for military reasons without regard to drainage or a safe water supply," Greenbie notes. "The great outdoors was the latrine. There was no general provision for cooking....Hardtack was bad enough if it was sound and fresh, [but it] was often mouldy [and] likely to be thoroughly riddled with weevils."[13]

Sanitation was especially bad in the early months of the war. Dr. Gordon W. Jones estimates that nearly 70,000 Union soldiers and about 30,000 Confederate soldiers died of enteric diseases (intestinal problems such as diarrhea, dysentery, and typhoid fever). Thus, around 100,000 soldiers' deaths could be attributed to poor sanitation. Camps often were littered with garbage and the entrails of animals slaughtered for food, which became breeding grounds for flies that spread disease. Nearby streams used for washing and drinking water became polluted by effluvia and excrement. "However," writes Dr. Jones, "it soon became obvious to the army high commanders that the dirtier the camp, the higher the sick and death rate."[14]

Hospitals often were equally filthy, and due to ignorance of the germ theory of infection and to poorly trained doctors (quite a few being only apprentice doctors), the mortality rate for soldier patients was high. Dr. Jones points out that the Civil War was the last American war fought before germ theory was understood and generally accepted. Most of the medical knowledge gained during the war, he said, was about how much injury the human body can endure in the absence of informed medical care.[15]

Civil War scholar Marilyn Mayer Culpepper reports that "Civil War field hospitals were spartan in the extreme, often hastily established in converted schools, hotels, churches, barns, private homes, boats. . . . Often the beds were boards set atop church pews or laid on the ground; mattresses were sacks of straw or corn shucks. . . . " Historian Earl J. Hess also comments on the primitive nature of field hospitals and the overworked and undersupplied medical personnel who staffed them:

> A regiment could suffer hundreds of casualties in a single morning
> with only a surgeon, an assistant surgeon, and a handful of untrained
> medical orderlies available to deal with the emergency. The system
> of field medical care was swamped after every serious engagement,
> overwhelmed by the enormity of battle. . . . The conditions in the
> field hospitals were unavoidably primitive. Barns, tents, and living
> rooms were improvised dressing stations, hardly fit for the surgical
> procedures needed during the hours immediately following a battle.[16]

No wonder then that wounded or ill soldiers often took extreme measures to avoid going to field hospitals, having observed the fate that befell their comrades due to poor hospital conditions, and sometimes due to untrained and careless doctors. A historian of Louisiana regiments reports that late in the war, Louisiana soldiers built theaters for entertainment during the winter where they organized and performed minstrel shows. Satirical plays were popular, "the most popular performance being a skit depicting army surgeons drinking and playing cards while nearby wounded suffered."[17]

In a postwar book, Union Major General Newton Martin Curtis (who himself was wounded and required emergency medical care during the war) devotes a chapter to "Medical Care and Hospital Life," terming the medical service during the war to be "in the worst condition of any branch of the public service."

> The camps were located ... without the advice of an officer of the engineer or medical branches of the service, no thought being given to sanitary conditions. These evils were augmented by bad cooking, the open sale in the camps by sutlers and "pie peddlers" of the most unwholesome trash, and the use of contaminated water. . . . The regimental hospitals had few facilities for properly caring for the sick, no special diet, no trained nurses, seldom cots, and, generally, a rubber and a woolen blanket as their only bedding. . . . General hospitals, to which the worst cases were sent, were better provided for, but the red-tape which had to be unwound left many to die in camp, whose recovery might have been speedily secured in a well-appointed hospital. The cases previously mentioned [in prior chapters] illustrate the difference between good hospital care under a competent surgeon, and the facilities and care of an ordinary field hospital.[18]

Curtis went on to note that the hospital care system improved as the war progressed; he gives special credit to the men and women of the U.S. Sanitary Commission and especially to "the inestimable services of the patriotic and devoted women who nursed and cared for the men disabled by wounds and disease."[19] His book, in fact, was sponsored and introduced by Mrs. Eliza Woolsey Howland, one of the seven Woolsey sisters who performed various services to the Union during the war (see Appendix A).

Each regiment had a "surgeon"—often a general physician—but more often than not he lacked essential equipment and supplies. Wounds would be treated, but no provisions were made for the sick. Ill soldiers were expected to take care of each other. No female army nurse corps existed early in the war. The "walking wounded" or slightly ill soldiers, or those who were smaller and less robust, were pressed into service as male nurses in hospitals. George R. Lee, an Illinois artilleryman by training, described his "introduction to war" in mid-February of 1862 when he was among a group of twenty-four men stationed in Cairo, Illinois, who were detailed to act as nurses on a hospital ship. Some 300 wounded or ill soldiers, including casualties from the Battle of Fort Donelson, were to be transported to hospitals in St. Louis aboard the steamship *War Eagle*.

Lee described the scene aboard ship as he walked down the narrow aisle between two rows of soldiers lined up like cord wood, their feet pointed toward the center aisle. They were lying on deck with no beds; not all had blankets and some used their coats as pillows. "They were crowded as closely as possible," he says, "many in pain, delirious with fever, moaning and muttering of wives, or home and mother. It was enough to make angels weep."[20]

A Union physician serving on the hospital ship *D.A. January* on the Mississippi River wrote a letter home on August 15, 1862, noting:

> I think I told you that our nurses are all men detailed from the army for that service (I think they are better than so many civilians).
> An order has been issued that all nurses and others employed in hospitals and belonging to the army must return to their regiments today.... We shall have to fill their places by convalescent soldiers or civilians. I have not much faith that convalescents will take care of the sick as they should be taken care of. But I feel the importance of having every man shoulder a musket these days that is able.... [21]

In addition to the poor state of medical care, ambulances were horse-drawn carriages; the bumpy ride to a hospital usually aggravated the soldier's wounds. Once there, his chances of survival were further reduced by the overcrowding, poor sanitation, and a shortage of doctors. Without anesthetics available, doctors routinely used chloroform or whiskey as painkillers. The art of first aid was yet to be invented. Drugs and medical supplies were normally in short supply.[22]

Recognizing these conditions, women began taking an active role along with men in planning and providing for the health care ("sanitation") and medical care of soldiers, for which no national organization existed. Out of their efforts grew the U.S. Sanitary Commission and the U.S. Christian Commission. English nurse and reformer Florence Nightingale served as a model for these women, and they built on her methods.

The U.S. Sanitary Commission was founded in New York in 1861. It faced the opposition of the existing army medical establishment, which not only resented civilian involvement but also questioned the use of women as nurses. Members of the commission began to inspect sanitary conditions at army camps and to provide nurses, ambulances, hospitals, and food. Additionally, the Commission used its influence to press for the recruitment of younger and better-trained doctors.[23]

Dorothea Dix was appointed Superintendent of Women Nurses for the War Department and personally supervised the recruitment, training, and deployment of all army nurses. Her authority was absolute. She made clear her preference for older, plain-looking women to be army nurses to avoid distractions, causing some younger and more attractive women to circumvent her regulations and go directly to the front as volunteers.[24]

Late in 1861 surgeon Charles S. Tripler, medical director of the Army of the Potomac, submitted a report responding to Major General George B. McClellan's request for recommendations for an army ambulance corps and nurse corps. Point 2 of his report concerns "the employment of an adequate corps of male and female nurses by the medical director, to act under his supervision," as suggested by the sanitary commission. Tripler comments:

In the plan to be submitted for hospitals it will be seen that a due proportion of male and female nurses is provided for. We can get female nurses through Miss Dix and from among the Sisters of Charity. It is a very damaging position for any one to take and avow, but in the honest discharge of my duties, though a Protestant myself, I do not hesitate to declare that in my opinion the latter are far preferable to the former, being better disciplined, more discreet and judicious, and more reliable. In the arrangement of the hospitals it might be judicious to assign one section to the Sisters of Charity and the other to the Protestant nurses. Male nurses are most readily obtained by detail from the troops. There are many men in the ranks who are the subjects of infirmities, disqualifying them for the active duties of the field, who could be usefully employed as nurses in the hospitals. Numbers have been enlisted with hernia and cirsocele [varicose veins and swelling of scrotum], and are being discharged on account of these, who would be very capable of doing the duties of nurses.[25]

In anticipation of the probable casualties from the first Union offensive against Richmond in 1862, the U.S. Sanitary Commission formed the Hospital Transport Service. A ragtag fleet of cast-off boats of all sizes and shapes were reconditioned into hospital ships, and they served as floating hospitals on the Virginia rivers for wounded soldiers transported to them by ambulance directly from the battlefields. The larger and more seaworthy vessels carried wounded and sick soldiers from docks on the Virginia coastal rivers along the seacoast to hospitals in Washington, Philadelphia, and New York. Hundreds of women served as volunteer nurses on the hospital ships, and many later published poignant memoirs of their experiences.[26]

When, as a young officer in the 16th New York Infantry, Newton Martin Curtis was wounded at West Point, Virginia, on May 7, 1862, he and a number of other soldiers were carried on board the Hospital Transport Service steamship *Wilson Small*. Among the nurses he found on duty aboard the ship were Eliza Woolsey Howland, Georgeanna M. Woolsey, Katharine Prescott Wormeley, Helen L. Gilson, and Harriet D. Whetten, all of whom served with distinction in the army nurse corps (see Appendix A). Curtis said that several of the wounded soldiers taken on board were thought to be mortally wounded, but only one died; "those who lived owed their lives to the care received from these patriotic and devoted women." He and the other wounded members of the 16th New York received special care from the Woolsey sisters. He also describes being evacuated to the North on the *Knickerbocker*, with nurse Helen L. Gilson in charge.[27]

Women in the North initially faced some opposition to serving as nurses on the basis of prevailing views about "proper" behavior for women but had less difficulty in dealing with the disapproval of society than did their Southern sisters.[28] Women in the South were slower to move into military nursing, mainly due to a strong tradition that nursing was employment acceptable only for lower-class people, and then mostly males. To work in a military hospital was a drastic departure from traditional female roles in the South. Army nurses were almost invariably relatively frail or disabled male soldiers detailed for that duty. Drew Gilpin Faust in *Mothers of Invention* cited the reasons this tradition was gradually overcome:

> Manpower shortages, escalating casualty rates, and patriotic
> ambitions, however, overrode custom and pushed southern women
> toward work with the sick and wounded, a movement encouraged
> by the innovative and much admired role Florence Nightingale
> had played in Britain's Crimean War of 1853–56. A woman of
> unchallenged respectability and high social standing, Nightingale had
> through her selfless actions and her widely read [book] ... established
> a conceptual legitimation for female nursing. The notion that woman's
> moral and emotional attributes uniquely fitted her for hospital work
> gained strength and currency, and women North and South found in
> Nightingale a model for female heroism.[29]

The acceptability of respectable women serving as military nurses became a matter of public debate in the South. Although it seemed to be natural for women to be "ministering angels" and caregivers, this tended to bring them into conflict with male authority in the form of army doctors. Also, forced intimacy with the male bodies of wounded or ill soldiers created a challenge to female "delicacy" or "modesty." For all these reasons Southern women who were called "nurses" were at first more often akin to general hospital workers than to modern-day nurses who actually treat sick or injured patients, apply bandages, administer medicines, participate in diagnosis, and change dressings. The only trained nurses in the South in 1861 were the Catholic Sisters of Mercy.

The growing medical care emergency overrode long-established gender conventions, but not quickly or easily. The conflict of authority also was noted by historian George C. Rable: "The flood of sick and wounded men overwhelmed the resources of most hospitals. . . . As matrons, nurses, and volunteers wrestled with these problems, [over time] they assumed ever greater authority. Becoming more efficient, self-confident, and impatient with routine and bureaucracy, they inevitably clashed with the physicians in the hospitals. The most conscientious nurses often received little cooperation from doctors who had little use for women in the wards."[30]

Civil War imperatives initiated the process of establishing nursing as a legitimate profession for women. In the South female nurses were viewed as a temporary phenomenon—not as an incipient revolution—due to the war emergency, as was the case of women working in public offices, factories, and schoolrooms. "The first Confederate nurses," says Rable, "simply opened up their homes to feed the convalescent and console the hopeless cases." Gradually they proceeded to set up makeshift hospitals near the army camps and, to treat sick and wounded men who were traveling home, at railroad depots. But they lacked the resources to handle the thousands of men who required extensive medical care.[31]

Many Southern women, however, openly defied conventions from the start and functioned as full-care nurses. Kate Cumming, whose family emigrated from Scotland to Canada and then settled in Alabama, was one of those who challenged the public attitude that nursing was "indelicate and unfitting work for a Southern lady." She described in her journal the horrors of war encountered in army hospitals: "Gray-haired men—men in the pride of man-hood—beardless boys—Federals and all, mutilated in every imaginable way, lying on the floor, just as they were taken from the battle-field; so close together that it was almost impossible to walk without stepping on them."[32]

The extremely violent war of an unprecedented large scale was creating an urgent need for a medical and health care system of national scope, with organized methods to furnish adequate training as well as supplies and equipment for medical personnel. Since most able-bodied men were away from home as soldiers in the ranks, women increasingly took the lead in organizing and staffing the system at all levels. In surprising numbers, women also increasingly took to the field and soldiered with the men as vivandieres and battlefield nurses, where they fully participated in all aspects of army life.

2

In the Field and on the March

These half-soldier heroines generally adopted a semi-military dress,
and became expert in the use of the rifle, and skilful shots.
Nurse Mary A. Livermore, My Story of the War *(1887)*

Hundreds of women served openly in female attire during
the Civil War as "half-soldier heroines," a term used by Civil
War nurse Mary Livermore in her reminiscences. For all practical purposes, they were soldiers. Many marched with the regiment—camping in the field and experiencing all the hardships
of military life, including extremes of weather and inadequate
food—and were exposed to enemy fire on or near the battlefield.
Others labored in frontline hospitals, at times having to flee from
advancing enemy columns or endure captivity when their hospitals were overrun. Both regular army nurses and other women
pressed into service as emergency caregivers often volunteered
to care for wounded soldiers where they fell on the battlefield.
Their stories include numerous examples of courage and endurance far beyond the call of duty, and several were buried with
military honors after death.

These soldiering women fall into four categories, though the
lines are not always sharply drawn and some individuals served
in more than one capacity:

- Daughter (or Mother) of the Regiment
- Vivandiere or cantiniere
- Battlefield nurse ("soldier-nurse")
- Field hospital nurse

In 1876, ten years after the end of the Civil War, author William W. Fowler made the following astute observations, primarily about women who participated in the American Revolutionary War:

In the great wars of American history, there are, in immediate connection with the army, two situations in which woman more prominently appears: the former is where, in her proper person, she accompanies the army as a *vivandiere,* or as the daughter of the regiment, or as the comrade and help-meet of her husband; the latter, and less frequent capacity, is that of a soldier, marching in the ranks and facing the foe in the hour of danger. During the War for Independence a large number of brave and devoted women served in the army, principally in their true characters as wives of regularly enlisted soldiers, keeping even step with the ranks upon the march, and cheerfully sharing the burdens, privations, hardships, and dangers of military life.[1]

With respect to the Civil War, Fowler added:

These women of the frontier during the late war may be called the irregular forces of the army, soldiers in all respects except in being enrolled and placed under officers. They fought and marched, stood on guard and were taken prisoners. They viewed the horrors of war and were under fire although they did not wear the army uniform nor walk in files and platoons. All these things they did in addition to their work as housewives, farmers, and mothers. Many others took naturally to the rough life of a soldier, and enlisting under soldiers' guise followed the drum on foot or in the saddle, and encamped on the bare ground with a knapsack for a pillow and no covering from the cold and rain but a brown army blanket.[2]

In the early part of the war it was not uncommon for wives to go along with their husbands into regimental life. For example, Lafayette L. Deming enlisted in the 10th Michigan Infantry late in 1861 as a captain, mustering into Company G in February 1862. His wife went with him into camp, where she wore a uniform, including a haversack, canteen, and

belt with revolvers, and served as Daughter of the Regiment (an all-purpose helper and mascot) and nurse. She continued in field service with
her husband in Alabama, Mississippi, and Tennessee until he resigned on
September 3, 1862, for unspecified reasons.[3]

The nineteenth-century stereotype of the role of women in wartime,
especially as memorialized in stories of Daughters of the Regiment, was
of young "ministering angels" who would provide inspiration to male soldiers, encourage them to fight, and take care of the sick and the wounded.
For the large majority of the reported Daughters of the Regiment, it is not
known whether they actually marched and "soldiered" with the men or
played only an ornamental role in camp. In all likelihood most were only
parade-ground ornaments before the regiments left training camp and
headed for the front lines.

Eliza Wilson was a typical Daughter of the Regiment, in the original
mold, for the 5th Wisconsin Infantry. "Her duties were to head the regiment when on parade, and to assuage the thirst of the wounded and
dying on the battlefield, where it was hoped that she would be a real
guardian angel of the regiment." That, at least, was the ideal. The parade
ground duties were common among young Daughters of the Regiment,
while the actual care of wounded soldiers on or near the battlefield was
not typically realized in practice.

Originally Eliza played the classic role in camp, indeed ornately cos-
tumed and serving as an inspiration for the male soldiers. As her uniform
was described in a soldier's letter, "the color is bright brown; no crinoline; dress reaches halfway between the knee and ankle; upper sleeve
loose, gathered at the waist; pantalettes same color, wide but gathered
tight around the ankle; black hat with plumes or feathers of same color;
feet dressed in morocco boots."

The daughter of a wealthy former state senator from Menomonie,
Dunn County, she was provided with her own tent and servant in the
camp and all necessary food supplies. She participated with the soldiers
during training, wearing the brown "Turkish" military-style costume. Judg-
ing by soldier letters, she also did inspire them by enduring some of the
hardships of camp life, marching along with them, and taking care of sick
soldiers at least during the training period. "It would do you good," said
one soldier, "to see her trudging along, with or after the regiment, her

dark brown frock buttoned tightly around her waist, her what-you-call-ems tucked into her well fitting gaiters, her hat and feather set jauntily on one side, her step firm and assured. . . . She came with one of the companies and remains with the regiment." The letters record her still being with the regiment at least into January 1862, but it is doubtful that her career continued beyond training camp and onto real battlefields.[4]

In the 7th Wisconsin Infantry Hannah Ewbank, a schoolteacher, served as Daughter of the Regiment in camp, elaborately garbed in "a Zouave jacket of blue merino [wool fabric], trimmed with military buttons and gold lace; a skirt of scarlet merino, trimmed with blue and gold lace; pants and vest of white Marseilles [cotton fabric]; balmoral boots; hat of blue velvet trimmed with white and gold lace, with yellow plumes, and white kid gloves." Again, it is doubtful that she went on to experience real battlefields or frontline dangers. The 39th New York Infantry reportedly had several vivandieres, but most likely they were of the transient variety that never ventured beyond campground life. One of the youngest Daughters of the Regiment on record was Lizzie Jones, who served in that position for the 6th Massachusetts Infantry at ten years old. In the regiment was a Sergeant Crowley of Lowell, who gave her recognition for her efforts.[5]

War, as everyone on both sides quickly learned, was far bloodier and less "noble" than they had imagined; and so young ladies of good intention but little worldly experience quickly dropped out or were removed from the scene by their concerned parents. The idealistic model of Daughters of the Regiment ran up against stark reality and did not survive much beyond early 1862. At this stage almost all Daughters of the Regiment of the original type faded away, and other women of substance and character stepped forward to assume important roles in the army.

A few Daughters or Mothers of the Regiment who remained in service typically did find themselves caring for wounded soldiers on or near the battlefield, usually without any special training or preparation for doing so. In modern terminology they served as "medics." Female vivandieres and cantinieres, literally suppliers of food and drink, respectively, to soldiers, were modeled after women in European armies. They were often exposed to enemy fire during the Civil War, and on occasion they were known to take up arms in the heat of combat.

One of the most storied Daughters of the Regiment who carried on as a battlefield nurse was Anna Etheridge (nee Anna Blair). Her thoroughly documented story provides a striking exception to the rule. "Gentle Annie," as the soldiers called her, went off to war with the 2nd Michigan Infantry and also served in the 3rd and 5th Michigan Infantry regiments when the 2nd was detached from the Army of the Potomac to serve in the west. She was under fire on several occasions and was awarded the Kearny Cross for gallantry. At times she set an example for the soldiers with her fearless behavior on the battlefield.

After the war, Frederick O. Talbot of the 1st Maine Heavy Artillery, who had been a sergeant at the time (later promoted to 2nd lieutenant), recalled seeing Etheridge in the midst of combat on June 22, 1864, when the II Army Corps was in a hot fight in the vicinity of Petersburg, Virginia, including an artillery duel. They had been nearly surrounded and forced to pull back, and the regimental lines became confused. Talbot was astonished to suddenly find himself alongside a "good-looking young woman" who stood there calmly, bandaging the wounds of one soldier after another. He had no idea who she was or where she came from, and so began making inquiries and learned her name (see Appendix B).

At the second Battle of Bull Run in August 1862, Etheridge could be seen helping wounded soldiers to safety under a rocky ledge while exposing herself to enemy fire. A cannonball killed a soldier while she was in the act of treating him. In 1863 at Chancellorsville an officer on a horse next to her was shot and killed, and a bullet grazed her hand, pierced her dress, and wounded her horse. She was revered by her soldiers and mustered out with them tearfully after a full three years of service.[6]

Another more-than-ornamental Daughter of the Regiment was Kady C. Brownell of Rhode Island. Kady accompanied her husband, Robert, into the three-months 1st Rhode Island Infantry. A "Jill of all trades," she trained with weapons and marched alongside her husband in the ranks. Her father had been in the British army and she was an "army brat" who knew about military life. At First Bull Run in 1861 she was a color bearer and led soldiers into combat, where they came under heavy fire, retreating in good order when the Union forces were routed.

When the 1st Rhode Island Infantry mustered out of service, Robert and Kady re-enlisted in a unit that was alternately designated as infantry and as artillery, the 5th Rhode Island, in October 1861. As Daughter of the Regiment in the 5th Rhode Island, Kady saw additional battlefield action. When the regiment was advancing into battle at New Bern, North Carolina, in January 1862, other units mistook it for a Confederate force and were preparing to open fire on them. Kady saw the danger immediately. She dashed forward into a clearing and waved the regimental colors until the 5th was recognized as friendly forces. Her courageous action helped to prevent a battlefield blunder that could have cost hundreds of lives. At other times she treated wounded soldiers, including her husband, who was severely wounded in action and given a medical discharge.[7]

A noted cantiniere or vivandiere turned battlefield nurse was Marie Tepe (sometimes given as "Tebe"), known as "French Mary," who initially enlisted along with her husband in the 27th Pennsylvania Infantry ("Washington Brigade"). Tepe marched and soldiered with the men, performing various chores in camp. Frequently under fire as a canteen woman and nurse on the battlefield, she was wounded in the ankle at Fredericksburg in December 1862. During the Battle of Chancellorsville the following May her skirt was riddled by bullets. She was awarded the Kearny Cross for gallantry at the same time as Anna Etheridge.[8]

A Civil War nurses internet web site on tripod.com has now identified her as Marie Brose, born August 24, 1834, in Brest, France (and therefore about twenty-seven at the outbreak of the Civil War). She emigrated to the United States at about age ten after her father died, and at about twenty she married Philadelphia tailor Bernardo Tepe. On June 1, 1861, Bernardo enlisted in Company I of the 27th Pennsylvania Infantry (confirmed by a roster check, where his name is given as "Bernard Tape"). She followed him into the regiment as a vivandiere. She left the regiment following a falling-out with her husband; according to one version, the conflict was about a theft of money from the vivandiere's tent. Bernardo continued in it and was mustered out on June 11, 1864.

Marie next joined the 114th Pennsylvania Infantry as vivandiere, and it was with this regiment that most of her famous exploits occurred. The online article reports that after the war, Marie moved to the Pittsburgh area and married Richard Leonard, a veteran of Co. K, 1st Maryland Cavalry. (A roster search confirms his service in that company from August 19, 1861, to August 27, 1864.) She divorced Leonard in 1897. The article shows a photo of her in old age and her grave site near Pittsburgh. She reportedly took her own life by ingesting poison in May 1901.[9]

Some women, such as Bridget Divers, who participated in the 1864–1865 Virginia campaigns as a battlefield nurse with Sheridan's cavalry, occasionally doubled as combat soldiers. She is reported to have been with the 1st Michigan Cavalry. Although no record of that could be found by the Michigan centennial commission, several well-known nurses testified to her exploits.[10]

At age eighteen, Sarah ("Sallie") Taylor was Daughter of the Regiment for the 1st Tennessee Infantry, in which her stepfather, a Captain Dowden, is reported to have served. Known as "Miss Captain Taylor," she carried a sword and pistols and traveled with the men, mounted on a horse. A Georgia newspaper reported her capture by Confederate forces in June 1862, and a postwar book describes her leading the regiment off to reinforce a Colonel Garrard. In all probability this was Colonel Theophilus T. Garrard of the 7th Kentucky Infantry (Union), who was campaigning in East Tennessee during the winter of 1862 (see Appendix B).

Susan Lyons Hughes, in a scholarly online article, has provided an important new bit of information, the precise identification of the unit in which Sarah reportedly served. Various units for the Union or Confederacy were known as the "1st Tennessee Infantry." Based on a July 18, 1863, newspaper story reporting her capture (apparently for the second time) and parole, Taylor served in the Union 1st Tennessee Infantry (also known as the 1st East Tennessee Infantry). The unit was called "Bird's" (actually Byrd's) regiment, in which, the story says, she was Daughter of the Regiment.[11] The regiment was mounted infantry at least part of the time and shows that designation during 1863 in the *Official Records*.

A Sarah Taylor—whether the same person or not is uncertain—also shows up on the provost marshal roster of prisoners at Gratiot Prison in St. Louis, Missouri, as being arrested at Westport, Missouri, on February 28, 1865. The 1st (East) Tennessee Regiment had formally mustered out during August 1864, but some of its later recruits consolidated into three companies that continued in service for another year. The circumstances of this arrest are not reported.[12]

Far more numerous than Daughters of the Regiment after early 1862 were women who served as nurses in field hospitals; a full account of their works would require encyclopedic treatment. Their situation tended to be highly fluid and dangerous. At times they were exposed to enemy fire, often caring for soldiers in tents or deserted buildings, on steamships, in railroad cars, and in other improvised conditions near the front lines. Sometimes they were forced by encroaching enemy troops to pack up hurriedly and evacuate a hospital, taking the patients and emergency supplies with them, or they were taken prisoner along with their patients. Harriet A. Dada of New York and Emeline McLellan of Maine were both in Confederate custody for a while when the town of Winchester, Virginia, was occupied by Confederate forces in May 1862 and their hospital was taken over.[13] More than any other category of women's activities or employment during the war aside from female combat soldiers, these pioneering nurses blazed new trails and set new standards.

The notion that female nurses during the Civil War were somewhat pampered, aristocratic women who lived in comfortable quarters and worked routine shifts in well-equipped hospitals is a misconception. Such cozy conditions were the very rare exception rather than the rule and were pretty much confined to the big-city hospitals. Far more common were makeshift, poorly equipped tent hospitals hastily assembled in the field, or ramshackle buildings in the combat zone that had been damaged by artillery fire. These meager facilities often were close to the front lines and exposed to dangers of all kinds.

Field nurses worked long hours with little or no time for rest and had very few amenities. Such basics as medical supplies and food were often in short supply, while nurses had to cope with an endless stream of badly wounded and very ill soldiers desperately in need of emergency care. A shortage of doctors often caused women to pitch in and become, in effect, assistant surgeons. Between long sessions of exhausting labors, a woman felt fortunate to catch a few hours' sleep wrapped in an army blanket on the floor and to have a few scraps of food to tide her over.

A nurse whose first experience was caring for wounded soldiers from the Battle of the Wilderness in May 1864 was Georgiana Willets of New Jersey. Although her length of service was comparatively short, it was extraordinarily intensive and highly praiseworthy. She joined the army nurse corps at a large hospital in Fredericksburg, Virginia, where the wounded from the Wilderness were being brought by the thousands.

Blankets stitched together and stuffed with straw served as mattresses, and coat sleeves filled with hay as pillows.

When Fredericksburg had to be evacuated, Willets assisted in loading the patients on hospital transport ships and caring for the soldiers on board as the ship headed up the Rappahannock River. At Port Royal an officer came on board and pleaded for nurses to help care for a thousand wounded soldiers lying on the ground, freshly removed from the battlefield. She and a companion disembarked and remained there four days doing what they could for the bedraggled soldiers, before Willets returned to her regular duty.

Willets then worked at army headquarters hospitals at White House Landing and City Point, Virginia. During July she helped care for 250 wounded soldiers from the siege of Petersburg aboard a hospital transport ship carrying them to hospitals in Washington, D.C. She continued in hospital service through late 1864, intending to return to service in the spring after a short break at home, but the war ended the following April.[14]

Many women who became nurses during the war began by accompanying their husbands (or occasionally a brother or a son) into military service, and once there, pitched in to help in any way they could. More often than not they had little or no training for nursing or medical care. But the sick and wounded became so numerous in 1862 that army medical personnel in the field, if sometimes not at the big-city hospitals, often welcomed their help. On-the-job training was the order of the day.

When the war broke out in 1861, Mrs. Fannie A. Beers was visiting her mother in Connecticut where Beers was raised. She and her husband, Augustus, had settled in New Orleans; he quickly enlisted in the Confederate 1st Louisiana Infantry Battalion and headed for the war in Virginia. Fannie volunteered for nursing duties in Richmond and was one of the first women to defy the convention—especially in the South—that being a military nurse was not an appropriate occupation for a woman.

When her husband's battalion was transferred out west to the Army of Tennessee, she followed him and continued working as a nurse, becoming a hospital matron. Her postwar memoirs report numerous instances of caring for wounded soldiers on the battlefields under trying and dangerous conditions. At times she lived in a rude log cabin and was exposed to severe extremes of weather. She sometimes foraged on her own for food to supplement the patients' diets and treated wounded soldiers whose only beds were straw on the ground or hard benches made from pews in a church pressed into service as a hospital. Beers had become a "soldier-nurse."[15]

On one occasion her hospital had to be evacuated on short notice due to the approach of the enemy. Boxes were quickly filled with bedding and clothing, and sick and badly wounded men were hurriedly carried on stretchers to a filthy cattle car. Some scraps of bacon and cold cornbread were the only food available in the cars, so Beers took a cauldron and some pails and filled them with leftover food from the day's meals—some soup, a few vegetables, and some mule meat; a little cold coffee and tea, and a small amount of milk. Next she requisitioned a cart and carried the meager supplies to the railroad cars. There she began feeding the neediest soldier patients in the cars.

> The men were silent, and looked jaded and ghastly in the lurid light [from pinewood fires kindled in the streets]. Some had bloody rags tied about head and hands, their breasts were bare, the panting breath could be heard plainly, their eyes shone fiercely through the grime of powder and smoke.... The faces of the officers were grave and troubled; none seemed to observe our frantic haste, but all to look forward with unseeing eyes. I did so long to have them rest and refresh themselves. During the whole of that eventful night my cheeks were wet, my heart aching sadly.
>
> Before daylight we were off. Railroads at that time were very defective and very rough. Ah, how terrible was the suffering of those wounded men as they were jolted and shaken from side to side! For haste was necessary to escape the enemy. About noon the train came to a full stop, nor moved again for many, many hours. [The enemy was in the vicinity, and the train remained silently hidden in a pine forest.] The small supply of cooked food was soon exhausted.... All were parched with thirst.... All through the night every one was on the alert, listening intently for sounds that might mean danger. No lights, no roadside fires could be allowed; but the moon shone brightly, and by its light the surgeons moved about among the suffering men, whose groans... served to make night dismal indeed. In the intervals of attending upon the sick, we slept as we could, leaning up against boxes, tilted back in chairs against the side of the car, or lying down, with anything we could get for pillows.... In the morning we were hungry enough to eat the stale corn-bread.[16]

On another occasion the surgeon Beers worked with called her out to the battlefield to help administer emergency care:

> Dr. McAllister silently handed me two canteens of water, which I threw over my shoulder, receiving also a bottle of peach brandy. We then turned into a ploughed field, thickly strewn with men and horses, many stone dead, some struggling in the agonies of death. . . . The dead lay around us on every side, singly and in groups and *piles*; men and horses, in some cases, apparently inextricably mingled. Some lay as if peacefully sleeping; others, with open eyes, seemed to glare at any who bent above them. . . . They [both Union and Confederate soldiers] seemed mere youths, and I thought sadly of the mothers, whose hearts would throb with equal anguish in a Northern and a Southern home. . . .
>
> Several badly wounded men had been laid under the shade of some bushes a little farther on; our mission lay here. The portion of the field we crossed to reach this spot was in many places slippery with blood. The edge of my dress was red, my feet were wet with it. As we drew near the suffering men, piteous glances met our own. "Water! water!" was the cry. . . . taking from my pocket a small feeding-cup, which I always carried for use in the wards, I mixed some brandy and water, and, kneeling by one of the poor fellows who seemed worse than the others, tried to raise his head. But he was already dying. . . .
>
> The next seemed anxious for water, and drank eagerly. . . . A third could only talk with his large, sad eyes, but made me clearly understand his desire for water. As I passed my arm under his head the red blood saturated my sleeve and spread in a moment over a part of my dress. So we went on, giving water, brandy, or soup; sometimes successful in reviving the patient, sometimes only able to whisper a few words of comfort to the dying. There were many more left, and Dr. McAllister never for a moment intermitted his efforts to save them.

After a while, more help arrived, more surgeons and attendants with stretchers. The wounded who could tolerate it gradually were carried off to hospitals, and Beers returned to her hospital, somewhat traumatized by the experience. Next day she was back at work in the wards helping to care for both Confederate and Union soldiers who had fallen on the battlefield.[17]

Mrs. Betsy Sullivan was another example of a soldier-nurse, one who traveled with and functioned as a member of the regiment. In May 1861 she went to war from Pulaski, Tennessee, along with her husband, John Sullivan, in Company K, Confederate 1st Tennessee Infantry. Known as Mother Sullivan, she shared all the hardships of army life. Her title of Mother of the Regiment was earned for nursing the sick and wounded soldiers, cooking for them, and mending and washing their clothes. According to an account by Mrs. Grace Meredith Newbill in 1917, "[Mrs. Sullivan] marched on foot with her knapsack on her back through the mountains of West Virginia, slept on the frozen ground, under the cold skies, a blanket her only covering, her knapsack, her pillow."

When one of the soldiers in Company K was killed in a skirmish at Cheat Mountain, Western Virginia, Mother Sullivan carried his body by wagon to a railway station and shipped it back to Pulaski. At the battles of Shiloh and Corinth in 1862 she was "on the battle ground with her boys, carrying bandages and with canteens of water suspended from her shoulders, she bound up wounds and stanched the life blood of many soldiers, moistened the lips of the dying, and closed the eyes of the dead."

At the battle of Perryville, Kentucky, in October 1862, Sullivan was on the battlefield when her husband received a severe head wound, and Lieutenant John H. Wooldridge suffered the loss of both eyes. As the army retreated from Kentucky, John Sullivan and John Wooldridge were among the wounded left behind at Harrodsburg, where they became prisoners. Mrs. Sullivan stayed with them and took care of them.[18]

Another soldier-nurse was Bettie Taylor Philips (Mrs. W. D.), who went to war with her husband in the Confederate 4th Kentucky Infantry, part of the famous "Orphan Brigade." She traveled with the regiment and cared for wounded soldiers on the battlefield. At one point she was arrested and held as a spy at Nashville. According to an early account, W. D. Philips entered the Confederate army in 1861 at the beginning of the war. Mrs. Philips joined him at Bowling Green, where he was appointed quartermaster of the 4th Kentucky Infantry. "She remained at his side...in camp, on long marches, often under shot and shell of the enemy," and ministered to the sick, wounded, and dying soldiers.

After two years in service her health began to fail, so she started from Tennessee for her home in Kentucky to recuperate. When she was arrested at Nashville and two soldiers started to search her, Mrs. Philips drew her pistol and demanded that they send a woman to search her. The searcher found sufficient cause to send Mrs. Philips to Louisville for trial as a spy. But lacking evidence for a conviction, the authorities released her. Eventually she found her way back to the brigade and stayed with it until the end of the war.[19]

Soon after the 1st Battle of Bull Run, July 21, 1861, a news story reported that the wife of Captain E. J. Magruder of the Rome Light Guards of Georgia, along with her husband's sister, was at her husband's camp caring for the wounded and sick soldiers. The article doesn't say so because its writing actually predated the battle by a few days, but other sources indicate that Captain Magruder was wounded in the left arm during the battle. The *Memphis Daily Appeal,* July 28, 1861 (from the *Rome Southerner,* July 18), reported: "Mrs. M. Is the same lady who was complimented several weeks ago in the Virginia papers, who went from Georgia with the Rome Light Guards, and who was 'armed to the teeth.' She says in a late letter to a friend in this city, 'I would rather be a soldier than a soldier's wife.'"[20]

Another Georgia woman, Charlotte S. Branch, a widow in Savannah, also became a field nurse after the 1st Battle of Bull Run in July 1861 when she hurried to Virginia to look after her children. She had three sons in the "Oglethorpe Light Infantry," Company B of the 8th Georgia, who had been in the battle. One was killed, one was taken prisoner, and the third had telegraphed her with the tragic news.

After a delay in Richmond, she was finally able to reach her son Hamilton, in camp near Manassas. There she was shocked to find so many young soldiers dying from wounds or disease far away from home. She stayed for months while trying to arrange to have her son John's remains disinterred and shipped home. While there Branch nursed some of the soldiers back to health, acquiring the nickname of Mother of the Oglethorpe Infantry. She also wrote letters attempting to help her son Sanford, who had been taken prisoner and was being held at Old Capitol Prison in Washington, D.C.

Eventually the grieving mother sadly returned home in December. Her son John's body was disinterred and sent to Savannah. Sanford was released from prison that month and finally paroled and returned to his regiment the following June. Hamilton's one-year enlistment expired in May 1862 and he returned home, but he reenlisted as a lieutenant in a militia unit called the Savannah Cadets. This unit saw service in coastal batteries of Georgia and South Carolina in 1862 and 1863.

At home, Branch became immersed in all kinds of war work, from sending food to the soldiers to acting as a nurse in local hospitals. Shortly after the Battle of Gettysburg in July 1863, she read about the battle in the Savannah newspaper, and listed under the casualties was Lieutenant Sanford W. Branch, who had been shot through the lungs, apparently mortally wounded. Once again she set out for Virginia to locate General Lee's army and there learned that Sanford had been taken prisoner again. His wound had been too severe to allow his evacuation from the field when the army retreated, so he had been left behind. Despite the intercession of politicians and officers, Branch was denied a pass to allow her to enter the Federal lines to be with her son. She was informed that he was recovering satisfactorily from his wound. Sanford remained in Yankee prisons for about eighteen months, but apparently received good medical care, because he survived.

During William Tecumseh Sherman's invasion of Georgia in May 1864, Hamilton Branch's Savannah Cadets were sent to help defend the state. As Mrs. Branch continued to seek an exchange for Sanford, who remained in Federal custody, Hamilton was now in harm's way, so she remained as a nurse in Atlanta and Marietta hospitals to be near the front. When Hamilton was wounded on July 24, she met him in the hospital where he was given a thirty-day furlough home. But he quickly returned to his unit and was slightly wounded again in September.

Sanford was finally released from Federal custody in December but was in very poor physical health upon arrival home: underweight, emaciated, and still coughing up blood from his lung wound. Then Savannah was occupied by Union forces and all families of Confederate officers were ordered to leave town. Mrs. Branch and Sanford took a horse and wagon and became refugees, seeking shelter in Effingham County, while Hamilton continued in the army. But Hamilton's health failed and he was sent to the Confederate hospital in Augusta, Georgia, in February 1865. By the time he recovered fully the war was over.[21]

Mrs. Branch's harrowing experiences were, in a sense, fairly typical of a mother who had sons in the army and was therefore motivated to become a nurse and to help the military cause in any way possible. She had many counterparts in both the North and the South. Quite a few wives of soldiers were similarly motivated.

On the Union side Mrs. Jerusha R. Small enlisted with her husband in the 12th Iowa Infantry and acted as a frontline battlefield nurse. She labored for months in the regimental hospitals caring for the wounded from the Battles of Belmont in November 1861 and Fort Donelson in February 1862, becoming known as an "angel of mercy." By the time of Shiloh in early April of 1862, the strenuous work had impaired her health. At that battle her husband was badly wounded and captured but later rescued. The tent in which she was caring for the wounded soldiers came under enemy artillery fire, and she and her wounded husband and many other wounded soldiers from the regiment were forced to flee for their lives, leaving all possessions behind other than a small supply of bandages.

The refugees found their way to an Ohio field hospital, where they were taken in and Small remained to nurse her husband and the other 12th Iowa soldiers. After her husband reached a stage of convalescence, she succumbed to fatigue and exposure and was bedridden. Told that there was no hope for recovery due to her frail condition, she asked to be sent home and was accompanied there by her husband, where she died a few days after arrival. She was buried with military honors, with many of the soldiers of the 12th Iowa who were home on furlough in attendance and taking part in her funeral procession. At her request, she was buried wrapped in the national flag.[22]

So-called regimental nurses like Jerusha Small originally went into the field to accompany a particular regiment from their own state with the intention of caring for their own soldiers. However, most served impartially wherever wounded or sick soldiers needed care: on battlefields, in field hospitals, and on hospital transport ships. They gave priority to soldiers from their own state, but casualties were not always that conveniently segregated in the aftermath of a battle. Jane E. Schultz reports that virtually every woman who originally accompanied a specific regiment into the war became a field nurse and inevitably was exposed to the dangers of battle. "At work in the field," she writes, "nurses encountered skirmishes; some were known to drag men out of the line of fire to attend to their wounds."[23]

Harriet P. Dame went out with the 2nd New Hampshire Infantry from Portsmouth in 1861 as a nurse and hospital matron, caring for wounded soldiers after the First Battle of Bull Run and staying with the regiment throughout the war except for occasional duty at field hospitals. The regiment first served in the defenses of Washington, then was among General George B. McClellan's army that began the first assault on Richmond in spring of 1862. Dame was in the trenches at Fair Oaks on the Virginia Peninsula in June 1862 while the soldiers were under bombardment. After the battle she marched a long distance with the soldiers and cared for the wounded along the way. At the Second Battle of Bull Run in August 1862 she was taken prisoner but was released and given a pass through the lines. She cared for the wounded at the Battle of Gettysburg in July 1863 and remained in service to the end of the war.[24]

Another early regimental nurse was Isabella M. Fogg, a thirty-seven-year-old widow whose only son enlisted in the 6th Maine Infantry. When the war broke out, she was earning her keep as a seamstress in a tailor shop. The 6th Maine consisted primarily of big, brawny lumberjacks of relatively mature age, whereas Isabella's son, Hugh, was nineteen years old and only 5 feet 4½ inches tall, and she was concerned about his welfare. After the 6th Maine marched off to war in summer 1861, Fogg attached herself to another Maine regiment and left for the battlefront that fall.

During the Virginia Peninsula Campaign of 1862, with McClellan's army trying to take Richmond, she served on the Hospital Transport Service ship *Elm City*. As the Seven Days Battles around Richmond unfolded, Fogg went onto battlefields to care for wounded Maine soldiers. During this campaign Hugh fell ill with malaria and was hospitalized for several months. At Chancellorsville in May 1863, where the 6th Maine took heavy casualties, Mrs. Fogg came under artillery fire. The chief surgeon of the regiment, F. S. Holmes, praised her for her "hazardous, arduous and untiring" services in the performance of her duties caring for the soldiers in the field (MacCaskill and Novak 1996, 35). She arrived in Gettysburg on July 4, 1863, one day after the battle, and spent nearly two weeks caring for wounded soldiers there.

Late in the war Hugh, who had reenlisted in a veteran regiment, the 1st Maine Veteran Volunteers, was severely wounded at the battle of Cedar Creek, Virginia, in October 1864 and had to have a leg amputated. Mrs. Fogg rushed to his aid and helped nurse him back to health. He was discharged on June 8, 1865. After the war, in 1866, Fogg was granted a government pension. She had fallen on a hospital boat and injured her spine and was crippled for the balance of her life. Both she and her son had performed courageous service for the Union.[25]

Since they lived in close proximity to the wounded and ill soldiers, the regimental and other field hospital nurses were also exposed to the diseases, such as typhoid fever, that swept the camps, and many were disabled or died from the exposure. A U.S. Civil War Centennial Commission report observed:

> As nursing quickly moved directly onto the battlefields, a number
> of women North and South faced challenging situations that taxed
> human endurance to the limit. Many set fractures and performed
> minor surgery with little knowledge and no guidance.... Practically
> all of the nurses were forced to improvise at one time or another.
> At Antietam Clara Barton used corn-husks for bandages, and
> Georgeanna Woolsey wrote after Gettysburg of making surgical pads
> from rags stuffed with sawdust.[26]

The conditions faced by regimental nurses early in the war were described by Mrs. M. V. Harkin, who served along with her mother, Mrs. Sarah A. M. Kenna, in the 17th Wisconsin Infantry in 1862. At St. Louis that spring they began getting a hospital ready.

> Soon we had plenty of work, for the measles attacked the boys,
> and we lost several.... At last the news came that there was every
> prospect of a fight at Pittsburg Landing [Tennessee], or Shiloh, as it
> is sometimes called, and the 17th [Wisconsin Infantry] was ordered
> to be ready at a moment's notice. Our worst cases were sent to the
> General Hospital, and everything was put in order. Then we were
> commanded to embark for Pittsburg Landing.... Along the Tennessee
> shore we watched for a masked battery, but, fortunately, we were not
> disturbed. When we reached Savannah [Hardin County, Tennessee]
> we could hear the noise and fuss of the hospital that they had close
> by the shore. Here we heard of the battle of Shiloh [April 6–7, 1862].
> The next morning we sighted the Landing, and disembarked about
> noon. Our soldiers were detailed at once to help bury the dead,
> the steamer was used as a hospital, and we were set to work. The
> doctors pitched hospital tents too.
> Here we saw some of the horrors of war. There were wounds
> of every description, and many a brave young life went out on the
> amputation table. The battlefield looked as if it had been ploughed in

deep furrows; for every inch, north and south, had been contested stubbornly; and the white wood was laid bare on every tree, as if it had been peeled by hand.... We had great hardships to contend against. There was great lack of hospital stores, and we were all on short rations. On account of the masked batteries [along the river banks] we found it hard to get supplies, and for one week all we nurses had to eat was hard-tack.... Then followed long, weary days, and night watches with poor suffering men. There was almost every form of sickness, and we had to do all the cooking, and we had to keep the soldiers clean and the hospital in order.... As the weather grew warmer sickness increased. The water was not very good, and the men lacked such food as would keep them in good health. The ground on which they had to sleep, with just a blanket wrapped around them, was damp and reeking with vile odors, and it was no wonder that so many died.[27]

During this period one of the other nurses at Pittsburg Landing, Mrs. Anna McMahon, fell ill with measles and after suffering for five days she died. A coffin was made for her out of cracker boxes, and she was buried beneath some large trees along the bank of the Tennessee River with a crude board bearing her name as a grave marker.

Mary J. Safford of Cairo, Illinois (who became known as the "Cairo Angel"), first worked in Illinois hospitals along with Mother Mary Bickerdyke. Mary A. Livermore of the Northwestern Sanitary Commission says of her, "I think she was the *very first woman* who went into the camps and hospitals, in the country; I know she was in the West." In their 1867 book, L. P. Brockett and Mary C. Vaughan describe her exploits:

The morning after the battle of Belmont [November 7, 1861] found her—the only lady—early on the field, fearlessly penetrating far into the enemies' lines, with her handkerchief tied upon a little stick, and waving above her head as a flag of truce—ministering to the wounded, which our army had been compelled to leave behind, to some extent— and many a Union soldier owes his life to her almost superhuman efforts on that occasion. She continued her labors with the wounded after their removal to the hospitals, supplying every want in her power, and giving words of comfort and cheer to every heart.

In a letter to the *Chicago Daily Tribune,* April 24, 1862, Dr. H. C. Gillett described the work done in the field after Shiloh by the surgeons and nurses sent by the Chicago Sanitary Commission:

The female nurses on the boats rendered themselves very useful.... Under the direction of Miss Mary Safford, they prepared food for the sick and wounded, bathed their wounds and washed their powder and blood-stained faces.... Since the commencement of the war, she has devoted her time and energies gratuitously to this labor of love. I can assure the benevolent that contributions sent to her care will be applied with economy, and distributed where most required, and when this wicked rebellion is crushed out, the name of Miss Mary Safford will be immortalized in American history like that of Miss Florence Nightingale in that of England.[28]

Teams of soldier-husband and nurse-wife serving in the field were common, especially early in the war. In one such case, although it is not known whether she continued as a nurse, a Mrs. Werner had accompanied her Union soldier husband to the Shiloh battlefield. As the battle started, she was urged to leave but refused to do so. Instead, she helped to carry off wounded soldiers from the battlefield to a place of safety. Another young woman with her who had also refused to leave was struck by a cannonball and instantly killed within a few feet of Werner. According to the *Daily Missouri Republican,* April 24, 1862, while caring for wounded soldiers, Werner tore her underclothing into strips to make bandages. Her husband was killed during the battle and she was left destitute.

A month later when the hospital ship *Empress* docked at St. Louis, it was carrying 448 sick and wounded soldiers, having also stopped at Evansville, Indiana, where it left off 371 soldiers, for a total of 819 casualties from Pittsburg Landing. The *Daily Missouri Republican* for May 18, 1862, reported that in addition to five surgeons, a steward, and an apothecary, the medical team on board included "five Sisters of Mercy and three lay sisters as female nurses, and twenty-eight male attendants."

Jane Hinsdale of Detroit, Michigan, whose husband, Hiram, was in the 2nd Michigan Infantry, went to war with the regiment as a nurse in 1861. At the First Battle of Bull Run she became separated from her husband, and while searching for him and caring for wounded soldiers on the battlefield, she was captured and detained by the Confederates. Left in an old barn with thirty to forty wounded Union soldiers, she tore up her underclothing to make bandages. Later she escaped and took information on Confederate movements to the generals in Washington, D.C. She continued in service throughout the war as a nurse in field hospitals and after the war was granted a pension. She could neither read nor write, and her pension papers are signed by her "mark."[29]

Mrs. Belle Reynolds (nee Arabella Macomber) also went into the field with her husband, Lieutenant William S. Reynolds, Company A, 17th Illinois Infantry, and traveled with the regiment. She sometimes rode in an army wagon, an ambulance, or on a mule and lived in a tent in camp. She saw combat while under fire at Shiloh in 1862, where she served as a nurse, and was later given a commission as Major by Governor Yates of Illinois. After the war Belle studied medicine and became a practicing physician.[30]

A number of officers' wives performed heroically. Nadine Turchin (Mrs. General John B.) accompanied her husband in the 19th Illinois Infantry, which he commanded as a colonel. Once when her husband became ill, she assumed command of the regiment and the soldiers accepted her leadership. She also served as a battlefield nurse and was frequently under fire.

Following a serious accident on the Ohio and Mississippi Railroad on September 17, 1861, Mrs. Turchin displayed extraordinary courage in rescuing members of Company I, 19th Illinois. While passing through Indiana their railroad car broke through a bridge and plunged into the water; 24 men were killed instantly and 105 injured. Some of the injured later died in the hospital, some were crippled for life, and others recovered and returned to the regiment. Robert Brand, the mayor of Galena, Illinois, paid her this tribute after thanking then-Colonel Turchin for his help:

> But to hear the wounded men speak of the heroic conduct of the brave Mrs. Turchin! When the accident occurred—when the dead, dying and mutilated lay in one mass of ruin—when the bravest heart was appalled, and all was dismay, this brave woman was in the water rescuing the mangled and wounded from a watery grave, and tearing from her person every available piece of clothing as bandages for the wounded—proves beyond all question that she is not only the right woman in the right place, but a fit consort for the brave Turchin in leading the gallant sons of Illinois to battle. Such misfortunes bring forth heroic women, whose services may be frequently needed if this fratricidal war shall continue to the bitter end.[31]

Enlisted men's wives sometimes accompanied their husbands, too. Lucy Ann Cox became a vivandiere and nurse in the 13th Virginia Infantry, reportedly traveling with her husband in Company A for most of the war. She marched with the soldiers, including their two long and dangerous journeys north during Lee's invasions of Maryland in 1862 and 1863, and she cared for wounded soldiers during combat. After the war she was buried with military honors.[32]

According to the regimental roster the only man named Cox in the regiment was William F. Cox, who had enlisted as a sergeant from Louisa County on April 17, 1861, and served in Company D (rather than Company A). He was reduced to private in March 1862 for some unreported infraction. Then in September, a few days before the Battle of Antietam, he was hospitalized for about five months, returning to duty on February 28, 1863. After remaining on duty for about a year, on February 8, 1864, he allegedly deserted and was recorded as a prisoner of war on February 9. He is listed as being a sergeant again at this point. Then he is shown as "confined" as of December 11, 1864, whether by the Union or the Confederacy is not reported. With this somewhat incomplete personal history, it appears that William Cox had a rocky career as a soldier, and that his wife had a more distinguished military record than he did. Lucy Ann Cox may well have carried on alone during her husband's absences.

Married couples combined in many ways to serve their country during the Civil War. At the outset of the war William H. Holstein and his wife, Anna Morris Holstein, were a wealthy and prominent couple living in Upper Merion, Montgomery County, Pennsylvania. When Lee invaded Pennsylvania in September 1862, William enlisted as a corporal in the 17th Pennsylvania Militia Infantry, which was called into service for defense of the state. For the time being, Anna worked at home in the Soldiers' Aid Society.[33]

Returning home after the Battle of Antietam, William told Anna of the drastic need for medical care for the soldiers. Together they gave up their comfortable home life and set out into the field to help, voluntarily accepting life in tents, the discomforts of exposure to the elements, and all the hardships of army life. In her journal Anna describes arriving at the Antietam battlefield and being horrified to see wounded men still scattered all over the field. Some of the more fortunate were in barns or log houses that had been pressed into duty as hospitals, where they at least had a little hay to serve as bedding. Decent food and medicines were scarce, and the medical personnel were overwhelmed by the sheer numbers of casualties.

Quite a few nurses like Anna were initiated into service when the war came near enough to their homes that they responded to the emergency call that went out from a major battlefield, and they traveled directly to the scene and pitched in to help. Another was Jane Boswell Moore of Baltimore, who rushed to the scene in Sharpsburg, Maryland, after the Battle of Antietam. Later she also served as a battlefield nurse in Virginia and Pennsylvania. Her memoirs provide graphic descriptions of what battlefield nurses experienced at this time (see Appendix B).

From Sharpsburg, Maryland, the Holsteins moved on to hospitals in Frederick, Maryland, and other places, often using makeshift beds or sleeping on someone's floor while traveling. Anna appears to have been hardier than William, who was subject to periodic attacks of fever or exhaustion and occasionally forced to take time out to rest and recuperate. The following year, after Lee's second invasion of the North, they went to Gettysburg shortly after the battle ended on July 3 and served at a field hospital where Union and Confederate casualties lay side by side. Anna noted in her journal, "The scenes around Gettysburg were horrible in the extreme: the green sod everywhere stained with the lifeblood of dying men...heaps of blood-stained clothing...shattered muskets...and the innumerable heaps of slain horses which literally cover the hard-fought field."

Arriving on the scene a few days later with a church party from Philadelphia carrying medicine and supplies, John Y. Foster was shocked at the carnage. About 30,000 wounded soldiers were still lying in the field, the army medical service completely unable to cope with the magnitude of the disaster. Makeshift hospitals were hastily established in damaged buildings or in tents, staffed by all-too-few army surgeons who had grossly insufficient medical supplies. Growing numbers of volunteer nurses began to appear on the grounds through their own initiative. At Round Top, Foster reported, "the slope was one horrid waste: far and near unburied corpses were lying for days afterward, scores of wounded rebels crouching among them unable to move. In some places bodies, caught in the thickets as they fell, were still hanging midway between the summit and the hill's foot, dense clouds of insects hovering over them."[34]

The spring 1864 Union campaign in Virginia found William and Anna Holstein working with the U.S. Sanitary Commission to care for the wounded following the Battle of the Wilderness on May 5–7. Almost 18,000 Union wounded were evacuated mostly to Belle Plains and the vicinity of Fredericksburg. When the Holsteins later arrived at the hospitals at Union headquarters in City Point, Virginia, on June 18, the town was overflowing with wounded soldiers, "wounded men at every step you take." Next day they were among the Sanitary Commission workers who fed and cared for 600 men. On June 20 the first boatload of wounded was sent off to hospitals in the North.[35]

In January 1865 William and Anna Holstein were immersed in caring for Union prisoners released from southern prison camps, most notably from Andersonville Prison, at hospital facilities in Annapolis, Maryland. They watched as the emaciated and starving soldiers tried to walk off the boats or were carried off by stretcher. Anna in her journal makes some pungent remarks about the Southern prison officials responsible for such cruelty. She describes "[sitting] by the bedsides of dying skeletons as they shudderingly recalled their prison life. . . . They appeared like a wretched bundle of bones, covered with a few filthy rags." Many were too weak and ill to survive for very long. "Every morning," she recorded in her journal, " a wagon was driven through the camp, to pick up those who had died during the night; the poor, emaciated bodies were caught up by an arm and foot, and pitched into the wagon as a stick of cordwood would be thrown . . . then taken to the shallow trenches which were to receive them."[36]

The couple remained in Annapolis until July 1865 finishing up their hospital work, then finally returned home for some hard-earned rest and recuperation.

Among the thousands of nurses who volunteered their services on both sides were Catholic nuns of several different orders, including the Daughters of Charity, based in Emmittsburg, Maryland, and the Holy Cross Sisters of South Bend, Indiana.[37] Other women of various religious or philosophical backgrounds flocked to the state hospital associations, which evolved into the U.S. Sanitary Commission, or to the Christian Commission, both of which supplied vital field hospital services.[38]

At a battle in the Southwest a wounded Confederate saw a group of women rushing to aid wounded soldiers on the battlefield, apparently oblivious to the bullets flying around. He exclaimed to a companion his concern that they would all be killed. The companion replied, "Oh, those are the Sisters. They are looking for the wounded. They're not afraid of anything." At Vicksburg the Sisters of Mercy wandered through the rubble of the city that had been devastated by Union artillery fire to care for wounded civilians in any structures still standing. The Vicksburg Sisters of Mercy also accompanied wounded Confederate soldiers in railroad boxcars to hospitals in Alabama, and their hospital at Jackson, Mississippi, came under Union artillery fire and had to be evacuated.[39]

One Union physician who served on a Mississippi River hospital ship thought the Catholic nurses too dour. In a letter home on August 18, 1862, he expressed a sectarian view:

> There are several catholic women (Sisters of the Holy Cross) about the establishment, who help to take care of the sick. They have a little room fitted up for their worship. There is also a protestant chaplain who deals in the genuine article of religious truth. These "sisters" no doubt do much good around here as they have charge of the cooking department, but I should not want them around my wards! They are a pale, forlorn looking set, with a down cast look which has anything but cheerfulness about it.[40]

On the other hand, a conservative Protestant Texas soldier was so impressed by what he experienced with the Catholic nurses in Georgia during 1863 that after the war, when he became a wealthy businessman and owner of several lumber companies, he donated large sums of money to the Sisters of Charity and helped to found a Catholic hospital. He did so even though he was severely criticized by his very conservative Protestant East Texas friends and neighbors. He had been reared in a strict Protestant environment where it was widely believed and preached that there was no place in heaven for Catholics. But his views were changed by his wartime experience.

William A. Fletcher, a private in the 5th Texas Infantry, had been wounded in the foot during the Chickamauga campaign. He hobbled to the field infirmary where more urgent cases received priority care, and so his untended wound bled all night. Later he was evacuated to Augusta,

Georgia, and placed in a makeshift hospital in a church, his "bed" a church pew. There his wound was periodically dressed and he was tenderly cared for. "The most of the dressing was done by Sisters of Charity—it was my first experience and I was in love with the women and the uniform at once and have not gotten over it yet; for there is a feeling of gratitude uppermost when and where my eyes behold them," Fletcher wrote.[41]

His great-granddaughter, Vallie Fletcher Taylor, wrote an afterword to his published memoirs in 1908:

> Bill had nurtured a special debt of gratitude to the Catholic Sisters of Charity. He was sure that the care given him by these compassionate women in Augusta, Georgia, had saved his leg from amputation. [His foot wound had become gangrenous.] ... in 1897, Bill began working with the mother house, St. Mary's Infirmary in Galveston, to plan a hospital for Beaumont. He secured land on the Neches River and donated funds and lumber to build their hospital. ... For his continuing contributions to the sisters, he received a great deal of criticism from Protestant pulpits in East Texas.[42]

The records of the Catholic orders include reports of female soldiers discovered in hospitals. Maher (1989) reports that Catholic Sisters were especially given two unusual duties: (1) acting as peacemakers between quarreling soldiers, and (2) attending to female soldiers who often were first discovered when wounded or sick. As to the female soldiers, "In hospitals where there were sisters, such cases were assigned to them and several different communities of sisters noted their care of such women."[43]

Regular army nurses also discovered female soldiers among their patients. Clara Barton, whose fame as a nurse spread across the country and around the world, was caring for wounded soldiers during the battle of Antietam in 1862 when a female soldier was brought to her attention (see Chapter 7). While giving one soldier a drink of water, a bullet tore through Barton's sleeve and killed the soldier. At Antietam Barton "had to sleep on the ground in the rain. ... after three days of round-the-clock work, she crawled into her tent, propped her head to avoid drowning, and lost consciousness"(Schultz 2004).

Early in the war, probably in 1862, an army nurse by the name of Adelaide E. Thompson (later Mrs. Adelaide E. Spurgeon) of New York City served in Washington, D.C., area hospitals, including work in a smallpox ward.

Eventually she was disabled by "blood poisoning" and was forced to give up the profession of nursing. She then entered the secret service at the provost marshal's headquarters. After the war she reported in her reminiscences:

> I was sent for one day by the judge advocate, who wished me to interview two parties who had been taken out of the ranks as a regiment was marching up the avenue. I went into a back room, where I saw two boyish-looking persons in uniform. After a short conversation they owned up to being of the gentler sex; but the deception was perfect. One was the wife of one of the men, and the other was engaged to one. They had traveled hundreds of miles with the regiment, and would probably have gone to the front but for the rascally behavior of one of the lieutenants, who was in [on] the secret. He offered some insult to the young wife, which she resented, and in a spirit of vengeance he signaled the provost guard, and had them taken out of the ranks. They both wept bitterly, not only at the disgrace, but at being obliged to return to their homes, leaving their loved ones, perhaps never to meet them again. With some difficulty clothing was procured, and they were sent home very much wiser women than when they left.[44]

In *Webster's Third International Dictionary*, the first definition of the word "soldier" is "a person engaged in military service: as (1) an officer or enlisted man serving in an army: a member of an organized body of combatants . . . (2) one that fights for a cause, endures hardships, or otherwise conducts himself gallantly. . . ." Clearly the women described here who performed military service under hardship conditions richly deserve the title "soldier." Then there were the women who formally enlisted as soldiers in male disguise and fought in combat alongside the men.

3

Foot Soldiers North and South

The most important qualification of a soldier is fortitude under fatigue and privation. Courage is only second; hardship, poverty, and want are the best school for a soldier.
Napoleon Bonaparte (1769–1821)

The frontline nurses who endured hardships and were exposed to enemy fire and other dangers were courageous soldiers. Even more remarkable in some ways were the women who adopted male disguise and enlisted in organized regiments as regular soldiers. They underwent formal military training and fought alongside the men, directly experiencing the violence and horror of war to the fullest as combatants. These women endured the same long marches, harsh weather, and bad food as the men. They also exchanged gunfire and engaged in hand-to-hand combat with the enemy and often became casualties under conditions identical to those of the male soldiers. Many of them advanced through the ranks to become sergeants—or in some cases, officers—until wounded, killed, or found out through some extreme circumstance, their promotions a testament to their military competence.

In September 1862 at the Battle of Antietam (Sharpsburg), Maryland, a young soldier in the 28th Ohio Infantry was severely wounded and an arm had to be amputated. After the war it was discovered that the soldier, who had survived the surgery, was a young girl named Catherine E. Davidson. Historical research has now discovered the probable male alias that she used (see Chapter 9 and Appendix B).

Female soldiers turned up in the earliest regiments to reach the field in 1861. At the beginning of the war when optimism was high that the conflict would be short, the typical term of enlistment for a regiment was three months. By the time of the First Battle of Bull Run on July 21, 1861, the earliest three-months regiments organized in April of that year were beginning to expire. Later the standard enlistment became three years, and numerous states had a three-months 1st, 3rd, or 5th Infantry regiment that by late 1861 or early 1862 had gone home and reorganized into a three-year regiment with the same designation.

"Charles H. Williams," a woman, is reported to have served three months in Company I of an early Iowa regiment. She was discovered when mustered out with the regiment. As she was described in newspaper reports, her hands were small and rather delicate, eyes large and lustrous, hair jet black. "She was born in Davenport where her mother now resides.... Capt. Cox learned her sex but allowed her to remain."[1] Her real identity has never been learned, partly due to confusion over the numerical designations of early regiments, and historical detective work has yielded mixed results (see Chapter 9).

Newspaper accounts early in the war suggest that female soldiers were fairly common. An unnamed woman said to be the mother of four children was reported to have served as "the most reckless daredevil" in the three-months 7th Pennsylvania Infantry regiment, which participated in several skirmishes and engagements in Maryland and West Virginia.[2] This newspaper report raises many questions, the answers to which probably will never be known. Where was her husband (if she had one)? Who was caring for her children while she was off engaging in "daredevil" activities? What were her motivations? All too often, we are left with tantalizing, and probably unanswerable, questions of this sort.

One little-known case of a female soldier early in the war occurred on what was then the western frontier. Miss Louisa Wellman of Iowa was born and raised on the frontier and was accustomed to outdoor life from childhood. She could ride a horse and knew how to use a pistol or a rifle. When the war broke out, she donned some of her brother's clothes and enlisted in an early Iowa infantry regiment. Her biggest problem was becoming accustomed to the rough language and profanity of many of the soldiers. Accordingly, she joined a group of more pious soldiers that came to be known as the "praying squad."

Louisa took part in the storming of Fort Donelson in February 1862, during which she was slightly wounded in the wrist. According to an 1877 account, "Afterwards she served often in the picket line and distinguished herself by her courage, vigilance, and shrewdness. . . . The battle of Pittsburgh Landing [Shiloh, April 6–7, 1862] was an affair in which she figured with a cool bravery that kept her company steady in spite of the terrible fire which was decimating the ranks of the Federal Army."

At Shiloh the regiment was slowly driven toward the river and was suffering heavy casualties when, just as they reached the shelter of the gunboats on the river, a shell exploded directly in their front and Louisa was thrown violently to the ground. She immediately jumped up onto her feet and was able to walk to the temporary hospital that had been established along the river bank. She had been wounded in the collar bone by a fragment of shell.

Because of the location of the wound, the surgeon asked her to remove her army jacket. When she refused to do so and blushed, the surgeon quickly guessed the truth. The wife of a captain was in camp at the time, so the surgeon wrote a note for the soldier to carry to the captain's wife with instructions on how to dress the wound. Louisa begged him not to disclose her secret so she could stay in the ranks, but he felt obliged to report the situation to the commanding officer. The commander expressed his admiration for her courage, but recommended that she serve in some other capacity and notified her parents.

With her parents' consent she was allowed to remain in hospital service in the ambulance department as a battlefield nurse, and she was furnished with a horse and saddlebags with medical supplies. "Whenever a battle took place she would ride fearlessly to the front to assist the wounded," the report continues. "Many a poor wounded soldier was assisted off the field by her, and sometimes she would dismount from her horse, and, aiding the wounded man to climb into the saddle, would convey him to the hospital." She was often exposed to enemy fire during this service.[3]

Although the story of Louisa Wellman is not documented by its author, it rings true and has numerous details that can be checked for historical accuracy. Among other things, if the story is true she would have been a member of the famous Iowa brigade that served with gallantry and distinction in Ulysses S. Grant's western army early in the war. The brigade comprised the 2nd, 7th, 12th, and 14th Iowa Infantry regiments, which were the only early Iowa regiments that saw action at both Fort Donelson and Shiloh.

An examination of the four regimental rosters and their casualty analysis data on the Civil War Database, interestingly but not conclusively, found only one hypothetical candidate for the male alias of Louisa Wellman who fits all the criteria. That was Pvt. Charles Cline, Company H, 14th Iowa Infantry, who was wounded at Shiloh and quickly discharged at that place without explanation.[4] Further, Wellman could not have been "Charles H. Williams," also of Iowa, because their military histories are very different.

Except where the military women survived the war and left interviews or memoirs, little is known about their motivations. By inference from their records of service, most simply wanted to be with their husbands or sweethearts at any cost and so adopted male disguise and braved shot and shell on the battlefields. Many female soldiers appear to have been motivated simply by patriotism or love of country and were willing to fight for the cause along with their loved ones. Some (probably a small minority) were adventurers, craving excitement and action, and in some cases they changed allegiances merely for the opportunity to remain a soldier.[5] Often women found in the ranks wearing a soldier's uniform were considered to be common prostitutes or spies and sent home in disgrace. However, camp followers and officers' concubines were one thing, while women who served in combat and risked their lives were quite another.[6]

Occasionally young women joined the army to get away from some disagreeable situation at home and to start a new life. Mrs. Jane Ferguson, who was married to a Confederate soldier, enlisted in a Union regiment and was arrested wearing a Federal uniform in Louisville, Kentucky, suspected of being a spy. During her trial in November 1863 she claimed in her defense that she had enlisted in the Union army to escape an abusive husband. She admitted that she had been sent as a spy but said she was using the occasion to escape and had no intention of returning to the Confederate side. She was convicted but later released after a review, and her ultimate fate is unknown.[7]

Frances Hook joined the army to escape a bad marriage; Sarah Edmonds ran away from home to escape a domineering father, later joining the army. A woman by the name of V. A. White was reported to have left a life of prostitution to join the army and start a new life, enlisting in Company D of the 1st Michigan Engineers and Mechanics and mustering out with the regiment in 1865.[8]

Skeptics often question how so many women, beyond a few huskier individuals whose bodies did not fit the female (or "feminine") stereotype, could have fooled the examining physicians and gained entry into the ranks. And when past this hurdle, how could they have continued to fool the men while living and working with them in close quarters? Or were they simply young women whom contemporary society would judge "immoral," present only to cohabit with the men rather than to serve their country, and therefore aided by the men in maintaining their male disguises? These are legitimate questions that occurred to the earliest postwar writers and commentators, some of whom were deeply skeptical about the stories of women fighting in the ranks. "Those who from whatever cause . . . donned the male attire and concealed their sex, " said Brockett and Vaughan in 1867, "are hardly entitled to a place in our record, since they did not seek to be known as women, but preferred to pass for men. . . . "[9] Individual case examples throughout the book will illustrate how a number of women (mostly young girls) came to be in the ranks and will demonstrate just how successful they were in maintaining their disguises.

Smaller, slimmer volunteers who doctors thought might not be able to carry heavy weapons and knapsacks typically were steered into accepting positions as drummer boys, buglers, or male nurses, and many a slender young girl entered the service in that way. Although originally intended to sound military calls during ceremonies and drills, drummer boys were not always left behind when the regiments went into the field. They were often in the heat of battle, sometimes sustaining wounds, and many "graduated" to become regular infantry soldiers once they saw combat.[10]

"Charles Martin," a girl of twelve, ran away from home "in the early part of the war," according to a postwar book, and joined an unnamed Pennsylvania regiment. Initially she served as a drummer boy but then became a regimental clerk. A Philadelphia newspaper reported in late 1863,

"She had evidently enjoyed the advantage of education, could write a good hand, and even composed very well." After participating in five battles and escaping unwounded, she contracted typhoid fever and her gender was finally discovered when she was hospitalized in Pennsylvania. Her parents resided in Bucks County. After she recovered she was sent home to her parents, who had assumed that she was dead (see Appendix B).

Three Charles Martins—each of them said to have been "discharged for disability" at about the right time to fit the story—appear on rosters of Pennsylvania regiments. Two of those regiments were organized at Harrisburg, one at Philadelphia, and all three were involved in heavy combat. The regiment that best fits the story, including the "early part of the war" reference and Philadelphia newspaper location, is the 114th Pennsylvania Infantry, organized in Philadelphia in August 1862. However, Company A, in which Charles Martin enlisted, had seen prior service as an independent company known as the Zouaves d'Afrique or "Collis's Zouaves" for about a year. He enlisted on August 17, 1861.

The 114th saw action at Cedar Mountain, Second Bull Run, Chantilly, Antietam, and Fredericksburg in 1862 during this Charles Martin's term of service. He was discharged for disability on April 6, 1863, about a month before the Battle of Chancellorsville. Interestingly, the 114th had two women openly serving in female attire: Septima Collis, the colonel's wife (see Appendix A) and the vivandiere Marie Tepe (see Chapter 2).[11]

Edmonia Gates is reported to have enlisted in a distinctly unusual and no doubt unique combination, first as a teamster and then as a drummer boy in another Zouave regiment, the 121st New York Infantry, or "Wilson's Zouaves." She was discovered in the latter regiment in March 1864 and sent to a Washington, D.C., workhouse.[12]

Historian Gregory A. Coco reports that Mrs. Abrev Kamoo came to the United States in 1862 after having attended the University of Heidelberg and enlisted in the Union army as "Tommy Kamoo." She served as a nurse and drummer, sustaining a slight wound to her nose at Gettysburg, and was not discovered during three years in the army.[13] No Union soldier by the name of Kamoo could be found, but there was a phonetically similar name: Thomas H. Kamouse. This soldier, a strong candidate to have been "Tommy Kamoo," enlisted as a private in the 8th New York Cavalry on September 4, 1862, and was discharged on June 7, 1865. The regiment was engaged at Gettysburg on all three days of the battle, July 1–3, 1863. Maria Lewis also served in this regiment (see Chapter 10).

Although a cavalry regiment would not be expected to have a drummer boy, the 8th New York Cavalry regimental history reports that when it headed to Washington, D.C., in late November of 1861, it was escorted by the "Union Blues," a band that included a drum corps of young boys dressed in Zouave uniforms. Additionally, 800 of the soldiers were originally unmounted. It is quite possible that at this early stage of the war, Kamoo worked her way through the ranks first as a drummer boy and then stayed on as a nurse or soldier.

Rebecca Peterman (a.k.a. Georgianne Peterman) from Ellenboro, Wisconsin, is reported to have served one or two years as a drummer boy with the 7th Wisconsin Infantry and to have seen action at Antietam in September 1862. Important recent research findings (Blanton and Cook 2002) indicate that Peterman joined the 7th Wisconsin Infantry in the fall of 1862 at age sixteen or seventeen and that her stepbrother and cousin were in the same regiment. Thus she, like many other female soldiers, likely had accomplices. Apparently her stepbrother's name was John F. Haney, according to new information from Census and Adjutant General Office data. The Civil War Database confirms that a John F. Haney from Dickeyville, Wisconsin, enlisted in Company C of the 7th Wisconsin on August 13, 1861. He is reported to have died of disease on November 11, 1862, at Washington, D.C.[14]

Part of the explanation for young women being able to deceive the male soldiers lies in the fact that manners and mores were very different then. Soldiers constantly on the march or in extended periods of combat usually wore the same uniforms and underclothes for weeks, and they slept fully clothed. During long periods of marching and fighting, they seldom took a full bath unless, during a break in the action, they came across a convenient stream or lake. Sarah Edmonds as "Frank Thompson" often slept beside the road while on frequent courier or mail-carrying duty. Even in camp, male soldiers often were slow to recognize that a fellow soldier had feminine characteristics, perhaps finding it unimaginable that a woman would have the audacity to masquerade as a man and have the endurance to succeed at it under hardship conditions. When it was reported that a woman had served in the ranks of the 14th Maine Infantry throughout the war, Lieutenant Colonel Ira B. Gardner said that she served under him for two years without being recognized as a female. "If I had been anything but a boy," he said, "I should probably have seen from her form that she was a female."[15]

Underage boy soldiers were not that uncommon, since the minimum age laws were seldom enforced and regimental officers had an almost constant shortage of soldiers. Unless a parent came looking for a runaway child, as they sometimes did, bearing a writ of *habeas corpus,* the officers were not inclined to ask questions as long as the boyish-looking soldier was performing well. The need to recruit replacements for casualties became more and more critical as the war progressed and many regiments became seriously short-handed. The officers needed warm bodies to fill the ranks.[16]

Civil War historian Elizabeth Leonard provides a cogent discussion of these issues.[17] In the first place, many would-be female enlistees *were* caught by the examining physicians. But others slipped through undetected because the physical examinations, especially during busy periods of enlistment and rapid processing of volunteers, were superficial. To be soldier material mainly required healthy limbs and acceptably good eyesight, which did not mandate close examination. The fact that so many Civil War soldiers were young, slender, and beardless and had high-pitched voices also helped the women in their deception. A typical regiment commonly had many soldiers fitting this description. As Leonard notes,

> Recruitment was rarely if ever followed by anything resembling
> modern-day boot camp with its intensive physical training. Rather,
> the focus was on learning how to drill. . . . Civil War soldiers lived
> and slept in close proximity to one another, but they rarely changed
> their clothes. Furthermore, they passed the bulk of their time, day
> and night, out of doors, where they also attended to their bodily
> needs. Thus, a female soldier could often maintain a certain amount
> of physical distance from her comrades, which was particularly
> important in connection with her toilet.

Army uniforms, being multi-layered and loose fitting, also helped young women to remain disguised. But perhaps even more importantly, the prevailing gender conventions and attitudes of the day were so ingrained in the men that they simply could not imagine a soldier wearing pants and doing the heavy work of a soldier being a woman. Soldiers handled weapons, carried heavy supplies, and performed tiring duties; women didn't. Unless the female soldier carelessly gave herself away in some manner, she had many factors working in her favor. Some male soldiers, as in the case of those who served with Sarah Emma Edmonds ("Franklin Thompson"), even joked about their comrades being girlish because they had slender bodies and small feet.[18]

Some female soldiers were discovered or accidentally gave themselves away in the confines of camp life (see Chapter 6 for examples). At the same time, many more maintained their disguises during all periods of the war, from the earliest battles in 1861 to the final siege of Petersburg and Richmond in 1865. How they managed to do this varies somewhat from case to case, but a number of the general factors that helped them succeed are known.

A great many, probably a large majority, of the female soldiers enlisted to be with their husbands or other loved ones and so had a partner to help protect and shield them. Other soldiers usually perceived these pairs simply to be close friends. The women who enlisted on their own tended to keep to themselves, quietly going about their business. Jennie Hodgers as Albert Cashier tended to sit by herself calmly puffing on a pipe, apparently lost in thought. According to a newspaper story in 1913, this seeming aloofness was overlooked by "his" comrades "in their admiration for Cashier's military bearing and reckless daring."[19] A soldier behaving in such "loner" fashion was generally left to himself. At the other extreme, some women in male disguise deliberately put on masculine airs, acting boisterous and swearing and drinking along with the other soldiers.

Regardless of how they managed it, women were in fact represented in all three main branches of the army: infantry, cavalry, and artillery. By far the most famous female infantry soldier was Sarah Emma Edmonds, who served for two years in the 2nd Michigan Infantry as soldier, spy, and nurse. After the war, when she applied for a pension, her former comrades confirmed her service, and she was made a member of the Grand Army of the Republic (GAR). She served in combat in several engagements but also acted as a mail carrier and courier and often was assigned to nursing duties.

After the war Edmonds briefly attended Oberlin College and in 1867 married Linus H. Seelye, a carpenter. During her efforts to obtain a pension in 1882 she made a surprise visit to her former friend and comrade in arms, Damon Stewart of the 2nd Michigan, by then a prosperous merchant in Flint, Michigan. When this matronly woman identified herself to him as "Frank Thompson," Stewart was flabbergasted. After searching his memory for events that had occurred twenty years previously, he invited her home to meet his wife and to stay as a house guest.

Stewart, who was wounded in action in Virginia in 1862 (Frank Thompson had helped to carry him off the battlefield), had served with distinction during the war, and was later promoted to captain commanding a company of the 23rd Michigan Infantry. He also was descended from Revolutionary War patriots. Stewart showed admirable honesty and self-confidence in his handling of what must have been an unprecedented and potentially risky situation. Fortunately for posterity he sent a letter to a newspaper correspondent friend in East Saginaw (whose initials were A.M.G.), notifying him that "while doing service in the Union army during the years of 1861 and 1862, I had a companion, chum, campfellow. I thought it was a man! I hope to die if it was not a woman! She's up at our house now. Come out!"

A.M.G. not only interviewed Edmonds, but also asked her additional questions about her youth in a follow-up letter. Edmonds's answers were so well written that they were incorporated intact into the newspaper story which appeared in the *Detroit Post and Tribune* on May 26, 1883, and the story was reprinted in other newspapers at least twice in later years. The article is a crucial source of information about Edmonds's early years and her motivation.

Edmonds was not aware that the reporter had incorporated her remarks in full into the story until another of her former comrades happened to read the story and got in touch with her. Albert E. Cowles of the 2nd Michigan, by then a judge, had performed hospital work with Frank Thompson in Washington, D.C. Cowles wrote Edmonds and enclosed the newspaper clipping. They continued to correspond, and Cowles's support was helpful in paving the way for Edmonds's reconciliation with the survivors of the 2nd Michigan. Stewart's testimony to Congress, along with that of other early members of the 2nd Michigan, was instrumental to Edmonds's success in obtaining a government pension.

During this period while the Congress was considering her application, Edmonds expressed some reservations about her spying activities.

Ultimately she preferred to be remembered as a nurse. Her gravestone in a Grand Army of the Republic plot at Washington Cemetery, Houston, Texas, reads simply "Emma E. Seely(e), Army Nurse."[20]

Enlistments of husband-wife teams were very common, especially but not exclusively early in the war. In some instances the wives were found out but were allowed to remain with the regiment. A Mrs. Watkins and a Mrs. Epping enlisted with their husbands in Company G of the 2nd Maryland Infantry (Union) in male disguise in 1861. After they were discovered they continued with the regiment as laundresses and participated in the unit's campaigns. A senior officer acknowledged after the war that the two women were found in his regiment.[21]

In a similar case a soldier by the name of John Finnern served three months in the 15th Ohio Infantry. When he reenlisted, this time in the 81st Ohio Infantry on September 23, 1861, his wife, Elizabeth, joined with him in male disguise. After she was discovered she remained with the regiment still in male garb and served as a battlefield nurse and surgeon's assistant for three years. She marched with the regiment and went through all of its battles.[22]

The story of another married couple in the Union army, previously garbled and inaccurately reported, has now been clarified and more completely documented. Martin Niles and his wife, Elizabeth, enlisted together in the 14th Vermont Infantry on September 2, 1862, and served together for ten months. They lived in Raritan, New Jersey, after the war. This probably accounts for previous erroneous reports that they had served in a New Jersey regiment.

The regimental roster now confirms that Martin C. Niles enlisted in Company K of the 14th Vermont as a private; was promoted to corporal February 28, 1863; and mustered out in Brattleboro, Vermont, July 30, 1863. The regiment was first sent to the defenses of Washington, where it helped to fortify the city and performed picket duty, participating in repelling Jeb Stuart's raid. The unit also was engaged at Gettysburg. Officially it was a nine-months regiment, and the roster lists only 78 soldiers on the roster (a regiment more typically contained 800–1,000 soldiers). As so often seems to be the case, no information could be found on the question of what male alias Elizabeth Niles used. Although Martin is the only Niles in Company K, there were two enlistments by this name in Company C, but no clues as to whether one of them might have been Elizabeth. Her husband died several years after the war, and she died October 4, 1920, at age ninety-two.[23]

A slice of Americana is portrayed in the remarkable story of Malinda Blalock and her husband, William McKesson ("Keith") Blalock. In addition to being a love story it contains extraordinary action and adventure related to nineteenth-century society and politics in the South. The Blalocks' biographer reported that Sarah Malinda Pritchard Blalock (alias "Samuel Blalock") enlisted in Company F ("Hibriter Guards") of the 26th North Carolina Infantry by posing as her husband's brother. The couple were residents of a western North Carolina mountain region with strongly divided sentiments about secession and the Confederate cause, and they were often pitted against neighbors and relatives.

A professed "Lincolnite," Keith was forced by community pressures into enlisting for the Confederacy. Although her sentiments originally were pro-South, out of loyalty to her husband Malinda planned to desert with him at the first opportunity. The circumstances never developed that would allow them to carry out this plan. As a result, Keith and "Sam" fought together in three battles, until in April 1862 Malinda was wounded in the shoulder. Keith carried her to the surgeon's tent, and in the process of removing the bullet the surgeon discovered that "Sam" was a woman. Upon Keith's pleading, the surgeon agreed to give him a short time to work out his next course of action.

Distraught about the probability of being separated from Malinda, Keith deliberately rubbed poison oak all over his skin. By next morning his skin was blistered and swollen and he had a high fever. Fearing that he had smallpox, the physician confined him to his tent under guard to avoid a contagion. It was quickly decided to give him an immediate medical discharge on April 20, 1862. Learning of this, Malinda immediately informed the incredulous Colonel Zebulon Vance that she was a woman and, after a surgeon verified her claim, she was immediately discharged on the same day. Keith and Malinda then slowly found their way home to the mountains to recuperate.

Under constant threat of recall to Confederate service, Keith and Malinda became outlaws and embarked on a much longer campaign as Federal partisans and guerrillas in the Blue Ridge and Great Smoky Mountains of western North Carolina and East Tennessee. They also became so-called pilots, guiding Union sympathizers and escaped Union prisoners through the mountains to safety in the North. Toward the end of the war they served as scouts and raiders with the 10th Michigan Cavalry.

Malinda was one of a very few women known (or suspected) to have fought on both sides during the Civil War, although she and her husband fought longest and most enthusiastically for the Union after April 20, 1862, until the end of the war.[24]

Among husband-wife teams, a somewhat garbled but evidently authentic case is that of Mary A. Brown, who on October 18, 1864, at age twenty-six, enlisted with her husband, Ivory Brown (age thirty-nine or forty-four; there is an age discrepancy in the records), in the 31st Maine Infantry. The regimental roster shows him enlisting as a private in Company M. He had previously enlisted in the 1st Maine Infantry at age thirty-six, according to the records, where he served for three months from May 3, 1861, to August 5, 1861. The married couple participated in the siege of Petersburg toward the end of the war. When Mary was discovered, she was allowed to stay with the regiment as a nurse and surgeon's assistant.

It was previously reported that Ivory Brown was injured when he took a bad fall in spring 1864 on a march during the Petersburg campaign. (There is some error or confusion here, since the Browns enlisted in the regiment in October 1864; the accident may have been in spring 1865.) When Ivory was sent to a hospital in Washington, D.C., Mary followed him there to take care of him. They returned to Maine after he was discharged from the hospital on June 1, 1865. The date of his military discharge is not on record. Mary received a government pension after the war for her military services. She claimed in a newspaper interview in 1930 that she had carried a musket in the army and participated in several battles, though there is no confirmation of this. She said that her brother-in-law was killed as she stood next to him at Petersburg.[25]

In what was a slight variation on the theme of husband-wife teams and possibly a unique case, a New York woman started off as a nurse and then became a soldier. Mary Siezgle (or Seizgle) of New York first served as a nurse at Gettysburg, then decided to join her husband in uniform in a New York infantry regiment, apparently the 41st New York. The unit identification could not be confirmed, but suggestive evidence was found.[26]

Soldiers' letters home sometimes contained news of female soldiers discovered in the ranks or encountered among the enemy during battle, incidents that often didn't make it into the official battle reports. A Union assistant surgeon wrote in a letter home that Union cavalry in Virginia on an expedition to Charles City Courthouse, December 12–14, 1863, took some Confederate prisoners. Among them was a female soldier about twenty years old dressed as a male who had fired her rifle at the cavalry before being captured. She was reported to have been in several engagements. The skirmish report on the expedition submitted to Major General Benjamin F. Butler by Brigadier General Isaac J. Wistar provides fairly detailed information about the operation but makes no mention of the female soldier who was among the ninety prisoners taken.

In a carefully planned combined forces operation, separate units of New York Mounted Rifles, New York Infantry, and U.S. Colored Troops marched as much as 76 miles from the vicinity of Williamsburg (the colored troops from Yorktown) "mostly through a severe storm," and traveled by day and night south and east of Richmond to rendezvous at Forge Bridge on the Rappahannock River. The 6th U.S. Colored Troops positioned ambulances and provisions strategically and served picket duty.

The complicated mission went off surprisingly smoothly, and the joint force caught members of the 42nd Battalion Virginia Cavalry totally by surprise at Charles City Courthouse in two camps. The first camp was overwhelmed and surrendered immediately, but the alarm was given and the other camp retreated into some buildings and put up a brief fight before also surrendering. The prisoners included eight commissioned officers and eighty-two enlisted men, along with a large number of weapons, munitions, and provisions. The Union forces then made their way back safely to Williamsburg.[27]

A peculiarity of service by women in the officer corps of the Confederate army is that apparently they sometimes served openly, without male disguise. Englishman Fitzgerald Ross, while traveling in the United States during the war, met a female Confederate captain on the train between Augusta and Atlanta, Georgia, who was said to have taken an active part in the war. Another female captain in uniform was seen traveling on a train between Charlotte, North Carolina, and Richmond, Virginia, in October 1864. She was said to have fought in several battles, receiving a field promotion for gallantry. Also, a female Confederate major allegedly was seen serving in General Hood's command during the Battle of Atlanta.[28]

The occasional overt service of Confederate female officers is not the only difference between South and North. Far fewer stories are known about unidentified Confederate female soldiers than about their Union counterparts (see Appendix A, "Unidentified Female Soldiers"). Otherwise, the patterns are similar for the two armies. The reasons for the differences are not clear. Two possible factors are disparate social attitudes in the North and South, and the fact that Federal records were better preserved than Confederate records. Also, many of the newspaper anecdotes about unnamed Northern female soldiers emerged only after the war, a period in which the victors dominated the news.

Sometimes young women joined the army to be with a brother or some other relative. A displaced Confederate soldier's wife, Elizabeth Meriwether, and her two young children, while seeking shelter as refugees from Federal-occupied Memphis, Tennessee, stayed overnight with a family named Peppercorn in rural Mississippi. The family consisted of a mother and three husky, tobacco-chewing daughters. While there in December 1862 or January 1863, Meriwether learned that Melverina Elverina Peppercorn, the youngest daughter, desired to enlist in the Confederate army where her twin brother, Lex (named after Alexander the Great), was serving. At one point Melverina dressed in male attire and fooled Meriwether into believing that she was Lex home on furlough, and the girl, convinced that she could pass as a man, said she planned to join right away.

When returning to Memphis in 1865, Meriwether stopped by the Peppercorn home and learned that Melverina had, indeed, joined the army and had fought in one battle. But when she learned that Lex had been wounded in the leg and taken to a hospital, she left the army to take care of him. The regiments that Melverina and Lex served in are not known, but it appears that Lex may have been in the 5th Texas Cavalry.[29]

Two female cousins, Mary Bell and Molly Bell, fought for the Confederacy as "Tom Parker" and "Bob Morgan," respectively. (The latter is sometimes reported as "Bob Martin.") They first enlisted in a cavalry company, were captured by Union forces, then were rescued by John Hunt Morgan's men. Next they enlisted in the 36th Virginia Infantry. In fall 1864 while serving in General Jubal Early's command in the Shenandoah Valley, the two were arrested and labeled by Early as suspected "camp followers" after serving for two years in his command. This glib labeling does not exactly do justice to the facts.

A regimental historian of the 36th Virginia reports that while on picket duty, "Morgan" [Molly Bell] "killed three Yankees and was promoted to corporal." At Belle Grove during the battle of Cedar Creek, Virginia, October 19, 1864, the Bells' captain (in whom they had confided) was captured. When they tried to confide in the lieutenant who took command, he turned them in to General Early, who put them on a train to Richmond. There they spent three weeks in Castle Thunder Prison before being sent home to Pulaski County, Virginia, still in their uniforms. Interviews with their former comrades confirmed that Tom Parker and Bob Morgan had been "valiant soldiers" who had never shirked their duty. During their interview with General Early upon being exposed, the Bell cousins told him that there were at least six other women in his army.[30]

When her sweetheart enlisted in the 1st Michigan Engineers and Mechanics regiment in fall of 1861, Marian Green saw him off to war in December. After a while she could not bear to be away from him any longer, so she made an "arrangement with a certain surgeon" and enlisted in a detachment recruited for the regiment. In summer 1862 she joined the regiment along with many other new recruits. At that time, the regiment was engaged in rebuilding bridges on the Memphis and Charleston Railroad. That fall the sweetheart was taken ill and sent to a hospital. A couple of days later Green showed up at his bedside, remaining for months to nurse him and other patients. She had kept her sex a secret in the regiment, but the boy wrote to her parents informing them of her presence and the parents arranged for her return home. Later when a portion of the regiment returned to Detroit for discharge, Marian met the young man there and they were married on November 17, 1864.[31]

Quite a few young women, like Sarah Emma Edmonds, enlisted on their own, though we seldom know much about the circumstances. Elvira Ibecker ("Charles D. Fuller") joined Company D of the 46th Pennsylvania Infantry as a private on September 2, 1861, when the unit was first organized, and served for about a month before being discovered. She was known to smoke and drink and apparently had a few confidants among the soldiers who knew her secret. Ibecker's military records indicate that she was eighteen years old and 5 feet 4 inches tall, with dark eyes, light hair, and a sallow complexion. The regiment was mustered in at Harrisburg on October 31, 1861, and sent to Harpers Ferry, where it was assigned to General Nathaniel P. Banks's army. Apparently Ibecker was detected in camp before the unit went into combat.[32]

Another solo operator, apparently, was Sergeant "Alfred J. Luther" of the 1st Kansas Infantry. The name of this female soldier was not reported in the original newspaper stories and other records. Instead, a Pennsylvania newspaper reported an anecdote told by a soldier who had witnessed the sergeant's discovery. The soldier said a sergeant in the 1st Kansas Infantry "encamped near us" was found to be a woman when she died in a hospital. The witness went to the hospital to see for himself and reported the facts in some detail:

> "I went to the hospital and saw the body after it was prepared for burial," he told the reporter, "and made some inquiries about her. She was of rather more than average size for a woman, with rather strongly marked features, so that with the aid of a man's attire she had quite a masculine look. She enlisted in the regiment after they went to Missouri. . . . She was in the battle of Springfield, where Gen. Lyon was killed, and has fought in a dozen battles and skirmishes."

DeAnne Blanton and Lauren M. Cook (Blanton and Cook 2002) identified the soldier's male alias as being Sergeant Alfred J. Luther and reported that she mustered into the 1st Kansas Infantry at Leavenworth, was wounded at the Battle of Wilson's Creek, Missouri, August 10, 1861, was promoted to first sergeant in 1862, and died of disease in a hospital on March 22, 1863. In this case the clear implication is that a woman sufficiently accomplished to be promoted to sergeant early in the war, and to lead soldiers in combat, probably would not have been found out except for her fatal illness.

One detail of the story could not be confirmed. The Civil War Database does confirm that Luther enlisted in Company A on May 30, 1861, from Elwood, Kansas, and was promoted to sergeant on May 1, 1862. However, she was not listed as being wounded at Wilson's Creek, though the regiment was there and had 71 killed, 185 wounded. The biography in the regimental roster indicates that she died of disease on March 22, 1863, at Lake Providence, Louisiana.[33]

Even though the attrition rate was high for would-be female soldiers and dozens were caught before they got very far, a surprising number fooled everyone (or almost everyone) for long periods of time, some until well after the war, and even for the rest of their lives. Among them were Sarah Emma Edmonds and Jennie Hodgers. As "Albert Cashier," Hodgers was one of the relatively few women known to have served a complete three-year term of enlistment disguised as a man without being discovered. She had arrived in the United States as a stowaway on a ship from Ireland at a young age, dressed as a boy, and had settled in Illinois. In September 1862, she joined the 95th Illinois Infantry at Rockford, where they trained at Camp Fuller. The regiment left camp on November 4 and traveled down the Mississippi River on transport ships to join the Army of the Tennessee in Mississippi.

During the battle of Vicksburg the regiment participated in two charges and held an advance position where, according to the unit history, it "encountered one of the most sweeping and destructive fires to which troops were ever exposed. The total loss to the regiment in these two charges was 25 killed, 124 wounded and 10 missing." Today the Vicksburg battlefield monument to some 36,000 Illinois soldiers who fought there includes the name of Albert D. J. Cashier.

In 1864 the 95th Illinois continued to be engaged in combat at Yellow Bayou and all the campaigns of the Red River expedition in Louisiana, and at Guntown, Mississippi, where the regiment was flanked, suffered fourteen casualties, and was forced to retreat to avoid capture. After a few weeks' rest, the 95th took part in the Battle of Nashville in December 1864 and the siege of Mobile in early 1865. Probably few if any female soldiers experienced more combat than Hodgers; she participated in forty battles and skirmishes and was never wounded.

After three years of hard service, the survivors of the 95th Illinois Infantry returned to Belvidere, Illinois, where Private Cashier and her comrades received a hero's welcome and were discharged from service. She settled into quiet civilian life, working as a farmhand and handyman in various small towns, finally settling in Saunemin. The ex-soldier was well known and popular. It was not until 1911 that a freak accident (she got hit by a car, breaking her leg near the hip) caused her secret to be revealed, though only a few people knew it for another two years.

After being admitted to a soldiers' home, her health gradually declined until she was adjudged "insane" and committed to an asylum. The story was reported in the national press on March 29, 1913. Once the news was out, many of her old comrades in the 95th Infantry reminisced about her service and shared personal stories about her exploits. The soldiers were supportive and protective of her, the bonds of shared combat being stronger than mere matters of gender. The tributes stressed Cashier's bravery and fortitude. He was cool under fire and tireless while on the march.

Former First Sergeant Charles W. Ives visited his old comrade at the asylum, where he "found [her] a frail woman of 70, broken, because on discovery, she was compelled to put on skirts. They told me she was as awkward as could be in them. One day she tripped and fell, hurting her hip. She never recovered." During one visit she told Ives, "Lots of boys enlisted under the wrong name. So did I. The country needed men, and I wanted excitement." "Al did all the regular duties," Ives recalled. "Not knowing that she was a girl, I assigned her to picket duty and to carry water just as all the men did." The medical staff at the asylum took special care of Hodgers, and she died there on October 10, 1915, at age seventy-one. The local post of the Grand Army of the Republic arranged for her burial with full military honors, clothed in her military uniform and in a flag-draped casket.[34]

The evidence is now overwhelming that hundreds, perhaps thousands, of young women did, in fact, manage to fool their male soldier colleagues for long periods of time. Even with rapidly expanding internet sites and new research methods it probably will be impossible to learn with any precision how many women fought in male disguise and escaped detection. All that can be said is that with the advent of the internet and intensive searching driven by interest in genealogy and the Civil War, more and more examples of female soldiers have come to light.

Various other lines of evidence also indicate that large numbers of female soldiers probably went undetected. In many instances female soldiers, when discovered, told the authorities that there were other women in the ranks known to them. A female soldier in the 101st Ohio Infantry who was discovered and discharged at Nashville in 1864 told the sergeant of the guard that there were five more women in the regiment.[35]

A Michigan cavalry soldier, John L. Ransom, kept a diary while imprisoned at Andersonville and Belle Isle. His diary entry for December 23, 1863, at Belle Isle notes: "A woman found among us—a prisoner of war. . . . She tells of another female being among us, but as yet she has not been found out." Others (including Sarah Emma Edmonds) told of burying female soldiers on the battlefield with no one else being aware of it. Edmonds (as "Franklin Thompson") was present with a detachment of doctors and nurses during the Battle of Antietam, September 17, 1862. While tending to the wounded on the battlefield, she came across a dying soldier who confessed to being a woman and asked "Frank" to conceal the truth and bury her on the battlefield.[36]

The truth about female soldiers in the Civil War has been, to some extent, obscured by social and psychological factors relating to gender discrimination. Nevertheless, it is becoming increasingly clear that the dubious arguments advanced to this day about women's alleged inability to perform as soldiers are refuted by history. Furthermore, the notion that women could not have concealed their gender during the Civil War is gradually succumbing to documented historical fact. Women not only fought as infantry soldiers, they also saw action in other branches of the army.

Horse Soldiers and "She Dragoons"

I was informed that there certainly were in the command two
females, that in some mysterious manner had attached themselves
to the service as soldiers; [one a teamster] the other a private
soldier in a cavalry company [on] escort duty. . . . the "she
dragoon". . . proved to be a rather prepossessing young woman.
  Major General Philip H. Sheridan, Personal Memoirs *(1888)*

The American Civil War was driven by horsepower (and mule-
power). In addition to the cavalry mounts, teams of horses pulled
supply wagons in wagon trains, ambulances, and other convey-
ances, including artillery pieces and caissons carrying ammunition. In the so-called horse artillery (horse-drawn field artillery),
cavalry and artillery soldiers worked closely together. Teams of six
horses pulled combinations of cannons on two-wheeled carriages
and two-wheeled limbers carrying ammunition. Artillery soldiers
sometimes rode on top of the caissons. Many Civil War regimental rosters list blacksmiths or farriers, who shoed the horses and
took care of the animals. At times there also were regiments of
Mounted Infantry when sufficient horses were available.[1]

Although there were approximately six times as many infantry
regiments as cavalry regiments in the Union Army, a surprisingly
large percentage of female soldiers served in cavalry units.[2] Recent research has discovered dozens of new examples of female
cavalry soldiers, including several new ones in Confederate ranks.
Some possible reasons for this large percentage are apparent.

Unlike infantry regiments, cavalry by their very nature tended to be highly mobile and relatively informal while in the field, not settled in any one place for long periods of time. Weather permitting, the soldiers might use a saddle and a horse blanket for a bunk around a campfire. Civil War historian Edward G. Longacre observes,

> Thanks to the mobility given to him by his horse, a trooper seemed to be in constant motion. While foot soldiers and cannoneers remained in camp for long periods between campaigns, horsemen served on a daily basis as pickets, couriers, escorts and provost guards. When allowed to make camp, troopers not only had to spend time keeping their uniforms, equipment and weapons in fit condition, but had to care meticulously for their mounts.[3]

In addition to skirmishing, quick strikes on vulnerable positions, and the other guard and escort duties, cavalry often acted as the eyes and ears of the army, probing the fringes of the opposing forces and monitoring their movements. J.E.B. ("Jeb") Stuart's cavalry command performed famously for Robert E. Lee with far-ranging scouting missions and hit-and-run attacks on Union supply lines. For the first two years of the war, the Confederate cavalry was far superior to that of the Union. A Federal Cavalry Bureau was first formed in July 1863, instituting monthly inspections and supervision of field units. Healthy and well-trained horses were then systematically acquired and housed in Union depots for the first time. Major General Joseph Hooker was particularly instrumental in developing an effective cavalry force for the Union.

The typical Union cavalry uniform had yellow trim, a crossed-saber insignia on the cap, reinforced trousers, boots and spurs, and a cartridge belt. The troopers carried a carbine slung over their shoulder (mainly for use when dismounted), a revolver, and a saber. In combat they often made saber and revolver charges. When dismounted and armed with repeating carbines, the Federal cavalry later in the war could deal with much larger Confederate forces.[4]

Historian Bell I. Wiley reports that Union cavalry regiments generally were not as well disciplined as the other branches, mainly due to their relative independence of operation in the field. This was especially true of units assigned to remote, outlying areas. When Federal inspectors conducted checkups, they were sometimes shocked by what they found and filed highly critical reports to higher command.[5]

In order to be self-sufficient in the field, cavalry soldiers carried all their fighting and camping equipment with them. Typical supplies included three days' subsistence for themselves and their horses, forty rounds of carbine ammunition, twenty rounds of pistol ammunition, shelter tent and camping equipment, and various tools and cleaning equipment. A cavalry horse usually carried about 270 pounds altogether. As a result of manhandling horses and supplies on a daily basis, cavalry soldiers had a higher than average incidence of back problems, frequent ruptures, and hemorrhoids.[6]

Despite the physical strain involved, a large number of women are known to have served in the cavalry branches of both the Union and the Confederate armies. Due to the hit-and-run nature of typical cavalry operations, whether scouting out the location of the enemy or skirmishing and withdrawing faster than infantry could pursue, cavalry soldiers—though obviously they also suffered casualties—were more likely than infantry soldiers to be captured alive, even if wounded by small arms fire.

During the Civil War the State of Illinois fielded seventeen numbered cavalry regiments, plus several independent cavalry companies and battalions. At least two of the early regiments had female troopers in male disguise. A young woman named Jane Short enlisted in the 6th Illinois Cavalry on November 23, 1861, under the name "Charley Davis." She is reported to have been wounded in the hand by a musket ball at the Battle of Shiloh the following spring. Then after recuperating, she rejoined the regiment and participated in various other engagements before falling ill and being sent to a hospital. There she was discovered and discharged.[7]

Meanwhile one Sarah Bradbury enlisted in the 7th Illinois Cavalry, Company C, under the name "Frank Morton," to be with her sweetheart. Also in this regiment was a female commissioned nurse and assistant surgeon named Sarah C. Clapp who served openly as a woman for nine months.[8] After two months Bradbury became an orderly to the general. But when her boyfriend was captured and she despaired of ever seeing him again, she shifted her allegiance and, in her own words, "becoming attached to a young man in the 22nd Illinois Infantry, I joined his regiment" (see Appendix B). She went on to serve in another regiment as well, the 2nd Kentucky Cavalry, as an orderly in General Phil Sheridan's escort.

As apparently happened with female soldiers on a number of occasions during the war, Short and Bradbury each subsequently hooked up with another female soldier and continued their adventures in other regiments. Louisa (Lou) Morris in St. Louis enlisted in the 10th Missouri Cavalry, a state militia cavalry unit. After serving nine months and surviving several engagements in Captain John Rice's Company G (the "Red Rovers"), Morris deserted and was living in Memphis as a woman. Somehow she met Jane Short and, supposedly out of patriotic fervor, the two decided to reenlist. This time they opted for the infantry and enlisted together in the 21st Missouri Infantry, Short as a drummer and Morris as a teamster. According to an 1874 book, when Short learned that the regiment was to be sent in pursuit of the feared Confederate cavalry leader Nathan B. Forrest, she became frightened and confessed her sex to an officer, also revealing Morris in the process. The two were arrested and hauled before the XVI Corps provost marshal and discharged from the army.[9]

Sarah Bradbury, meanwhile, left the 7th Illinois Cavalry and joined the 22nd Illinois Infantry to be with her new male friend, who didn't know she was a female. She finally confided in him, but his reaction upset her (reading between the lines of her formal statement it appears that he began making unwelcome romantic overtures), and she "became satisfied that he was not a gentleman." Some time thereafter she found her way into the 2nd Kentucky Cavalry, Company L, as a member of General Philip Sheridan's escort. There she somehow became acquainted with Ella Reno, a teamster. When the two got drunk on apple cider and fell into the river, their rescuers discovered that they were women and Bradbury's career came to an ignominious end (see Chapter 9).

Another pair of female cavalry soldiers was discovered just before the Second Battle of Bull Run in August 1862. The Union 2nd Maryland Cavalry was in camp near Harpers Ferry, when two privates were discovered to be female and were drummed out of the regiment.[10]

Then late in 1863 two female Union cavalry soldiers were captured separately following a combined forces battle in Tennessee. During the Civil War Tennessee was a sharply divided state, with East Tennessee loyal to the Union and West Tennessee generally supporting the Confederacy. Long campaigns and major clashes of the armies had taken their toll on Tennesseans both in casualties and in devastation of their homeland. By late 1863 most Confederate forces, other than some raiding cavalry contingents, had been cleared from the state.[11]

When Ulysses S. Grant's long siege of Vicksburg, Mississippi, finally was successful on July 4, 1863, and the Confederate army some 20,000 strong surrendered, among the prisoners from the garrison was Ellen Levasay, a female trooper with the 3rd Missouri Cavalry. According to National Archives records she was first sent to prison in St. Louis and later transferred to Camp Morton, Indiana, in August 1863, where she was held for eight months before agreeing to take the oath of allegiance to the United States and being freed.[12]

In October 1863 a brigade of Union troops headed by Colonel Frank Wolford was attacked by a group of Confederates under the command of Brigadier General John C. Vaughn at Philadelphia, Tennessee. Wolford was colonel of the 1st Kentucky Cavalry ("Wolford's Cavalry"), and he also commanded the 11th and 12th Kentucky Cavalry, the 24th Indiana Light Artillery, and the 45th Ohio Mounted Infantry (later known as the 45th Ohio Volunteer Infantry). Vaughn's brigade consisted of four Confederate Tennessee infantry regiments that are known to have served as mounted infantry at times.[13] Catching Wolford short-handed after he had deployed nearly half of his force on a supply train rescue mission, Vaughn overwhelmed the Kentuckians in a sharp engagement.

Wolford's brigade had 7 killed, 25 wounded, and 447 captured. The prisoners were taken to Virginia and incarcerated on Belle Isle in the James River near Richmond, where by the end of 1863 about 7,000 Union prisoners were held. A remarkable coincidence came to light there. Two of the prisoners from the battle proved to be women who had been serving in two different Union cavalry units. A soldier named "Tommy" in the 45th Ohio (Mounted) Infantry became ill in the prison and, when her sex was discovered in early February 1864, she was released.[14] The other, Mary Jane Johnson, had served in the 11th Kentucky Cavalry for about one year. She was discovered to be a woman some time during her imprisonment at Belle Isle[15] (see also Chapter 7).

Another "Soldier Tom" was a woman (actually a very young girl) who served in the Illinois cavalry early in the war and later as a scout. A postwar newspaper story offered only a sketchy report of her activities, but it remains the most complete account to date. In 1990 the journal *Minerva* contained a very brief item about a female soldier from Illinois who served as a scout ("one of eighteen") and as an attaché in General Frank P. Blair, Jr.'s, XVII Army Corps.[16] The *Emporia News,* Illinois, May 13, 1870 (see "Soldier Tom" in Appendix B) carried a story from the *St. Louis Times,* where it was headlined "A Degenerate Female Soldier." (The reason for the derogatory adjective in the headline is not clear from the story.) The Illinois paper headlined it "Soldier Tom." A court reporter had apparently interviewed a young woman who was appearing as a witness in a court case, a tall woman about twenty-two years old who, he said, had "served over two years in the Federal army during the war—fifteen months as a private in the Illinois cavalry, and over nine months as a teamster in the noted "Lead Mine Regiment." She had been at the siege of Corinth in 1862, was present during the campaign against Vicksburg (probably during the operations occurring June 20–July 24, 1862), and campaigned in Tennessee and Georgia.

"At Lookout Mountain," he reported, "she formed one of a party of eighteen" who scouted the position of General Bragg's forces. This may or may not be a reference to the Battle of Lookout Mountain (November 23–25, 1863), as a lot of skirmishing and campaigning occurred at various times in the vicinity of the mountain. Her time as an attaché "of Gen. Blair's 17th [Army] Corps" in the Army of the Tennessee can be dated as between April and September 1864, the period when Blair was corps commander.

Finally, the court reporter noted that she was involved in "reconnoitering operations around the Chattahoochie [*sic*] River [when] she was connected with Gen. Davis' 14th [Army] Corps." A lot of campaigning occurred around the river throughout July 1864, but this appears to be a reference to the operations on July 6–10. General Jefferson C. Davis was commander of the 2nd Division, XIV Corps, at this time, later promoted to corps commander.

The regiments that "Soldier Tom" served in and an approximate timeline for her alleged two-plus years of army service can be reconstructed from clues in the newspaper story. The "Lead Mine Regiment" was the 45th Illinois Infantry, which was recruited in the vicinity of Galena, Illinois; mustered in on December 25, 1861; and served in the Western Theater. The regiment was in camp near Fort Henry, on the Tennessee River, in February 1862. Her reported military activities included:

April 29–May 30, 1862: Siege of Corinth, Mississippi

June 20–July 24, 1862: Vicksburg and vicinity operations

November 23–25, 1863: Chattanooga and Lookout Mountain,
    Tennessee, and Ringgold, Georgia

April 23–September 22, 1864: Army of the Tennessee campaigns

July 1864: Reconnoitering operations around Chattahoochee River,
    Georgia

We do not know whether "Soldier Tom's" service was continuous, or if there was a hiatus between her time in the infantry and her enlistment in an unidentified cavalry regiment. The 1862 engagements fit the history of the 45th Illinois Infantry. Her nine months' infantry service would have been in 1862. Her second career of approximately fifteen months in the cavalry most likely started about November 1863. It was not possible to figure out what cavalry regiment she served in, but she may well have been on detached duty as a scout for Gen. Thomas.

In the 1st Michigan Cavalry, part of George Armstrong Custer's famous Michigan Cavalry Brigade in which Bridget Divers also served late in the war (see Chapter 2), another woman was present in camp at the outset and soldiered with the men. When Private Richard C. Ostrander mustered into Company M on September 7, 1861, his wife (whose first name is not reported) arrived in camp with him from their home town of Dowagiac, Michigan. Mrs. Ostrander set up housekeeping in his tent, "defying the efforts of regimental authorities to evict her." The officers apparently came to accept her as a member of the regiment, allowing her to act as a vivandiere. "Entering fully into the role, the lady donned a specially tailored uniform and clasped a brace of pistols around her waist." She followed her husband in and out of combat for two years, until he deserted and fled to Canada. She was reported in an 1864 newspaper story to have been "daring in the face of the enemy."[17]

A female cavalry trooper from Iowa reportedly had an extraordinary career. Although her story is controversial and not well documented, Elsa J. Guerin is said to have enlisted in an Iowa cavalry regiment at Keokuk in 1862 as "Charles Hatfield." According to the story as reported, she became an orderly to Major General Samuel R. Curtis's assistant adjutant general, and also went on spying missions behind enemy lines. The army under

General Curtis gathered along the Big Blue River near Westport, Missouri, during 1864 to oppose an invading Confederate army of about 12,000 commanded by General Sterling Price. The two armies clashed for several days, concluding with a climactic battle near Westport on October 22–23.

"Charley" at this time was a headquarters aide and courier on the staff of a Major Charlot, carrying orders and messages all over the battlefield area, often at the front, and was praised by his officers for "coolness and bravery." General Price's Confederate force was finally driven from the field, and Curtis pursued him hoping to destroy his army. In one of several rear-guard actions Union cavalry charged across the prairie to attack and the Confederates turned at bay, forming a line of battle. After heavy losses on both sides, the Federals pulled back. Scores of casualties were scattered across the landscape. Among them, it was reported, a group of Confederates found "Charley" on the ground beside his dead horse, weak from loss of blood. He had sustained a gunshot wound in the leg and a saber cut on the shoulder.

The wounded trooper was evacuated from the field and taken to the headquarters of General Shelby's brigade where a Confederate surgeon tried to revive the diminutive Yankee soldier who appeared to have fainted. In the process, he removed the soldier's jacket to inspect the shoulder wound and was surprised to discover that his patient was a female. Quietly, he dressed the wound and replaced the jacket, not telling others of his discovery. When "Charley" revived and was feeling better, the doctor told her, "Your secret is safe with me until you are able to tell me your story. There is not time now and this is no place to hear it." Later during an exchange of wounded prisoners, "Charley" was freed and taken to Fort Leavenworth, Kansas. There she learned that General Curtis had recommended her for a promotion, and a commission of first lieutenant eventually came through. "Charley" was then assigned as an aide-de-camp to General Curtis and served until the end of the war. Elsa Guerin's story as outlined here was first published in 1885.[18]

Is it a true story? Historical research in various databases yielded mixed and inconclusive results. Only one of the handful of Iowa cavalry regiments was formed in Keokuk, and its history perfectly matches "Charley's" story. That was the 3rd Iowa Cavalry, which was engaged in and around Big Blue River and Westport, Missouri, in late October of 1864.

Major Charlot, the assistant adjutant general on whose staff Guerin allegedly served, was verified as a former Missouri militia adjutant general who transferred to the regular army with the rank of major and position of assistant adjutant general on the staff of Major General Curtis. However, no Charles Hatfield was found on the roster of the 3rd Iowa Cavalry and the regiment had only one missing in action/prisoner of war soldier captured during this battle, whose history does not fit "Charley's" story.

There was a Jacob C. Hatfield, a private in Company D, whose age at enlistment was given as eighteen, but he did not enlist at Keokuk in 1862. Also, a search of the Civil War Database Personnel Directory yielded a Charles Hatfield who on some unspecified date had enlisted in Company F of the 23rd Iowa Infantry (rather than cavalry). Based on Iowa state records, the entry is suggestively annotated, "Rejected on 9/19/1862 . . . by Mustering Officer." No reason is cited for the "rejection." A possible answer that would be consistent with a number of other cases is that Elsa Guerin failed on her first attempt to enlist, but succeeded on the second attempt. But if so, no historical record of it could be found. Although "Charley's" story sounds authentic and generally fits the facts of the battle, no personal record could be found to support it.[19]

On the other hand, historical research has confirmed a number of similar reports and even supplied some of the originally missing information (see Chapter 9). As one example, an unnamed woman was reported to have enlisted with her unnamed husband in the 1st New York Cavalry. When he was wounded during the Seven Days Battles around Richmond in June 1862, she carried him off the field and received a flesh wound herself in the process. After the field hospital at Savages Station was overrun by Confederate forces on June 29, 1862, they were both taken prisoner. National Archives records indicate that by mid-August she and her husband had been exchanged and were at Camp Parole, Annapolis, Maryland, a way station and hospital for returning Union POWs. The account contained sufficient clues to allow investigation that has at least tentatively, but highly probably in this case, identified the husband's name and the wife's male alias.[20]

Sometimes the documentation and supporting testimony is very complete. A case in point was recently published in detail involving a woman, who, like Frances Jamieson (see Chapter 5), served in the U.S. Cavalry

(Regular Army). Martha Lindley, disguised as "Pvt. Jim Smith," enlisted in Company D, 6th U.S. Cavalry, along with her husband, William D. Lindley. They mustered in on August 12, 1861. The muster roll gives "Smith's" age as twenty-seven, height 5 feet 8 inches, brown eyes, black hair, dark complexion. The couple saw action together during the Virginia Peninsula Campaign, March–June 1862, after which Martha Lindley was detailed to hospital duty as an orderly for the regimental surgeon. She served through August 1864, mustering out with the company. Additional information was obtained from a postwar newspaper interview and an oral history from a descendant.[21]

In September 1864 another pair of women, this time apparently sisters or cousins, was discovered in the 1st West Virginia Cavalry. Their names were given as Kate Frances and Eliza Frances. As in a number of other cases, they told authorities that one or more additional women were still concealed in the ranks. Regrettably, no roster could be found for the regiment to check on the reported male aliases "James Johnson" and "Frank Glenn." The annotated provost marshal letter reporting the incident leaves it ambiguous as to whether Kate and Eliza were genuine soldiers or only camp followers (see Appendix B). Several additional examples of female cavalry soldiers, whose identities are not known, appear in Appendix A, "Unidentified Female Soldiers," for the years 1862 through 1864.

Female cavalry soldiers in the Confederacy were surprisingly numerous, but as previously noted, the Confederacy was more advanced in cavalry organization throughout the first two years of the war. As Edward G. Longacre observes, the Confederacy avidly recruited cavalry soldiers early in the war while the Union was slow to recognize the importance of cavalry. Major General Joseph Hooker in 1863 was first to make important reforms in the Union cavalry that led to successes later in the war. General Julius Stahel was an early cavalry commander for the Union in 1862, before the Union had attained some degree of parity.

The following story is difficult to evaluate, but it is claimed that in early December of 1862, Stahel's troopers were engaged in reconnaissance around Upperville, Virginia, when they met a squad of rebel cavalry and gave pursuit. According to the *Nashville Dispatch* of December 12, 1862, "When closely in contact with them, two females on horseback were descried riding with the cavalry. These women were supposed to be spies in disguise," (which of course makes no sense at all). The Confederate soldiers were ordered to halt and surrender, but instead wheeled around into position to fight, and carbine and pistol shots were exchanged. Casualties were sustained on both sides, and one of the Confederate women was shot in the leg, the projectile badly fracturing a bone. "While she lay bleeding on the ground," the newspaper story said, "her rebel companions fled from her, and she was left to the mercy of her captors." She was removed to a private home and provided with medical care.

About the same time (late December 1862), it was reported in Arkansas and Texas newspapers that a young woman named Diana Smith was serving in the Virginia "Moccasin Rangers," having joined Captain Kelser's company. Her father (first name not reported) had "raised the first company of guerrillas" from Jackson County and commanded them until he was captured and imprisoned at Camp Chase, Ohio. Diana, whose exploits were reported to have included being captured and escaping several times, was said to be "accompanied by Miss Duskie, who has also earned the proud distinction of a heroine."[22]

Numerous guerrilla bands, "rangers," and similar independent paramilitary outfits were raised and operated in a somewhat freelance fashion early in the war, in Virginia, Tennessee, and elsewhere, but official records or rosters of them are nearly impossible to find. Confederate commanders preferred to have the "irregulars" merged into the regular volunteer companies. The only reference found to Moccasin Rangers was the name assigned to Company A of the 3rd Virginia State Rangers. No officer by the name of Kelser appears in the available records of that unit.

A better documented case is that of Mary Ann Pitman, who served first in a Confederate Tennessee regiment and then as "1st Lt. Rawley" in Nathan Bedford Forrest's cavalry brigade. Her home was in Chestnut Bluff, Tennessee, and disguised as a man she recruited a company of cavalry soldiers at Union City, then saw action with them at Shiloh and was wounded in the side during the battle. She later was deployed as a secret agent and gunrunner for Forrest, resuming female attire and using the name Mary (or Mollie) Hays. In that capacity she was captured by Union forces and, in effect, became a double agent. Hers is a complex and interesting story (see Chapter 9).

General Phil Sheridan began his famous Shenandoah Valley, Virginia, campaign in August 1864, officially on August 7, with battles and skirmishes raging up and down the valley through November 28. When it was over, the Confederate army had been driven from the valley in tatters, and the area, known as the "breadbasket of the Confederacy," had been devastated—crops burned and mills and buildings destroyed. It was a crushing defeat for the Confederacy. Sheridan's personal charisma inspired his soldiers, but it was his understanding of how to use cavalry for maximum effect that made a big difference.

"The fiery, former cavalry officer [Sheridan] stood pre-eminent among army commanders in his use of the mounted arm," says historian Jeffry D. Wert, who cites the comments of two Union cavalry officers about how skillfully Sheridan blended the use of cavalry with infantry and elevated the role of the cavalry. When Sheridan's cavalry (which included George Armstrong Custer) routed the Confederates at the Battle of Tom's Brook on October 9, Wert reported, "[it] epitomized the Confederate cavalry's descent from the glorious days of 1862 to this autumn of attrition and blighted dreams." Elsewhere Wert notes that Sheridan's use of cavalry provided a model for armored operations in World War II. "The contribution of the Union cavalry to the outcome of the [Shenandoah Valley] campaign was decisive and attributable to Sheridan."[23]

National Archives records show that on August 8 a Union cavalry soldier wearing the uniform of a sergeant was arrested at Sandy Hook, Virginia, and incarcerated at Old Capitol Prison in Washington, D.C., upon suspicion of being a Confederate spy. She used the male alias of "Charles Wilson," but her real name was Sarah E. Mitchell, a sixteen-year-old girl from Winchester, Virginia. Mitchell was later sent to prison at Fitchburg, Massachusetts. When authorities attempted to exchange her, Confederates said they did not know her and rejected the exchange.[24]

Another rather different version of this incident, reported in the *New Orleans Daily Picayune* on August 31, 1864, said that "a female spy was captured in Pleasant Valley [Maryland], dressed in male attire. . . . She claimed to be a member of Imboden's cavalry." When examined by a doctor at brigade headquarters she admitted her name was "Sarah E. Mitchel" [*sic*] and said she was a native of Winchester, Virginia. The *Nashville Dispatch* for January 4, 1865, reported that Mitchell claimed to have been a lieutenant in the Confederate army. She was transferred to a female prison at Fitchburg, Massachusetts, on October 13, 1864.

The Civil War Database provides some confirmation of her apparently complex story, which is yet another that must be pieced together from garbled reporting. "Imboden's Cavalry" was a multiforce brigade headed by Brigadier General John D. Imboden that served in the Virginia Shenandoah Valley. It comprised the 18th Virginia Cavalry, the 62nd Virginia Infantry (Mounted), and McClanahan's Battery. A roster check of the 18th Virginia Cavalry shows a Charles Wilson in Company G, but offers no information on either the date of enlistment or date and method of discharge. The roster of the 62nd Mounted Infantry also shows a Charles Wilson (the two units were somewhat interchangeable) who enlisted as a private in Company L on November 1, 1863, at Richmond. The records further indicate he was in the hospital at Staunton, Virginia, on October 31, 1864, and, without further explanation, "Absent, arrested 12/31/64 [place not stated]."

Though additional research is needed to clarify her story, it appears that Sarah E. Mitchell may well have been both a Confederate cavalry soldier and a spy. On the other hand, Sandy Hook, Virginia (vicinity of Richmond), and Pleasant Valley, Maryland, are about 200 miles apart. (While there are three Pleasant Valleys in Maryland, the most likely candidate is the one in Carroll County, which had a lot of cavalry activity during the war.) The discrepancy in location of capture is puzzling.

Several reports have also been found of women serving in the artillery of both armies, though generally less is known about them. Artillery during the Civil War included many different types of guns (both smoothbore and rifled), a variety of projectiles, and also several different kinds of fuses. The 12-pounder Napoleon gun was one of the most popular for field artillery because it was relatively trouble-free; among the standard muzzle-loading rifles were 10- and 20-pounder Parrott guns. Field artillery commonly operated in support of infantry on the battlefield. A regulation-size battery consisted of six guns, each with an ammunition chest, drawn by a team of six horses hitched in pairs. Each battery was supplied by four-wheel carts (caissons) carrying ammunition chests, which also were drawn by six-horse teams. The artillery soldiers marched alongside their horse-drawn guns or rode on the caissons.

An artillery piece in combat was operated by a ten-man team. (Or perhaps we should say "ten-person team.") In some units known as "horse artillery," such as the example in Imboden's Cavalry, all the cannoneers were mounted and they operated along with the cavalry, using somewhat lighter guns for more rapid movement. But in all cases, field artillery required large numbers of horses (and sometimes mule teams) to transport the guns and ammunition. Muddy roads often bogged down the wagon wheels; and the teams also had to overcome other obstacles such as hilly and rocky terrain. Projectiles of grapeshot or canister (iron balls, plates, and cylinders in various combinations) were commonly used against infantry, their shotgun effect often decimating the ranks of charging soldiers when used at ranges of about 300 to 600 yards.[25]

"Artillery was a headache to us one way or the other a lot of the time," said infantry soldier Robert Hale Strong of the 105th Illinois Infantry. "We had to help get ours out of the mud, then defend our batteries against Rebel charges. In the meantime their artillery would give us fits." During the 1864 Atlanta campaign, Strong described observing the artillery in action as members of his infantry company protected a battery. "We were expected to repulse any charge the Rebs might make on the battery," he said. "While it was easy sitting it was dangerous work, because the enemy's batteries were shelling ours and our battery was shelling them." He then gave this graphic description of the artillery in action:

> Each man at the cannon is numbered, and each number has just
> certain things to do. He does this with the regularity of clock work,
> and does nothing else. The caisson holding the ammunition is brought
> up to a few feet in rear of the cannon, the horses are unhitched and
> taken a short distance to the rear and hidden if possible, and firing
> begins.
>
> One man brings the powder cartridge from the caisson. Another
> man shoves it into the cannon muzzle. Another one rams it down.
> By this time, the first man has returned from the caisson with a shot
> or a shell. If it is a shell and the fuse is already cut to the required
> length, the shell is passed on to the cannon, inserted and rammed
> home. If not properly fused, the fuse is adjusted first.
>
> Then the priming is inserted in the touch hole and the string that
> fires the cannon is pulled. After the shell screams out and the cannon
> recoils, the cannon is run back into position. Then one man puts his

Table 4.1 Women Who Served in Artillery Units

Margaret Leonard	2nd Massachusetts Heavy Artillery	Unit overrun 1863, captured, imprisoned at Andersonville and Castle Thunder (see Chapter 7)
Mrs. John Bahr	Washington Artillery, New Orleans	Served as vivandiere and nurse in camp with husband (Larson 1992, 44; Lonn 1940, 379–380)
Ella H. Gibson	1st Wisconsin Heavy Artillery	Served as chaplain for nine months (Massey 1966, 86; Wiley, *Life of Billy Yank*, 1978, 337)
Unidentified	Confederate Army	Sergeant captured manning gun in June 1864 at Cold Harbor, Va. (see Appendix A, Unidentified Female Soldiers)
Sallie Curtis	2nd Kentucky Heavy Artillery (Union)	After serving twenty months in another regiment, enlisted in artillery but was discovered after a week (see Chapter 7)
Bridget Higgins	Confederate Army	Captured with husband after a battle in 1862 (see Chapter 7)
Florena Budwin	Pennsylvania Battery	Captured in male disguise with husband, sent to Andersonville; later died in Florence, S.C. (see Chapter 7)
Mary A. Loomis	1st Michigan Light Artillery	Served as nurse, camped and marched with husband (see Appendix A)
Eliza C. Porter	1st Illinois Light Artillery	Served as nurse in husband's regiment (see Appendix A)
Unidentified	6th New York Heavy Artillery	Artillery corporal stationed in Virginia gave birth to baby boy (see Appendix A, Unidentified Female Soldiers)

finger over the touch hole to keep out air. Another with a swab or a sponge on a pole wipes out the cannon. Another shell is inserted and fired. And this is done two or three times in a minute, everybody is on the jump. Every so often, the end of the swab is dipped in a bucket of water and the cannon thoroughly washed out. If an artilleryman is killed or wounded, another stands ready to take his place. Each is trained to do the next man's job when needed.[26]

In one of the classic Civil War memoirs, Edward A. Moore, a Confederate artilleryman who served under Stonewall Jackson, describes life in the field artillery, including his experiences in combat. Once while marching with his battery of the Rockbridge Artillery through the Shenandoah Valley of Virginia in 1862, shortly before the Second Battle of Bull Run or Manassas, there was a clash with Federal troops in the vicinity of Middletown. He reported,

> As the rest of us came up we met a number of prisoners on horseback. They had been riding at a run for nine miles on the pike in a cloud of white dust. Many of them were hatless, some had saber-cuts on their heads and streams of blood were coursing down through the dust on their faces. Among them was a woman wearing a short red skirt and mounted on a tall horse.[27]

It is not clear from this brief description what the woman's role might have been, but the circumstances (and the red skirt) suggest that she was with the Federal soldiers in combat, probably as a vivandiere.

Among the women who enlisted in artillery units was Sarah Jane Perkins, who served for three years in a Virginia battery before being captured by Union forces and imprisoned at Point Lookout, Maryland, in 1864 (see Appendix B). Table 4.1 includes other examples.

Neither the harsh conditions of military life nor the physical danger of combat appear to have deterred women from active and meaningful participation in the American Civil War. Instead, women went where their men did or enlisted on their own in the artillery, cavalry, or infantry and performed faithfully as full-fledged soldiers. They also volunteered for other forms of dangerous military duty.

5

The Secret Service: Spies, Scouts, and Saboteurs

Both the Confederacy and the Union took advantage of skilled, courageous women who acted as couriers, or spies appropriating official secrets. In the South, it was not uncommon for women to work as blockade runners or Confederate agents, using treachery and "feminine ways" to acquire needed supplies.
Jeanne M. Christie, in Confederate Women *(2004)*

During the Civil War the term "secret service" was rather loosely applied to anyone who engaged in clandestine activities in support of military goals. Although those activities varied widely in practice and included spying, detective work, and courier duty, the operatives in a generic sense were said to be in "secret service." Other than the work done by agents fielded directly by the Union and Confederate governments, these information-gathering and -transmission activities usually were unsupervised and uncoordinated efforts by patriotic individuals. Freelance spying efforts, such as most of those described by Loreta Janeta Velazquez in her memoirs, were not at all uncommon. Velazquez allegedly was employed by the Confederate government at certain times, but more often acted on her own (see Chapter 9).

Various official Union and Confederate "detective," "secret service," or espionage agencies were formed during the war, sometimes operating on behalf of a particular general and sometimes more truly national in scope. Often a government-paid spy would operate in a particular theater of the war and report to the commanding general or his staff in that area. More than once operatives from different spying agencies got in each other's way, including incidents of arresting members of a competing agency. In the view of historian Rhodri Jeffreys-Jones, "Neither side developed an effective espionage or counterespionage network in the course of the war."[1]

A large number of women officially or unofficially served as spies, smugglers, couriers, or saboteurs for the Confederacy and for the Union. Many of them made major contributions to the war efforts of their governments, often at great personal risk to their lives. It was not unusual for them to take on a male disguise to carry out their missions. "Scouting" was another distinct category of wartime spying activity, the primary mission being to search out (typically on horseback) crucial tactical information about the daily status of the opposing army. Jeffry D. Wert states that army scouts "operated on the fringes of an army with the purpose of obtaining enemy locations, movements, and strength." The scouts might be individuals or groups, "often operating at or even behind enemy lines."[2]

In September 1862, Colonel William A. Phillips, commanding a regiment of Indian Home Guard in the southwest, submitted a report to the general commanding the department, in which he explained a change in tactics he had adopted: "As they [the Confederates] have female spies and other means of information, I have always chosen one position (not defensible) in the day-time and a strong position at night." Brigadier General Grenville Dodge created a large western network of spies for Ulysses S. Grant early in the war that included several women. One of his female operatives, Mary Mainard, was arrested and held in a Confederate prison until the end of the war.[3]

By 1864 the use of women military operatives (whether called "scouts," "spies," or "detectives") in the trans-Mississippi states and territories seems to have been common. Brigadier General John B. Sanborn, on May 28, 1864, instructed his Union field officers in Missouri to "send out women spies or good scouts and ascertain, if possible, what the enemy's force is and what he intends to do and who is in command" (his order is reprinted in Appendix B, page 316). Major Jeremiah Hackett of the 2nd Arkansas Cavalry (Union) reported to his commanding officer on June 15, 1864, about the results of a scouting mission in the vicinity of Cassville, Missouri:

June 13, I made with the cavalry of my command a scout to the east of the road as far as Packet's Mills, on Prairie Creek. Saw 4 men, well mounted and armed, who on sight of my command scattered and escaped. Crops are looking fine in this vicinity. I returned and intersected the Wire road at Pea Ridge, overtook the infantry at the head of Little Sugar Creek, where I encamped, catching 2 women, Mrs. and Miss Gibson, engaged in an attempt to break the telegraph wire near the forks of the Bentonville road. I brought the women with me, prisoners.[4]

Early in 1865 a woman named Nora Winder was reporting directly to Major General William T. Sherman on Confederate forces, positions, and troop movements. In a letter dated February 12, 1865, from Hilton Head, South Carolina, she informed Sherman of her travels through Georgia with her young son, during which she observed and named the locations of powder works, artillery batteries, concentrations of soldiers, and fortifications. She also mentions having missed connections with "the young man who was to hand me the money the day I left Milledgeville...." At almost exactly the same time, Major James M. Moore addressed a letter to Brigadier General Sanborn from Cassville, Missouri, February 11, 1865, saying: "I have received information from a female spy that I had employed that the rebels are concentrating their forces, 500 strong, on the Dry Fork of Osage, in Arkansas." Mature women as well as younger girls were on the government payrolls as spies, especially in the North.[5]

Both men and women engaged in smuggling of weapons, drugs and medicines, clothing, food, and other essential supplies, concealed in their luggage or clothing or on their person. Smugglers often doubled as couriers by carrying concealed military messages that transmitted vital information about enemy positions, force strengths, and movements. Women sometimes concealed messages in their hair or sewn into their clothing.

In one instance, two women with Confederate sympathies successfully smuggled clothing and other goods from Baltimore to Harpers Ferry in 1861. "One of them...attired herself in two full suits of uniform, over which she wore her appropriate female garb, while the other lady concealed beneath her crinoline twenty-five thousand percussion caps, which are of inestimable value to us just now." Similarly, a young Maryland woman named Nannie Webster smuggled various goods through Union lines to Richmond. On one occasion in 1861 she arrived there alone, "with her petticoats quilt with quinine, her satchel full of letters, many of them containing money, and with no end of spool thread, needles, pins, and other little conveniences now so hard to get in the blockaded south."[6]

In North Carolina, twenty-five-year-old Emeline Pigott attended to sick and wounded Confederate soldiers, sometimes bringing them home to her parents' farm on the Atlantic coast. Pigott collected mail, food, clothing, and medicine in several counties to support the Confederate cause, delivering the goods to a network of prearranged drop-off points such as hollow trees. After her lover was killed at Gettysburg, she became a courier for the Confederate secret service in the vicinity of New Bern, North Carolina, carrying mail and dispatches concealed underneath her hoop skirt, narrowly avoiding capture several times. She was once jailed in New Bern in 1865, but managed to obtain her release.[7]

The *Nashville Daily Union,* December 21, 1862, cautioned women about the likelihood of being searched if they tried to pass through the military lines:

To the Ladies.—We are informed that the Military Police of this city have adopted a rule to examine all females passing through the lines, who may be suspected of carrying contraband goods, letters, &c. The practice has become so common, that they have deemed it absolutely necessary to adopt this course. We understand some cases of the above character transpired yesterday, and we would warn all females to avoid anything of the kind in the future, if they would escape exposure. We understand that they have employed ladies for the purpose of examining any who may be suspected.

An extraordinary pair of sisters who did not at all fit the stereotype of the Southern belle became spies and smugglers for the Confederacy. Ginnie (Virginia) and Lottie (Charlotte) Moon, daughters of a physician, were born in Virginia but were moved to Ohio while young. Although for the most part they outwardly maintained the dress and other social customs of the time, in some ways they were very rebellious. According to Harnett T. Kane, "They were, everybody said, perfect ladies, and at the same time hellers in their own special fashion. . . . Miss Ginnie toted a gun during most of her life—a pretty pearl-handled revolver that she knew very well how to use." In later life Ginnie became a chain smoker, and both sisters were outspokenly in favor of women's rights.[8]

While living in Oxford, Ohio, the sisters astonished their neighbors by reading biographies and serious books on science, including Charles Darwin. The older sister, Lottie, was romantically involved with future Union general Ambrose Burnside but eventually married James Clark, who became a judge, and the much younger Ginnie was sent to live with the pro-Southern Clark family. Judge Clark was active in the Knights of the Golden Circle ("Copperheads"), a pro-Confederate, antiwar movement that flourished in the western states bordering the Mississippi River.

Confederate couriers often visited the Clark household while carrying secret messages. One time a courier arrived carrying dispatches that needed to be delivered to Confederate General Kirby Smith in Kentucky. At this point Lottie began her career as a Confederate spy by volunteering to deliver the dispatches. Donning the disguise of an old woman, she succeeded in passing back and forth through the lines and accomplishing the mission. Thereafter she conducted several other spying missions in Virginia.

Ginnie, meanwhile, had moved to Memphis, Tennessee, to be with the sisters' mother after their father died. Ginnie and her mother joined with other women in preparing bandages and providing medical care for wounded Confederate soldiers as Federal forces threatened the city. Ginnie began passing back and forth through Union lines carrying messages and medical supplies, and she and her mother teamed up to deliver some urgent information to the Knights of the Golden Circle in Ohio. Once there, they gathered papers and supplies to carry back to the South, but by this time they had come under the suspicion of Union agents.

As they boarded a boat in Cincinnati for the return trip, a Union officer appeared and confronted them with orders to search them. Ginnie reportedly was found to be carrying forty bottles of morphine, seven pounds of opium, and a supply of camphor. She and her mother were promptly arrested and confined in a hotel. Despite the serious evidence obtained, no legal action was ever taken against the Moon sisters. The charges against Ginnie were dropped, but she was required to report regularly to Union authorities. Eventually she was ordered to leave the North.[9]

Mary Ann Pitman, a soldier in male disguise who became a secret agent and procurer of ordnance and ammunition for Confederate General

Nathan Bedford Forrest, had a rocky career in the latter occupation. When captured by Union forces she served time in at least three Union prisons. Whether due to a philosophical conversion of her beliefs about Yankees (as she claimed) or to fear about the potential punishment for her actions, she became a turncoat and cooperated with Federal authorities to the point of changing her former allegiances to the Confederate cause and supplying the Federal authorities with vital information. In the latter part of 1864 she was deployed as a double agent while masquerading as a Union prisoner. Eventually she was pardoned and well compensated by the U.S. government (see Chapter 9).

Spying was an exceedingly dangerous activity, punishable by death if the perpetrator were caught in the act and convicted. As H. B. Smith, a chief of detectives for the Union, noted in 1911, "Any citizen or soldier from the Confederacy found within our lines was considered a spy; some were executed. To escape such treatment it was necessary to report to the nearest officer and take the oath of allegiance. Even then we were not protected, but had to examine the purported refugee, or deserter, to ascertain their possible honesty. We captured a great many spies."[10]

Official government espionage agencies also took many forms. A small Confederate army signal corps was formed in 1862. The Signal Bureau provided cover for a highly secretive "Secret Service Bureau" and courier network known to insiders as the "Secret Line," which was run by the Confederate War Department.

> All combined, some 1,500 men are estimated to have served the Confederacy as signalmen. Pledged by oath to secrecy, they were responsible for signal communication and official cipher correspondence. Both through direct observation and the interception and "breaking" of enemy signals, they made their contribution to military intelligence. Yet their service is virtually unknown and their role seldom is counted in the study of campaigns and battles.[11]

The memoirs of Dr. Charles E. Taylor about his activities in the "Secret Service Bureau," from the foreword of which the above quote is taken, were published in 1903, about forty years after the fact. He asserted that the bureau was headquartered in Richmond and served as a nerve center for military intelligence communications, while giving the appearance of being a small headquarters for the Signal Corps. According to Taylor, the Bureau network effectively monitored shipping traffic on the Potomac River, and their signal stations provided timely information to Confederate commanders in the field.

In the North, Allan Pinkerton, chief of the self-named United States Secret Service and a protégé of General McClellan, supervised a "large corps of men and women, white and black, then engaged in obtaining information" during the Virginia Peninsula Campaign in 1862. These espionage agents often undertook dangerous missions such as penetration of secessionist groups in the North who were plotting various schemes, including the assassination of President Abraham Lincoln. One of these secret service women was Mrs. Kate Warne, whom Pinkerton in his postwar memoirs describes as "the lady superintendent of my agency." Posing as a secessionist from Montgomery, Alabama, she worked closely with Pinkerton gathering information that helped Lincoln to reach Washington, D.C., safely on his trip from Illinois to Washington, D.C., to begin his presidency.[12]

Lafayette C. Baker ran what was in some respects a rival "secret service," which he later named the National Detective Police. He was originally employed by General Winfield Scott, the able but elderly senior Union general, to obtain information in Richmond in 1861, then was placed in charge of the secret service bureau with plentiful resources at his command. In February 1862 the bureau was transferred to the War Department. Its primary mission was to protect the capital city and the government against spies and traitors.[13]

Among the Confederate spies that Union authorities monitored were Miss Fanny C. James, Rose O'Neal Greenhow, and Antonia Ford. Miss James, a Baltimore resident, was arrested in May 1863 and committed to the Baltimore jail for "treason." A letter to her from Richmond was intercepted by authorities, showing that she had smuggled goods and supplies, including quinine, to friends in Richmond.[14]

In Washington, D.C., Mrs. Greenhow, a widow, ran a major Confederate spy network out of her home in the city while under constant surveillance by the Union detective corps headed by Allan Pinkerton. She lived in the heart of the city and had social and political connections that reached high in government circles and into northern Virginia. As a spy, she was resourceful and very successful. Her exploits have been well reported and documented by numerous authors.[15]

Detective chief Lafayette C. Baker kept tabs on another female spy in northern Virginia, just outside of Washington, D.C. Antonia J. Ford, a young woman from an aristocratic family in Fairfax, professed to be a loyal Unionist, but was secretly operating as a Confederate spy. Union officers boarded with the family and carried on government business there. In his postwar book Baker referred to her as "Miss A.J.F."

> Fairfax Court-House was for two years within our lines, and occupied as an outpost by our army. Here lived a citizen by the name of F., with whom boarded several of the staff officers. His daughter, Miss F., was a young and decidedly good-looking woman, with pleasing, insinuating manners. She discoursed fluently, and with enthusiasm, of the Union cause, impressing her admiring guests with her loyalty and intelligence. Meanwhile, she carried out her commission as a rebel spy. This document [the Confederate commission], in its original form, was found through the confidence reposed by Miss F. in a female subordinate in my bureau, who played the part of a Southern lady going to her friends. Miss F. opened her heart to the young adventurer, and also her bed, in which, between the mattress and its nether companion, was concealed the prized and useful paper. It was found there when the fair spy was arrested by my order.[16]

Baker had sent one female spy to catch another. (The Union counterspy, "Frankie Abel," discussed below, was colorful in her own right.)

The Children of the Confederacy (an auxiliary organization of the United Daughters of the Confederacy) has an Antonia Ford Chapter #885 that offers an online article titled "Who Was Antonia Ford?" The biographical sketch describes Ford's life and career in some detail. As the Federal officers talked among themselves, "she listened carefully to all that was said and watched all that was done and reported as much as she could to J.E.B. Stuart, whose troops operated in the area of Fairfax Court House."[17]

Just before the Second Battle of Bull Run, Ford herself drove a carriage twenty miles through the Union lines to deliver important information to Stuart about Federal plans, information that is credited with having avoided a "certain disaster." The following December when Union Brigadier General Edwin Stoughton established his headquarters at Fairfax Court House, she began monitoring his activities and reporting them to

Stuart and John Singleton Mosby. On March 8, 1863, she was instrumental in helping Mosby and his men to raid the quarters and capture Stoughton and a number of other Union officers.[18]

Frances Jamieson (a.k.a. "Frank Abel") served in many capacities during the war in a long and checkered career, beginning in the Union cavalry. Originally she joined her husband, a U.S. cavalry captain, and served with him as a lieutenant at First Bull Run. When he was killed in the battle, she left the army and served as a nurse in army hospitals.[19] Thereafter she spent a longer career as a spy and detective. In September 1862 she went to work for Major General Nathaniel P. Banks, an army corps commander, as a spy. On October 1 she was captured by Confederate cavalry and sent to a Richmond prison. In December she was released, exchanged for famous Confederate spy Belle Boyd, but Banks had moved on to command in the Department of the Gulf.[20]

Jamieson then joined Lafayette Baker's Union detective force, working in the Baltimore, Maryland, area, but was arrested and imprisoned at Old Capitol Prison, Washington, D.C., on various "morals" charges. In the summer of 1863 she was released into the custody of Baker, who often used women for spying activities and detective work. She sometimes wore a male disguise while conducting spying operations for Baker in the Washington, D.C., area.[21] Baker sent Jamieson ("Abel") to infiltrate the Ford home in Fairfax and gain Antonia Ford's confidence. "Frankie Abel," wearing a faded calico dress, played the role of a destitute refugee from New Orleans, and she succeeded in fooling everyone at the Ford household.

She was taken in by the Fords, who gave her stylish clothes to wear and a place to stay. She and Antonia Ford traded stories of their service to the Confederacy, and after two months, "Frankie" had so gained Ford's confidence that Ford showed the woman her commission from Stuart. After Jamieson's departure for New Orleans a few days later, Federal agents moved in quickly and placed Ford and her father under arrest. The elder Ford was released shortly thereafter, but Antonia was held until May 20, when she was exchanged. She was, however, soon rearrested and escorted to Old Capitol Prison in Washington, D.C.[22]

In January 1864 Jamieson was arrested again in Norfolk, Virginia, by the provost marshal and ordered out of the city. She was reported to be working part-time in Norfolk as a prostitute. Where she went after that is not documented.[23]

A notorious and highly controversial alleged spy was Annie E. Jones, who, according to some reports, was a consort of several Union officers in Washington, D.C., and Virginia-area camps. Jones was a native of Massachusetts, where a newspaper-style online publication in 2004 contained a feature article about her. "Miss Jones was obviously a nineteenth century Mata Hari who traded her womanly charms for sensitive information," said the author. The article reported that Anna Elinor Jones was an orphan living in Cambridge, Massachusetts. She left there in 1861 at age nineteen intending to become an army nurse in Washington, D.C., but was turned down because of her age.

Undaunted, she seems to have begun a life as a charmer and manipulator of men in authority, both military and civilian, influencing them by offering her companionship and, no doubt in some cases, sexual favors. In return she was supplied with passes through the lines, horses, plush quarters, and various amenities, occasionally even military escorts. Apparently she started out in the guise of a Daughter of the Regiment with the 135th New York Infantry, but was soon engaged in far more than ceremonial roles.[24]

Union detective chief Lafayette C. Baker, who clearly considered her to be a spy, devoted several pages to Annie Jones ("A.J.") in his postwar memoirs. "One of the most strangely romantic female histories of the war, which came within the investigation of the bureau, was that of Miss A.J.," he stated. He refers to her as being of a particular type of woman, euphemistically termed "female visitors to the army." He continued: "Much of the information communicated to the rebels was given by these irresponsible characters passing through rebel and Union lines. The condition of morals among officers who found congenial companionship in the society of such women, is apparent, and needs no coloring from pen or pencil."

Baker reports that this "unfortunate and degraded young woman" violated her parole—she had sworn not to cross the Potomac into Virginia—and was arrested while trying to pass the Confederate pickets. Massachusetts politicians interceded on her behalf and obtained her release. She then gave the Union authorities a sworn statement that included a confession and much more.

In the fall of 1862 I went to the Army of the Potomac, with
no different object in view; spent some time at General S.'s
headquarters at Fairfax Court House. During this time was the guest
of the general and his staff officers. After General S. Left Fairfax
Court House I went to Centreville. . . . In June or July last I attempted
to pass the Federal pickets, for the purpose of visiting Drainesville,
then outside our lines; was arrested, and taken to General S.'s
headquarters, and by him sent to General M., who at once released
me, and sent me back to General S.'s headquarters, where I
remained until the army returned from Maryland.[25]

Jones, possibly due to her "political clout" both inside and outside the
army, seems to have been handled like a hot potato whenever she got into
trouble or violated the military conventions. "General S." apparently was
Edwin Henry Stoughton, who served in the defenses of Washington early in
the war, and as of December 1862 made his headquarters at Fairfax Court
House until March 1863, when he was captured as described above.[26]

Jones's formal statement then continues, linking her with Custer and
Custer's superior at the time, Gen. Judson Kilpatrick.

General S. was then relieved, when I joined General K[ilpatrick]'s
command, and went to the front, as the friends and companions
[sic] of General C[uster]. We made our headquarters near Hartwood
Church. Stopping at this point, General K. became very jealous of
General C.'s attentions to me, and went to General M.'s headquarters
and charged me with being a rebel spy. I was then arrested and
sent to General M[eade], Military Governor of Washington, who
committed me to the Old Capitol Prison. I have spent two years
and a half in the Union army, and during that time have been the
guest of different officers, they furnishing me with horses, orderlies,
escorts, sentinels at my tent, or quarter rations, &c. I have invariably
received passes from these officers, to go and return when and
where I pleased. . . . I have repeatedly passed the outside pickets of
the Federal army, several miles beyond, into the rebel lines; and was
once captured by Moseby [sic]. . . . I was detained one or two days,
then allowed to return.

These allegations created a controversy that ultimately led to a formal
inquiry and came to the attention of the commander-in-chief of the Army
of the Potomac. Her formal statement continues:

On the 7th day of November, 1863, I was released from Old Capitol Prison, by order of the Secretary of War.... On my discharge from prison, I signed a parole, one of the conditions of which was "that I should not enter the state of Virginia" without proper permission, during the rebellion; but, notwithstanding this obligation, I have made several ineffectual attempts to do so.... During the entire time since my leaving home in 1861, I have led a very roving, and, may be, questionable life. I am now very unwell, owing to my long confinement and other causes, and desire to be released from custody, in order that I may return to my home and friends; and, if released, I pledge myself not to return to Washington during the present rebellion.

Historian D. A. Kinsley characterizes the allegations in this statement as "Annie's Revenge." Although the statement is factual in a number of respects, there is more to the story that casts it in a different light. Kinsley makes the case that Jones was for a time General Judson Kilpatrick's mistress, a *femme fatale* and a generally dangerous and troublesome adventuress, and that Custer was innocent of the charges. Kinsley reports that Custer first met Jones when she was brought to his tent by Kilpatrick, a notorious womanizer, and introduced to him as an aspiring nurse. In fact, she had become Kilpatrick's mistress and he had presented her with a horse, a major's uniform, and a pass allowing her to roam around pretty much at will, whereupon she "played havoc with inlying and outlying pickets [and] exposed herself to Rebel snipers...."

Finally she went off into Confederate John Singleton Mosby's lines and remained there for two days. She claimed to have been captured by Mosby's men, but Kilpatrick suspected otherwise and kicked her out of camp. About a month later she turned up at Custer's camp with a military escort and an ambulance, showing Custer passes from the Medical Department and the War Department authorizing her to visit the army as a "sister of mercy." She claimed to have been officially placed as a hospital nurse in the 3rd Cavalry Division, but Custer disputed the validity of her passes and banished her from camp, saying that the signers of the passes had no authority in his camp. Custer was adamant and she was forced to leave.[27]

On March 22, 1864, Kinsley reported, a confidential packet came down the chain of command from General George Gordon Meade and was delivered to Custer by an aide to Kilpatrick. It contained a document titled "Report respecting a young lady calling herself Annie E. Jones, supposed to be a Rebel Spy." The packet included various allegations about her associations with Kilpatrick and Custer but also contained a provost marshal investigation report about her activities. General Meade asked Kilpatrick and Custer for any comments they cared to make.

The provost marshal investigation report noted that although she had been arrested twice under suspicion of being a Confederate spy and finally sent to Old Capitol Prison in Washington, D.C., she had been exonerated both times. The investigator stated that he had yet to find anyone who considered her to be a spy and suspected that the anonymous charges that had been made against her emanated from "a female who is jealous of her," someone whose lover she had spirited away.

Custer, knowing full well that Jones had been Kilpatrick's mistress, was furious about the allegations directed at him and responded immediately with a formal statement. However, he side-stepped the issue of his superior Kilpatrick's culpability and protected him in the process. Annie Jones had been at his camp for only one week, he said, and was never allowed outside the lines. Her statements about consorting with Kilpatrick and himself and being allowed to come and go through the lines freely, he said, were "simply untrue," adding "I do not believe she is or ever was a spy." He too considered her simply a young woman seeking excitement and adventure.[28] Finally, she was sent away to a prison in Barnstable, Massachusetts, far away from the army camps.

Annie Jones certainly was a feminine force to be dealt with and somewhat of a mystery figure. Apparently very physically attractive and with an engaging personality, she took what fate gave her and made the most of it. She apparently left jealousies in her wake, whether deliberately or not, and was fully capable of manipulating people in positions of authority to serve her own ends. The temptation is to write her off as simply an exploitative woman of "loose morals," but the historical record leaves us with a complex portrait of an unusual person who is not easy to delineate. While denying that she had ever engaged in spying activities, Jones candidly admitted to being "a companion to the various commanding officers, as a private friend or companion." Although this statement may have been partly her "revenge" for being snubbed, it also appears to have been more than a little true.

A lot of her "companionship" may well have been purely social, non-sexual—if somewhat opportunistic and self-serving—behavior. The composition and vocabulary of her formal statement indicates that she was very literate and articulate. Her extensive influence with politicians and Union authorities also suggests that she had certain qualities that made her appealing, a pleasant companion. By all accounts she apparently was not a spy, and so her motivation seems to have been accurately characterized by D. A. Kinsley as the desire for excitement and adventure. Probably she also enjoyed the red carpet treatment given to her, the amenities provided, and the influence she had.

If she had been a male, behavior of this sort perhaps would have been considered an "ego trip" and she probably would have been viewed as an adventurous, politically skillful, and clever but self-centered person. Her story is unusual for the times and not at all typical of women with her demonstrated intelligence, yet fits a pattern of scandalous behavior by male army officers who often were found to have female consorts or concubines in camp with them under various guises, some more discreetly than others. In February 1864 Colonel Theodore Lyman, an officer on General Meade's headquarters staff and later a congressman from Massachusetts, had said, in colorful language: "There are perfect shoals of womenkind now in the Army [many living] a sort of Bedouin life." Later in March, no doubt with the Annie Jones affair currently in mind, General Meade issued an order saying that until further notice, "The employment of females as officers' servants is prohibited." The situation apparently had become notorious.[29]

One of the most intriguing characters among women who served as spies in the Civil War is Cuban-born Loreta Janeta Velazquez, whose story has been viewed with great skepticism by historians and social commentators. Other than a few scattered contemporary references, her 1876 memoirs have long been the primary source of information about her alleged adventures as soldier and spy for the Confederacy.[30] Her memoirs are quoted from and extensively paraphrased in *Patriots in Disguise* (Hall 1993). Basically, they tell the story of a young girl from a wealthy family who, in 1849, was shipped from Cuba to live with her aunt in New Orleans and attend Catholic school. There she learned fluent English, married an army officer, and ran away with him at fourteen years old, experiencing army life at various western frontier posts.

When the Civil War broke out, her husband (whose name is not known) defected to the Confederate army. Against his will, she adopted male disguise, practiced walking and talking like a man, and served as an independent officer with her husband in Pensacola, Florida. In order to impress her husband, she traveled to rural Arkansas and recruited a battalion of soldiers that she brought back to Florida for training. After her husband was killed in a training camp accident, she continued in service, later becoming engaged to and eventually marrying Thomas C. DeCaulp, an officer who had served with her husband.

At the First Battle of Bull Run, July 21, 1861, Velazquez fought in the front lines in male disguise as "Lt. Harry Buford." At first buoyed by the Confederate victory there, she gradually became disillusioned by her combat experiences at Balls Bluff, Virginia, on October 21, 1861; Fort Donelson, February 13–16, 1862; and Shiloh, April 6–7, 1862. After the battle at Shiloh she was severely wounded by an explosion on the battlefield where she was helping to bury the dead, and when evacuated to the south on a train, a doctor discovered that she was a woman. Initially she had used a girdlelike garment to disguise her female form, but it gradually deteriorated until it no longer worked properly, and thereafter she was arrested several times and imprisoned on suspicion of being a woman. At the time, a woman in male soldier disguise was automatically suspected of being a spy.

Tiring of military life and the constant hassle of trying to maintain her disguise, Velazquez began experimenting with spying activities. At times she freelanced, but at other times she appears to have been authorized by Richmond authorities as an official secret service agent. One of her more dangerous reported exploits was penetrating the Federal detective corps headed by Lafayette C. Baker and acting as a double agent, pretending to work for him while actually carrying out Confederate operations.

After the war, by her own account and confirmed by scholarly writings, she was part of a Confederate expedition to settle in Venezuela. When that failed and she had exhausted her wartime profits from sales of bogus bonds and other money-raising schemes, she traveled around the western

United States seeking a new fortune in mining operations. A mining entre-
preneur became her third husband and the father of her son. Eventually
the mining schemes and her marriage failed, and she once again struck
out on her own.

Except for one or two brief mentions of her after 1876, what became of
her and her son remains a mystery. She apparently died in obscurity, but
no date or place of death is known. Historical evidence has been found
that supports some of the key elements of her story, though in certain
portions fact and fiction appear to be inextricably entwined (see Chapter
9 and Appendix B).

Undoubtedly the most famous Confederate female spy was Belle Boyd,
who had begun to attract attention in early 1862. Her life and career
have been extensively reported.[31] While passing through Richmond in
mid-October of 1862, Boyd was interviewed by the *Southern Illustrated
News* newspaper and a local artist contributed a sketch of her to go with
the story on October 18:

> This young lady, who has, by her devotion to the Southern cause,
> called down upon her head the anathemas of the entire Yankee press,
> was in our city last week. . . . Miss Belle is the daughter of Benjamin
> B. Boyd of Martinsburg, at which place he was for a long time
> prominently engaged in the mercantile profession. He afterwards
> removed to Knoxville, Tennessee, where he lived about three years,
> but returned to Martinsburg about two years previous to the breaking
> out of the present war. Her mother was the daughter of Captain
> Glenn of Jefferson county. Miss Belle is the oldest child of her
> parents, and is about 23 years of age.

The editors then quoted an article about Belle Boyd from the *Philadel-
phia Inquirer* by an unnamed correspondent who had seen her in action.
The correspondent's reporting seems to be reasonably objective and fair.
His story describes how Southern women arranged to be introduced to
Northern officers while using various assumed names and proceeded to
pump them for information:

> By such means they are enabled to frequently meet combinedly,
> but at separate times, the officers of every regiment in a whole
> column, and by simple compilation and comparison of notes, they

achieve a full knowledge of the strength of our entire force. . . . The chief of these spies is the celebrated Belle Boyd. Her acknowledged superiority for machination and intrigue has given her the leadership and control of the female spies in the valley of Virginia. . . . Belle has passed the freshness of youth. She is a sharp-featured, black-eyed woman of 25, or care and intrigue have given her this appearance. Last summer, whilst Patterson's army lay at Martinsburg, she wore a revolver in her belt, and was courted and flattered by every Lieutenant and Captain in the service who ever saw her. There was a kind of Di Vernon [a "horsey, dashing heroine" of early-nineteenth-century English fiction] dash about her, a smart pertness, a quickness of retort, and utter abandonment of manner and bearing which were attractive from their very romantic unwontedness.

The correspondent reported watching Boyd charm the young officers, and later warning them about who she was. He learned that she had been introduced to them under different names, such as "Miss Anderson" or "Miss Faulkner." He continued:

She is so well known now that she can only practice her blandishments upon new raw levies and their officers. . . . She has, however, a trained band of coadjutors, who report to her daily— girls aged from 16 upward—women who have the common sense not to make themselves as conspicuous as she, and who remain unknown. . . . The reports that she is personally impure are as unjust as they are undeserved. She has a blind devotion to an idea, and passes far the boundary of her sex's modesty to promote its success.

While attempting to run the Union blockade and travel to Europe in May 1864, Boyd was captured by a U.S. ship, brought back to Fortress Monroe, and imprisoned. After obtaining her freedom she again traveled to Europe, where she married a former American sailor by the name of Samuel Harding on August 25, 1864. Harding had been on the crew of the ship that had captured her at sea and had apparently fallen in love with her during the trip back to the United States. Harding was taken into custody in Martinsburg, Virginia, by the provost marshal on December 2, 1864, and sent to Washington, D.C.[32]

Perhaps a degree of eccentricity, along with shrewd intelligence and an "unfeminine" zest for independence, were prerequisites for being a fe-

male spy during the Civil War. Belle Edmondson, who undertook extensive spying operations around Memphis, Tennessee, for the Confederacy,
sometimes used the alias "Brodie West." Edmondson also smuggled
through the lines dispatches, equipment, and medical supplies concealed
in her petticoats. She appears to have been a "liberated woman" who
had constant trouble with human relationships but nevertheless was an
accomplished musician, a Mason, and a skillful chess player. Edmondson
makes frequent references in her diary to playing chess against men.

Among Edmondson's collected correspondence are letters back and
forth between her and Captain Thomas H. Henderson, a Confederate
scout with whom she shared information, and other Confederate officers
that record some of her spying activities. In a March 16, 1864, diary
entry, she recorded an incident of smuggling uniforms through the lines
concealed in her clothing, along with buttons and money. The contraband
was so heavy that she had difficulty walking.

> At one o'clock Mrs. Fackler, Mrs Kirk & I began to fix my articles
> for smuggling. We made a [petticoat] of the Gray cloth for uniforms,
> pin'd the hats to the inside of my hoops, tied the boots with a strong
> list, letting them fall directly in front.... All my buttons, brass
> buttons, money &c in my bosom.... started to walk, impossible that,
> hailed a hack—rather suspicious of it, afraid of small-pox. Weight
> of contrabands ruled—jumped in with orders for a hurried drive to
> corner Main & Vance. Arrived found Anna not ready had to wait for
> her until 5 o'clock, very impatient started at last. Arrived at pickets,
> no trouble at all—although I suffered horribly in anticipation of
> trouble. Arrived home at dusk.

On April 20 and 21, 1864, she records in her diary being threatened
with arrest by the Yankees "for carrying letters through the lines and
smuggling, and aiding the Rebellion in every way in my power." On April
22 she went out disguised by a thick veil to purchase some supplies, but
avoided the pickets because she had heard that detectives were out looking for her. Yet the next day she succeeded in penetrating the lines again.
The Union authorities, with the military situation very fluid, seemed content for the time being to keep an eye on her, and she continued her activities as best she could under the circumstances. She recorded the comings

and goings of Union and Confederate soldiers in her diary on a daily basis and noted (April 29) that "I beat Maj. Crump at chess."[33]

In addition to battlefield nurse Fannie Beers and Loreta Janeta Velazquez, the state of Louisiana produced several other extraordinary women soldiers or spies. Mrs. William Kirby, wife of one Confederate soldier and mother of another one, smuggled weapons through Federal lines at Baton Rouge, Louisiana. She was caught, convicted as a spy, and imprisoned in a Federal stockade on Ship Island where she died near the end of the war. Her son was killed at Gettysburg, but her husband survived the war.

Citing a report by John McGrath, a Baton Rouge, Louisiana, historical society officer, Matthew Page Andrews (1920) reports that William Kirby was a wheelwright by trade. "At the outbreak of the war, father and son, the latter a lad of tender age, joined the Confederate army of northern Virginia to die [the son] finally upon the hillside at Gettysburg." From the start, Mrs. Kirby (whose first name is not known) devoted herself full time to the Confederate cause. Aside from constantly urging young men to enlist, she gathered clothing, medicine, and supplies for the soldiers. After Baton Rouge was occupied by Federal troops, she became a very successful smuggler by spiriting quinine and other medicines through the lines into the South.

Mrs. Kirby then undertook the more dangerous mission of smuggling arms and ammunition out of the city, skirting around Union cavalry pickets by avoiding public roads and traveling through the fields and woods. After successfully fooling Union authorities for a long time, she finally came under suspicion and was detected and arrested. "When arrested," Andrews reports, "she had just secured two cavalry rifles which she had placed under her top dress. The butts reached nearly to her arm pits.... [they] were long enough, however, to reach to the soles of her shoes, and at each step struck the brick pavement, with a loud metallic sound."

Two soldiers, hearing the tapping sounds, stopped and questioned her, discovering the rifles. She was taken before a military tribunal, convicted as a spy, and sentenced to confinement on Ship Island for the duration of the war. The island, off the Mississippi coast near Pensacola, Florida, had a Union military stockade for housing suspected spies and Confederate collaborators and sympathizers. While confined there, Mrs. Kirby was informed of her son's death. Near the end of the war her health failed and she died in prison. William Kirby lived four or five years longer.[34]

Young girls often became messengers, scouts, and occasional spies to support the cause (see Chapter 2 and Appendix A). At the age of sixteen or seventeen, Melvina Stevens was a trusted scout and spy for the famous Federal scout, Dan Ellis, a so-called pilot who helped guide Union prison escapees, Confederate deserters, and escaping slaves to safety through the mountains of East Tennessee. Ellis and his guerrilla band provided information to Federal authorities about Confederate activities and acted as couriers.[35]

Nancy Hart, a young Virginia girl, at various times acted as a scout, spy, guide, messenger, and nurse. According to an online web site biography, she never learned to read or write but was an expert rider. She grew up in the country in Roane County, where she learned how to use a rifle and generally became accustomed to outdoor life. Early in the war when she was about nineteen years old, Hart is reported to have joined a cavalry unit known as the Moccasin Rangers, in which Diana Smith also served about the same time (see Chapter 4). However, her term of service in that unit is not clear, and she seems to have operated more as an independent scout and spy. She carried messages back and forth between elements of the Confederate army, traveling alone at night, and served as a guide for Confederate detachments.

Hart also led wounded Confederate soldiers to hiding places with sympathetic families, sometimes nursing them back to health. She also peddled food to Union camps and hung around in order to spy on them and report their strength to General Stonewall Jackson. On occasion she led Jackson's cavalry on raids. Eventually Union authorities offered a reward for her capture. In July 1862 she was surprised in her hiding place and captured by Lieutenant Colonel William C. Starr of the 9th West Virginia Infantry and briefly imprisoned in a dilapidated building that served as a jail. But she seized a gun and shot her guard, escaping on Starr's horse. A few days later she led a large Confederate raiding party that captured Starr and his men.[36]

The exploits of these Southern women and their Northern counterparts, though noteworthy, daring, and indicative of strong character traits and dedication to a cause, still do not compare to those of perhaps the most amazing female soldier of all: Harriet Tubman. Out of slavery came a black woman, lacking the education and privileges of the many white women of the South and North, who through individual grit and determination almost single-handedly "conducted" the underground railroad before the war that led thousands of African Americans to freedom and independence in the North. Then during the war Tubman served as a soldier, leading raids and scouting missions and spying for the Union in South Carolina (see Chapter 10).

Several other female Union army scouts are listed in Appendix A, including Susan Bond and Katie Smith. Others whose names have been lost to history are mentioned in the "Unidentified Female Soldiers" section of Appendix A.

Pioneering women served as nurses in primitive field hospitals like this one. From *Sparks from the Camp Fire*, 1895

Women nurses served on hospital ships like these shown at Pittsburg Landing during the Battle of Shiloh in April 1862. From *Century War Book*, 1894.

Helen Gilson was a Hospital Transport Service nurse on the Virginia peninsula in June 1862 and field hospital nurse after major battles in 1863. From *Our Army Nurses*, 1897.

Wounded soldiers being evacuated from the Seven Pines/Fair Oaks battlefield in Virginia; women nurses served on both sides at this 1862 battle. From *Century War Book*, 1894.

Annie Etheridge, a famous battlefield nurse for Michigan regiments in the Army of the Potomac, is shown here in a postwar photo wearing the Kearny Cross for valor and a regimental badge. Courtesy State Archives of Michigan.

Marie Tepe, a battlefield nurse from Pennsylvania, was frequently under fire and was wounded in 1862. She is shown here wearing the Kearny Cross for valor. Photo by Robert P. Swiatek from *Music on the March*, 1892.

Kady Brownell (left), 1st Rhode Island Infantry, in vivandiere costume. From *Women of the War*, 1866. Belle Reynolds (above), battlefield nurse at Shiloh, became a doctor after the war. From *Women of the War*, 1866.

Mary Jane Safford, the "Cairo Angel," a pioneering frontline nurse. From *Women's Work in the Civil War*, 1867.

Albert D. J. Cashier (Jennie Hodgers), who saw heavy combat as a soldier in the 95th Illinois Infantry, is shown here (on the right) with a fellow Illinois soldier. After the war Cashier continued to live as a man, and her true identity was not discovered until 1911; two years later the story made national news when she was discovered in a veterans' home. The poster below shows 1864 (left) and 1913 (right) photographs. Top: courtesy of Spencer H. Watterson; bottom: courtesy of Illinois State Historical Society.

Jennie Hodgers's gravestone in Saunemin Cemetery, Illinois, bears the name under which she fought. Courtesy Illinois State Historical Society.

Sarah Emma Edmonds, famous soldier and spy who served as Franklin Thompson in the 2nd Michigan Infantry, later married Linus Seelye. She was honored by the Grand Army of the Republic; her grave is maintained to this day in Washington Cemetery, Houston, Texas. Courtesy Mrs. Leona Zaboroski, Concerned Citizens for Washington Cemetery Care.

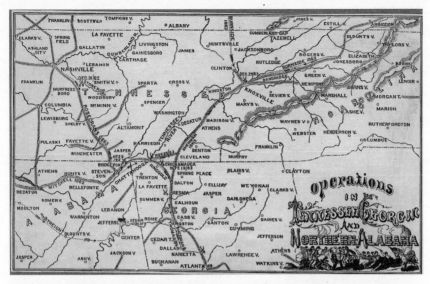

This map of operations in Tennessee, Georgia, and Northern Alabama shows campaign and battleground areas where women soldiers, including Loreta Janeta Velazquez and Mary Ann ("Amy") Clark, served. From *The Women in Battle*, 1867.

Civil War–era military map of Washington, D.C., a major hub of army activity and spying operations during the war. The city was surrounded by military camps and field hospitals where numerous women served. Published by Charles Magnus, New York, N.Y.

Elizabeth Van Lew, effective Union spy in Richmond. From *On Hazardous Service*, 1912.

Margaret E. Breckinridge, army nurse
who became a casualty of the war. From
Woman's Work in the Civil War, 1867.

Clara Barton, Civil War "ministering
angel" and Red Cross founder, in postwar
photograph. From *Our Army Nurses*, 1897.

Sophronia E. Brecklin of New
York served as a field hospital
nurse in Virginia and Maryland
and was the first nurse in a
field hospital after the battle
at Gettysburg, Pennsylvania,
in July 1863. From *Our Army
Nurses*, 1897.

Mary "Mother" Bickerdyke,
of whom Gen. William T.
Sherman reportedly said,
"She ranks me." From
*Woman's Work in the Civil
War*, 1867.

Loreta Janeta Velazquez (left) served as a lieutenant in the Confederate army and as a spy and counterspy. She was wounded at Shiloh and imprisoned several times. From *The Woman in Battle*, 1876. Unidentified Confederate widow (right, probably Velazquez) who served as a spy. According to the caption in *Confederate Operations in Canada and New York* (1906), she was a messenger for St. Alban's Raiders and procured the "proper papers" from the Confederate government.

Elida Rumsey Fowle, too young and attractive to meet Dorothea Dix's army nurse standards, volunteered for hospital service in Washington, D.C., for three years. From *Our Army Nurses*, 1897.

6

They Were Determined to Serve

A widow McDonald has been detected in several [Confederate] regiments and discharged as many times.
  Austin State Gazette, *Texas, February 22, 1862*

From the opening artillery fire of the Civil War at Fort Sumter in 1861 through the Appomattox Courthouse surrender of Robert E. Lee's army in April 1865, women continuously used guile and resolute determination to join the army. They did not always succeed, but they never stopped trying through four long years of war. They cut their hair short, wore loose-fitting clothes, practiced male mannerisms—whatever it took to perfect their disguises. These women were not easily discouraged. One by one they donned male clothing and risked embarrassing exposure and public censure to enlist in the army, and if found out, often turned right around and tried again in a different regiment.

Society had mixed feelings about the women as the reports of their discovery multiplied. Initially, the most common military reactions to the discovery of a woman wearing male army clothing were to label them prostitutes, or spies, or mentally disturbed individuals, or devious people of some kind, up to no good in any case since they were violating conventional sensibilities. Newspapers often termed them "Amazons"; in contemporary usage the general meaning of "Amazon" was simply a "bold and daring woman," and in the early years newspapers reported their efforts admiringly. Later in the war, after the romance had worn off, newspapers sometimes suggested that the cross-dressing soldier-women were "coarse" or "ugly." Though some of the women were rugged and stoutly built, they were not necessarily physically unattractive.

In the final analysis gender conventions and prejudices of the mid-nineteenth century on the home front dictated that by virtue of their bold and cheeky behavior, these women must be abnormal in some socially significant way. They were, indeed, outside the norm; but this was only circular reasoning. Another discordant factor was that the male soldiers who had lived and soldiered with the women usually did not depict them in physically unflattering terms in the way that outsiders did. To the contrary, the soldiers often found them to be "rather prepossessing," as General Philip Sheridan said of the "she dragoon" found in the ranks of his cavalry escort, and the men admired their courage. Still, their exploits became fodder for the nineteenth-century press, and a sensational story was often more important to competitive editors than accurate reporting.

The women—mostly teenage or young adult—who joined the army (or the war effort in one capacity or another) came from all walks of life. They included poor working girls, runaways seeking a new life, young women from middle-class families of moderate means, and well-to-do, highly educated society women. They might be single, or attached to a young man who had "gone for a soldier," or married and accompanying their husbands to war. Some, like Jane Hinsdale and Jennie Hodgers, were illiterate. Others, like Sarah Edmonds, had hardscrabble early lives but attained a good public education and were articulate. And some from the more privileged segments of society were conversant with good literature, music, philosophy, and social niceties. Clearly there were strong undercurrents in society behind the phenomenon; the women were not simply an unrepresentative sample of nineteenth-century womanhood consisting entirely of mannish Amazons.

On a hypothetical spectrum of lower- to upper-class women, the former tended to become soldiers, soldier-nurses, or army scouts while the latter tended toward hospital work as nurses, matrons, or administrators in the hospital system. There were, of course, many exceptions to this general rule, and women who engaged in spying or smuggling activities came from all across the spectrum. Also, their education level played an important role in how much of a historical record an individual woman left behind. Sarah Emma Edmonds is known to history primarily because she was intelligent, articulate, and a good writer. Jennie Hodgers is known to history only because of her admirable army service and hard-earned reputation that ultimately was placed on the record by her comrades in arms, not by her.

What all of these women had in common in addition to their personal courage was their indomitable will and their perseverance in the face of adversity. They were unwavering in their determination to take part in the war, no matter what obstacles were thrown in their way. As for the female soldiers in male disguise, only death or accidental discovery of their gender could thwart their purpose, and even when discovered, many quickly went elsewhere and enlisted again. The battlefield nurses, scouts, and spies regularly risked their lives in the performance of their duties, and others, such as the smugglers, risked at least imprisonment and disgrace.

The majority of would-be female soldiers were probably discovered very early in their enlistment while still in camp, before seeing any field service. Sometimes they didn't even get that far. The hospital matron at Benton Barracks, St. Louis, Missouri, one day detected a young woman in male disguise applying for enlistment. Questioned by the provost marshal, the applicant confessed that her real name was Lizzie Cook, from Appanoose County, Iowa. Her father, she said, was in the 1st Missouri State Militia Cavalry and was killed in a skirmish at Walnut Creek, Missouri. Her brother was a sergeant in the 5th Kansas Infantry. She said she was trying to reach her brother and wanted to serve her country. She had registered in a St. Louis hotel as "William Ross." Lizzie was described as about twenty years old, "tall, fine-looking, intelligent, animated in conversation."[1]

While serving on recruiting duty, apparently late in 1862, Sergeant Lewis B. White of the 3rd New York Cavalry, Company H, received a volunteer recruit one day in Rochester. The volunteer was dressed in dark clothes and a soft hat with a gilt cord around it. White later reported that the recruit "had the general air of a soldier" and claimed to have served eighteen months in the infantry until wounded in a limb, hospitalized, and discharged. White thought the recruit was too slight for the rigors of cavalry service and suggested the position of bugler, which was immediately accepted. But when he started to lead the recruit to a surgeon for an examination, the recruit balked, and finally confessed to being a female. Others who talked with the recruit thought "he" was rather slight in build and possibly underage, but none suspected that "he" was a "she."[2] There is no way to tell whether the girl had actually served in the infantry previously as she claimed, but the incident demonstrates her determination to serve in the army.

The true gender of some apparently male soldiers or enlistees came to light when they were unable to fool a nurse or a physician who interviewed them, by accidentally displaying "female mannerisms," or as a result of random or chance occurrences such as being recognized by a relative or friend. In one unusual case, a young girl's avarice overpowered her judgment. It began when a boy named "Charles Norton" volunteered to be servant to Captain Reeves of Company E, 141st Pennsylvania Infantry. Norton marched with the company, cooked for the captain, and took care of his possessions. At the Battle of Chancellorsville in May 1863, Captain Mercur, who had small feet, found his boots missing. Charles was caught and confessed, and during questioning was found to be female, but exactly how was not reported.[3]

A more typical case was that of Sarah Collins, of Lake Mills, Wisconsin, who was reported to have enlisted with her brother, Mason, in a Wisconsin regiment. She was quickly detected by her mannerisms and sent home before the regiment departed for the front.[4] As might be expected, perceived feminine behavior was a fairly common means by which female soldiers in disguise were discovered and exposed. In the course of living in close quarters, one of the men might happen to notice certain body language, perhaps a gesture or mannerism, and begin to suspect something. Many young teenage boys in the army had high-pitched voices or were relatively small in stature and beardless, so those factors alone would not particularly attract attention. But a manner of dressing or a toss of the hand might.

One of the more amusing failures to masquerade successfully as a male soldier occurred late in 1862 when a young woman, accustomed to pulling on a skirt over her head, gave herself away by trying to pull her army pants on in that way. In another case a young soldier was discovered to be a woman after serving about two months in the Union 1st Kentucky Infantry as a private when she aroused suspicion about the way she pulled on her stockings. She was using the male alias "John Thompson." The regiment was in the Western Virginia Kanawha Valley Campaign late in July 1861, and a newspaper correspondent covering the campaign reported: "She performed camp duties with great fortitude, and never fell out of the ranks during the severest marches. She was small in stature, and kept her coat buttoned to her chin."

This woman (whose real name is not known) proved to be a spy when a letter that she had written to Confederate authorities was found and she confessed to the crime. She was expecting to be hanged and was reconciled to her fate, but instead she was sent to prison in Columbus, Ohio.[5] The *Savannah Republican,* Georgia, August 8, 1861, editorialized:

> Don't hurt that woman.—The papers speak of a Georgia woman who has been detected in what is known as the "First Kentucky Regiment" (Lincoln), in Western Virginia, and arrested as a spy. When interrogated as to her object, she boldly avowed that she was in the service of her native and beloved South, and desired the vengeance of its invaders; she knew her fate, and as a patriot she was ready to meet it. She was sent to Columbus, Ohio. We hope our Government will see to it that this patriotic woman does not suffer the penalty of death, whatever may be the ransom. Spare two spies on our side, or exchange five hundred prisoners of war, before a hair of her head shall be touched.

Noteworthy in this case is the fact that the Georgia newspaper saw no reason to criticize this "belle of the South" for masquerading in male disguise. Instead, they applauded her daring and patriotism.

One of the earliest female soldiers on record enlisted in the 3rd Ohio Infantry in 1861, apparently in April, in an attempt to join her lover, who she knew was stationed at Camp Dennison. She joined the regiment in camp near Cincinnati, where she "assisted in all the duties of forming a new camp, handling lumber, standing sentry, etc." Then when her lover was nowhere in sight, she discovered that there was another Camp Dennison in Pennsylvania where he was, so she requested a transfer to one of the companies in the 2nd Ohio Infantry at that location. At this point Colonel Morrow (spelled "Marrow" in some sources) somehow recognized that the soldier was a woman, female clothes were obtained to send her off in "proper attire," and she was discharged.[6]

As many of these reports illustrate, the circumstances leading to exposure are often not stated explicitly in the newspaper stories, which report only the fact that a soldier had been found to be a woman. In those cases we can only speculate as to what gave them away. Sallie Curtis enlisted in an unnamed Indiana Union regiment early in the war and served for twenty months before being discovered and discharged. She quickly reenlisted, this time in the Union 2nd Kentucky Heavy Artillery. Her second enlistment lasted only a week before she was found out and discharged again.[7]

Means of their discovery were not reported for a young woman in the 63rd Illinois Infantry who told authorities that she simply wanted to be with her sweetheart. She was discovered on board a steamship with her regiment en route to Nashville. A woman named Kate in the 116th Illinois Infantry, who was discovered while on picket duty, was reported to be the girlfriend of a lieutenant; he was reprimanded by the colonel for allowing her to continue service in the regiment.[8]

Throughout the first two years of the war women continued doggedly in their efforts to join the army. Starting in 1861 and continuing off and on for four years, Louisa Hoffman enlisted (or tried to) in all three major branches of the army. She is reported to have served in the 1st Virginia Cavalry at First Bull Run and through August 1862, then as a cook in the three-months 1st Ohio Infantry. Finally, she was arrested after enlisting in Battery C of the Union 1st Tennessee Light Artillery and was brought before the provost marshal at Nashville, Tennessee, on August 16, 1864. After being dressed in normal female attire she was sent under guard to Louisville, Kentucky, and from there to her home in New York City.[9]

An unnamed woman said to be the mother of four children was reported to have served as "the most reckless daredevil" in the three-months 7th Pennsylvania Infantry regiment, which participated in several skirmishes and engagements in Maryland and West Virginia.[10] As is frequently the case, the shallow and sensational reporting in this September 1861 newspaper story immediately raises questions about how the woman was able to be away from her children for three months, not to mention why she would "recklessly" risk her life in battle. Where was her husband (if she had one)? Who was caring for her children? What were her motivations? All too often, we are left with tantalizing and probably unanswerable questions of this sort. However, such newspaper reports this early in the war—despite their shortcomings—tend to be essentially accurate.

Another example is "John Williams," who enlisted as a private in Company H, Union 17th Missouri Infantry ("Western Turner Rifles"), on October 3, 1861, in St. Louis, and later that month was discovered to be a woman and discharged (see Chapter 9, "John H. Williams").[11] However, another "John Williams," whose true name was said to be Sarah Williams, was reported to have been arrested late in 1864 as a private in the 2nd Kentucky Cavalry after serving for three years. Information is lacking to shed light on her motives, means of discovery, and whether in fact there was more than one female soldier using the name "John Williams."

Sometimes the regimental officers knew that a soldier was female, but looked the other way because the individual was a good soldier. In fact, there are reasons to suspect that this was true far more often than has been reported. Regiments often were severely thinned by combat casualties and rampant diseases in camp, reduced from the standard of about 1,000 down to 200 or 300, and recruiting of replacements was a continual problem. A female soldier from Cincinnati, Ohio, who was detected in the ranks by an officer in late 1861, pleaded to stay in service. The officer did not report her and she remained in the ranks. "She looks as brave as any soldier in the division," he reported, under a newspaper *nom de plume.* "I say bully for her, and if I only could get 100 of such I would send a company."[12]

The civil and military authorities often didn't quite know what to do with the women who were arrested when found in uniform away from camp, and so shuffled them around from place to place hoping someone else would deal with the unwelcome problem posed by their presence. Immediate discharge was the usual response when women were discovered in the ranks, but depending on specific circumstances many were arrested on suspicion of being enemy spies. Prostitutes or spies—what else could they be by contemporary standards? The historical record includes instances of women in Confederate uniforms held in jail by Confederate authorities, and women in Union uniforms held in jail by Union authorities. But the opposite situation prevailed when women in uniform were captured by the enemy during combat. Then female Union soldiers usually were incarcerated in Southern prisons and vice versa, although the prisoners of war typically were paroled when their sex was discovered (see Chapter 7).

Discovery of female soldiers from Ohio, New York, and Illinois also made the news in the spring and summer of 1862. A teamster with an Ohio regiment was hospitalized with measles in Nashville, Tennessee, during May 1862. The *Nashville Dispatch* for May 31 reported that she had first served in the regular army, then later joined the Ohio regiment. "She is represented as about eighteen years old, and made rather a handsome boy. She has three brothers in the army, but not in the regiment to which she was attached." Another young woman from Chenango County, New York, was discovered in male disguise in a Pennsylvania regiment. According to *Frank Leslie's Illustrated Newspaper* for July 19, 1862, she had previously served as a nurse in the 61st New York Infantry along with her husband, but for unspecified reasons she had become separated from that regiment.[13]

Harriet Brown (alias "Harry Brown"), meanwhile, was found in an Illinois regiment, where she had been for three months before being discovered. She was arrested for unknown reasons in 1862 at Union Depot in soldier's uniform en route from Lexington, Kentucky, to Chicago and placed in a Kentucky hospital to serve as a nurse. Not being happy in that position, she once again tried to don a uniform. This time she was arrested in Indianapolis, but let go after being supplied with "suitable apparel." Later, apparently resigned to the fact that she could not be a soldier, Brown became matron of an army hospital in Quincy, Illinois.[14]

The examples reported here and elsewhere indicate that the most commonly stated motivation for enlistment in the army was to be with a loved one. When discovered in uniform in the 89th Ohio, Mary Corbin told the authorities that she wanted to be with her sweetheart. It is not clear whether she actually had been serving as a soldier, or was simply trying to join the regiment when discovered. She was caught on August 27, 1863.[15]

Revenge as the primary motive for a young woman to enlist in the army also is a recurring theme. Another girl who was discovered in the ranks late in 1861 told the authorities that she had enlisted to avenge the death of her only brother, who was killed at the First Battle of Bull Run in July of that year. Mary Smith enlisted in the 41st Ohio Infantry ("McClellan Zouaves") in the fall of 1861 and went into training at Camp Wood, Ohio. There she was found out to be female by her mannerisms. The soldiers noticed that she was unusually skillful at sewing, and there was something about the way that she wrung out a dishcloth. She was said to be "intelligent, good-looking, full of patriotism, pluck, and aged about twenty-two years."[16]

Persistent would-be female soldiers also showed up in the South, in several different states, where even stricter taboos were in place about the socially acceptable roles of women. Reports began as early as 1862. The *Charleston Mercury,* South Carolina, for January 16, 1862, reported: "A young widow named McDonald was discharged from Col. Boone's regiment [Confederate 28th Kentucky Infantry] at Paraquet Springs, Kentucky last week, where she had been serving as a private, dressed in regimentals, for some time. This was her second offence, she having once before [presumably in 1861] been discharged from a regiment."[17] No information is available about Mrs. McDonald's motives, but since she was a widow it is possible that she, too, was seeking revenge.

On May 30, 1862, the *Southern Confederacy* newspaper in Atlanta, Georgia, published a letter signed with the initials G.W.A. He had taken the train from Atlanta to Montgomery, Alabama, early in the morning on May 26. During a stop at the small town of Loachapoka in eastern Alabama, a group of soldiers in uniform boarded the train. One, the informant noted, was "a fair blue-eyed girl" with an obvious feminine voice. She was from Hayneville, Alabama, but all the boys in town had gone off to war so she decided to go with them. "She also stated that other girls from her section had already gone to war," the writer said. On arriving in Montgomery, he reported, the girl was turned over to the provost marshal.

The *Weekly Columbus Enquirer,* Georgia, August 19, 1862, reported that a young woman was found among a group of new conscripts in a North Carolina regiment in mid-August.

A Female Volunteer.—In calling the roll of a regiment of conscripts who had just entered the camp of instruction at Raleigh, N.C., last week, one more "man" was present than called for by the list. The *Winston Sentinel* says: "This, of course, involved an investigation, when it was discovered that the features of one claimed to be a conscript were quite too fair and fine for one of the sterner sex. The soldier was charged of being a female, when she confessed the truth and acknowledged that she had determined to accompany her friends in the perils of war, and avenge the death of a brother who fell in the fight near Richmond. We have heard nothing in any degree to implicate the good character and standing of this gallant heroine."

About the same time that the North Carolina girl sought revenge for her brother's death in the war, a young woman in the North was discovered in Captain Gerard's company (Company I) of the 66th Indiana Infantry after fooling the soldiers for some time. One day by chance her uncle visited the camp and accidentally met and recognized her. She was immediately discharged. Her motives are not known.[18]

By 1863 all notions of a short war had passed, and the depleted armies needed more and more soldiers. Short-handed regiments also recruited intensively to fill their dwindling ranks, and female soldiers turned up regularly. Archival records show that "a friend of William Hertzog's wrote [November 21, 1863] not to his family, but to Will, describing a splendid new recruit his company [encamped in Pulaski, Tennessee] had picked up. However, the new volunteer turned out to be a woman and much to the men's disappointment had to be discharged" (see note 8).

During 1863 and 1864, revenge for the death of a family member was cited frequently as a reason for trying to join the army. In February 1863 a female cavalry trooper by the name of Henrietta Spencer was discovered in the camp of the 10th Ohio Cavalry at Cleveland. The *Peoria Morning Mail,* Illinois, February 14, 1863, reported that her home was in Oberlin, Ohio, and that she had enlisted to avenge her father and brother, who were killed at Murfreesboro, Tennessee, in December 1862. The regiment had not yet been completely organized, so she was sent home before it left for the front. Regimental records show that the 10th Ohio Cavalry was organized at Camp Cleveland and Camp Chase and did not leave camp until July 25, 1863.

The *Cincinnati Dollar Times* for August 11, 1864, reported a story taken from the *Cleveland Herald* about a young woman who said that she had lost three brothers in the war and that she was determined to enlist and avenge their deaths. Since she was too well known in Cleveland she traveled to Windsor, and there donned male attire, had her hair cut short, and walked around the streets of Detroit as a young boy.

> She offered herself as a "substitute" to an enrolled man, who took her to four different recruiting offices, where papers were made out; but the "boy" was each time rejected on surgical examination as being "too short," the real state of the case not being explained to the "principal." At last the "boy" started for the provost marshal's office to "volunteer." The venerable examining surgeon proceeded to strip the "boy" and was so much astounded at what he discovered that he rushed in alarm from the room and proclaimed the unlooked-for sex of the recruit. The girl was severely reprimanded for her conduct, but she declared that she was "bound to be a soldier or die" and was determined to get into the ranks somewhere. She says other girls have got into the army, and she could not see why she should not.

While visiting the camp of the 19th Illinois Infantry at Camp Douglas one day in 1863, the famous Civil War nurse Mary Livermore had a certain soldier pointed out to her by a captain, who asked her if she noticed anything peculiar about the soldier. "It was evident at a glance that the 'man' was a young woman in male attire," she reported, and she told the captain so. The captain replied that he had heard rumors to that effect and suspected it to be the case. The young woman was called out of ranks and questioned. She pleaded to remain in the army, saying she had joined to be with her husband, but she was escorted out of camp. Livermore took the young woman in charge, but she jumped out of the carriage and fled, jumped off a bridge in a suicide attempt, and when rescued, ran away and disappeared.[19]

Some young women simply could not conceal their gender from the penetrating gaze of a veteran officer. A former Illinois lieutenant acting as an army recruiter for the 124th Illinois Infantry was escorting a group of volunteers from Galesburg to Quincy, Illinois, by railroad car during March 1864 when one of them caught his eye. The soldier appeared "too raw" for military life. Investigating further, the lieutenant discovered that the recruit was a young woman named Mary Ann West. She had previously tried to enlist in the 66th Illinois Infantry at Monmouth. West was turned over to the Sisters of Charity in Quincy to be returned home.[20]

To avoid betraying themselves, some female soldiers aggressively displayed "masculine" (or at least unfeminine) habits. Loreta Janeta Velazquez, who served as a Confederate junior officer, wore a false mustache and practiced a swagger. At first she also wore a chain-metal corset-like affair to disguise her female form, but in her memoirs she reports ruefully that her specially designed outfit kept getting "out of order" and she was frequently stopped and questioned. Once while in jail in Lynchburg, Virginia, under suspicion of being a woman in Confederate uniform, she propped her feet up on a windowsill, turned her head, and spat just as some unfriendly visitors arrived at her jail cell, in order to convince them she was not a woman.[21]

Others were known to smoke and drink to blend in with the group. In 1862 a woman disguised as a man enlisted in Captain Jackson Brand's company of the 107th Pennsylvania Infantry. According to a newspaper that reported the incident, "He [she] could smoke a cigar, swagger, and take an occasional 'horn' [drink] with the most perfect sang froid." The unidentified woman lived in Path Valley, Franklin County. About a month later she returned home and resumed female attire without explanation, but said she was determined "to try it again."[22] Elvira Ibecker (a.k.a. "Charles Fuller") of the 46th Pennsylvania Infantry also smoked and drank along with the boys (see Chapter 3).

Another woman who was said to have tried this preemptive approach was Mrs. Frances Clayton. She was reported (apparently incorrectly) to have served in a Minnesota regiment along with her husband, and according to newspaper reports "the better to conceal her sex, she learned to drink, smoke, chew, and swear with the best, or worst, of the soldiers."[23] Like so many other stories of female soldiers reported in contemporary newspapers, the facts of her military service were badly garbled. She could not have served in a Minnesota regiment, none of which served when and where she said she did (see Chapter 8).

Occasionally a young woman simply decided that she had had enough of army life, for whatever reasons, and resigned voluntarily. A girl who had served two years in an Indiana regiment (dates not reported) and was wounded twice apparently tired of army life, donned female apparel, and informed her astonished colonel who she was and departed for home. Initially she had enlisted to be near a sweetheart, but he had proved to be a coward and the relationship had ended.[24] In another case, reported by the *Mobile Register and Advertiser,* Alabama, for May 18, 1864, "a Detroit cavalry captain was astounded a few days since when one of his new recruits walked up to him and declared that soldiering was rather disagreeable, and that said recruit, being a female, would quit the business."

Sometimes overly aggressive behavior led to an indiscretion that sabotaged the otherwise successful deception practiced by a woman in male disguise who had been in service for a relatively long period of time. A female cavalry soldier in Sheridan's command, together with a female teamster from Tennessee, got drunk on apple cider and fell into a river; both were discovered to be female when rescued. Sheridan personally interviewed them and records the incident in his memoirs (see Sarah Bradbury and Ella Reno, Chapter 9 and Appendix B).

In one case a woman's discovery ended in tragedy. A female soldier in the 14th Iowa Infantry, when exposed in camp during April 1863, shot and killed herself. She may have considered it a fate worse than death to be found out. Like many others, she had wanted to be with her lover and apparently could not bear the thought of being separated from him.[25] A few other cases are on record in which the exposed woman was extremely distraught and even suicidal, including the young woman at Camp Douglas identified by Mary Livermore and a New Jersey girl exposed in the 39th New York Infantry in 1861 (see Appendix A, Unidentified Female Soldiers for 1861).

Even as some young women accidentally gave themselves away or were exposed by chance, others succeeded in maintaining their disguises for long periods of time. Almost invariably the long-term female soldiers eventually were exposed due to a calamity: severe illness requiring hospitalization, being wounded or killed in action, or capture and imprisonment by the enemy. A genealogical web site based in Indiana, apparently no longer operative, contained something called the "Thornburg Newsletter" which identified a Mary A. Thornburg as the daughter of Nathan Thornburg and Phoebe Beals/Bales living in Randolph County, Indiana, during the Civil War. The newsletter reported that she "dressed as a man and joined the

Union Army." She was discovered when she contracted smallpox. Later she married Eduard DeForest and lived a normal, conventional life.[26]

A "drummer boy" who turned out to be a girl was discovered in a Pennsylvania regiment. A local newspaper reported, "She had evidently enjoyed the advantage of education, could write a good hand, and even composed very well." After participating in five battles and escaping unwounded and undiscovered, she contracted typhoid fever and finally was exposed when hospitalized in Pennsylvania. Her parents resided in Bucks County.[27] (See other examples of female "drummer boys" in Chapter 4.)

Malinda Blalock in the 26th North Carolina Infantry was among several other infantry soldiers discovered after being wounded in action (see Chapter 3). Others for whom battlefield wounds disclosed their secret included Confederate soldiers Mary Ann Clark, Charlotte Hope, and Lucy Matilda Thompson and Union soldiers Lizzie Compton, Catharine Davidson, Mary Galloway, Mary Owens Jenkins, and Annie Lillybridge (see especially Chapters 7 and 9).

Female soldiers whose names are not known, including numerous casualties, also have been reliably reported. After the Battle of Gettysburg, July 2–3, 1863, among the battlefield casualties found on the field were two Confederate women (one dead, one seriously wounded). One had participated in Pickett's famous charge and was killed at the so-called high-water mark on the slopes of Cemetery Ridge. The other casualty at Gettysburg was reported by a wounded Union soldier from Michigan, in a hospital at Chester, Pennsylvania. After the battle he wrote a letter home saying that there was a female Confederate soldier there with them in the hospital who had been wounded severely and lost a leg. He thought this was "romantic" and felt sympathy for her.[28]

The following year a Union female officer was found to have fought in the Battle of the Wilderness, Virginia (May 5–7, 1864). Margaret Hamilton, a Catholic sister from New York State, reported that while serving at the U.S. Military Hospital in Philadelphia, "we received a large number of wounded after the battle of the Wilderness, and among them was a young woman not more than twenty years of age. She ranked as lieutenant. She was wounded in the shoulder, and her sex was not discovered until she came to our hospital. It appeared that she had followed her lover to the battle; and the boys who were brought in with her said that no one in the company showed more bravery than she. She was discharged very soon after entering the ward."[29]

Among the diverse reasons that women disguised as male soldiers were suddenly exposed, none was more dramatic than giving birth to a child. To put it mildly, this was a certain giveaway and caused a sensation every time. Yet few, if any, of the soldier-mothers were ever identified by name. One can only speculate that the male soldiers of all ranks may have adopted a protective posture and deliberately kept the women's identities secret—a paternalistic attitude, if you will. Quite a few examples of soldiers giving birth were reported by their fellow soldiers in the field in letters to their homes and in other records such as nurses' memoirs. Civil War nurse Harriet Whetten recorded in her diary on August 21, 1862, that she had discovered a woman among the hospitalized Union soldiers in her care who was pregnant and had to be sent home.[30]

A female soldier serving in a New Jersey regiment with her husband had been in four battles before being discovered in 1863 when she gave birth to a baby. At Johnson's Island prison camp on Lake Erie, Ohio, a Confederate officer prisoner gave birth to a baby boy during the first week of December 1864. "This is the first instance of the father giving birth to a child we have heard of," said the *Sandusky Register,* Ohio.[31] The December 1864 date is rather late in the war for a female soldier to be discovered, especially a Confederate officer in male disguise. It is truly extraordinary that, as cited above, a female Union officer had been discovered about six months earlier after being wounded at the Wilderness battle. To have become officers and be trusted to lead others in combat, both women must have displayed well-above-average courage and ability.

Taking the record for perseverance as soldiers were Frances Hook and Elizabeth Compton for the North and Mary Ann Clark for the South. Each was discovered more than once, was wounded in combat, served in more than one regiment, and persisted in service for several years, sometimes in cavalry and sometimes in infantry. (See their case studies in Chapter 9 and contemporary reports in Appendix B.)

Starting in 1861 and for a period of four years, Frances Hook apparently served in five different Illinois regiments (one cavalry), plus a Tennessee cavalry regiment and a Michigan Infantry regiment! During this time she used the name "Frank" as an alias, but with several different last names. During the Murfreesboro–Stones River campaign in Tennessee, December 1862, she was wounded in the shoulder and was discovered and discharged. She managed to serve in three more regiments after that.

"Lizzie" Compton, after being wounded and discovered, claimed to have first enlisted at age fourteen and to have served in seven different regiments, "leaving one and enrolling in another when fearing detection" or actually being detected. Three Michigan infantry regiments are among those named, along with the 11th Kentucky Cavalry. She was wounded in the shoulder at Tebbs Bend, Kentucky, on July 4, 1863. Her documented record is less complete than Hook's, and her male alias or aliases have not been reported.

Mary Ann Clark's record in the Confederate army was for many years incomplete and garbled, but recent research (Blanton and Cook 2002) has fleshed out the details substantially so that a fairly complete picture has emerged. In 1861 she enlisted in the army to escape from a bad marriage and served for four months (apparently in a Louisiana cavalry regiment). She then reenlisted in another regiment, possibly then a third, served in Bragg's army in Kentucky, was wounded, captured, and later paroled.

Sarah Edmonds had served for two years in the 2nd Michigan Infantry before she became ill with malaria, contracted early in the war on the Virginia Peninsula, and was about to be sent to the hospital. Fearing exposure, she deserted, and her story was not fully known until long after the war. Jennie Hodgers completed a three-year enlistment in the 95th Illinois Infantry and was only accidentally exposed long after the war. Both saw hard service and experienced combat. This impressive group of combat veterans, it should be noted, came from diverse backgrounds and included several women who were married either at the time or later, once again refuting the stereotypes suggesting that female soldiers had to be mannish, or even lesbians.

From the earliest months of the war in 1861 and constantly from then on, young women kept trying over and over to pass muster. Although they were often detected early and sent home—or so the authorities intended—quite often they would leave camp and head directly to another regiment to try again. They would sometimes succeed on the second or third try and serve for extended periods of time. Others, barring some catastrophe, sustained their disguises all along and served with distinction, often being promoted to sergeant or lieutenant and leading men in combat.

Whether there were more women who went undetected altogether than who were found out is impossible to say, but it is crystal clear that throughout the war, from start to finish, women were determined to be soldiers. Those who succeeded experienced all the rigors of field service, engaged in combat, and became casualties just like the men. Many were wounded or killed in action, or suffered the inhumane conditions of enemy prison camps. The women prisoners almost certainly would have been paroled if they had only revealed their gender to the prison guards, but many courageously chose not to do so voluntarily. They accepted their fate just like the men.

7

Casualties of War: Battlefield, Prison, and Hospital

> I am sick and tired of war. Its glory is all moonshine. It is only those who have never fired a shot nor heard the shrieks and groans of the wounded who cry aloud for blood, more vengeance, more desolation. War is hell.
>
> *William Tecumseh Sherman, graduation speech at*
> *Michigan Military Academy (June 19, 1879)*

The Union army marched off to Manassas, Virginia, in July 1861 with visions of a quick, decisive, and glorious victory over the "insurrectionists." The pulse quickened to hear the roll of the drums and see the bright colors fluttering in the breeze. Quite literally they thought it was going to be a picnic, and civilians streamed out from Washington in their carriages carrying their lunches with them to watch the spectacle. But something unexpected happened when the armies clashed along Bull Run Creek. The Union army was sent reeling in defeat, fleeing in total disarray back to Washington City. Over 1,700 Union soldiers were dead or missing, another 1,000 or so wounded. The victorious Confederates had about 400 killed or missing and about 1,600 wounded.

The last major war on the American continent had been the War of 1812, and that was some fifty years earlier. At that time the United States had won a largely defensive victory against Great Britain with casualties (killed and wounded) totaling 6,765 over the full term of the three-year war. At First Bull Run alone the casualties were about 4,000, and there were almost four more years of bloody battles still to come in the Civil War. The Medical Department of the army in 1861 was poorly organized, understaffed, and lacking in resources to deal with casualties on this scale, so the wounded suffered beyond imagination. First Bull Run shattered a lot of illusions about the romance of war, and a far more realistic view took hold fairly quickly.

One of the consequences of a rapidly growing army and an escalating war is a need for more and larger prisons. Times of widespread public disorder commonly lead to declarations of martial law, more sweeping arrests, and rapid expansion of penal institutions to accommodate the influx of prisoners, both military and civilian. In the process, civil liberties tend to get trampled underfoot. After President Abraham Lincoln suspended the writ of habeas corpus in some regions of the country, military tribunals became common and civilian courts often were trivialized. Under habeas corpus, when a person perceived that he was being unjustly detained by authorities and wished to appeal it, a civil judge could issue a writ requiring that the prisoner be brought before the court and his detention justified. In practice, during the Civil War federal judges often were pitted against military authorities in regard to the handling of prisoners and became ineffective at constraining the harsh effects of martial law and military tribunals on civilians.

Lincoln's suspension of habeas corpus has been the subject of extensive discussion by historians, but less noticed is the fact that Confederate president Jefferson Davis did the same thing. Special Orders No. 1 issued on March 30, 1862, from the headquarters of the Confederate Army of the Mississippi declared: "Martial law is hereby established at Jackson and Grenada . . . and their respective environs for a circuit of 5 miles. The inspector-general . . . will appoint suitable persons at each place to act as provost-marshals." A letter the next day to Major General E. Kirby Smith on behalf of General Robert E. Lee noted that "the attention of the President has been called to . . . the necessity for martial law. In reference to the latter you will please report the exact limits of the country over which you desire the establishment of martial law and when you desire it to go into effect." President Davis made it official on April 8, 1862, with the following proclamation:

By virtue of the power vested in me by law to declare the suspension of the privilege of the writ of habeas corpus, I, Jefferson Davis, President of the Confederate States of America, do proclaim that martial law is hereby extended over the Department of East Tennessee [a hotbed of pro-Union sentiment], under the command of Maj. Gen. E. K. Smith; and I do proclaim the suspension of all civil jurisdiction [with specified exceptions], and the suspension of the writ of habeas corpus in the department aforesaid.[1]

As historian Louis Fisher observes, "The widespread use of military tribunals throughout the Civil War marked a turning point in America's experience. Hundreds of tribunals operated with little supervision by Congress or the courts." In December 1861 Union Army headquarters in St. Louis declared martial law, and while paying lip service to the legitimate role of civil courts in regard to wartime litigation, still tended to view the civil courts as both subordinate to military affairs and unreliable. The army was concerned not only with guerrillas, but also with "insurgents" and "disloyal" citizens.

An army circular was issued on February 14, 1862, announcing that "persons in arms against the United States were to be arrested and held for trial before a military tribunal." The circular authorized military seizure of the personal property of anyone found to be assisting the Confederate cause. The Congress, in effect, ratified Lincoln's actions after the fact, ultimately passing laws that brought the actions into accord with statutory law. Also, Lincoln was acutely aware of both the legalities of the situation and the potentially harmful effects on civilians. He monitored the situation via the Adjutant General's Office and often overturned sentences of the military tribunals, especially those involving the death penalty.[2]

Civil War author Peggy Robbins reports, "At the very beginning of the war, because there were no places to detain prisoners, both sides released them on parole, on oath to take up arms no more." During the war each side took more than 200,000 prisoners.[3] Although women had served time in prison before, for crimes ranging from drunk and disorderly to murder, the numbers imprisoned as a direct result of the civil crisis were unprecedented. Perceived political crimes, treason among them, added to the population of overcrowded detention centers.

At the seat of government in Washington, D.C., the Federal government operated Old Capitol Prison, which became the unwanted temporary home of many political dissidents, Confederate spies, and other sometimes colorful characters, including many women. As indicated in Federal correspondence recorded in the *Official Records of the Union and Confederate Armies,* outlying military departments sometimes unloaded their troublesome prisoners by sending them to the nation's capital for safekeeping. In *Official Records,* Series 2, Vol. 2, there appears a "List of prisoners confined in the Old Capitol Prison, Washington, D.C., March 17, 1862" in the form of a table, with headings of "Name," "Date of arrest," and "Nature of offense."

At that date we find not only the notorious Confederate spy Rose O'Neal Greenhow in residence for almost seven months, but also Mrs. Augusta H. Morris, "Spy; actively connected with Walworth, Smithson and others. Sent to Washington by General Johnston"; and Mrs. L. A. McCarty, "Spy, as shown by the papers found upon her." Additionally, we find Mrs. C. V. Bexley (a misspelling for "Baxley) charged with "Carrying information to Richmond" and already resident for two and a half months, also found with the goods concealed upon her person. When arrested, she was carrying a surgeon's commission in the Confederate army for a doctor friend in Baltimore, numerous other incriminating letters, and a personal journal (see "Mrs. C. V. Baxley" in Appendix B).[4]

Women, especially in border states, often were arrested and thrown in jail simply for displaying pro-Confederacy sentiments too strongly in public, perhaps adorning themselves with Confederate flags, so that big-city prisons at times had numerous female inmates. Prisoner rosters for the Gratiot Street Prison and Chestnut Street Prison in St. Louis, Missouri, from 1862 through early 1865 show dozens of female prisoners, some held on the flimsiest of charges or no stated charges at all. A few examples:

Miss Jennie M. Spencer, February 26, 1865, prisoner of war

Mrs. T. A. Ryder, February 28, 1865, disloyal practices; to be sent beyond Union lines

Mary E. Bowles, January 4, 1865, feeding and harboring guerrillas

Imogene Brumfeld, released December 27, 1864, banished from department

Isadora Morrison, July 12, 1862, female spy

The prison rosters sometimes contain ages and physical descriptions, showing females ranging from fourteen to fifty-seven years old. Miss Clarinda P. Mayfield of Vernon County, Missouri, who was arrested during July 1864, is described as 4' 8," age 16, light hair, blue eyes." Somehow it is difficult to imagine her posing any serious threat to the Union. As an interesting sidelight, virtually all of the women appear to have been 5 feet tall or under. One who must have stood out from the crowd was Mrs. Elizabeth Price of Jefferson County, Missouri, who is described as 5' 8," age 50, gray hair, hazel eyes." She is listed as being there on order of the provost marshal general.

Gratiot Street Prison served primarily as a clearinghouse for prisoners of war from battles and surrenders in the Mississippi River area. Most prisoners were processed there and forwarded to Alton, Illinois, about twenty-five miles away or to other longer-term holding areas for military and political prisoners. The female prisoners at Gratiot apparently ran afoul of the St. Louis area provost marshals for one reason or another, often for alleged spying or "disloyalty." Their stay typically was about two months before being released and often banished from the area, with more serious cases being forwarded to Alton Prison.[5]

Historian Louis S. Gerteis, writing about life in St. Louis during the war, notes:

> For conditional Unionists, the imposition of martial law created distinct new dangers. With Confederate and Union armies in the field, any opposition to Federal policies became potential violations of military law.... Martial law and the use of military commissions to punish civilians clearly denied Missourians ordinary civil rights. Efforts by Lincoln and his commanders in Missouri to distinguish between arenas of martial and civil law never fully succeeded, nor did efforts to distinguish between criticism of the federal government and overtly disloyal acts....
>
> For the wives of Confederate soldiers who remained in St. Louis under martial law, the rigors of life in the field with their husbands may well have seemed preferable to the scrutiny of provost marshals. But as Mary Bowen (wife of Confederate general John Bowen) discovered, the fortunes of war could be very harsh.... She and her children remained with General Bowen during the painful siege of Vicksburg. [After her husband died of dysentery] Mary Bowen buried her husband and traveled to Atlanta, where she and her children

lived until they were driven from the city by Sherman's advancing federal army.[6]

Women whose loyalties did not lie with the governors of the regions they lived in often were subjected to harassment and threats when they lent their support to the "enemies." A postwar Union claims commission investigated the claims of a group of women living in the strongly secessionist state of South Carolina who were loyal to the Union. Mary W. Carlisle (nee Mary DeGraffenreid) of Chester County stated that she lost ten mules worth $1,750 and was harassed by the local population for her pro-Union sentiments. Her reputation as a Yankee woman was widely known. "As a northern woman she was threatened during the war and received anonymous letters of an insulting character." Sherman's army in 1865 burned the buildings on her property and took the mules. The Federal government awarded her $1,250 based on supporting testimony about her loss of property.

Charlotte A. Smith Grant of Marlborough County testified to having concealed her first husband, Thomas Smith, and her brother-in-law from Confederate authorities who were trying to conscript them into the army:

> They threatened to put me in jail if he [Thomas Smith] did not come in.... They had already taken Mrs. Mary Chan & put her in jail because her husband and son were lying out. And my husband said he would come in rather than I should go to jail. He came in and they got him off. He lay out 2 years and said he would not fight. He would never shoot a gun—that he would just as lief go out here at home and shoot his brothers—that there was no more harm in it.... I also fed and protected William D. Cromwell, a deserter, Georgian, and he gave me this paper on leaving [inserted into record as an exhibit].

In August 1864 a Confederate detachment led by a Captain Hawthorne (possibly Captain Robert A. Hawthorne of the 1st South Carolina Infantry, "Orr's Rifles") terrorized her home. "He sauced me and I sauced him," she told the commission. "He said he would destroy everything I had and would not leave me bread enough to feed my children, because I would not inform on deserters and harbored them. He frightened my children almost to death by shooting." She was awarded $290.

Another Marlborough County resident, Eleanor Quick, a widow about fifty years old, testified:

I don't know the names of all...this was the last year of war. And a while before Sherman's Raid some Yankee prisoners came to where I lived and the rebels were hunting them and I showed them into the swamp or my children did and they staid [sic] there around a week or a fortnight till Sherman's army came along. And I fed them all the time. They were prisoners that escaped from rebels who were ahead of Sherman's army. My children got acquainted with them and can remember their names. I can't.[7]

Mrs. Quick was awarded $761. Primarily the commission made awards for properties seized and used by Union soldiers, but her efforts on behalf of escaping Union prisoners apparently were considered a worthy exception.

With martial law in effect in many cities, women living in the war zone who expressed "disloyal" views in public or were caught engaging in any activities that the authorities deemed suspicious were summarily arrested, sometimes placed under house arrest and sometimes in jail, depending on the local circumstances. This was especially true of Confederate women in occupied territories, but also of Union women in the border states at times. In some situations when their properties were confiscated, women were forced to become refugees and wander through the countryside seeking food and shelter.[8]

In late September 1864, Mrs. Alice Gordon Bennett was arrested while trying to pass through the Union lines near Louisville, Kentucky, and sent to the city jail under guard. She had passed into Union territory near Atlanta in disguise and had obtained information from Union officers, which she was endeavoring to carry back to the South. Mrs. Bennett said that her husband was a sailor and requested to be tried in New Orleans. She was interviewed while passing through Bellville, Texas, just west of Houston, en route to New Orleans.[9]

Women who were caught in soldier uniforms by members of the provost guard or city police officers usually were treated like criminals and thrown in jail, typically suspected of being spies. Without question, they sometimes were spies, but more often they clearly were not. In most cases the women simply wanted to be soldiers, something beyond the imagination of most police at that time. Private "John Thompson" in the Union 1st Kentucky Infantry was one exception who was found to be a spy.[10] The local provost marshal's main concern was to get rid of the troublesome women, and so he found some way to transport them elsewhere when there was no overt evidence of spying on their part. Female inmates often were shipped from jail to jail, sometimes remaining behind bars for the duration of the war.

A woman identified only as Mrs. Custis (or Curtis), a Daughter of the Regiment from Rochester, New York, said to be in the 2nd New York Infantry (more likely the 13th New York Infantry), was captured at the First Battle of Bull Run in July 1861 while on horseback and wearing quasi-military attire. She was taken by members of the 8th Louisiana Infantry to Richmond and was detained there by Confederate authorities. Her captors didn't quite know what to do with her. According to Agatha Young, "She was not in the least frightened by her predicament, and having a fluent tongue, she told her captors in detail what she thought of them and their cause."[11]

As early as 1862 reports began circulating about girls being found wearing soldier uniforms. A Pennsylvania newspaper story reported, "Two Maryland girls, 18 and 20 years old respectively, were arrested in Washington on Wednesday, in soldier's uniform. They said that they had been in the army some time, and one of them was at the battle of Bull Run. They were admonished by Gen. Wadsworth and sent to their homes in Hagerstown, Md."[12]

According to a report by Joseph Darr, Jr., Union Provost-Marshal-General, dated Wheeling, West Virginia, January 5, 1863, he had in custody in a Sutton, Virginia, jail one Mary Jane Green "charged as a spy for the guerrillas." By order of General Rosecrans she was released to her home in Braxton County, but was caught destroying a Union telegraph line and returned to military custody. Green was a repeat offender, an outspoken pro-Confederate who wore male disguise and engaged in spying, sabotage, guerrilla activities, and other provocative acts. Her reconstructed career indicates that she was arrested seven times by 1863. She was shuttled by one local provost marshal to another, finally spending the remainder of the war in Old Capitol Prison, Washington, D.C.[13]

A female soldier was arrested by General Jeremiah C. Sullivan two to three miles from Harpers Ferry, West Virginia, while serving in the same company as her lover late in 1863. Her parents were reported to be wealthy. She was said to be one of eight to ten female soldiers brought to Harpers Ferry about that time, ages sixteen to eighteen.[14] The following year a female soldier by the name of Lizzie Hodge was arrested on August 25, 1864, in Nashville, Tennessee, and brought to the office of the provost marshal. "She will be held until this morning, when she will be sent to her sister," it was reported.[15]

Because of the growing number of civilian female prisoners, special prisons for women were established in several locations. The *Nashville Dispatch,* January 4, 1865, and a similar article in the *New Orleans Daily Picayune* (from the *Boston Journal*), January 15, 1865, contained a feature about the Union's female prison in Fitchburg, Massachusetts. A portion of the Fitchburg prison had been used since 1863 to house secessionist women, including captured soldiers, spies, and smugglers. Among the inmates reported at Fitchburg were Annie E. Jones and Mary Jane Johnson ("both camp followers, and suspected of being Rebel spies"), though Jones had since been transferred elsewhere; Jane A. Perkins and Sarah Mitchell ("prisoners of war"); and Mrs. Mary E. Sawyer of Baltimore. Sawyer had been convicted by a military tribunal of sending letters and contraband through the lines and "sentenced to be imprisoned until the termination of the present rebellion" (*New Orleans Daily Picayune,* August 11, 1864).

Female soldiers in male disguise also became prisoners. As in all wars, thousands of soldiers in the Civil War were captured by the enemy during battles and became prisoners of war (POWs). The capture could occur when a position was overrun and the soldiers were forced to surrender, or when a soldier was wounded and could not be evacuated. Quite a few women soldiers became POWs and were sent to military prison camps. Sometimes they were discovered due to their wounds, and sometimes their disguises remained intact until later. Union women are known to have been imprisoned at Castle Thunder and Belle Isle, in Richmond, and the Florence, South Carolina, prison. Apparently several women also were incarcerated at the notorious Camp Sumter, Andersonville, Georgia.

At times a particular commander would immediately parole a captured female soldier upon her discovery. A "stout and muscular" female Union soldier in her twenties was wounded at Chickamauga (September 19–20, 1863) and captured. When her gender was discovered by the Confederates, she was released under a flag of truce carrying a note to the Union commander: "As the Confederates do not use women in war, this woman, wounded in battle, is returned to you." She had been with her regiment for a year.[16] The Confederate commander, whose name has been lost to history, may well have been clueless about women in his own ranks.[17]

When Newton Leonard enlisted in the 2nd Massachusetts Heavy Artillery in November 1863, his wife, Margaret, received permission to go along with him as a laundress in Company H. On April 20, 1863, Companies G and H were overrun by the enemy at Plymouth, North Carolina. Margaret ended up in the Andersonville, Georgia, prison and eventually in Castle Thunder at Richmond. The *Unconditional Union,* Little Rock, Arkansas, on August 11, 1864, reported a story: "Late and Interesting from Castle Thunder. Mrs. Margaret Leonard, of Boston, Mass., arrived in this city yesterday from Castle Thunder, Richmond...and makes the following statement of the circumstances attending her capture, her treatment while in the rebel lines and her experience in other respects":

[The company was ordered to Plymouth, North Carolina.] This place was captured on the 20th day of April by the rebels, with all that was in it, including my trunks, over which the rebels and our own men had a quarrel for the possession but the rebels got them. The rebels gave me nothing back, not even a hat for my head. I had nothing only what was on my back. They seized all the money, goods and everything else they could take from our men. There was a good many wounded at Plymouth after the battle, and they left me there four weeks in the hospital as a nurse. At the end of that time I was taken to Andersonville, Ga., in a hog cart. They kept me ten days there and treated me kindly. My husband was allowed to visit me every day. This was the only place at which they showed me any kindness.

At the end of ten days they took me to Richmond and lodged me at Castle Thunder. I arrived in Richmond the 9th of June and remained there till the 12th of August. All the rations the prisoners have in Castle Thunder is corn bread and water and rotten bacon. They have not half enough to eat. For the last five weeks they gave me no soap not as much as would wash my hands. They kept what they called deserters, spies and Yankee bushwhackers in Castle

Thunder. There are not many prisoners in Richmond now; but there are 27,000 at Andersonville and Macon, Ga., and they are dying very fast of scurvy, chronic diarrhea and dropsy. If they are not soon released there will not be many left to release.

While I was at Andersonville, I saw them burying our prisoners every day. There are no prisoners now at Belle Isle, and very few in the other Richmond prisons. There were only two other prisoners in the female department of the castle with me. We had mattresses of straw to sleep on. . . . We used to get the *Richmond Examiner* every day, and read in it that Grant was dead. The rebels thought he was for about a fortnight. The people of Richmond have nothing to eat but corn bread and bacon.

Among the more notorious prisons other than Andersonville were Libby Prison in the South, and Elmira Prison, New York, and Point Lookout, Maryland, in the North. Lack of adequate shelter, food, and sanitation in the crowded prisons, especially late in the war, caused great suffering, disease, and death. Photographs of Andersonville survivors, indeed, tragically show emaciated humans indistinguishable from those found in Nazi German prison camps at the end of World War II. A number of women experienced the hard life of some of the worst of Civil War prison camps when captured. The following examples of women held at military prison camps along with male soldiers are arranged chronologically, where dates are known, in order to demonstrate the patterns of events as the war progressed.

In July 1862, five Confederate women were imprisoned at Camp Douglas, Illinois, all captured after the battle for Island No. 10 in Missouri during April, having accompanied their husbands into camp. One of them was Bridget Higgins, an Irish immigrant whose husband had been impressed into service in a Confederate artillery company in October 1861. She went with him and was taken prisoner along with him after the battle.[18]

Sarah Rosetta Wakeman (alias "Lyons Wakeman"), disguised as a male soldier, was on guard duty at Carroll Prison in Washington, D.C., during August of 1863. In a letter home she reported seeing a female Union major confined there who had been in battle.[19] Margaret Underwood, a native of Washington, D.C., enlisted in her sweetheart's Confederate regiment to be with him. Her length of service is unknown, but eventually her sex was discovered and she was imprisoned in Castle Thunder,

Richmond, under suspicion of being a spy (circa 1863). After about six months she was released and sent north.[20]

A soldier named "Tommy" in the 45th Ohio (Mounted) Infantry was captured at the battle of Philadelphia, Tennessee, October 20, 1863, and imprisoned at Belle Isle Prison near Richmond. Her sex was discovered early in February 1864 when she became ill, and she was released.[21] Mary Jane Johnson, who served in the 11th Kentucky Cavalry (Union), was also captured in the same battle after serving about one year. She was discovered to be a woman while at Belle Island Prison, Richmond, in 1863. Long after the war a Massachusetts soldier published an excerpt from his wartime diary in the *National Tribune,* July 11, 1889, that dated Johnson's discovery. W. W. Sprague's diary entry for December 9, 1863, reads: "This morning a young woman was discovered in camp on Belle Isle, belonging to the 11th Ky. Cav., named Mary Jane Johnson, 16 years of age. She has been in the Union army a year; has neither father nor mother, and was induced to join the army by the Captain of her company, who was killed in the same battle where she was taken prisoner. She was sent over to Richmond to be sent North."[22] Just how he would know Johnson's background and the circumstances of her army enlistment is not clear, and this information may be nothing but camp scuttlebutt.

Florena Budwin was captured and imprisoned at Andersonville in early 1864 while serving in male disguise along with her husband, a Pennsylvania artillery captain. Her husband died there. She acted as a nurse for the prisoners. After later being transferred to a Florence, South Carolina, prison she became ill. When a doctor discovered her secret, she was given special care, but died of pneumonia on January 25, 1865, and is buried at the Florence National Cemetery, South Carolina.[23]

One of the more famous wartime prisoners held by the Confederacy was Mary Walker. Although a trained physician, she was at first allowed only to serve as a nurse in the Union army, where she labored for more than two years before finally being hired as a contract surgeon by the 52nd Ohio Infantry regiment.[24] Walker was born into an abolitionist family in Oswego, New York, on November 26, 1832. She graduated from Syracuse Medical College at age twenty-two in June 1855, and the following year married another physician, Albert Miller. They set up a joint medical practice in Rome, New York, but it was not successful. They were later divorced.

At the commencement of the Civil War, Walker went to Washington, D.C., to join the army but was denied a commission as a medical officer. Instead, she volunteered her services as an unpaid nurse in the army hospital located at the U.S. Patent Office. After that she worked as a surgeon in frontline army field hospitals at Fredericksburg, Virginia, and after the Battle of Chickamauga, at Chattanooga, Tennessee. In September 1863 she finally was officially appointed as an army assistant surgeon and assigned to the 52nd Ohio Infantry. According to an American Association of University Women chapter web site, "During this assignment it is generally accepted that she also served as a spy."

Walker was captured in Georgia in 1864 while treating a Confederate soldier on the battlefield and was imprisoned for four months in Castle Thunder, Richmond. While there, her wearing of trousers and boots attracted unusual attention. The citation for her Medal of Honor award by President Andrew Johnson, dated November 11, 1865, acknowledges her confinement as a prisoner of war from April 10 to August 12, 1864.[25]

A story from the *Macon Telegraph* was reprinted in the *Memphis Daily Appeal* of Atlanta, Georgia, on May 18, 1864. "One of the Federal prisoners in Camp Sumter gave birth to a young solon of humanity yesterday. It is reported there are five women among the captive warriors at Andersonville." A postwar letter confirmed the presence of this woman at Andersonville during 1864, though she was not in male disguise. John L. Richard, a former soldier in the 111th Ohio Infantry, inquired in a letter to the *National Tribune,* August 15, 1889:

> [I] would like to ask any comrade who was a prisoner at Andersonville if he knows anything about the woman who gave birth to a child at that place. Her name was Baxter, and her husband was a soldier who had been home on furlough. On his return his wife accompanied him, and while passing down the Mississippi the boat was captured and all on board made prisoners and sent to Andersonville. [I think] that the child was the youngest prisoner of war on record, and would like to know if it is yet alive. It was born in August, 1864.

A female Union prisoner from East Tennessee who was identified only as Mrs. Collier was imprisoned in male disguise at Belle Isle Prison near Richmond at the same time as Mary Jane Johnson. Her sex was discovered on December 23, 1864, by a fellow captive, who turned her in to the officer in charge, after which she was released and sent North. She told the authorities that she had enlisted to be with her lover and said there was another female among them still to be discovered. Unless the diary date mentioned above is wrong, the other woman still awaiting discovery could not have been Mary Jane Johnson.[26]

A woman named "Canadian Lou" (or "Low") serving in a Missouri regiment was arrested in Memphis, Tennessee, for being drunk and disorderly in December 1862.[27] Very little is known about her, and she may or may not have been a real soldier. Nor is much known about Mary Wright and Margaret Henry, two Confederate soldiers who were arrested in uniform and imprisoned in Nashville near the end of the war (1865).[28] However, Mollie Bean (a.k.a. "Melvin Bean") was a real soldier who served in the 47th North Carolina Infantry for about two years and was wounded twice. For unknown reasons she was picked up on February 17, 1865, taken to Richmond for questioning, and imprisoned in Castle Thunder. Her captain was reported to be named John Thorp.[29]

Disguised female soldiers often were killed or wounded in combat. While Clara Barton was caring for the wounded on the battlefield at Antietam in September 1862, Surgeon F. H. Harwood of Wisconsin suspected that a soldier wounded in the upper chest was a girl, and asked for Barton's help because "she won't let me examine her." Barton took the soldier to her wagon and confirmed the doctor's suspicions. Harwood was then allowed to examine her, and found that the bullet had penetrated her body and lodged just under the skin of her back. He made a small incision and removed the bullet.

The soldier turned out to be a young woman named Mary Galloway, who had enlisted to be with her future husband. "She [Barton] shepherded and shielded the girl, and subsequently located her lover in a Washington hospital." Later Barton reported that the couple had named a daughter after her. Galloway had attached herself to an army wagon train just prior to the Battle of Antietam, intent on locating her boyfriend, who was a lieutenant.[30]

As confirmed in the Army *Official Records* of the war, "the unidentified body of a female Confederate soldier was discovered by a burial detail on the west side of the stone wall at the angle on Cemetery Ridge, at Gettysburg in July 1863. A participant in Pickett's Charge, she was one of the 12,000 courageous souls that stepped off Seminary Ridge and marched across a mile of open ground th[r]ough a hell of enemy fire. The fact that her body was found in such an advanced spot is testimony to her bravery. However, except for an unverified story that the woman had enlisted in a Virginia regiment with her husband and was killed carrying the colors during the charge, Hays' notation is the extent of acknowledgment she received for having given her life for her country."[31]

An equally romantic story that appears to be true is that of "Frank Mayne" (a.k.a. Frances Day) of Pennsylvania, who enlisted in Company F of the 126th Pennsylvania Infantry on August 9, 1862. "When he enlisted," said the regimental historian, "he was a stranger to all of the men of that company, but in a few days he had so ingratiated himself with his comrades and officers as to be promoted to Sergeant." On the day that William Fitzpatrick, another soldier in Company F, died in a Washington-area hospital, Sergeant Mayne "unaccountably deserted." That was the last they heard of Mayne until much later when a soldier was mortally wounded in a battle out west and before dying told of enlisting in the 126th Pennsylvania to be with her sweetheart, William Fitzpatrick. In her despair, she had first deserted and then reenlisted in another regiment. Members of that unfortunately unnamed regiment, the historian said, wrote letters to the officers of Company F to verify her story, and the mystery of Sergeant Mayne's desertion was solved.[32] Except for her death-bed confession, her story would never have been known.

Occasionally forensic evidence has been discovered belatedly. An unidentified female soldier was killed at Shiloh (April 6–7, 1862) and buried on the battlefield. In 1934, seventy-two years later, a gardener working on the fringes of the battlefield found some human remains and notified authorities. Nine bodies were exhumed, along with fragments of military uniforms and gear. One was identified as a woman, and with her remains was the minié ball that apparently had killed her.[33] Like the story of "Otto Schaffer" (see National Archives, Record Group 94), a hermit farmer in Butler County, Kansas, who had served as a soldier in the Union army and was only discovered to be a woman at death, her secret remained intact until long after the war.

The remains of a female soldier were found in the grave of a Union soldier exhumed in 1886 near Resaca, Georgia, where a battle was fought in May 1864. The grave marker reportedly identified the soldier as "Charles Johehous, Private, 6th Mo." Although this identification is dubious, the story apparently is true (see Appendix A, "Unidentified Female Soldiers"). Reports of this type suggest that for every known female soldier, there may have been on the order of five to ten that went undiscovered. The very fact that such discoveries almost were lost to history suggests that many others probably were.

Quite a few other cases emerged only following a soldier's arrest for various causes. When Marian McKenzie ("Harry Fitzallen") was arrested by the army in West Virginia in December 1862, she said she had served in the 23rd Kentucky Infantry regiment (Union) at the start of the war, and she was reported to have both served and been arrested in several regiments. She also allegedly served in the 5th Virginia Infantry at one point (see Appendix B). The West Virginia provost marshal requested instructions from his superior on how to deal with her and was told to prosecute her if there was evidence of spying, and otherwise to release her. She was said to have been a prostitute before the war.[34]

Regimental records indicate that she enlisted in the 23rd Kentucky on October 4, 1861, and was discharged and sent to the provost marshal December 20, 1862, after about fourteen months' service. The Civil War Database indicates that the unit was organized at Camp King near Covington, Kentucky, in 1861 but remained in camp until February 1862, then was sent to Tennessee and Kentucky. Henry (not Harry) Fitzallen is shown enlisting in Company B on October 4, 1861. Her alleged service in the 5th Virginia Infantry cannot be confirmed. That regiment served from May 7, 1861, to April 9, 1865, so it is possible that McKenzie joined it before October of 1861. A roster search found a large number of soldiers who had left the regiment before October 4 for one reason or another. The most likely candidates to have been Marian McKenzie using a male alias were narrowed down to about five based on various clues, but could not be narrowed down further.[35]

Margaret Underwood, a native of Washington, D.C., enlisted in her sweetheart's regiment to be with him. Her length of service is unknown, but eventually her sex was discovered and she was imprisoned in Castle Thunder, Richmond, under suspicion of being a spy (circa 1863). After about six months she was released and sent north.[36] In addition, a female Union major was observed by a Union guard (who happened to be a woman) in 1863 as she was being held at Carroll Prison in Washington, D.C.[37]

The report of an inspection made of the Point Lookout, Maryland, prison camp dated July 9, 1864, and signed by C.T. Alexander, Surgeon, U.S. Army, states that "among the prisoners is a woman, Sarah Jane Perkins, whose removal is desirable." (See Appendix C.) Some time in 1861 she enlisted in a Virginia artillery unit, where she served until 1864 when she was captured by Union forces. At some point she apparently abandoned her male disguise, but was allowed to continue in service. Whether or not she ranked as a lieutenant is controversial.[38] A Confederate prisoner of war at Point Lookout, Maryland, wrote in his diary on June 9 that a woman was among the new prisoners brought into camp that day. She had been in an artillery unit with her brother since the start of the war. This apparently was Sarah Jane Perkins.[39] A Southern woman imprisoned at Fitchburg, Massachusetts, noted in her journal the arrival there on October 17, 1864, of a Miss Jane Perkins from Danville, Virginia. Like many other female prisoners during the war, Perkins was shuttled around from jail to jail.[40]

The historical record leaves little doubt about the combat services of these women, and in many cases the documentation is substantial. At the same time, other reports of female soldiers have proven to be either outright frauds or highly questionable. For the sake of historical accuracy it is important to establish which cases are genuine and which are dubious.

8

Myths and Apocryphal Stories

Truth will come to light...at the length truth will out.
William Shakespeare, The Merchant of Venice

Civil War history abounds with tall tales, especially ones that began appearing fifteen to twenty years after the war and on to the turn of the century. Veteran soldiers in their later years often were inclined to swap yarns during their reunions, and a very strong interest in the Civil War by the younger generation encouraged a spate of books chock-full of "war story" anecdotes. Stories of female soldiers are no exception. The cases discussed here are, for one reason or another (or for many reasons), of doubtful credibility. Women were assigned to this mythic category if it appeared that there were serious contradictions or demonstrably false information in their stories; further verification is needed to justify their inclusion on the Honor Roll of Civil War Service (Appendix A) alongside those women whose stories are well documented.

At a minimum, basic factual information often is lacking or inadequate in these stories, and important details could not be verified or were established to be false. Garbled newspaper reporting and careless popular writings may be responsible for some of the problems, but all the cases reported here need clarification and better documentation in order to be taken seriously. As originally reported, the details of Amy Clark's adventures as a Confederate heroine in combat were more mythical than true, yet there was a true story underlying the myth. So it is important to keep an open mind about what future research might reveal. Although verification may yet be found for a few of the stories presented in this chapter, still most of them appear to be simply tall tales—stories told to entertain or written to sell newspapers or books.

Charlotte Anderson

Occasionally a story that has been generally accepted as true for decades turns out, upon closer examination, to be false. Such erroneous information needs to be weeded out in order to obtain a better understanding of the truth. DeAnne Blanton and Lauren M. Cook have demonstrated that one such case—which was reported by a seemingly unimpeachable source (the provost-marshal-general of the Army of the Potomac) and remained unchallenged in the literature for a long time—of a prisoner found to be a female was in fact a case of a male soldier pretending to be female so he could get out of the army!

General Marsena Patrick recorded in his diary on January 18, 1865, at City Point, Virginia, "Then I had to examine a woman, dressed in our uniform—Charley (or Charlotte) Anderson, of Cleaveland [sic], Ohio, who is, or has been, with the 60'Ohio. She has told me the truth I think, about herself." On January 22 he added, "I have also sent off several persons, including my woman dressed in men's clothing, for Cleveland." About a month later a newspaper reported that the authorities in Cleveland suspected the truth and discovered via a physical examination that "Charlotte" was a man after all. Further, he had previously enlisted in a Pennsylvania regiment in 1863 and used the same ruse to escape, that time dressing in women's clothes and representing himself as a woman.

A further curiosity in this instance is that no one by the name of Charles or Charley Anderson appears on the rosters of the 60th Ohio or the Pennsylvania regiment. This raises the question of whether Anderson was even a soldier at all, or possibly instead a scam artist of some kind who worked the army for transportation and other benefits. As mentioned elsewhere, however, the published rosters in any given case might be incomplete, or inaccurate, or may even have been expunged after the fact in some circumstances. Yet the Ohio and Pennsylvania regimental rosters generally are complete and well documented.[1]

Sarah Stover and Maria Seelye

Nothing is more frustrating to a historical researcher than to discover what appears to be a spectacular, detailed new example (in this case of a female soldier) that strongly supports a thesis, only to learn upon follow-up investigation that it contains serious factual errors and cannot be verified. Thus, discovery of the following case was initially exciting. A book published about ten years after the war that otherwise contains reliable and independently verifiable information reported an instance of two young women who enlisted in a Missouri regiment in male disguise. They were said to have served for about a year without being discovered, participating in several battles. Their names were given as Sarah Stover and Maria Seelye. The story at first seemed plausible:

> Being homeless orphans, and finding it difficult to earn a subsistence on a small farm in Western Missouri, where they lived, [they] determined to enlist as volunteers in the Federal Army. Accordingly, having donned male attire and proceeded to St. Louis early in 1863, they joined a company which was soon after ordered to proceed to the regiment, which was a part of the army of the Potomac. Within two weeks after their arrival at the scene of conflict in the East, the battle of Chancellorsville was fought [May 1–3, 1863], the two girls participating in it and seeing something of the horrors of the war in which they were engaged as soldiers. In one of the minor battles which occurred the following summer they were separated in the confusion of the fight, and upon calling the muster, Miss Stover, known in the regiment as Edward Malison, was found among the missing. Her comrade, after searching for her among the killed and wounded in vain, at last ascertained that she had been taken prisoner and conveyed to Richmond.[2]

Miss Seelye then was reported to have boldly deserted and set out in borrowed female clothing to locate and help Miss Stover. After a circuitous journey and a complicated series of transactions in which she had to obtain passes or talk her way through military lines, she managed to find Stover in Richmond's Libby Prison and gain entry by claiming to be closely related to her.

She found her friend just recovering from a wound in her arm. The secret of her sex was still undiscovered; and after her wound was entirely healed they prepared to attempt an escape which they had already planned. Miss Seelye contrived to smuggle into the prison a complete suit of female attire, in which, one night just as they were relieving the guard, she [Stover] managed to slip past the cordon of sentries, and joining her friend at the place agreed upon, the two immediately set out for Raleigh, to which city Miss Seelye had obtained two passes, one for herself, the other for a lady friend.

En route they were reported to have had a few close calls, including an encounter with a cavalry soldier who initially thought they might be spies, but they managed to talk their way out of difficulty. After a week they finally made their way to Washington, D.C., by steamship. This, says the report, "was in the autumn of 1863." At this point their normal term of service was due to expire in two months.

After due consideration of the dangers, they decided to rejoin their regiment, then encamped near Washington, D.C., and say that they had just escaped from Richmond. Again disguised in male clothing they re-ported for duty, and since Seelye's desertion was accounted for in this manner, they received no punishment, and both were soon afterwards regularly discharged from service.

Detailed as it is, the story has a ring of authenticity to it. Certainly it contains ample specific dates, circumstances, and other facts that can readily be checked. For example, the male alias, the early (implicitly short-term) Missouri regiments that served in the Army of the Potomac and participated in the Battle of Chancellorsville, the imprisonment, and the arm wound, among others. These details were checked by various means. The Civil War Database alone has several useful investigative tools such as a Personnel Directory, a Regimental Casualty Analysis (including names of all killed, wounded, or captured in each battle, and typically the type and location of the wound), as well as regimental histories and rosters.

A check was made in the Personnel Directory for a Union soldier from Missouri by the name of Edward Malison (including alternative spell-ings). None was found. The Regimental Histories volume of Frederick H. Dyer's *Compendium of the War of the Rebellion* was consulted to find any Missouri infantry regiments that served in the Army of the Potomac.

None was found. All of the Missouri regiments had served in the western armies. The Union army official Order of Battle for Chancellorsville showed that no Missouri regiments were there.

The story, therefore, is patently false as reported. The events could not have occurred at the times and in the places named. The two young women could not have been serving in a Missouri regiment. It remains faintly possible that the author may have somehow gotten the state wrong, but this seems unlikely. The most likely explanation is that the author accepted as true a story that was false and simply repeated it. He does not indicate his source or sources.

The postwar yarns more typically began to show up fifteen to twenty years after the war at the same time that the veterans in general began to talk more openly about their combat experiences and to produce a rich literature of personal histories, often quite eloquent and heartfelt, for posterity. Historian Earl J. Hess notes that it took some time for the soldiers to process their traumatic experiences and that "few memoirs were published for at least 15 years after the end of the war."[3]

The growing public interest in memoirs and reminiscences of the war, unfortunately, also created an opportunity for unscrupulous individuals to peddle fake stories for a profit. The "romance of war" theme was a popular one among those who were too young to fully understand the real nature of war as the veterans did. For those who were on the front lines in combat, the "romance" dissipated very quickly.

Kate W. Howe

A woman named Kate W. Howe showed up on the lecture circuit in 1885 claiming to have performed service in the 27th Massachusetts Infantry using the male alias "Tom Smith." She claimed that her sex had only been discovered when she was wounded at the Battle of Lookout Mountain in Tennessee, and said that she received a government pension. The veterans were skeptical of her. Research has indicated that no soldier by the name of Tom Smith served in the 27th Massachusetts, and no pension file was found for Kate Howe. In fact, the regimental history shows that the 27th was not even at Lookout Mountain. In this case a motive for the fraud is not difficult to imagine. Her colorful story drew large paying crowds.

"Frank Stanhope"

Also in 1885, a newspaper story reported that a husband-wife pair had served together in the 10th Georgia Infantry. The husband's name was Charlie Stanhope and, according to the story, the wife used the name Frank Stanhope, pretending to be Charlie's brother. When Charlie was killed at the Battle of Bentonville, North Carolina (March 19–21, 1865), the story said, Frank fainted. And when the surgeon loosened Frank's collar, he discovered that Frank was a female. This almost certainly was another postwar yarn. Neither the 10th Georgia Infantry regiment nor the separate 10th Georgia Infantry battalion included any soldier by the name of Stanhope, and neither unit was present at the Battle of Bentonville. Here, as in many other cases, the suspect is an unscrupulous newspaper editor trying to appeal to a public yearning for romantic stories.[4]

Lieutenant Bland

Not all apocryphal stories can be traced to aging veterans, yarn-swapping, and a quest for newspaper or book sales. Captain John Truesdale published an immediate postwar book titled *The Blue Coats, and How They Lived, Fought and Died for the Union, with Scenes and Incidents in the Great Rebellion, Comprising Narratives of Personal Adventure, Thrilling Incidents...* (it goes on for 30 more words!). Some online investigation revealed that Truesdale was a Presbyterian minister who served as a chaplain in the 57th and 105th Pennsylvania Infantry regiments from 1863 to 1865. Although *Blue Coats* otherwise contains many independently verifiable stories of the war, and Truesdale seems to have made a conscientious effort to accurately report real incidents, his total lack of documentation leaves a lot to be desired. The following story, which is quoted verbatim from his book (Truesdale 1867, 169–171), where it appears in quotation marks without any attribution, is a case in point:

HOW A CAPTAIN WAS CAPTURED

I was officer of the guard, on as bright a July day as ever dawned on creation; and though it was oppressively warm, as early as guard mounting, eight o'clock, yet that interesting ceremony had passed off magnificently, and I was preparing to go the grand rounds immediately after the call for the second relief, when Lieutenant H., the old officer of the guard, sent his respects, with an earnest request for me to call on him at his marquee [a large field tent] for special consultation. "H__l is brewing at post number twelve," said he, as he took me by the hand, "and this fellow will tell you what he saw there; and you may rely upon trouble there before to-morrow."

"And I saw nothing at all, at all, but a ghost sure," said the Irish soldier; "it came out of the hill forenent [sic] the old graveyard, shook its fist at me as it passed, and went into the bush towards the fort."

"How did it look," inquired H.

"Look? Indade [sic], how should it look, but like a woman draped in white, with eyes of fire?"

"An hour after, I was carefully searching the ground in the vicinity of post number twelve, when my ears were saluted with the well-known cry of, 'Buy any pies 'n cakes?—all clean and new; twenty-five cents for the pies, two cakes for a penny.'"

"Where is your pass, my good lady, if you are a camp follower; and why are you here among the rocks and bushes, if you wish to sell your marketing?" said G.

"I am the honest wife of Pat Maloney, of the fourteenth Maryland, and shtopped [sic] here to rest me weary limbs afther [sic] coming five miles down from me home in the hill, your honor!"

"Very likely," said I, "but you will please march down to the camp, and submit to a slight inspection of your basket and papers, if you have any."

"I have no papers, sir; and why should you put a loyal woman, and a wife of a Union soldier, to this trouble, bad luck till ye?"

"You will not be harmed, madam. If you are a loyal woman, as you say, you will see the propriety of so doing." Cakes and pies, sure enough, but no papers; and I began to believe that there was no connection between her and Pat's "ghost;" but why should she wear a pair of men's boots?

"Och, those were the boots me husband wore before he 'listed, sure!"

And so the captain, somewhat given to gallantry, volunteered to accompany her to her friends, two miles toward her "home in the hill," where she was to give positive proof that she was "neither a spy nor a ghost." And away they went, a single soldier only accompanying them, amid the ill-suppressed laughter of the regiment.

Noon, one o'clock, two o'clock, and no tidings of the captain! What was to be done? A squadron of cavalry was ordered to dash up the hill, reconnoitre, and report. And then time wore heavily away for an hour, when the cavalry charged into camp and up to headquarters, when instantly the long roll was beat, and in five minutes the regiment was under arms in line of battle. A perfect silence ensued, and the adjutant read the following note:

"Colonel D.: I am willing to exchange the pies, cakes and basket for the soldier and the d____d fool captain whom I caught with crinoline. Peddlers and ghosts are at a premium in these parts just now. Yours, *in haste,* BLAND, First Lieutenant C.S.A."

The soldier's musket was found four miles from camp, with the note from the *woman lieutenant* sticking on the point of the bayonet; and so the captain was captured.

A marvelously detailed and clearly apocryphal story! Note that, for purposes of investigation, almost no factual information is given. The story emanates from an unnamed officer of the day of an unnamed regiment and gives no date, location, or other identifying details, except for the alleged Pat Maloney of the 14th Maryland Infantry (Union). A cursory check revealed that there was no 14th Maryland Infantry; only thirteen Union infantry regiments were fielded from that state. A check in the Civil War Database found sixty-two Patrick Maloneys that served in the Union army, none of them in a Maryland regiment. The one bit of information in the story that could be checked proved to be false.

Emily of Brooklyn

In one of the more famous reported examples of a female soldier discovered only after receiving a mortal wound, an early postwar book (Moore 1866) reported that a young woman named Emily, from Brooklyn, New York, was killed in Tennessee sometime after the June 23–July 7, 1863, Tullahoma campaign while serving in a Michigan regiment. After reading Moore's account (see Appendix B), if you are of a cynical bent you might exclaim, "Cue the violins!" The story exemplifies the saying, "If it sounds too good to be true, it probably isn't true."

According to the story, in early 1863 at the age of nineteen, Emily had expressed a desire to be the Joan of Arc of the Civil War and was obsessively determined to join the army. In order to dissuade her from taking some rash action, her parents had sent her to Michigan to live with a maiden aunt. Though her aunt had tried to prevent her, Emily finally had disguised herself as a boy and run away, enlisting at Detroit as a drummer boy in a Michigan regiment that served in Kentucky and Tennessee. She went with her regiment into the Chattanooga campaign, serving in Van Cleve's division of General Rosecrans's army. Different versions of the legend have her being mortally wounded at Chickamauga or at Lookout Mountain. After sending a heart-rending message home at the urging of the wounded colonel of the regiment whose tent she was taken to, she died and was buried on the battlefield.[5]

Contemporary author Frazar Kirkland reports that Emily was killed at the Battle of Lookout Mountain (November 24, 1863, two months after Chickamauga), which contradicts the story as originally reported. Blanton and Cook also report it as Lookout Mountain and cite the Brooklyn *Daily Times,* February 19, 1864. Frank Moore reports that she was "buried under the shadow of the cloud-capped mountain [Lookout Mountain]," not necessarily during the battle of the same name, which may account for some of the confusion.

The published reports provide ample specific clues that lend themselves to investigation, but first a chronology of events helps to put the story in perspective:

June 23–July 3, 1863: Rosecrans's army's Tullahoma campaign, Tennessee
August 16–21, 1863: Rosecrans's army besieges Chattanooga, Tennessee
September 18–20, 1863: Battle of Chickamauga, Tennessee
September 23–25, 1863: Battle of Chattanooga, Ulysses S. Grant's army
November 23–25, 1863: Battle of Lookout Mountain, Tennessee

The narrative plainly states that Emily's death occurred after the Tullahoma campaign. During the Battle of Chickamauga in September, according to the Order of Battle for Rosecrans's army published in the *Official Records of the Union and Confederate Armies,* General Van Cleve was commander of the Third Division of XXI Corps. That division had no Michigan regiments. Assuming the accuracy of the reported information, this would appear to bracket her death—if the story is true in the first place—as most likely having occurred during Rosecrans's August assault on Chattanooga. Since the story of Emily had already appeared in several newspapers in late October and early November, the Battle of Lookout Mountain can be ruled out conclusively as the location of the alleged incident.

The timing of the newspaper stories was consistent with the Battle of Chickamauga, but in addition to Van Cleve having no Michigan regiments in his division, the only Detroit regiment engaged in that battle (the 9th Michigan Infantry) had only one casualty in that battle, a twenty-year-old lieutenant who was wounded but survived the war. Also, the 9th Michigan was at that time serving provost guard and train-guard duty and was not directly engaged in the battle.

Two Detroit cavalry units (which did not have drummer boys), the 2nd and 4th regiments, fought at Chickamauga. Each had one casualty and their names and identities are on record: Lieutenant James Hawley of Hillsdale and Private Charles E. Rickard of Bangor, respectively. The 13th Michigan Infantry and the 22nd Michigan Infantry (neither organized in Detroit) were engaged for at least part of the battle, the 13th for both days. Neither had a wounded colonel. All of this militates strongly against Chickamauga as the place of Emily's death.

That leaves the week-long August assault on Chattanooga as by far the most likely setting for Emily's story, if true, but trying to locate a Michigan regiment whose colonel was wounded in Tennessee during that time period becomes a search for a needle in a haystack. While researching my previous book, *Patriots in Disguise*, I retained a genealogical researcher who searched Census records for a family on Willoughby Street in Brooklyn in 1863 who, according to the news reports, had a daughter named Emily and a son named Eph[riam]. The researcher was unsuccessful in that worthy quest.

Although it is possible that there is some truth underlying Emily's story, it contains far too many contradictions and is not credible as it now stands. Before it can be accepted as valid, much stronger supporting evidence is needed.

Frances Clalin

Frances Clalin initially was said to have served in a Missouri or a Maine militia cavalry unit but is not traceable to either. The famous photos of her from the Boston Public Library showing her in a cavalry uniform and in a dress have been widely reproduced, and the information with them, as has been published in various places, was that she served for three months in Company I of the 44th Missouri Artillery (or Company F of

the 4th Missouri Heavy Artillery) and then nineteen months in Company
A of the 13th Missouri Cavalry. According to Dyer's *Compendium,* there
was no such unit as the 44th Artillery. Missouri had only two numbered
artillery regiments, plus quite a few independent batteries. There was a
13th Missouri Militia Cavalry that served from May 1862 (therefore after
Fort Donelson) to February 1863 in the District of Rolla, but no rosters
are available for it.

Authentication of the story is severely lacking, and all we have are
two photographs of her, one in uniform and one in female dress, with no
evidence whatsoever that she actually performed military service. Other
than the similarity in names, there appears to be no reason to think that
Frances Clalin and Frances Clayton were the same person (see next entry). Even if Clalin did serve in the 13th Missouri State Militia Cavalry,
that unit was not at Fort Donelson, where Clayton claimed to have been
wounded, or at Stones River, so the stories do not match. Furthermore,
Civil War reenactor and historical researcher Wendy King, in a private
communication, has informed me that a *carte de visite* in the possession
of a friend of hers shows that her name was Clatin rather than Clalin.

Frances Clayton

Mrs. Frances Louisa Clayton was reported in several newspaper stories in early October 1863 to have enlisted in a Minnesota regiment to be
with her husband. She was said to have been wounded and her husband
killed at the Battle of Stones River, December 31, 1862, and January 1,
1863 (so I reported in *Patriots in Disguise*), or at Stone Mountain, according to another story.[6] The *Nashville Dispatch* for May 22, 1863 (citing the
Louisville Journal of the previous day), without naming her, reports a
woman at headquarters seeking transportation to Minneapolis. She had
been in battles at Shiloh and Stones River, and wounded twice (see Appendix B).

A recent book provides extensive coverage of Clayton and includes the
two photographs of Clalin or Clatin captioned as "Frances Clayton." The
authors report that she served with an unidentified Union regiment from
Missouri and was discharged in Louisville, Kentucky, in 1863. In a newspaper interview in November 1863, they report, she set the record straight
that she had been wounded at Fort Donelson rather than at Stones River,

but was later at Stones River; however, she did not identify her regiment.[7] Most newspaper stories stated that she had joined a Missouri (rather than a Minnesota) regiment, and one said she used the male alias of "Jack Williams." An online search turned up a site that asserted (without providing any documentation at all, an aggravatingly common feature on the internet) that Clayton used the name "Hillarius Schmitt" at one point.

The Order of Battle for Fort Donelson shows only the 8th and 13th Missouri Infantry regiments present. The 8th had only one killed at Fort Donelson, a captain, and no name matches other than two John Williams, both sergeants, whose records don't match the story. No casualty data was available for the 13th Missouri Infantry, but there were no name matches. On May 29, 1862, the regiment was merged into the 22nd Ohio Infantry, which also was at Fort Donelson, where it had one killed and one wounded. Private Joseph Colvin of Company B was killed.

Although it is a bit of a stretch, there may be some significance to the fact that there were two other Colvins in the same company. One, William, continued in service into 1865. A Marion Colvin who enlisted and was mustered into the company on the same dates as Joseph is listed, with no further information as to length of service or date of discharge. This may leave a slight crack in the door for the possibility of a husband-wife team like the Claytons, but it could easily be purely coincidental.

Some other interesting bits of information emerged during a general search in the Civil War Database Personnel Directory for any soldiers with the given names of Clayton or John Williams (Missouri units), or Hillarius Schmitt. Two Francis Claytons were found for Missouri, but the stories did not match, and as might be expected there were many (116) soldiers named John Williams in Missouri units. A soldier by the name of Hillarius Schmidt (with a "d") was found who served as a private in the Minnesota 2nd Artillery, but he was mustered in on March 21, 1862, after the Battle of Fort Donelson and was discharged for disability on January 3, 1863. Since this battery was at Stones River, someone under the impression that Clayton's connection with that battle was a valid assumption may have hypothesized for some reason that Schmidt was Clayton's male alias.

Something is clearly very wrong, or badly garbled, about Clayton's story. The Stones River connection is obviously not valid, and there is no evidence to support her participation in the Battle of Fort Donelson in a Missouri regiment. Altogether, there is no support at all for her claims outside of the belated newspaper reports, long after both Fort Donelson and Stones River, in which she is quoted and/or misquoted. If she traveled to Minnesota to recuperate from her alleged wound at Fort Donelson, that would have been early in 1862 (not 1863). And if, as the May 22, 1863, newspaper story implies, she was leaving the army at that point (see Appendix B), her secret identity exposed, where was she and what was she doing between then and October when her Minnesota trip made all the newspapers? Additional documentation of some kind is needed to rescue this story from the apparent tall-tale category.

Ellen Goodridge

Ellen Goodridge and her sweetheart, James Hendrick, allegedly served together for three or more years in a Wisconsin regiment. The story, long accepted at face value, is that Hendrick enlisted in 1861 in a Wisconsin regiment and fought at Bull Run (by context a three-month regiment), then rejoined for three years and received a commission as lieutenant, serving in the Army of the Potomac. Ellen then joined him and went on various "raids" with him, serving until the end of the war when he was killed in 1865 (see Appendix B).

This is a widely repeated story that apparently lacks even rudimentary confirmation.[8] The only three-months regiment from Wisconsin was the 1st Infantry, which did not serve in Virginia, was not at First Bull Run, and was mustered out August 21, 1861. A three-year 1st Wisconsin Infantry was then formed in October 1861, but it served in the Army of the Ohio. The 2nd, 3rd, 5th, 6th, and 7th Wisconsin Infantry regiments did serve in the Army of the Potomac, but their rosters do not show any James Hendrick or Hendricks.

The National Park Service Civil War Soldiers and Sailors database shows no James Hendrick(s) for early Wisconsin regiments. Even more conclusively, the Civil War Database Personnel Directory shows only one officer by that name in the entire Union army, a captain from New York who survived the war.

Someone who has access to Frank Moore's papers might be able to shed some light on the origins of this story. Otherwise, the only conceivable explanation is that Ellen Goodridge either lied or gave the wrong name for her male companion and husband-to-be.

Emma Hunt

Evidence of a woman's possible service in Indiana cavalry is contained in a photograph captioned "Emma Hunt and her Uncle, Rockport Parke City, Ind." Both of them are in uniform.[9] However, some further documentation is necessary. I have seen a photograph of my mother dressed in a sailor's uniform during the 1920s and she was never in the Navy!

Madeline Moore

Madeline Moore ("Albert Harville") is said to have joined the army to be with her lover, was elected lieutenant, and served with Gen. George B. McClellan in West Virginia. She and her boyfriend, Frank Ashton, were both reported to have been wounded in a battle and became separated. Later Moore fought at the Bull Run and Wilderness battles, was reunited with Ashton, and they ultimately married. All this according to legend.

Most historians are dubious about the authenticity of the story.[10] The Personnel Directory on the Civil War Database shows two soldiers named Frank Ashton, but both served only briefly in the emergency Pennsylvania militia formed when Lee invaded Maryland in September 1862. No soldier was found by the name of Albert Harville.

Mary Walters

Mary Walters is reported to have served with her husband, William, in the 10th Michigan Infantry. She allegedly was wounded at Antietam in September 1862, discovered by the doctor who examined her, and advised to go home. Instead, she rejoined the regiment after recuperating and continued to serve. When her husband later disappeared on a scouting expedition, according to the story, she applied for a discharge and went home. The newspaper story, written some thirty-five years later, reported that her husband had been wounded in the head and lost his memory. By remarkable circumstances they were reunited and planned to live out their lives together.[11] Unfortunately, this story appears to be totally unfounded.

Aside from suspicions aroused by the fact that the story only surfaced near the turn of the century, when romantic reminiscences about the war were popular, objective research casts serious doubt on it. The 10th Michigan Infantry was not at Antietam, and there is no William Walters on the regimental roster. The Personnel Directory of the Civil War Database shows only two Michigan soldiers by the name of William Walters, both of whom enlisted after Antietam (one in 1864), and neither was wounded.

Mary Ellen Wise

According to contemporary newspaper stories, Mary Wise served two or more years as a private in the 34th Indiana Infantry using the alias "James Wise." She was said to have been wounded in action three times. At Lookout Mountain (November 24, 1863) she was taken to the hospital with a shoulder wound and was discovered and discharged.[12]

The 34th Indiana Infantry was not in action at Lookout Mountain. Considering that the wrong unit identification may have been reported (not uncommon in newspaper stories), a roster search of the Indiana units that were present at Lookout Mountain yielded one standout candidate to have been Mary Wise. A private named John W. Blankenship, no age given, was one of the nineteen members of the 6th Indiana Infantry wounded that day. He (possibly she) enlisted on October 10, 1861, in Company K. The entry further states, "Date and method of discharge not given." This identification, however, would require further evidence in order to be credited.[13]

Additionally, evidence has been found suggesting that Wise may have been mentally unbalanced, and therefore of questionable veracity, possibly exploiting her war service story for personal gain. In September 1864 she married a veteran soldier at a hospital in Washington, D.C., but by the following February her husband had her arrested for following him around with a pistol and threatening his life. A judge ordered her to leave the city. It is also possible that she may have had a legitimate grievance of some kind with her husband.[14]

9

Case Studies: Historical Detective Work

The devil is in the details.
German proverb

Since many reports of women in Civil War military service required either clarification or additional historical confirmation, an extensive search was conducted on internet databases such as the Historical Data Systems Civil War Database and Cyndi's List, two of the most comprehensive sources of Civil War unit histories and rosters. As appropriate, other searches were conducted in the Army *Official Records* on CD ROM, in Frederick H. Dyer's *Compendium of the War of the Rebellion* (a print source), and on the internet at large, using the powerful Google search engine (www.google.com). Sometimes no unit rosters were found, but often they were. The research occasionally yielded mixed results, but in many instances either shed additional light on a particular story or eliminated some portion of it from consideration. Also, I had the good fortune at times to hear from descendants or relatives of some of the female soldiers in question, who provided important new information.

These case studies illustrate how the use of online databases can supplement and clarify (or debunk) information available from traditional sources and standard reference works. It must be emphasized that muster rolls or regimental rosters are not always 100 percent complete or accurate, especially for Southern units and for very early regiments when everyone thought the war would be over in three months, only a brief interlude in American life. Failure to find a name on the roster must be interpreted carefully in the context of all available information.

The case histories presented here are arranged in alphabetical order by last name, and are pieced together from numerous sources. They have been investigated as thoroughly as time and resources have permitted.

Sarah E. Bradbury

Sarah Bradbury (alias "Frank Morton") was the "she dragoon" who was hauled before General Phil Sheridan for an interview after being discovered in the ranks of his cavalry in 1863. The basic story is reported in Chapter 4 and in the Ella Reno entry in this chapter. Before being discharged Bradbury gave a sworn statement about her background and soldier life (see *Nashville Dispatch* article in the Sarah Bradbury entry in Appendix B).

Although there appears to be no doubt that Bradbury served in the cavalry, extensive checking of the specific units she claimed to serve in yielded very little confirmatory evidence. To be on the safe side, I checked for the name "Frank Martin" as well as "Frank Morton," since they are so phonetically similar. Taking the claims to specific units in order:

"I first went into the 7th Illinois Cavalry, in Company C." Neither name shows up in Company C or in the entire regiment. Since she stated that a "Mr. H" induced her to enlist in Company C and that he was captured, a further check was made indicating that of all soldiers in that company whose names began with "H," none went missing while on a scouting mission during 1862 or early 1863. A soldier by the name of Michael Hay did desert on March 8, 1862. However, Bradbury said that as of the time of her statement in March 1863, "I have been in the service 6 months," which (unless a false statement) would date her first enlistment, where she said she served for two months, as September 1862.

Bradbury says that next she joined the 22nd Illinois Infantry, presumably about November 1862. Neither name appears on the roster. Allowing some latitude for the date of enlistment, which is only approximate, one soldier was found who fits Bradbury's profile. A John Ford enlisted as a private in Company E on October 25, 1862, then deserted on December 4, 1862. The record based on Illinois state data gives Ford's place of residence as Monroe County, Kentucky, rather than Nashville County, Tennessee, but she could have lied about that. Monroe County is on the border with Tennessee, about 100 miles from Nashville.

Bradbury says she then became a member of Sheridan's escort, 2nd Kentucky Cavalry, Company L. Even though we know this was true from Sheridan's biography and the official record, there is no trace of "Morton" or "Martin" on the roster and no evidence of a soldier leaving under unusual circumstances at that time. Although this might be indicative of the muster roll records being expunged, it seems more likely in this case that Bradbury was not entirely truthful in the portions of her statement about following various male friends.

Bradbury would make an interesting psychological case study if more were known about her life. In her formal statement she portrays herself as being strongly dependent on being attached to a male, yet she must have had good soldierly qualities to become part of Sheridan's escort and had capabilities for acting independently to be able to serve in the cavalry at all. The language of her statement indicates an intelligent and literate person. It is quite possible that she understood male biases and social conventions would make her appear to be an abnormal specimen of femininity, and so she deliberately painted herself as a lovesick girl merely following a man around in order to conform her disguise to the prejudices of the times.

Mary Ann Clark

Some very important new information has been reported by Blanton and Cook bearing on the name and identity of the famous Confederate soldier whose name in the past commonly has been reported as Amy Clarke (a.k.a. Anna or Annie Clark[e], Mrs. William Clark; aliases "Henry Clark" and "Richard Anderson"). Evidence is cited based on archival records that Mary Ann Clark (her real maiden name) enlisted in the army in October 1861 (unit not identified) under the name "Henry Clark" while fleeing from a bad marriage. In the process, she resumed using her maiden name. She left this unit in February 1862.

Based on a December 17, 1862, letter of her mother and other archival information, Clark left home again in June 1862 following some unknown personal tragedy and reenlisted in the army. Later that year a letter arrived home from her describing being wounded and captured and her impending exchange. She was held prisoner in various places for almost three months, finally at Cairo, Illinois, and then exchanged in December 1862. In August 1863 she was a lieutenant in Bragg's army and her fate after that is unknown.[1]

Apparently the earliest published version of her story was in December 1862 in a Cairo, Illinois, newspaper at the time of her exchange after being wounded (see Appendix B). The level of inaccurate or garbled information in this story, as it turns out, is very high. The kindest thing that can be said of the information in the story is that someone of approximately her name did serve as a soldier and may have experienced some of the reported adventures in some of the named units. The newspaper story reported that a Confederate prisoner by the name of Private Richard Anderson was actually Anna Clark, wife of Walter Clark, born in Iuka, Tennessee. She fell in love with a Louisiana hussar (cavalry soldier) and enlisted in his regiment, serving four months (this suggests that she first served in a Louisiana cavalry regiment). She then enlisted in the 11th Tennessee Infantry and was captured. Her husband, the story continued, was killed at Shiloh, where she also fought, at one point standing on dead soldiers to get a better sight of the enemy. She was reported to be not yet thirty years old and was said to be "well informed upon politics, literature, and other general topics." The authorities gave her a dress to be worn during the prisoner exchange.[2]

Several pieces of the puzzle are still missing, mainly in regard to the regiments she served in, most commonly cited as an unidentified Louisiana cavalry regiment and the 11th Tennessee Infantry, and in what order. Blanton and Cook more recently found that Clark was a casualty in the battle at Richmond, Kentucky, on August 30, 1862, "wounded in the thigh a considerable piece above the knee," and was captured. This no doubt would have been the subject of her letter home late in 1862 and the occasion for her imprisonment and eventual exchange. The 11th Tennessee Infantry was not at the Battle of Richmond, Kentucky. The 1st Louisiana Cavalry was in action there, but an online web site that contains complete company rosters for the 1st Louisiana shows no "Henry Clark" or "Richard Anderson" in the regiment.

We also now know that the 11th Tennessee was not at Shiloh (Crute 1987), though the 1st Louisiana Cavalry was there (Bergeron 1989). In addition, Clark's husband was not named Walter Clark, and she was not wounded at Shiloh. However, she had been wounded in battle, held in custody, and finally exchanged. Presumably the newspaper at least got her male alias right, but that is not certain either. The obvious lesson is that contemporary newspaper reports of this kind need to be analyzed very carefully to weed out errors and establish elements of truth.

Shortly after being exchanged Clark showed up in Jackson, Mississippi (if this newspaper story about her can be taken at face value). The Mississippi newspaper story appeared on December 30, 1862 (see Appendix B). However, it may have been reprinted from an Atlanta newspaper and perhaps the editor carelessly left in the reference to "this city." Otherwise, she was reported to have been in Atlanta late in 1862 or early in 1863 on furlough after being exchanged. This story contained the standard mythical version of her serving with her husband at Shiloh, and after he was killed there continuing in the ranks of Bragg's army in Kentucky, until she was twice wounded—"once in the ankle and then in the breast, when she fell a prisoner into the hands of the Yankees." Her sex was then discovered and she was paroled as a prisoner of war after being required to don female apparel.[3] It was General Kirby Smith's army at Richmond, Kentucky, not Braxton Bragg's, but that's another story.[4]

The following August, Clark was seen wearing lieutenant's bars at Turner's Station, Tennessee, this time in Bragg's army, and was recognized as the heroic "Amy Clarke." A Texas cavalry soldier wrote a letter home to his father saying that he had heard of her brave deeds and repeated the story of her husband being killed at Shiloh and she being wounded and released by the Yankees while required to wear a dress.[5] The persistence of this mythical version is striking, and similar mythical elements have clouded the facts in other cases, too.

Some major and minor discrepancies are evident in the various published accounts, but there appears to be little doubt about the basic story of her service. The 1st Louisiana Cavalry was organized in Baton Rouge on September 11, 1861, and served in Tennessee, Mississippi, and Georgia. The 11th Tennessee Infantry served in the Army of Tennessee, commanded by Bragg after June 1862, at Murfreesboro, Chickamauga, and the Atlanta campaign.

Muster rolls were found for the 1st Louisiana Cavalry, known as "Scott's Cavalry Regiment," and a search was conducted for any Anderson or Clark(e), finding one of each. A Private James B. Anderson served in Company C, and a Private George Clark served in Company D. No records were found for a Richard Anderson or a Henry (or Walter) Clark.

In the case of Mary Ann (Amy) Clark, there are several independent confirmations of an apparently true basic story which, as in many other examples throughout this book, have been garbled so seriously in contemporary newspaper reports as to almost completely obscure the facts. Her name and her marital situation were reported incorrectly, the units she served in were confused, and the oft-repeated story of her being with her husband at Shiloh (or with her husband in the army at all) is purely a myth.

Elizabeth ("Lizzie") Compton

The basic story is that when wounded and discovered, Lizzie Compton claimed to have enlisted at age fourteen and served eighteen months in seven different regiments, "leaving one and enrolling in another when fearing detection." Among the regiments mentioned are the 11th Kentucky Cavalry, the 125th Michigan Cavalry (no such unit existed, this possibly being a mistaken reference to the 25th Michigan Infantry), and the 8th Michigan Infantry. She was reported to have been wounded at Fredericksburg, Virginia, in 1862, but recovered and moved from the Army of the Potomac to the Army of the Cumberland (see Appendix B).[6]

The 11th Kentucky Cavalry was organized a few companies at a time during July and September of 1862 at Harrodsburg and Louisville. They served in Kentucky and Tennessee from November 1862 to July 1863, including the Knoxville Campaign in November–December 1863, and then in the Atlanta Campaign the following spring and summer. Compton could not have been at Fredericksburg with this regiment.

According to several sources she was wounded again when shot in the shoulder in the Battle of Green River Bridge (or Tebbs Bend), Kentucky, on July 4, 1863. An undocumented source on the internet reported that a battalion of 25th Michigan, 8th Michigan, and 79th New York infantry was attacked by a large Confederate force under John Hunt Morgan, and among the casualties was "16 year old Lizzie Compton of London, Ontario who was then posing as a man." She reportedly had last served in the 11th Kentucky Cavalry. ("Last served" here probably does not refer to her service prior to being wounded in Kentucky in 1863, but instead to the last regiment in her service career. That would fit the facts as originally reported in 1867.)

The Civil War Database confirms that the 25th Michigan was engaged in the battle at Tebbs Bend and had sixteen wounded that day. Several of the wounded could be eliminated as candidates to have been Compton, based on internal evidence such as mustering out with the regiment in 1865. Among the remaining candidates one stands out: For Jonathan Walburt of Company D, age eighteen, the entry (based on Michigan Volunteers "Record of Service") states, "Date and method of discharge not given....No further record." However, this is only suggestive, and additional documentation would be needed to authenticate it.

There is no evidence in the regimental history that the 8th Michigan had personnel at Tebbs Bend. The 25th Michigan, which was in 1st Brigade, 2nd Division, XXIII Corps, throughout, was at Tebbs Bend. On the other hand, the 8th Michigan was in the Battle of Fredericksburg; the 25th Michigan was not. The Civil War Database regimental Casualty Analysis indicates that only one 8th Michigan soldier was wounded at Fredericksburg: Nathan M. Healey, who enlisted in the regiment at Flint, Michigan, as a private on September 10, 1861. Healey was reported "discharged for disability 10/18/1862 at Washington, D.C."

Since neither Compton's male alias or aliases nor names of anyone she served with have been reported, further roster checks are not possible at this time. Unless more information turns up we can only imagine, based on these clues, that she may well have served in the 8th Michigan at Fredericksburg in 1862, the 25th Michigan at Green River (Tebbs Bend), Kentucky, in 1863, and the 11th Kentucky Cavalry in the latter part of the war. That leaves four unidentified regiments still to be discovered if the basic story is true. One 1863 newspaper story quoted in Appendix B suggests that she also may have served in the 2nd Minnesota Infantry.

Sophia Cryder

Teenager Sophia Cryder, described as "a plump lass of only 16 years of age" from the area of Carlisle, Pennsylvania, served as a soldier in

Company A of the 11th Pennsylvania Infantry in 1861 at Camp Curtin, according to a newspaper report. The commander of Company A ("Sumner Rifles") was reported to be a Captain Kuhn. Her disguise was exposed when two men showed up at Camp Curtin and said they were looking for "a girl who had strayed away." In less than an hour, she was found "on guard doing duty as a sentinel."[7] A roster check confirms that Christian Kuhn was captain of Company A. The regiment was organized in August 1861 and posted at Camp Curtin, Pennsylvania, until November 27, when it moved to Baltimore, Maryland.

A soldier by the name of Coutney (perhaps Courtney) H. Early is reported to have enlisted in Company A on September 30, 1861, and to have been discharged via a writ of habeas corpus on October 18, 1861. This would have been nearly a month after the "discovery" date reported in the newspaper, but the official discharge date could have been delayed for many reasons. Underage soldiers sometimes were removed via a writ of habeas corpus, so this mention is interesting and suggestive. Another soldier in Company A by the name of Armstrong Robinson, who enlisted October 15, 1861, also was reported to have been discharged via a writ of habeas corpus on November 7, 1861.

The available clues are sufficient to suggest that further record searching might eventually result in "full disclosure" in this case.

Catherine Davidson

Catherine Davidson enlisted in the 28th Ohio, serving in male disguise, and was severely wounded at Antietam and had her arm amputated. Hers was a late-nineteenth-century postwar "romantic" story that apparently was true (see Appendix B). Reportedly she had followed her lover into service, though he was in a different regiment, but he was killed at Antietam and she was severely wounded there.

The Civil War Database Casualty Analysis record shows that the 28th Ohio had three killed and eleven wounded at Antietam. Of the eleven wounded, six can pretty well be ruled out as candidates to have been Davidson on the basis of internal evidence such as continued service into 1864 and 1865. One soldier stands out as a highly probable candidate to have been Catherine Davidson's *nom de guerre*: Private William

Holzhuch, twenty-one, of Company F (no place of residence given) was reported to have been discharged for wounds on March 9, 1863 ("lost arm"). This is the only entry that lists the exact nature of the wound.

Four other soldiers cannot be ruled out entirely since no information is given about their wounds and they otherwise fit the profile. Genealogical research might eliminate some of them as candidates in the long run. One of them, Private Joseph Doerr of Company A, has no age reported but was not discharged for close to seven months; most women were promptly discharged when discovered in the hospital. On the other hand, Private Holzhuch was not discharged for almost six months, possibly because of the hospital care required for an amputation.

Private William Illbrock of Company C, twenty-seven, was discharged on November 21, 1862, at New York City, barely two months after the battle. Private Jacob Mueller, twenty-eight, of Company F, the same company as Private Holzhuch, was discharged on January 10, 1863, a little less than four months after the battle. And Private Otto Mueller of Company D, twenty-one, was discharged on March 10, 1863. Still, the specific reference to "lost arm" seems to be fairly conclusive.

Frances Hook

The story of Frances Hook is one of the most extraordinary of all. At various times she is reported to have used the male aliases "Frank Miller," "Harry Miller," "Frank Martin," "Frank Henderson," and "Frank Fuller" (see Appendix B). The narratives about her contain many clues as to dates and events. Based on these, intensive research into regimental histories and unit rosters has narrowed down the possibilities to the outfits that she most likely served in and the probable sequence. Some of the information reported about her military service, typically, appears to be muddled or incomplete, but a coherent picture begins to emerge. The sequence of enlistments reconstructed from all the various stories appears to have been:

(1) 11th Illinois Infantry
(2) 65th Illinois Infantry (?)
(3) 3rd Illinois Cavalry

(4) 2nd Tennessee Cavalry

(5) 8th Michigan Infantry

(6) 90th Illinois Infantry

(7) 19th Illinois Infantry

She (and her brother) reportedly first enlisted in June 1861, served three months, and then mustered out. Her only brother was reported to have been killed at Pittsburg Landing (Shiloh) in April 1862. These statements indicate that her first service almost certainly would have been in the 11th Illinois Infantry. A three-months 11th Illinois Regiment was organized in Springfield and served from April 30 to July 30, 1861. The three-years 11th Illinois Regiment was at Pittsburg Landing. Complete rosters exist for both regiments, and there is no one by the name of Hook or any of the other reported male aliases listed. The three-months regiment had no battle casualties. The three-years regiment had sixteen killed and six wounded at Shiloh, whose names and places of residence are listed.[8]

The next enlistment may have been soon after the Battle of Shiloh. Some reports say that early on Hook enlisted in the 65th Illinois "Home Guards." There were no Home Guard units in Illinois, though there were numerous units so designated in Missouri. The regular 65th Illinois Infantry ("Scotch Regiment") served from May 1, 1862, to July 13, 1865, and cannot be ruled out. However, no one by the name of Hook or any of the male aliases was found on the unit roster.

An early postwar author (Kirkland 1867) reports that after leaving the 11th Illinois Infantry Hook enlisted in the "3d Illinois regiment." For some reason there was no 3rd Illinois Infantry; the 3rd Illinois Cavalry served from September 21, 1861, to October 10, 1865, the timing of the organization date being correct to fit the profile of this being the second unit that she served in. The regimental roster contains no one by the name of Hook or any of the male aliases.[9]

Somewhere in this sequence (probably third or fourth) it seems clear that Hook served in the 2nd East Tennessee Cavalry (later known simply as the 2nd Tennessee Cavalry). She is reported (Middleton 1993) to have enlisted in this unit in July 1862 at Louisville, Kentucky, about a year after leaving the 11th Illinois Infantry.

The Tennessee Civil War Centennial Commission reports that the 2nd Tennessee Cavalry was organized in East Tennessee during July to November 1862; however, its individual companies were organized in various locations in Tennessee and Kentucky.[10] Hook was reported to have been wounded in the shoulder at Murfreesboro/Stones River, Tennessee (December 26–31, 1862). The 2nd Tennessee Cavalry regiment was the only one of the candidate regiments that served in the Murfreesboro campaign, during which it had eighteen casualties. Hook was discovered at this time and mustered out. However, none of the reported aliases appears on the regimental roster.

Martha Baker, a hospital worker associated with her husband's 40th Indiana Infantry at Nashville, Tennessee, late in 1862, reported after the war that while serving in Nashville "I met two soldier women who donned the blue. One, Frances Hook, alias Harry Miller, served two years and nine months; the other was called Anna. She was put under our charge until the military authorities could send her North" (Holland 1897, 228–231). Encountering Frances Hook at a Nashville hospital at that time fits perfectly with her story as otherwise reconstructed.

According to Kirkland's narrative, after Hook left Tennessee, when she arrived in Bowling Green, Kentucky, she found the 8th Michigan Infantry there, enlisted, and was given the position of regimental bugler. This most likely would have been in the first few months of 1863. Kirkland reports: "The pretty bugler stated that she had discovered a great many females in the army, and was intimately acquainted with one such—a young lady holding a commission as Lieutenant in the army. She had assisted in burying three female soldiers at different times, whose sex was unknown to any but herself."[11]

The history of the 25th Michigan Infantry (from John Robertson's *Michigan in the War*, 1880) contains an unattributed quote confirming Hook's presence in Louisville, Kentucky, in 1863 as a member of the 8th Michigan. She arrived with a captain in charge of some rebel prisoners and was detailed for duty with the 25th Michigan then garrisoning the city. At this time she was using the name "Frank Martin." While there, a soldier from her home town recognized her and exposed her, as a result of which she was assigned to hospital duty. The same account mentions her prior service in "an East Tennessee cavalry regiment" and her being severely wounded at Stones River, discovered, and mustered out. She was said to have reenlisted in the 8th Michigan Infantry after Stones River. However, no "Frank Martin" appears on the regimental roster. A Francis Miller served in Company B of the 8th Michigan Infantry from October 5, 1861, to July 30, 1865, but his record does not fit with Hook's reported service in other units during this time period. No other Miller, Henderson, or Hook is listed on the regimental roster.

Next in the sequence and possibly her next-to-last service, Hook was reported to have enlisted in the 90th Illinois Infantry under "Col. O'Mara" and served in "all the battles" of that regiment, an unlikely claim since the unit was formed in 1862 and she had been occupied elsewhere into 1863.[12] A regimental roster check found that the colonel of the 90th Illinois was Timothy O'Meara. The regiment was formed on September 7, 1862, and served in Mississippi, Tennessee, and Alabama, including the Chattanooga campaign (September 27–November 23, 1863).

Hook was captured near Florence, Alabama, in early 1864, after she was shot in the thigh "during a battle" (not necessarily fought at or near Florence, Alabama) and left behind with other wounded (Blanton 1993). Her sex was discovered while she was imprisoned in Atlanta. She was exchanged at Graysville, Georgia, February 17, 1864, hospitalized in Tennessee, then discharged in June.[13] According to the description of the prisoner exchange (Kirkland 1867), she was serving in the 19th Illinois Infantry at this time.

Kirkland reports two contradictory accounts of Hook's capture. First he has her as "Frank Henderson" in the 90th Illinois passing through Florence, Alabama, accidentally left behind while obtaining a meal, and captured (but not wounded) by two Confederates concealed in the house. Her wounding, he reports, happened after she was taken to Atlanta and was attempting to escape. Later she was exchanged and recuperated in a hospital.[14]

In a separate section of his book, Kirkland has her being taken prisoner in a battle near Chattanooga and, while attempting to escape, being shot through the calf of one leg. When examined by her captors she was found to be a woman. She was then given a separate room at the prison in Atlanta, Georgia.[15] Clearly, the story of her wounding and capture in 1864 is somewhat confused. Still it is documented sufficiently to ensure a strong factual basis rather than being simply a romanticized yarn, as some of the stories that emerged thirty or more years after the war are likely to have been.

Hook later married. On March 17, 1908, her daughter wrote to the Adjutant General's Office seeking confirmation of her mother's service, and some was found.[16] Further confirmation of her service in the 90th Illinois late in 1863 was reported (Middleton 1993) in the form of a letter from a soldier, Nat Mullin, Company H, 10th Illinois Infantry, which was published in the *National Tribune*, August 29, 1895. Mullin recounted being captured December 18, 1863, and taken to a prison in Atlanta. Among the wounded prisoners there was a girl using the alias of "Frank Miller," of Company G, 90th Illinois Infantry, who was eventually exchanged.[17] A roster check confirms that Nathaniel Mullin did serve in the 10th Illinois, Company H, until August 1864. However, the roster of the 90th Illinois, Company G (or any other company), shows no "Frank Miller," no Henderson, and no Hook.

Hook is described by several witnesses variably as "about medium height, with dark hazel eyes, dark brown hair, rounded features, and feminine voice and appearance," or as having "auburn hair, which she wore quite short, and large blue eyes, beaming with intelligence . . . complexion naturally very fair, became somewhat bronzed from exposure . . . exceedingly pretty and amiable . . . very refined in her manners."[18]

Despite the puzzling fact that the male aliases seem to be impossible to confirm objectively (the names are always what she claimed when discovered), little doubt remains that Frances Hook richly deserves her place on the Honor Roll of Civil War Service (Appendix A). Sometimes it appears that when they were exposed, female soldiers may have lied about the male names they were officially known by in regimental records! Either that or, at certain times during the war, some records were expunged to avoid embarrassment or criticism of the officers in charge when a woman was found in the ranks.

Mary Owen(s)/Jenkins

The basic story is that Mary Owens from Danville, Montour County, Pennsylvania, enlisted in a Pennsylvania regiment as "John Evans" to be with her husband, William Owens. As reported in 1867, "She was in the service eighteen months, took part in three battles, and was wounded twice—first in the face above the right eye, and then in her arm; this required her to be taken to the hospital, where she was obliged to confess her true sex and the circumstances of her being in the ranks.... [she] saw her husband fall dead by her side, and returned home wounded and a widow." Her discovery was in 1863.[19]

Various stories have been reported about Mary Owen Jenkins, Mary Stevens Jenkins, and Mary Owens ("John Evans"), probably all the same person. According to the core story, she served in a Pennsylvania regiment with her husband (Jenkins was reportedly in the 9th Pennsylvania Cavalry). A 1901 newspaper story reports that Mary Owens served eighteen months as "John Evans" and was discovered when she was wounded in the arm.[20] An earlier account quoted from *Frank Leslie's Illustrated Newspaper* for March 7, 1863, gives her name as Mrs. Mary Owen (rather than Owens) and links her with Huntingdon County (rather than Montour County). It reports that she served with her husband and continued in disguise after he was killed by her side in their first battle. "She then participated in three battles and was wounded twice, whereupon she was discharged from service."[21]

One would tend to assume from these contemporary and early postwar reports that her husband was named Owen or Owens. Other variations of the story create some confusion. Mary Stevens Jenkins (apparently the second married name of Mary Owens) was reported to be a Pennsylvania schoolgirl who served two years in a Pennsylvania regiment, and was wounded several times but never discovered. According to an 1896 news story she was married to Abraham Jenkins of Massillon, Ohio, and died in 1881.[22]

Betty Ingraham reports that Mary Owen Jenkins served in the 9th Pennsylvania Cavalry. Leonard (1999) reports her serving in Company K of the 9th Infantry (instead of cavalry). Extensive searching of several databases failed to yield any strong confirmation of the story. Unfortunately, no roster was found for the three-years 9th Infantry regiment. Neither the three-months 9th Infantry regiment nor the 9th Infantry Militia regiment, which served less than a year, had anyone on their rosters named Owen(s) or John Evans, though Leonard cites Record Group 94, National Archives records which appear to confirm the infantry service.

The 9th Infantry also was known as the 38th Volunteers (9th Reserve). The roster of the 38th shows a William Evans in Company E (no John Evans), but this William Evans was still serving in 1864 when he transferred to the 190th Pennsylvania Infantry. A search for a Pennsylvania cavalryman named Owen(s) who was killed in action was unsuccessful for the 2nd, 3rd, 9th, and 11th cavalry regiments.

The search for verification is complicated by the question of which version of the story to accept: that her husband was killed and she was severely wounded in the same battle, or that she continued in service after he was killed and was wounded in later battles. The utility and research value of the Civil War Database for approaching such questions from several different angles was put to work.

On the first assumption, the Personnel Directory was used first to examine all Pennsylvania soldiers named Owens or Owen who did not survive the war. There were eleven, most of whom could be eliminated on the basis of internal evidence such as dying as a prisoner at Andersonville in 1865 or dying of disease. Three remaining candidates fit the profile of the story fairly well. Soldiers named Oscar Owens, Owen K. Owens, and Thomas Owens all served about the right amount of time and were killed in action. Next a search was conducted for another soldier by the name of John Evans (or anything close) in the same regiment and/or company who was wounded at the same battle.

The closest thing to a match was the case of Oscar Owens, who enlisted as a private in Company D of the 36th Pennsylvania Infantry on April 24, 1861, and was killed in action about fourteen months later at Gaines Mills, Virginia, on June 27, 1862. Mary Owens was reported to have served in the army about eighteen months. Then the regimental Casualty Analysis feature was used to examine the names and other available details of all soldiers from that unit who were wounded in the same battle. No one named Evans was on the list and only one other fit the profile: a Private Daniel Edwards. He had enlisted in Company F of the 36th on July 5, 1861 (a little over a month after Oscar Owens's enlistment date), was wounded at Gaines Mills on June 27, 1862, and (apparently after having spent some time in the hospital) was "discharged for wounds" on February 5, 1863. His service time, therefore, would have been about nineteen months.

Though it is possible, as has been suggested by other cases, that Mary Owens falsely gave her male alias as "John Evans" instead of "Daniel Edwards," the original story reports quite specifically that she "enlisted in the same company with her husband"; Owens and Edwards served in different companies. However, if the *Frank Leslie's Illustrated Newspaper* version of the story cited above is accurate and she was wounded in later battles after her husband was killed, then a totally different search strategy will be needed to pin down the facts. The inability to find stronger evidence for the first hypothesis suggests to me that the latter version probably is more accurate.

This case provides a strong illustration of the problems caused by nineteenth-century garbled newspaper reporting, which is clearly in evidence here. There are strong underlying indications of the basic truth of her story, but the newspaper inaccuracies (possibly combined with deception on the woman's part) severely complicate the search for truth. Still, given the number of specific references and details in the case of Mary Owens Jenkins, it should be possible to obtain clarification eventually.

Annie Lillybridge

As reported in 1863 (see Appendix B), Annie Lillybridge's parents lived in Hamilton, Ontario, Canada, she in Detroit. According to the story, she served in Captain Kavanagh's company of the 21st Michigan Infantry to be with her sweetheart, Lieutenant W. The regiment went to Kentucky and later fought in the Battle of Pea Ridge (March 7–8, 1862), or according to some versions, Prairie Grove, Arkansas (December 7, 1862). Colonel Stephens frequently detailed her as regimental clerk, which brought her near now-Major. W, adjutant. A few weeks later (which would have been late March or early April), she was wounded in the arm while on picket duty and taken to a hospital in Louisville, where she remained several months. Her arm was disabled, and she was discharged by the surgeon. One report says that she swapped discharge with Joseph Henderson to reenlist.[23]

During a roster search for the 21st Michigan, I found a 2nd Lieutenant George W. Woodward in Company G, thirty-seven years old, from Wright, Michigan. He mustered out June 8, 1865, in Washington, D.C., as brevet major. No one by the name Lillybridge was in Company G. More importantly (since she probably would have used a false name), no one in Company G was discharged in Louisville around March or April of 1862.

Several basic points of the story do check out. The regimental colonel was reported to be "Stephens"; Ambrose A. Stevens of Saranac was colonel. Captain "Kavanaugh" was reported to be the commander of Company B; James Cavanaugh of Grand Rapids was captain of Company B, but there was no Lieutenant W in that company. The adjutant at the time the unit was organized was Morris P. Wells, twenty-seven, of Ionia, who had previously served in the 16th Michigan Infantry as a second lieutenant from July to December of 1862, in the Army of the Potomac. Wells (very possibly the "Lt. W" of the story) was commissioned a field and staff officer in the 21st Michigan on July 26, 1862, was wounded at Stones River on December 31, 1862, and, having attained the rank of lieutenant colonel, was killed at Chickamauga on September 20, 1863.

During these roster checks, I discovered that the battle of Pea Ridge was fought in March 1862, and the 21st Michigan wasn't mustered into service until September 4, 1862! Since Lillybridge could not possibly have fought at Pea Ridge in the 21st Michigan and the regiment was not at Prairie Grove, the story somehow has been distorted, perhaps by careless reporting. Nevertheless, the numerous specific details suggest the likelihood of a basically true story that either has become muddled or was embellished in the first place.

When the regiment first left Detroit it traveled via Cincinnati to Louisville, Kentucky, and its first major battle was at Perryville, Kentucky, on October 8, 1862, where it had twenty-four wounded. Since she was taken to a hospital in Louisville, Kentucky, after being wounded, this may well have been the location. The regiment was then transferred to General Rosecrans's army at Nashville, Tennessee; its next major engagement was at Stones River in December, where it suffered heavy casualties, including fifty-five wounded. Adjutant Wells, the apparent object of Lillybridge's affections, was wounded at Stones River on December 31, 1862.

At this juncture there are insufficient clues to narrow down the search any further. The 21st Michigan Infantry fits the facts insofar as named people are concerned but doesn't fit Lillybridge's being in combat in Arkansas. She could have been among the wounded at Perryville. If it had happened at Stones River it would seem more likely that she would have been sent to a hospital in Nashville, not Louisville, considering only the relative distances of the two cities, but other military factors could have been involved in the decision. Both the 1863 *Nashville Dispatch* story and an 1867 book (see Appendix B) state that she arrived in Chicago in June 1863 from the hospital in Louisville. Except for the confused information about battle dates and locations, the story apparently is basically true.

Nellie A. K.

A woman with this first name and initials reportedly enlisted in the 102nd New York Infantry with her brother, fought in a number of major battles "right up to Ringgold," and was discovered and discharged near Chattanooga, Tennessee.[24] A roster search has established that the regiment contained ninety-five soldiers whose last name began with "K" (a large number of them named Kelly), none of whom was indicated to have been discharged at or near Chattanooga, or in Tennessee. We don't know for sure what last name she used, and it may not have begun with "K."

The regiment served first in the Washington, D.C., area and in Virginia, in the Army of the Potomac until October 1863, and then in the Army of the Ohio and Army of the Cumberland for the duration of the war. It was involved in the Chattanooga, Lookout Mountain, and Ringgold campaigns, November 23–27, 1863. The regiment had one killed and two wounded at Lookout Mountain, November 24, 1863. The wounded were Captain Robert Avery from New York City and Private James Hunter (Hunter had enlisted in Company A in New York City August 11, 1861). The entry for Hunter concludes: "Date and method of discharge not given," but this is a fairly common notation.

The regimental information, at least, appears to be accurate. However, without additional clues about her name or other details, further identification will be difficult.

Mary Owen(s). See Mary Owen(s)/Jenkins

Mary Ann Pitman

Mary Ann Pitman is reported to have been a native of Chestnut Bluff, Tennessee, who at the outset of the war masqueraded as a man and, with the help of an otherwise unidentified "Lt. Craig," traveled to Union City,

Tennessee, where they raised a full company of Confederate cavalry soldiers, she serving as "2nd Lt. Rawley." According to her own statement to Federal authorities in 1864, "We took [the company] into Freeman's regiment. I was second lieutenant in the infantry" (see Appendix B). This casts doubt on the assertion that she fought in a cavalry company at the Battle of Shiloh in April 1862, where she is said to have received a wound in the side that temporarily disabled her.[25]

Some historical detective work using the Google search engine and the Civil War Database—after discarding the notion of cavalry service, which had been dominating the search—found that Colonel Thomas J. Freeman was commander of the 22nd Tennessee Infantry (Confederate). Furthermore, the regiment was in action at Shiloh, and a First Lieutenant W. H. Craig, Company I, shows up on the regimental roster. Yet, no "Lt. Rawley" appears on this roster or any other early Confederate Tennessee regiment. However, as is the case with several border states, the histories of early regiments and battalions is both incomplete and chaotic, due to repeated consolidations, mergers, and changes of unit identifications.

After recuperating from her wound, Pitman rejoined her company, which she said was then assigned to Nathan Bedford Forrest's cavalry brigade. Presumably her company of the 22nd Infantry then became mounted infantry. At the time of the siege of Fort Donelson in February of 1862, Forrest's brigade comprised the 1st Kentucky Cavalry, the 3rd Tennessee Cavalry, and George Gantt's 9th Battalion Tennessee Cavalry. Because the cavalry often operated independently by company or battalion, and consolidations were taking place regularly, it is difficult to trace individuals and to search all the various temporary rosters. At Shiloh in April, Forrest was commanding the 3rd Tennessee Cavalry regiment.

In June 1862 Forrest was made a brigade commander of cavalry in the Army of Tennessee and was formally promoted to brigadier general on July 21. By late July Forrest's brigade included the 4th, 8th, and 9th Tennessee Cavalry regiments. In a battle report on skirmishes around Nashville, Tennessee, on July 21, 1862, Forrest specified other units that were under his command: "On my arrival at Alexandria with a portion of my command (the Texas Rangers) I was advised that during the day some 700 Federal cavalry had been sent from Nashville to Lebanon. I immediately ordered forward the balance of my command, being portions of the First and Second Georgia Cavalry and the Tennessee and Kentucky squadrons."[26]

It is not clear what Pitman was doing in Forrest's command for the balance of 1862 and in 1863. After being captured in 1864, she stated in her formal deposition: "While with Forrest's command I was, a large portion of the time, occupied on special service, much of which was of a secret character and in the performance of which I passed in the character of a female. Whilst so employed I was detailed to procure ordnance and ammunition and came to Saint Louis as Mary Hays" (see Appendix B). Apparently Pitman never was a cavalry trooper in the conventional sense (except possibly as mounted infantry at Shiloh), at least no documentation of that has been found. Instead, she seems to have acted as an all-purpose spy, agent, and smuggler for Forrest, and by her own story, Forrest knew that she was a female.

Forrest, meanwhile, was promoted successively to more responsible commands during 1863, first heading a cavalry division and then by September becoming a corps commander, officially attaining the rank of major general on December 4, 1863. He operated for a while under General Braxton Bragg in the Army of Tennessee during 1863, but quarreled with him and was given an independent command in December. Early in 1865 he was promoted to lieutenant general. Yet according to Pitman's deposition, Forrest remained in close communication with her and was personally trying to recover her from the Union forces after her capture in April 1864. Given his immense responsibilities at this time, her story on this point seems very unlikely and could easily be an embellishment on her part to inflate her value in the eyes of her captors.

Pitman's story after her capture is an extraordinary one in its own right, and has been capably reported by other researchers.[27] A convincing case has been made that, whether she feared for her life or—as she claimed in her deposition—she had "seen the light" and wanted to make amends for her errors, Pitman embarked on a new career as a double agent for the Union. The evidence of that seems clear, whether due to "getting religion" or to genuine contrition. The valuable information she provided about Forrest and the Confederate secret society operations of the Order of American Knights won her freedom.

Living in Saint Louis under Union protection, at first she met with a Confederate officer sent to persuade her to return, but she declined on the grounds that she could be more valuable where she was. Then, apparently by prearrangement, she was rearrested and shuttled from prison to prison on various pretexts, once failing in an escape attempt that probably was faked in order to conceal her work for the Union. In prison she had many opportunities to obtain valuable information from other Confederate prisoners.

Late in October 1864 Pitman took the oath of allegiance to the United States, and she was pardoned by President Lincoln on November 24, 1864. Finally, at the conclusion of the war she received a substantial sum of money from the U.S. government for her efforts, a clear indicator of her important contributions to the Union cause in 1864.

Ella Reno

Ella Reno served in the Union 5th Kentucky Cavalry for four months and then was transferred to the 8th Michigan Infantry by request, becoming a highly regarded soldier. She was reported to have served in other regiments as well and was discovered and dismissed each time. Reno was once jailed for two weeks for using abusive language to a superior (based on Daniel Larned files). She served later as a teamster. After Reno (the teamster) and her friend Sarah Bradbury (the "she dragoon") were exposed while serving in Sheridan's command and were interviewed by him, they were sent home.[28] The *Nashville Dispatch,* March 8, 1863, reported "Army Police Proceedings":

Before the Chief of Army Police, Nashville, March 7, 1863. . . . Miss Ella V. Reno and Miss Sarah E. Bradbury, who exhibited their martial ardor and love of country by enlisting as young men and serving faithfully as soldiers for several months each were, upon the discovery of their sex, honorably discharged, and were sent from Murfreesboro by Capt. Wiles, Provost Marshal General, to the Chief of Police to be forwarded to their friends—those of Miss Ella residing in Cincinnati, Ohio, and those of Miss Sarah residing in this county. After being provided with proper female apparel they were placed en route for their homes.

Three days later the newspaper followed up with "The Romantic Story of the Female Soldiers," including the information that Sarah Bradbury had been using the name "Frank Morton." The newspaper published lengthy extracts from a sworn statement by Bradbury made before the judge advocate, including specific information about the regiments in which she had served (see Appendix B).

Lucy Matilda Thompson

The story of Lucy Matilda Thompson, who served in the 18th North Carolina Infantry, along with her husband, Bryant Gause, is a fairly typical example of garbled reporting that then gets repeated and perpetuated through the years. In *Patriots in Disguise,* I repeated information from a seemingly reliable source that contained several errors or distortions.[29] According to previous reports, her husband's surname was "Gauss," she used the male alias "Bill Thompson," she was 49 years old at time of enlistment and lived to be 112 years old, and she was wounded at the Battle of Bull Run and again around Richmond. Almost none of this is accurate, including the spelling of her husband's name.

Two descendants or relatives by marriage of Thompson have since corrected me on these errors. Her married name was Gause (not Gauss). She married Bryant Gause when she was eighteen and had four babies (two sets of twins) before the war, all of whom died as infants or were stillborn. Even the reported military records were not entirely accurate. Roster checks in the Civil War Database showed that Bryant Gause enlisted in Company D (not Company B) of the 18th North Carolina Infantry. He is listed as a twenty-four-year-old farmer from Bladen County. He was wounded at Frayser's Farm, Virginia, on June 30, 1862, during the Seven Days Battles, but not mortally, as previously reported. Instead, he returned to service and was wounded again (this time mortally) at Fredericksburg, Virginia, on December 13, 1862. The official North Carolina records cited in the Civil War Database indicate that he died of his wounds at Scottsville, Virginia, on January 1, 1863.[30]

The descendants have supplied a wealth of information about Thompson's life and career and have assisted me with ongoing research to pin down elusive details. Thompson told family members that she was first wounded slightly in a skirmish in the spring of 1861, then more seriously some time after the Seven Days Battles around Richmond in June 1862 and before the Battle of Fredericksburg, in which her husband was mortally wounded. Because she was pregnant at this time, she left the unit to go home when they were ordered to go to Fredericksburg.

The male alias that she used apparently was not "Bill Thompson" (at least no confirmation of that name can be found in the records), and a search is being conducted to try and identify her male alias based on records of wounded soldiers from the regiment during the time period in question.

"Tommy"

A soldier named "Tommy," who was with the 45th Ohio (Mounted) Infantry, was captured on October 20, 1863, during the battle of Philadelphia, Tennessee. Imprisoned at Belle Isle near Richmond, she became ill and was discovered to be a woman. James E. King, who reported the discovery that "Tommy" was a woman and was taken prisoner along with him at Philadelphia, Tennessee, was confirmed to be in Company A, 1st Kentucky Cavalry as reported in a memoir (see Chapter 7).

Four soldiers by the name of Tommy who were captured at this battle were found in the regimental roster of the 45th Ohio. For two of them, the dates for their release and/or return to regiment do not fit the story. One who was released about the right time is ruled out by continued service under the same name until the end of the war. By process of elimination, the most likely candidate to have been "Tommy" the female soldier was Thomas Shannon, Company I, who enlisted as a private on August 6, 1862. The record indicates that Shannon died at Andersonville Prison in Georgia on April 28, 1864. If he/she was released from Belle Isle in February or March of 1864 when discovered, Shannon (if "Tommy") could have been recaptured while still in uniform or while in the process of trying to reenlist in another regiment, and sent to Andersonville.

See also Mary Jane Johnson, 11th Kentucky Cavalry, in Chapter 4. Apparently more than one Union female soldier was captured during this battle!

Loreta Janeta Velazquez

My previous research on Velazquez was reported in detail in *Patriots in Disguise,* including the discovery of an apparent photograph of her during a trip to Canada in which she was helping Confederate soldiers who were prisoners there. In her memoirs she reports meeting a one-armed major in charge of Tod Barracks at Camp Chase, Ohio, where her brother was imprisoned.[31] A contemporary newspaper story was found about a one-armed major named John W. Skiles who was camp commandant. His military service records were obtained from the National Archives confirming his position there.

Much more has been learned about Velazquez after ten additional years of research, and many of my more recent findings were included in a chapter contributed to Phillip Thomas Tucker's book *Cubans in the Confederacy* (2002). Verification of her story in terms of official records and witness testimony is now more complete, and includes the following documentation (in chronological order):

1861

October. The *Louisville Daily Journal* (October 9, 1861) reported the arrest of a "Mrs. Mary Ann Keith" of Memphis, Tennessee, in Lynchburg, Virginia, where she had registered at the Piedmont House Hotel as "Lieutenant Buford" wearing a soldier's uniform.

November. In the book *A Rebel War Clerk's Diary,* the author reports in his diary entries for November 20–21, 1861, an encounter with a "diminutive lieutenant" who applied for a passport and travel without appropriate authorization. He became suspicious of the lieutenant's feminine mannerisms and reported the incident to the provost marshal. Next day she was arrested "and proved, as I suspected, to be a woman." (Velazquez reports in her memoirs being arrested under identical circumstances.)

1862

April. A wounded female Confederate soldier who gave the name "Arnold" surrendered in Augusta, Georgia, on April 29, 1862, and was sent before the provost marshal. She said that she formerly lived in Arkansas where she owned a plantation. She was wounded in the hand and foot in battles earlier in the month (Shiloh, April 6–7) and was returning to the city with other wounded soldiers (*Daily Chronicle & Sentinel,* Augusta, Georgia, April 30, 1862; *Southern Watchman,* Athens, Georgia, May 14, 1862).

May. A woman in army uniform who gave her name as "Mrs. Arnold" surrendered to the mayor of New Orleans on May 13 and was sent to the provost marshal. She stated that she owned a plantation in Arkansas, and that she had been arrested in Richmond on suspicion of being a spy. "She claims to have been in the battles of Manassas and Belmont, and to have been with the army in Kentucky"(*Southern Watchman,* Athens, Georgia, May 14, 1862, from the *New Orleans True Delta*).

Note: The previous two stories are nearly identical, leaving it ambiguous whether the venue of surrender was Augusta, Georgia, or New Orleans, Louisiana. One of the two newspapers has garbled the location. The following stories suggest that the location was most likely New Orleans.

June. The *Chicago Times* for June 11 reported a story from the *New Orleans Delta* (unspecified date) about a woman named Anne Williams being brought before the provost court for trial. She is said to have "resided in this city [New Orleans] several years ago in a house of questionable character" and to have married an Arkansas planter. Later she left the planter and showed up "with our army at Utah, where she became acquainted with many under the name of Mrs. Arnold." She is reported to have served with the 7th Louisiana regiment at Manassas, then was wounded and brought to public attention after the Battle of Shiloh. She then visited New Orleans and was arrested for wearing male attire, but was released with honor because of her patriotic conduct. Then about two weeks before the date of the story (presumably in May) she was arrested for alleged theft. She was found living with a soldier named Williams at Camp Lewis. She claimed to have switched her allegiance to the Union. She was convicted of the theft charge and sent to parish prison for six months.

December. Essentially the same story but with more details was reported six months later by the *Peoria Morning Mail,* Illinois, for December 17, 1862, based on a court report from the *New Orleans Delta.* The story records the arrest of Velazquez (as "Anne Williams") in New Orleans for alleged theft and her incarceration in parish prison for six months. She was arrested at Camp Lewis, where she was living as the wife of a Connecticut soldier (variously reported as the 13th or 18th Infantry) named James Williams. (If so, he was not an officer. No officer named Williams is listed in the roster of the 13th or 18th Connecticut Infantry. The 13th Connecticut was, in fact, serving under Banks in Louisiana at this time and did perform provost guard duty in New Orleans.) The story added that prior to the war she had been married to an Arkansas planter and later was "with our army in Utah" using the name "Mrs. Arnold."

1863

June. The *Richmond Whig* for June 19, 1863, reported a story taken from the *Jackson Mississippian* that a "Mrs. Laura J. Williams" had arrived in Jackson from New Orleans. She was described as a former resident of Arkansas who had served in the Confederate army as "Henry Benford" and raised a company of troops in Texas for the 5th Texas Volunteers. Her husband was said to be in the Union Army. The same story with additional details was reported in the *Spectator*, Staunton, Virginia, for June 30, 1863. At the outbreak of the war her husband, a native of the North, moved to Connecticut and joined the Union Army in the 18th Connecticut Infantry. The story includes mention of her being imprisoned in New Orleans by General Benjamin F. Butler, an incident also reported in her memoirs.

July. The *Savannah Republican,* Georgia (July 15, 1863), and the *Richmond Dispatch* (July 16, 1863) reported the release of "Mrs. Alice Williams" from Castle Thunder. The *Spectator,* Staunton, Virginia (July 21, 1863), reported that "Mrs. Alice Williams," who had served as "Lieutenant Buford" and had been imprisoned at Castle Thunder in Richmond upon suspicion of being a spy, "was sent South last week." The Savannah newspaper reported: "Her real name is Mrs. S. T. Williams and her husband is a 1st Lieutenant in company E, 13th Connecticut regiment, under Banks, in Louisiana. Her father is Major J. S. Roche, of Mississippi...." The *Savannah Republican* (July 24, 1863) reported: "'Lieut. Buford,' alias Mrs. Williams, was sent from Richmond to Atlanta on the 16th." Some comments about her are quoted from the *Richmond Sentinel.* "Loretta Janeta Valesquez" [*sic*] was reported by the *Richmond Examiner* (July 25, 1863) to be imprisoned in Richmond's Castle Thunder prison. A mention of her imprisonment in Castle Thunder is included in a book about Richmond's Civil War prisons (Parker, 1990), where her name is spelled as "Valasquez."

Summer. Union counterspy Felix Stidger reported seeing the Confederate spy, Madame Velazquez, in St. Louis that summer (Horan 1954, 106).

July 27. Application dated June 16 received by Confederate War Department in Richmond from "Mrs. Lauretta Fennett Williams," a.k.a. Lieutenant H. T. Buford, C.S.A., for an officer's commission. Apparently the department never acted on the application and returned it to her (Blanton and Cook 2002, 69).

September. The *Spectator*, Staunton, Virginia (September 22, 1863), quoting from the *Richmond Examiner*, reported a new development about "Mrs. Williams," a.k.a. "Lieut. Harry Buford." After leaving Richmond last summer, the story says, she went to Chattanooga where she joined General Bragg's army and served for a time on the staff of Gen. A. P. Stewart and in secret service. "The other day she visited Richmond again, not as gay Lieutenant, but in the garments more becoming her sex, and bearing the name of Mrs. Jeruth DeCaulp, she having, in the interval, married an officer [Confederate]...first obtaining a divorce from her first husband, Williams, who is in the army of Gen. Grant." She is reported to have received the rank of Captain and $1,600 in back pay and to be en route to her husband's home in Georgia.

September. The *Savannah Republican,* Georgia (September 25, 1863), reported that "Harry Buford, nee Mrs. Williams [*sic*]" had married a gentleman from Georgia by the name of DeCaulp who ranked as a captain. She was said to be a native of Mississippi.[32]

October. The *Weekly Columbus Enquirer,* Georgia (October 6, 1863, attributed to the *Richmond Examiner*), expanding on the marriage story, noted that "last summer the Lieutenant got into Castle Thunder [prison], her sex not corresponding with the dashing uniform she wore." This time she was in female garb and was "bearing the name of Jeruth DeCaulp, she having, in the interval, married an officer...of that name, first obtaining a divorce from her first husband, Williams, who is in the army of General Grant." She was reported to be en route to her new husband's home in Georgia.[33]

1864

March. Major H. Winslow, in a memo to General Leonidas Polk in Mobile, Alabama, on March 15, 1864, reported placing a female secret service agent in the field who would be operating in the West and North. (*Official Records,* Series 1, Vol. 24, Part 1, 634. See Appendix B. Velazquez reports this assignment and the circumstances in her memoirs.)

July–December. In his history of the Confederate Army of the Tennessee, an aide-de-camp to General A. P. Stewart reported an incident in the last half of 1864 in which "Lieutenant Buford" reported for duty as a scout, but was found to be a woman and her orders were rescinded.[34]

1865

October 10. A letter from New York City by Sanford Conover to Brigadier General Joseph Holt, Judge Advocate General in Washington, D.C., refers to three potential witnesses to implicate Jefferson Davis directly in a plot to assassinate President Abraham Lincoln, "one of whom is a Miss Alice Williams, who was commissioned in the rebel army as a lieutenant under the name of Buford."[35]

1866

Mrs. "Loretta De Camp" (also identified as "Lt. Roach") was reported, in a highly distorted news story about her career, to be passing through St. Louis in April 1866 (see below and Appendix B).

1867

January. A 1960 Civil War centennial study cites a number of references, including the *New Orleans Picayune* (January 5, 1867), indicating that a "Mrs. Mary de Caulp" who had served in the Confederate army as "Lieutenant Bufort" was participating in a Venezuelan colonization scheme for former Confederate soldiers and their families[36] (Velazquez in her memoirs, 537–552, describes this expedition).

The December 1862 newspaper story, based on New Orleans court proceedings, provides a number of potentially important clues about Velazquez's personal life and marriages. Along with other clues in the literature about her, it suggests a possible sequence of five or six marriages. Although like the rest of her story there are some date and sequence problems in this hypothetical reconstruction of events, it begins to make some sense out of previously confusing references. Her married names may have been, successively: Roach (or Roche), Arnold, Williams, De-Caulp, Wasson, and that of an unidentified Nevada miner.

First, before the war she may have been married to a Louisiana planter by the name of "Roach" (possibly Roche or La Roche), a name which pops up here and there in the stories about her. Some accounts say that her family settled in St. James Parish.[37] According to another version Roche was her maiden name and her father was a Major J. S. Roche (see below).

Her own story reports her marriage as a very young girl to a U.S. Army officer with whom she reportedly lived at various "frontier posts" and who defected to the Confederacy when the war started and was killed in a training accident in Florida. His name may have been Arnold, and Utah, where she was reported to have lived as Mrs. Arnold, certainly was a frontier post.

The name of Williams, which she used at various times and is documented in several records and newspaper stories, is given as her husband's name in New Orleans following her December 1862 arrest there. Numerous references report her once having been married to a Yankee officer, and the name Williams is typically mentioned in that context. Next is the story in 1863 of her marriage to an officer by the name of DeCaulp, who died soon thereafter.

When Velazquez was investigating the possibility of emigrating to South America after the war, she reported another brief marriage to a Major John Wasson, who died of disease soon afterwards. The Personnel Directory of the Civil War Database shows a Captain John M. Wasson who served in Company B of the 21st Arkansas Infantry, but no other information about him is available. Finally in 1868, she is reported to have married an unidentified miner in Nevada, with whom she had a son, but she apparently was later estranged from her husband; the Nevada connection also crops up a few times, including in a postwar letter by General James Longstreet (see Appendix B).

The "true account of her remarkable career" recorded in several newspapers during June 1863 (see Appendix B) is false in many particulars, and badly garbled in others. First of all it must be understood as a "heroine of the Confederacy" story making the rounds of Southern papers, showing her defying "Beast Butler" and repudiating her Yankee husband while battling nobly for the Southern cause. The flag-waving account of her arrest is reported differently elsewhere.

Other confusing and garbled stories about Velazquez include the following. Despite occasional references to her raising troops in Texas and serving with them, no evidence has been found to support this. In her memoirs she claims to have done so in Arkansas, but there are problems with that story, too. Unfortunately, no roster could be found for the 5th Texas Infantry to check for the presence of a Henry Benford.

The name Roach or Roche frequently appears in stories about her, but in contradictory ways. Katherine Jones (1955, 290) reports, without supplying any source, that Velazquez married "a New Orleans planter named Roach" (Roche?) and was living in Saint James Parish, Louisiana, in 1861. The July 1863 story from Richmond, Virginia, states, "Her father is Major J. S. Roche, of Mississippi, but she was born in the West Indies." Checks in Crute's *Confederate Staff Officers, 1861–1865* and Carroll's *List of Field Officers, Regiments and Battalions in the Confederate States Army, 1861–1865* (1983) show no Major Roche in the Confederate army. No one by that name is listed in the Civil War Database Personnel Directory from Mississippi. A Major E. M. Roach was the only field grade Confederate officer by that name, and he served in the 15th Arkansas Militia Infantry early in the war.

In the June 1863 newspaper story from Jackson, Mississippi, it is said that "she saw her father [Major J. S. Roche] on the field" at Shiloh. That, too, is a highly problematical statement because no evidence has ever been found to suggest that her father served in the Confederate army and no such thing is mentioned in her memoirs. In fact, her memoirs report her serving with her lover, Captain DeCaulp, at Shiloh.

Velazquez's arrest in Richmond and imprisonment at Castle Thunder is well documented, but the July 15, 1863, *Richmond Examiner* story also contains some surprising and questionable information. Alice Williams, Anne Williams, Mrs. Lauretta Williams, Mrs. James J. Williams . . . and now Mrs. S. T. Williams, whose husband was reported to be a lieutenant in the 13th Connecticut Infantry. Although "Williams" clearly was one of her favorite cover names, the 13th Connecticut roster contains no officer named Williams at all. Nor is there any evidence, as that story also claims, of her ever riding around in an ambulance and acting as a field nurse. These sorts of assertions are puzzling, and it becomes problematical to account for them.

Then there is the even more curious, and again badly garbled, postwar story carried in the *Bellville Countryman*, Texas, April 13, 1866, and the *Carroll Parish Journal*, Floyd, Louisiana, June 23, 1866, which never once mentions the name Velazquez or "Lieutenant Buford" (see Appendix B). Attributing the story to the *St. Louis Republican,* June 7, 1866, the Louisiana editors report that "Mrs. Loretta De Camp" [*sic*] moved with her parents from the West Indies and settled in St. James Parish. When the war broke out she raised a company of cavalry (not infantry), proceeded to Virginia, and fought there in the Peninsula Campaign (not at First Bull Run and Balls Bluff). Furthermore, her maiden name again was reported to be Roach. In one place she is referred to as "Lieutenant Looch" and in another as "Lieutenant Roach."

This strangely convoluted—or highly embellished—story also has her traveling to Fort Pillow in 1863, "where she was elected first lieutenant in Captain Phillips's company of Independent Tennessee Cavalry." With this unit she fought at Shiloh, and when Captain Phillips fell mortally wounded "the command then devolved upon her." She led the company in a charge, and "was twice wounded and carried from the field." Since Shiloh occurred in April 1862, we first have to assume a date error, and then wonder about the origins of the entire story of service in Tennessee cavalry instead of Arkansas infantry.

The story then gets better and better as she is appointed to the adjutant general's department in Atlanta and "assigned to duty with the provost marshal, as chief of detectives and military conductor." There are other details too, some containing elements of her previously reported story but with all sorts of new twists and unlikely details.

Perhaps some history of journalism research might determine whether the *St. Louis Republican* (a *St. Louis Missouri Republican* dating to that period was found online) was the *National Informer* tabloid of that era; or is it more likely that Velazquez's story improved with age? Given her track record for using false names and cover stories, one has to suspect some possible yarn-spinning on her part that is then seized upon by newspaper reporters and further garbled by them, as the legend grows and spreads.

Another dubious and at least partly fictitious account of Velazquez concerns her association with secret service chief Lafayette C. Baker. A 1960 book written by a former newspaper man from New Jersey, Jacob Mogelever, portrays (complete with dialogue) an encounter between Baker and Velazquez in a Washington, D.C., bar where he allegedly spotted her for the first time and saw through her male disguise.[38] In this version Baker first accuses her of being a Confederate spy, but in a spirited exchange with her he realizes that she would make a good Union agent. According to the story, he had her locked up at the Old Capitol Prison, but after a while had her released, and they sparred with each other for some time before she was employed in his detective bureau. Mogelever quotes extensively from her memoirs, but takes considerable liberties at times with the facts. Her own story in her memoirs of how she came to be employed by Baker is quite different from Mogelever's version.

Loreta Janeta Velazquez remains one of the most fascinating female soldier-spies of the Civil War and a real challenge for historical research. Much more detective work will be required to obtain definitive answers. Clearly there is a hard core of truth to her story: she was a soldier in uniform and did engage in military and spying activities. Many of her anecdotes about specific incidents have been verified. Evidently she also engaged in considerable deception, and possibly some embellishment, severely complicating the effort to pin down the whole truth about her. The problem centers around the difficulty of filtering out the myths, the garbled and distorted information in newspaper stories, and her own deceptions, and then of isolating and more clearly establishing the facts. At least some of this should be possible, especially obtaining more accurate information about her family and married names, places of residence, and postwar activities. In time and with continued intensive research, more reliable details may also come to light about her military and spying activities.

"Charles H. Williams"

A female soldier (real name unknown) using this male alias was reported to have served three months in the 1st Iowa Infantry, Company I, under "Capt. Cox" in order to be with a lieutenant sweetheart. The *New York Tribune,* September 1, 1861, identified her regiment as the 2nd Iowa Infantry. In a recent book she was reported to have been arrested once in St. Louis in August 1861 while walking down the street and turned over to the provost marshal. He released her after she promised to leave the army. The book also reports a Nellie Williams who enlisted in the 2nd Iowa Infantry, saying that she did so because she enjoyed soldier life. The authors cite several newspaper stories published in 1861, including one dated August 22.[39]

The 1st Iowa Infantry, the only three-months regiment from the state, was organized at Keokuk and served from May 14, 1861, to August 20, 1861, mustering out at Rolla (about sixty miles from St. Louis). The first news story is dated four days later, picked up from a St. Louis newspaper a day or two previously. Since the three-months 1st Iowa Infantry was mustered out on August 20, 1861, this story more likely refers to someone in that regiment rather than in the 2nd Iowa Infantry.

The 2nd was organized May 27, 1861, so it is conceivable that Nellie Williams served in it for a few months and then was discovered. On the other hand, no Captain Cox was listed in the 1st Iowa. Hugh P. Cox was listed as captain of Company I of the 2nd Iowa Infantry as of May 6, 1861. The 2nd Iowa also was organized at Keokuk and served from May 27, 1861, to July 20, 1865, mustering out at Davenport. Curiously, no Charles H. Williams is listed on the rosters of either regiment. Thus, part of the story fits perfectly with the history of the 1st Iowa, and part with that of the 2nd Iowa. This suggests some garbled newspaper reporting on a basically true story. However, one suspects that Charles Williams and Nellie Williams were one and the same, and that she served in one or both of the two regiments.

Fanny Wilson

Fanny Wilson and her friend, Nellie Graves, were reported to have served in male disguise in the 24th New Jersey Infantry along with their boyfriends early in the war. The unit reportedly saw combat in West Virginia in 1861, and was later transferred to Mississippi. There Fanny's boyfriend was wounded and she took care of him, but he died. When Fanny and Nellie became ill, they were sent to a hospital in Cairo, Illinois, where hospital personnel discovered their sex and they were discharged.

The *Nashville Dispatch*, August 26, 1864, reported that "Fanny Wilson, aged 19 years, and an actress in the Memphis Theatre, was arrested a few days since while attempting to be a soldier. She had shorn her locks and donned the Federal blue—but it would not do." Fanny later served briefly in the 3rd Illinois Cavalry, but was found out again and discharged (see Appendix B).[40]

The intricate details of this story suggest that it may well be essentially true. However, there is a very serious problem with it as contemporaneously reported. The 24th New Jersey Infantry (a nine-months regiment) was mustered in on September 16, 1862, and did not serve in West Virginia, but instead in the defenses of Washington until late 1862. The regiment then joined the Army of the Potomac and was involved at Fredericksburg in December and Chancellorsville the following spring. It mustered out on June 29, 1863, and was not at Vicksburg, instead serving out its time in the Army of the Potomac.[41]

Since some partial documentation of portions of the story have been found, it may well be a case of newspaper garbling and resulting misidentification of the regiment in which she allegedly served. Fanny Wilson and her companion, Nellie Graves, have been assigned a provisional status on the Honor Roll of Civil War Service in Appendix A, pending further research and investigation.

10

African American Women at War

There are many people who do not know what some of the colored
women did during the war.... There were hundreds of them who
assisted the Union.... These things should be kept in history before
the people.

Susie King Taylor, A Black Woman's Civil War Memoirs *(1997)*

On October 16, 1859, John Brown sent shock waves throughout the South when he executed his ill-fated plan at Harpers Ferry,
Virginia. Brown and twenty-one followers raided the Federal ar-
senal in an effort to capture the armory and inspire and arm a
slave rebellion. The plot failed quickly, and Brown was injured
and carried to Charles Town to stand trial; he was eventually
executed. Yet the implications of his insurrection reverberated
through slave-holding states long afterward. His plot exacerbated
the anger, frustration, and fear that smoldered across the South
in the months preceding the Civil War. That is why, on January 4, 1860, several South Carolina citizens met at Black Oak
Church near Charleston to establish the "Vigilance Association of
St. Johns Berkeley."[1]

Abolitionist sentiments had long menaced the slave-holding
states, but the events at Harpers Ferry prompted many citizens to take a more offensive stance. "The disclosures following
the recent Harpers Ferry affair leave no room for doubt...that
the course of the Abolition party will become ever more daring,"
the founders of the St. Johns vigilance committee declared. "[It]

now threatens to invade our very homes with its vile machinations." Racial tension and suspicion mounted, as many believed that abolitionists would send agents disguised as "the school master" or "the book or map agent" and "leave the germ of insubordination & insurrection among our domestics."[2] African Americans in South Carolina were fully aware of the vigilance committee's watchful eye. "It would have been very dangerous for a slave to say anything in favor of the Union cause," Harry Quick explained. "He would have been taken up right off & hung on charge of endeavoring to raise an insurrection." One free black woman experienced firsthand the wrath of the committee "when she was robbed and driven from her home by them."[3]

In fact, slaveholders' fears may have been well founded. Whether or not inspired by secret agents posing as booksellers, many black women in the South did conspire against their Confederate enemies, once war became a reality. Considering the anxiety and suspicion that the "domestic" enemy evoked in every household, it seems that some of the most daring acts of the Civil War were the secret activities of black women in the South. Whether they took a direct role in the events of the war, such as those women who posed as men in order to don a uniform and fight, or played a less conspicuous role as frontline nurses, scouts, or spies, black women faced increased peril just because they were born without the same rights as their white counterparts.

While many white women were able to pass as men for many years and serve in the military, that opportunity was less available to black women. "Colored" regiments were fewer in number and they appeared after the war began. One woman refused to let the race hurdle stop her, however. Maria Lewis (apparently light-skinned) served in the 8th New York Cavalry, successfully posing as a white man, until she turned herself in to a group of Northern abolitionists who visited her camp to help the freed slaves. She was apparently ready to turn in her uniform, and her wish was granted. The abolitionists promised to find her a safe place. Other black women did follow in her footsteps, once the Union began to enlist black soldiers, though records are scanty. Lizzie Hoffman enlisted in the 45th U.S. Colored Infantry, but her plans were interrupted when she was discovered and arrested as she attempted to board a steamer with her fellow recruits. Another African American woman enlisted—this time successfully—in the 29th Connecticut Infantry (Colored), only to be foiled by Mother Nature. Her baffled sergeant asked his wife in a letter: "One Question I wish to ask Did you Ever hear of A Man having a child[?]"[4] While her fate is unrecorded, that soldier's career was certainly short-lived.

The U.S. Navy may have shown more tolerance for women serving in hospitals and on naval ships during the war. Historian Lisa Y. King has found that many women apparently followed their husbands when they enlisted. The navy may have found itself in short supply of cooks and nurses by the time it began recruiting African American sailors; therefore, the women were accepted aboard ships where they filled those much-needed roles as "lady volunteers." Surprisingly, some women's names have appeared on muster rolls as enlisted personnel. Harriet Ruth served as a nurse on the U.S.S. *Black Hawk,* and Harriet Little, also a nurse, served on the U.S.S. *Hartford.* Additionally, Lucy Berington of North Carolina was enlisted as a "first-class boy" (lowest official naval rank) as a washerwoman. She was employed at the U.S. Naval Hospital in New Bern, North Carolina. Most interesting, however, is the case of Ann Stokes. She was also listed in official documents as a "first-class boy," but she is extraordinary because, after the war, she received a Navy Invalid Pension. A handwritten note on her Declaration for Invalid Pension specifically states "For a Woman." The words were underlined for emphasis, so there can be no doubt that the navy recognized her gender during and after her service.[5]

Some women chose to serve in more creative ways. As the war burned ever deeper into the Southern lands, it must have seemed insignificant to the president of the Confederacy, Jefferson Davis, when a new servant joined his Richmond, Virginia, household. Sent to the Davis estate from the household of a wealthy Richmond heiress named Elizabeth Van Lew, the new servant was a seemingly simple young woman who went by the name of Ellen Bond. To the rest of the household, Ellen seemed to be a little feeble-minded, but she was apparently competent enough when it came to household chores, because she remained in the Confederate White House for some time. Long enough, it seems, to put the president at ease when it came to divulging military intelligence in her presence. That turned out to be a serious mistake. The wealthy Miss Van Lew and Ellen Bond were both spies for the Union Army. Each night, the "simple" young servant would convey intelligence to Mrs. Van Lew, who passed it along to Union officials.

In fact, the real name of the young servant was Mary Elizabeth Bowser. She was a former slave of the Van Lews, and she had gained her freedom at age eighteen before receiving an education in Philadelphia. Through the wily schemes of Van Lew and Bowser, the Union Army gained access to valuable Confederate correspondence and military documents. Miss Bowser has been credited for playing a role in the fall of Richmond in 1864.[6] While the case of Mary Elizabeth Bowser is certainly extraordinary, for it seems incredible that a black woman would have had the steely nerve to spy on the Confederate president, it was, in fact, her high-society connections and her unique access to the Confederate White House that really set her apart from her peers. In truth, it was not unusual for black women to help the Union cause.

Oddly, espionage may have come easily to black women because they were such unlikely candidates. The very existence of slavery in the South depended on the belief that blacks lacked the intelligence necessary to carry off anything that required so much skill and acumen. So, naturally, some women took advantage of their so-called disadvantage. One woman's actions in the early months of 1863 so impressed Union officials that they recorded her exploits in a book shortly after the end of the war. Unfortunately, they were not impressed enough to record her name. She is known only as Dabney's wife.

While quartered on the banks of the Rappahannock near Falmouth, Virginia, a Union camp was approached by a "contraband" couple—a runaway husband and wife who, like many, had abandoned their plantation tasks to join the Yankees.[7] The man was called Dabney, and he brought with him two very special talents that were always in short supply to a wandering band of soldiers: the ability to cook and the knowledge to navigate the local topography. Dabney and his wife were welcomed into the camp, but before long, Dabney's wife disappeared. This strange behavior may have gone unnoticed at first, but before long the entire camp discovered the shocking truth: Dabney's wife had left to offer her laundry services to a Confederate camp on the other side of the river. She wasn't a double-crosser, however; she was a double agent, and her weapon of choice was a clothesline. She and her husband had devised a method to communicate signals and convey critical military secrets as she dried her laundry. The method is best explained in Dabney's own words, as he explained it to one of the Union officers:

> That clothes-line tells me in half an hour just what goes on at Lee's headquarters. You see my wife over there; she washes for the officers, and cooks, and waits around, and as soon as she hears about any movement or anything going on, she comes down and moves the clothes on that line so I can understand it in a minute. That there gray shirt is Longstreet; and when she takes it off, it means he's gone down about Richmond. That white shirt means Hill; and when she moves it up to the west end of the line, Hill's corp has moved up stream. That red one is Stonewall. He's down on the right now, and if he moves, she will move that red shirt.[8]

According to the postwar account written by a Union officer, the Dabney family's clothesline telegraph proved to be one of General Hooker's most valuable resources.

As the war progressed, Union camps found themselves inundated with runaway slaves, eager to grasp at the freedom that lay behind Union lines, no matter how tenuous or hazardous that freedom was. Many African American women fled to the Federal lines to stay close to their husbands, while others arrived, merely hoping for a respite from slavery. Officials established refugee villages where, in theory, women and children could find food and shelter from the ravages of war. Unfortunately, the shells and bullets might have been preferable to some of the perils women faced in refugee villages. Food was scarce, disease ran rampant, and the climate was sometimes brutal. In Kentucky, for instance, women and children died in significant numbers, due to exposure to the cold. Perhaps the greatest threat was the attitude of mean-spirited Union officers. Brigadier General Speed S. Fry was the commander of Camp Nelson in Kentucky, and he quickly gained a reputation for extreme cruelty. Upon occasion he took it upon himself to expel all of the women and children from the fort. One cold day in November 1864, he drove 400 helpless women and children from the only security they knew. Many died as a result.[9]

Women in Mississippi's freedmen villages also met with hardship. Camps were sometimes left vulnerable when troops were called away to battle. Women and children fell victim to guerrilla attacks by Confederate soldiers who abused them and sometimes kidnapped them and sold them off elsewhere. Freedmen's villages of the Vicksburg and Natchez areas of Mississippi were particularly dangerous in 1864, as guerrillas attacked on a daily basis.[10] That year, more than a thousand African Americans disappeared at the hands of the "bushwhackers."

A freedmen's village in Arlington, Virginia, suffered the same agony from Confederates out of nearby Maryland, only that camp was a little different. "The Marylanders tormented them by coming over, seizing, and carrying away their children. If the mothers made a 'fuss,' as these heartless wretches called those natural expressions of grief in which bereaved mothers are apt to indulge, they were thrust into the guard-house."[11]

These women suffered unthinkable pain, having reached a freedmen's camp only to watch their children disappear back into slavery. Yet the women in Virginia had an advantage that others did not, in the person of Sojourner Truth. When this fiery abolitionist heard of this awful treatment, she soon put a stop to it.

Sojourner Truth was born on the property of Colonel Ardinburgh as Isabella Baumfree, a slave child, to parents James and Betsey in Ulster County, New York. She was freed under the New York act of 1817, which freed all slaves aged forty and above. Little is known about her childhood, except that she suffered cruel treatment and yet developed deep religious conviction as she grew into a young woman. It was a religious experience, in fact, that prompted her to change her name in 1843 to one that would reflect her self-perceived destiny: to sojourn the countryside as an itinerant preacher. She sermonized the "truth" in a distinctive and powerful manner, demonstrating her clever and frequently shocking wit. She soon encountered others on her travels who preached another kind of truth, and one that fanned the fire inside her. She joined the fight to abolish slavery and embarked on delivering moving speeches that made her audience tremble. Of course, the listeners trembled for differing reasons. Some were not so pleased about her speeches on slaves' rights, or women's suffrage. One angry white man once told Sojourner Truth that her speeches were no more important than a flea bite, to which she responded, "Maybe not, but the Lord willing, I'll keep you scratching."[12]

By the time the Civil War began, she was in her sixties and had earned unprecedented fame as an inspirational speaker. Even President Lincoln was impressed upon meeting her, as she explained in a letter to a friend: "I told him that I had never heard of him before he was talked of for president. He smilingly replied, 'I heard of you many times before that.'"[13] Despite her late age and her celebrity, She placed herself in harm's way to support the Union and the freedmen. She quickly went to work, raising money and food contributions for the black regiments. She was working to aid the refugees in the freedman's village in Virginia when she heard about the horrible acts of the Confederate guerrillas. She encouraged the women to fight against the attackers, and they apparently did. "Her electrifying words seemed to inspire them...the exasperated Marylanders threatened to put Sojourner into the guard-house. She told them that if they attempted to put her in the guard-house, she 'would make the United States rock like a cradle.'"[14] Sojourner Truth fought on, after the guns of the war quieted, for the rights of women and African Americans alike. She died in Battle Creek, Michigan, on November 26, 1883.

The southeastern states contained a very large number of freedmen's camps, since the coastal islands of South Carolina had been occupied by Federal troops early in the war and most of the landowning whites had fled the area. Additionally, in April 1862, Major General David Hunter carried out a successful assault on Fort Pulaski in coastal Georgia. Upon victory he proclaimed that all slaves in the vicinity should be regarded as free. Hundreds of African Americans gained quasi-freedom there, under the supervision of U.S. officials. Some remained on their coastal plantations to harvest the crops, while others joined the new regiment of black soldiers being organized by General Hunter. One woman who benefited from the events in the Southeast was a fourteen-year-old girl from Savannah, named Susie.

Susie King Taylor was born a slave in Savannah, Georgia, but her insatiable love of learning prevented her from living a life of obscurity. Against heavy odds and contrary to the laws of the state of Georgia, Taylor learned to read and write at a young age. Every day at nine o'clock she would wrap her books in paper "to prevent the police or white persons from seeing them" and visit a clandestine school on Bay Street.[15] She was an eager student who quickly absorbed as much as her instructor could offer. By the time the Civil War began, she was ready to become a teacher in her own right.

One day in 1862 Taylor sat at her mother's house and listened to "the roar and din" of distant gunfire. "They jarred the earth for miles," she explained. Little did she know that this gunfire would soon rattle more than land. It would change her entire life, by taking her out of slavery and thrusting her into a new existence as a free woman. Only days later, her family would flee aboard a Union gunboat to St. Simon's Island, where they found protection and freedom in one of the many refugee camps. Before long, Taylor's reading abilities made her a valuable asset to Federal authorities. Under their direction and with their funding, she opened a school on the island where she taught children and adults alike. Taylor enjoyed her role as teacher, but she was undoubtedly intrigued by other events taking place around her. The first regiment of black soldiers developed from the men living within the black coastal settlements, and the regiment became official under the leadership of Colonel Thomas Wentworth Higginson as the First South Carolina Volunteers.[16] Several of Taylor's family members joined, so she herself volunteered as a laundress. It wasn't long before she was doing more nursing and teaching than washing and ironing, however.

Within a few months, Taylor was on the move with her regiment, and her love of learning surfaced again. "I learned to handle a musket very well while in the regiment, and could shoot straight and often hit the target. I assisted in cleaning the guns and used to fire them off, to see if the cartridges were dry...I thought this great fun."[17] Sometimes her adventurous nature put her a little too close to the action: "Some mornings I would go along the picket line, and I could see the rebels on the opposite side of the river... [they] would shoot across at our picket, but as the river was so wide there was never any damage done." In another instance, Federal authorities had to see to her safety. "The shelling was so heavy that the colonel told my captain to have me taken up into the town to a hotel, which was used as a hospital.... I expected every moment to be killed by a shell, but on arriving at the hospital I knew it was safe, for the shells could not reach us there."[18]

Despite her enthusiasm, Taylor was fully cognizant of the horrors of war, but she approached them with her usual passion. "It seems strange...how we are able to see the most sickening sights, such as men with their limbs blown off and mangled by the deadly shells, without a shudder; and instead of turning away how we assist in alleviating their pain."[19] Lovingly, she nursed her "boys" to health and fed them with whatever supplies she could garner as they traveled. Sometime during the war, Susie married Edward King, a sergeant in the regiment. The couple stayed with the regiment until the end of the war. Afterward, Susie returned to Savannah where she started a family. It wasn't long, of course, before she opened a school for free black children.

Harriet Tubman was born into slavery in the vicinity of Dorchester County, Maryland. She was one of eleven children born to Benjamin Ross and Harriet Green. She suffered firsthand the horrors of slavery as she watched her siblings "carried off weeping and lamenting" by slave trad-ers, to disappear from her life forever.[20] This great heartbreak, as well as the abuse she suffered at the hands of cruel neighbors who "rented" her time as a house maid, instilled a venomous hatred of slavery. At age fifteen Tubman suffered a severe head injury when she stepped into the path of an angry overseer, about to punish a fellow slave. Tubman had not realized that the overseer had thrown a lead weight at the subject of his ire until it was too late. She sustained a head wound so severe that her parents feared for her life. She never fully recovered and suffered peri-odic "sleeping fits" and bouts of pain. Her tragic early years set the stage for a lifetime of activism against the institution of slavery.

Tubman gained her freedom as a young adult when she ran away in 1849, prompted by the fear that she too would be sold away to the dreaded Deep South. She set out on foot, navigating by the night sky toward the North, until she reached Pennsylvania. She went on to Philadelphia and managed to secure a job and began to save money. Her joy upon discovering this wonderful freedom inspired her to seek the freedom of other slaves. For the next several years she made forays into the South to rescue slaves from bondage, beginning with her own family members but soon branch-ing out with her scheme until she earned the title of "conductor" of the Underground Railroad. By 1860 Tubman had made at least nineteen trips into slave country and had earned a bounty on her head of $40,000.

By the time the Civil War broke out, Tubman's reputation was widely known. Nonetheless, the fearless freedom fighter went back into the South to assist the escaped slaves who attached themselves to Union camps. She worked as a teacher and nurse until the Federal Army realized the value of her knowledge and experience, demonstrated in her years of moving about the Southern states without detection. She was recruited as a spy in 1863 and placed under the direction of Edwin M. Stanton, secretary of war. She enlisted a number of local men from the southeastern coastal area, including at least one river pilot skilled in navigating through southern swamps. This band of spies carried out a highly effective system of scouting and spying against Confederate operations. Not surprisingly, Tubman also used the web of spies to encourage more slaves to leave bondage and escape to Union lines.

In July of 1863, Tubman carried out one of the most significant missions of her remarkable life when she led Colonel James Montgomery in the Combahee River expedition. This military operation would ultimately lead to a devastating blow to the South with the raid and destruction of several of its wealthiest and most successful cotton estates. In the process, the mission also freed more than 750 slaves in one night. Many of those freedmen quickly joined up with the newly formed black regiments, a fact which added humiliation to the South's devastation.

Harriet Tubman lived nearly fifty years after the passage of the Thirteenth Amendment and the end of the Civil War. She faced the challenges that followed and endured with the same determination she had shown as a young woman, leading African Americans through the disappointing turns of Reconstruction and beyond. She eventually applied for a military pension, but her application was denied, despite support from Secretary of State William Seward and Colonel Higginson. She died on March 10, 1913, and was buried with full military honors.

Sometimes women set out with the intent to help the Union cause, and those leaders, like Sojourner Truth and Harriet Tubman, couldn't be quieted by mere bayonets or bullets. But more often, women in the South stumbled upon the opportunity by chance. Elizabeth Geary was a free woman living in Darien, Georgia, when she happened upon a Union camp near her home. She and her family were visiting an area called the "salts," where several lumber mills were operating. Upon seeing the Union troops, she realized that they were in danger of walking straight into the snare of Confederate scouts.

We notified the Union soldiers when they came up that the Rebels were near & there was danger of the Union soldiers being surprised

& taken. They then sent to the boats & got a stronger force & returned. A skirmish ensued & the Rebels retreated. The rebels' plot was to have cut off the smaller force from the vessels & then capture or destroy them, after enticing them far enough back into the woods from the shore. But from the information given...the plot was broken up by the reinforcement from the boats.[21]

Mrs. Geary's actions did not go unnoticed by the Confederate troops or her Southern neighbors. "I was threatened with death & injury to my person, family and property on account of my Union sentiments, and so was my husband. They threatened to hang me for telling the Union soldiers that the Rebels were near." The Geary family was "molested & injured by being driven from place to place & out of [their] house." Shortly after this incident, the city of Darien was burned by Union troops. The Gearys managed to escape by boarding a Union boat and riding to Beaufort, South Carolina, where they found refuge in a Union camp.[22]

Like many Southern black women during the Civil War, Elizabeth Geary was forced to make a heartbreaking decision—whether to support the Confederacy and perhaps betray her own race, or to act in a way that would be perceived as betrayal to her former friends and neighbors and support the Union cause. Her decision in this case, to risk her life and those of her family, is significant because Mrs. Geary was a successful free black woman with considerable land holdings.[23] When she warned Union troops about the rebel scouts, she chose to support other African Americans who were not so fortunate as she. Yet things are not always so clear cut, and sometimes the fog of war blurred the line between white and black, and friendships prevailed over politics.

Sarah Ann Black was born a slave, but gained her freedom when her own mother purchased her for $500. When Black was old enough, she began to sell milk for a living. By the time the Civil War engulfed the South, Black had earned enough money to buy a house and purchase six good milk cows. She supported herself in a neighborhood that apparently consisted of friendly, sympathetic, and racially diverse working women.

Black lived in Savannah, Georgia, during the war, and she suffered a severe blow to her livelihood one day when Confederate troops seized a good portion of her possessions. "My cows were taken by the Confederate authorities & driven to the cattlepen to be driven across the river the next day," she explained. The soldiers planned to use her milk cows for beef, to feed the troops. When one of her neighbors found out, the whole neighborhood went into action. "I had a friend, a white lady living near me & she went to the pen and claimed the cattle as hers & they let her drive them off. . . . I took them & put one of them in each of my neighbor's yards as each person was allowed to have one cow. When they came round afterwards they, seeing only one cow in each yard, left it & so I kept them from the Confederates."[24]

One of the neighbors who took part in this scheme, Caroline DeWillis, was the granddaughter of a white woman, though her parents both "were of Indian blood."[25] She and the others demonstrated considerable courage as well as loyalty to their friend in need in creating their own small, racially diverse rebellion and defying Confederate authorities.

While historians may forever debate the many causes for war and the varied intentions of the politicians involved, one thing is clear: much of the testimony from slaves and free blacks in Georgia indicates a belief that the Yankees were at war to free the slaves. "The colored people were all [of] one mind, one feeling," said former slave Edward Hornsby. "I do not think the colored men could be doubted for their Unionism. . . . I could tell you what would fill a book of what I have seen and knew of the courage in the efforts to aid the Union."[26] Primus Wilson described the tension that mounted along with suspicions that Savannah's slaves were siding with the Yankees: "I heard about 4 years before the Yankees came that the war was going on for our freedom. . . . I was on the side of the Yankees all the time. We were watched as a hawk watches a chicken all the time and we had to be very careful."[27]

Yet another former slave described the danger his community faced as they defied the rebel officials. "They told me if they heard me talking about the Yankees they would whip me severely & put me in the stocks—afterwards in their presence I kept my mouth shut—I kept my mind inside . . . [and] they couldn't punish my mind."[28]

Savannah became a unique arena for would-be spies and activists when a trainload of Union prisoners arrived from the overpopulated and notorious Andersonville prison. In July 1864, Confederate officials transported several captives to a fort in Savannah, where they would stay until the end of the war. As the train entered the Savannah station, Yankee prisoners were surprised to discover that their presence had sparked a great deal of interest from city slaves and free blacks. One prisoner recalled that a very large crowd greeted them, which had apparently "manifested an interest in us such as we had not seen before in any city of the South."[29] Indeed, the spectators were fascinated to see the Yankees. For years they had quietly monitored their progress and prayed for their success. "All the colored people were in favor of the Yankees . . . every one," said former slave Peter Miller. "The first thing in the morning was to learn where they were. Samuel Bowen—one of us—could read a little, and when we heard of the guns firing at Ball's Bridge, that was the first time that our feelings lifted up in our hearts."[30] Georgianna Kelly also described her feelings during the war: "Every time that I heard they were in battle I sympathized with the Union, Ho! I guess I did. I didn't know what manner it would end and I felt sad. I wanted every time the Union to gain it. I knew that they were on our side. I had knowledge enough to know that they were working for us. If they were on our side we were on their side."[31]

But when the beloved Yankees arrived at the train station, many of Savannah's supporters were saddened and deeply touched by their miserable condition. "Those prisoners were in very bad condition," one slave reported. "They were full of vermins & starving."[32] Perhaps it was the shock of seeing their heroes in such wretched condition that prompted them into action. Over the next several months, Savannah's slaves and free blacks carried out coordinated efforts to feed, clothe, and set free their despondent friends, risking their own lives in the process, as witnessed by Susie King Taylor:

> When I went into Savannah, in 1865, I was told of one of these stockades which was in the suburbs of the city, and they said it was an awful place. The Union soldiers were in it, worse than pigs, without any shelter from sun or storm, and the colored women would take food there at night and pass it to them, through the holes in the fence. The soldiers were starving, and these women did all they could toward relieving those men, although they knew the penalty, should they be caught giving them aid.[33]

Georgianna Kelly was a free-born seamstress living in Savannah during the war. She told how she conspired with the women and children of the city to provide food for the prisoners. "All my colored friends used to bring their things to me to give to the prisoners. I have had as much as 300 loaves of bread in my house at one time to give the prisoners from Andersonville. We would send the colored boys all around the city to collect the bread & they would bring it to my house & then they would ride past the stockade and throw them a bag."[34]

At the risk of certain severe punishment, Georgianna Kelly provided a makeshift distribution center where the city's black population could contribute food in a covert way. Of course, Kelly and the others could not have managed such an organized campaign if not for their financial resources. The African American community in Savannah was actually well situated because of the distinctive form of slavery that had evolved in the coastal city.

Slavery was not a static system; it varied a great deal from one region to another, depending very much on local economic systems and conditions. As in many cities in the South, the role of many slaves in the city of Savannah was to earn wages. From those wages, they would pay the urban master a set fee, providing him or her with extra income. Whatever amount the slave earned in excess of their masters' fees could be saved or used to pay rent or to accumulate property. As a result, many slaves accumulated significant holdings.[35] Slaves in Savannah often lived in their own homes, largely unsupervised, worked at specialized jobs, and paid their masters a weekly sum of $3 to $8 a week. Many slaves, both men and women, were able to accumulate significant estates by working for themselves. Phoebe Rutledge explained that she "got [her] property by hard working. I was as hard working a woman as there was in the county." Although she was in her seventies during the war, she risked her life for the prisoners, explaining, "I felt good in my heart for I had children sold all about and scattered everywhere and I knew [they] would end it all and I was willing to do my part for the cause."[36]

Savannah women earned wages in a wide variety of jobs, including nursing, sewing, laundering, cooking, and making baskets and other goods. Many established themselves in businesses and enjoyed free movement about the city, day and night. While some slaves were able to purchase their freedom through hard work, some could not. That decision was entirely in the hands of the owner. Judy Rose explained that, despite twenty years of hard work and her ability to acquire a household full of furniture, she was a slave until General Sherman arrived in Savannah at the end of his famous march. "I was born a slave," she told the commission. "At the beginning of the war I was a slave. I was made free when [Sherman] came to the city. I was a washer and ironer. I hired my time—I paid seven dollars a month in summer and eight dollars a month in winter.... I bought the horse the year Lincoln was elected [and] I bought the mule about the time the Union prisoners were brought into the city."[37]

Despite her status, Rose rented a house and claimed a wagon, harnesses for the horse and mule, kitchen furniture, three bedsteads, three bureaus, a sofa, and "one doz. and a half good chairs besides some old chairs in the kitchen."[38]

One of the most successful slave entrepreneurs in Savannah was Rachel Bromfield. Incredibly, she claimed to have lost $16,000 in cash during the war. This amount, she claims, was stolen during the panic as General Sherman approached the city. When Union officials researched her claim after the war, they found it to be true. She also owned a horse, two cows, a wagon, a house full of furniture "necessary to accommodate 13 regular boarders and comers and goers," mahogany tables, walnut chairs, woolen carpets, and bed clothing for thirteen beds. She had rented a large, sixteen-room house on Bryan Street in Savannah and ran it as a boarding house. She risked all her holdings when she decided to join other slaves and free blacks by helping the Union prisoners.[39]

Bromfield paid $40 a month for the house she used until rumors began to circulate that she "was a Union woman & harboring Union men." In fact, the rumors were true. "I secreted 6 soldiers for 7 months & fed & clothed them & kept 2 others one month," she later revealed. In response to the rumors, and in an effort to put her out of business, her landlord raised her rent to $100 a month. His efforts failed, as she managed to pay the higher rent. All the while, Bromfield was sneaking food to the prisoners in the stockade. She was actually caught a few times and threatened with death. Nonetheless, she persisted. "I was threatened with the bayonet by Charlie LeMar—a rebel—for carrying bread & milk to the Union soldiers.... He kicked it all over & threatened to run the bayonet into me.... I was threatened again at the stockade by the guard, with their guns—for carrying tobacco & old clothes to the soldiers of the Union there confined." She also paid money to help prisoners escape to safety. "I paid the [river] pilot $10 in gold for each of them," she explained. She carried out her covert activities without the support of her husband. He was away "waiting on his master in the Rebel army."[40]

Bromfield wasn't alone in her efforts to help prisoners escape. Francis Keaton "stowed away 11 soldiers that came down from Andersonville. I kept them one week & feed [sic] them and took care of them."[41] The slaves and free blacks seemed to have gained the trust of the Andersonville prisoners after a time. Larry Williams told how he "met four escaped prisoners on the outside edge of town. They were hiding themselves in the tall weed; I was working in that vicinity and they saw I was a colored man & they knew they could trust to speak to me."[42]

On December 13, 1864, five months after the Andersonville prisoners arrived in Savannah, Major General William T. Sherman and his army approached Fort McAllister near Savannah as the famous "march to the sea" came to an end. The sight of the procession was quite moving to local African Americans who had risked so much to secretly support the Northern army. It wasn't just soldiers who marched to the seaside city of Savannah, for all through Georgia, slaves had abandoned their belongings and the only homes they knew to join the march.[43] "I did all I could for the Yankees when they first came in I was so glad to see them," recalled Herb Strafford. "We all went to cooking breakfast for them [and] they told us we were free."[44]

But the celebration was short-lived. The war-weary troops had sustained a long, rugged march through the South before reaching Savannah. They were exhausted, hungry, and in need of shoes, clothing, and provisions. The Union troops were unaware of the difficult and risky work the African Americans had carried out for the prisoners. Unfortunately, the danger wasn't over for the city's slaves and free blacks, as Union soldiers considered their property as fair game for seizure. "They came into our house and took possession of everything I had, did not allow me a blanket, not a thing," Phoebe Rutledge explained. "They took what I had in the pot cooking for our supper."[45] Nevertheless, slaves believed that freedom had finally come with the arrival of the Federal troops, and any price seemed acceptable to them that December in 1864.

"When they first came, if I had had 3 times as much property I would have enjoyed their taking it if I could have got my freedom," said Peter Miller. "I will be in favor of the Union until I die. Slavery is death."[46] His feelings reflected most of the testimonies of slaves who spoke in 1871 of the day Sherman's troops arrived. Jerry Brown returned Yankee threats with a giddy response:

> At the beginning of the rebellion I was a hard down slave and never became free until the union army came here. . . . When they first came up to me I went to them and they said—hey! Old man—ain't you afraid I will kill you? I said if you do kill me you can't kill me but one time, but I don't think you will be so bad. . . . I told them I didn't think that Mr. Lincoln would send them to shoot me.[47]

Many of Savannah's slaves and free blacks did receive recognition for their wartime efforts, eventually. More than forty African Americans received compensation for losses they sustained during the war. But in his own words, Peter Miller summed up a common sentiment: "I was satisfied whether I got anything or not because [the Yankees] delivered me from bondage."[48] Susie King Taylor's grandmother mirrored his thoughts, after she lost her life's savings when the Freedmen's Bank failed. "I will leave it all in God's hand. If the Yankees did take all our money, they freed my race; God will take care of us."[49]

Just a few short years after the Civil War ended, Phoebe Rutledge became a widow. She later reminisced about her husband: "On his deathbed [he] begged me to read the 15th amendment to him & I read it all. He was quite taken with it & thanked God that he lived to see the end of it. He was loyal to the U.S. throughout the war."[50] The roles that black women played during the Civil War—the risks they took, whether carrying bread through back alleys or stashing runaway prisoners in their back rooms, whether by nursing, spying, or teaching—were as risky and significant as the activities of any soldier in the war. African American women were not just victims of the Civil War—they were active participants and valiant fighters.

New information obtained in the past ten years via a more thorough and comprehensive search of the records along with the "historical detective work" reported here has given us a far more complete picture of the roles of women in the American Civil War. The findings have allowed correction of some past errors, elucidated many previously garbled or incomplete stories, and discovered more examples of women active in the war. Women's participation in the war is now seen to have been on a far larger scale than previously believed.

Rich and poor, educated and uneducated, black and white, women from all walks of life performed military service in the war. They marched and fought as infantry soldiers, cavalry troopers, and artillerists. They performed as spies, scouts, couriers, detectives, and saboteurs. Additionally, women became frontline and battlefield nurses in large numbers for the first time in American history.

How did this come about? It is now apparent that the social reform movement that was under way early in the nineteenth century, partly fueled by women's desire for more freedom and independence, laid the groundwork for a quiet revolution. The mores of society dictated that women confine themselves to home, family, and church. Men headed the families, voted, participated in politics, and fought wars. Though women had made some progress toward equality by midcentury, they remained subordinate to men for most practical purposes. When the war inadvertently created a need for large armies and vast numbers of medical care personnel on an unprecedented scale, women were ready and willing to fill the gaps and seized the opportunities.

Ironically, the war otherwise stalled the momentum of the women's movement, dissipating its energies in the enormous task of fulfilling the immediate needs of the war effort. The overall impact of the war on Northern and Southern society was overwhelming. It was like a hurricane that brings all other human

Honor Roll of Civil War Service

Women Known to Have Served

In the cases of women whose identities are known and who have been assigned to the Honor Roll, there is little or no doubt of actual military service even though some details of their records may be questioned. Apocryphal cases have been excluded from this list (see Chapter 8).

These are among the more compelling stories of women serving as soldiers, nurses, spies, or scouts during the Civil War. Clearly, they were soldiers in the fullest sense of the word. Those who served as combat soldiers in male disguise were willing to fight incognito and to risk life and limb in the process, and so cannot be accused of having selfish or frivolous motives. The records of the women who otherwise soldiered with the men speak for themselves.

Following in alphabetical order by last name is as complete a list of known female soldiers or nurses who fit the stated criteria, North and South, as could be compiled on the basis of current information. The high percentage of casualties among these women is due to the fact that so many were only discovered to be female as a result of being wounded or killed.

Key to Symbols

† = wounded, killed in action, or died of service-related illness

ᴾ = prisoner of war

() = provisional status (questionable authenticity, additional documentation needed)

ALLEN, Mrs. Patrick (nee Mary Wilson). Union spy arrested in Richmond, Virginia, July 24, 1863, for transmitting Confederate military information to the Federal government. Damning correspondence was found in her possession. She was committed to the care of the Sisters of Charity asylum and kept under surveillance *(Weekly Columbus Enquirer,* Georgia, July 28, 1863; from the *Richmond Examiner).*

ATWOOD, Nancy M. (later Mrs. Nancy M. Gross). A widow working as a seamstress at the outbreak of the war, she became a regimental nurse with the 6th Maine Infantry. She lived in a tent while in camp, and was exposed to hardships and dangers. Marched with the soldiers and cared for the wounded in the field and in hospitals. She was granted a pension after the war (Holland 1897, 309–311; Sudlow 2000, 59–61).

BAHR, Mrs. John. In the famous Confederate Washington Artillery of New Orleans where her husband was a hospital steward "she bore the hardships of camp life," serving as a nurse and taking care of the wounded soldiers. With the approval of the colonel, she wore the uniform of a vivandiere (Larson 1992, 44; Lonn 1940, 379–380).

BAKER, Mrs. E. H. "One of the more adept female agents" employed by Allan Pinkerton, she was sent to Richmond as a spy to inspect the iron works and fortifications. Due to her social connections in that city, she also was able to witness a test of a Confederate submarine at the Tredegar Iron Works and report back on its characteristics. Her report alerted U.S. Navy ships to an unsuspected threat (Pinkerton 1883, 396–403; Kane 1954, 71–74; Markle 1994, 171–173; Axelrod 1992, 160–161).

BARLOW, Arabella Griffith (Mrs. Francis C.). [†] Campaigned with her officer husband, Francis C. Barlow, in the 61st New York Infantry and served as a nurse in the Sanitary Commission. Cared for wounded and sick soldiers at Harrison's Landing during July 1862. Also at Belle Plains, Fredericksburg, and elsewhere in 1863 and 1864. Her health impaired from her labors, she died of fever in Washington, D.C., on July 27, 1864[1] (Brockett and Vaughan 1867, 225–233).

BARRON, Lucy Fenman. Enlisted as a regimental nurse in the 111th Pennsylvania Infantry, serving in Pennsylvania, Maryland, and West Virginia. She came under enemy fire in West Virginia and often experienced the hardships of field service, once forced to live under Confederate occupation, and hospitalized for typhoid fever. She survived it all and retired to Eureka, California.[2]

BARTON, Clara. Cared for wounded soldiers on several battlefields, including Antietam and Fredericksburg, while exposed to enemy fire and extreme hardship conditions. She performed extraordinary labors for the soldiers both during and after the war. Her almost superhuman efforts to keep track of individual casualties at Andersonville and elsewhere, and to help families locate missing soldiers, are legendary (see Chapters 2 and 7).

BAXLEY, Mrs. Catherine V. [P] Served as a spy and dispatch carrier for the Confederacy. She was arrested in 1862 at Baltimore while carrying correspondence and documents concealed in her clothing and incarcerated at Old Capitol Prison in Washington. Baxley was deported to the south along with Rose Greenhow. In 1865 she was arrested again and imprisoned in Washington.

BEAN, Mollie (alias "Melvin Bean"). [†][P] Reported to have served in the 47th North Carolina Infantry for about two years and was wounded twice. She was arrested on February 17, 1865, and taken to Richmond for questioning and imprisoned in Castle Thunder (see Chapter 7).

BEATTIE, Katie. A noted Confederate saboteur, smuggler, and spy in Missouri who helped prisoners to escape and burned Federal boats and warehouses. She became a local heroine for her resistance to "Yankee invaders" (Massey 1966, 105; Leonard 1999, 72).

BEERS, Fannie. Nurse and wife of a Confederate soldier who served in the 1st Louisiana Infantry Battalion, she overcame prejudices against female nurses and became a hospital matron. She experienced extreme hardship conditions in the field, was exposed to enemy fire, and treated wounded soldiers under makeshift circumstances and on the battlefield (see Chapter 2).

BELL, Mary (alias "Tom Parker"). [P] See Molly Bell.

BELL, Molly (alias "Bob Morgan"). [P] Molly and Mary Bell were cousins who served together as Confederate soldiers, first in a cavalry company and then in the 36th Virginia Infantry, including extensive combat experience. Molly attained the rank of corporal. When they were discovered in the ranks, Gen. Jubal Early suspected that they were prostitutes and sent them to Richmond where they were imprisoned for three weeks, then sent home (see Chapter 3).

BENNETT, Mrs. Alice Gordon. [P] Confederate woman arrested as a spy while attempting to pass through Union lines near Louisville, Kentucky, in September 1864. She was sent to New Orleans for trial (see Chapter 7).

BICKERDYKE, Mrs. Mary A. ("Mother Bickerdyke"). Served as a nurse both in hospitals and in the field and cared for wounded soldiers at Fort Donelson, Shiloh, and Vicksburg. Bickerdyke stopped at nothing to obtain necessary supplies for the wounded, including the bending and breaking of army regulations. She was highly respected by Generals Grant and Sherman, who tended to give her whatever she requested.[3]

BLACK, Sarah Ann. Free black woman in Georgia who defied Confederate authorities (see Chapter 10).

BLALOCK, Malinda (Sarah Malinda Pritchard Blalock; alias "Samuel Blalock"). [†] Served in 26th North Carolina Infantry posing as her husband's brother, including combat. In March 1862 Malinda was wounded in the shoulder and discovered to be a woman. Later the couple served as Federal partisans and guerrillas (see Chapter 3).

BOND, Ellen. See Bowser, Mary Elizabeth.

BOND, Mrs. Susan. An official army scout employed by the Union in Missouri late in 1864, as documented by government records (Leonard 1999, 231, *Official Records of the Union and Confederate Armies*, Series 1, Vol. 41, Part 4, 512).

BOWEN, Mary. Wife of Confederate General John Bowen; lived in St. Louis, Missouri, under Federal martial law in 1863. She also was with her husband in Vicksburg while under siege from Grant's army. Traveling to Atlanta after her husband's death, she and her children were forced to flee from Sherman's advancing army (see Chapter 7).

BOWSER, Mary Elizabeth (a.k.a. Ellen Bond). Black servant woman in the household of Jefferson Davis who acted as a spy for Elizabeth Van Lew (see Chapter 10).

BOYD, Belle. ᴾ One of the most famous Confederate spies, whose escapades have spawned an extensive literature. She used "feminine wiles" and native shrewdness to extract military information from Union officers (see Chapter 5).

BRADBURY, Sarah (alias "Frank Morton"). Served in two regiments of Union cavalry and one infantry regiment until exposed along with another woman while on duty in General Phil Sheridan's command as cavalry escort. Her sworn statement after exposure says that she served successively in the 7th Illinois Cavalry, Company C; the 22nd Illinois Infantry; and the 2nd Kentucky Cavalry (see Chapters 4 and 9 and Appendix B).

BRADLEY, Amy M. Served in the field as a nurse with the 3rd and 5th Maine Infantry regiments in 1861, living in a tent and subsisting on army food. She also served as superintendent of nurses on Hospital Transport Service ships during the 1862 Virginia Peninsula Campaign and assisted with several amputations. She continued in hospital service as a U.S. Sanitary Commission agent until the end of the war (Moore 1866, 415–452; Brockett and Vaughan 1867, 212–224; Cashman 1990; Greenbie 1944, 165–168; Sudlow 2000, 47, 65–71).

BRADY, Mrs. Mary A. † A founder of the Soldiers' Aid Association of Philadelphia, she first participated in local hospital work. In 1863–1864 she visited field hospitals and helped care for wounded from the battlefields of Chancellorsville and Gettysburg. Brady was exposed to enemy fire and extremes of weather during the 1864 Virginia battles, and acquired a heart condition that restricted her activities. She died May 27, 1864, from ensuing complications (Brockett and Vaughan 1867, 647–649).

BRANCH, Mrs. Charlotte S. She had three sons in the Confederate army and served as a nurse on the battlefield and in field hospitals, finally becoming a refugee fleeing Sherman's army late in the war (see Chapter 2).

BRECKINRIDGE, Margaret E. [†] Served as a volunteer nurse in field hospitals in Kentucky and Missouri and on hospital boats on the Mississippi River, transporting sick and wounded soldiers north from the battlefields. During these trips the boats were endangered by Confederate guerrillas and had some narrow escapes. Weakened and exhausted by her labors and exposure to contagious illnesses, she died July 27, 1864.[4]

BRECKLIN, Sophronia E. See Bucklin, Sophronia E.

BROMFIELD, Rachel. Black woman in Georgia who at great personal risk helped Union prisoners to escape (see Chapter 10).

BROWN, Harriet (alias "Harry Brown"). Served in an Illinois regiment for three months before being discovered. She was arrested at a Union depot in soldier's uniform en route from Lexington, Kentucky, to Chicago and assigned to serve as a nurse in a hospital (see Chapter 6).[5]

BROWN, Mrs. Josephine Lovett. Wife of Confederate operative Robert W. Brown, she reportedly was a highly effective Confederate agent and courier in 1864 and 1865 (Tidwell 1988, 406–407).

BROWN, Kate. See Slater (or Slator), Mrs. Sarah.

BROWN, Mary A. Enlisted in male disguise in the 31st Maine Infantry with her husband and served with him at the siege of Petersburg, Virginia, in January 1865. When discovered, she continued with the regiment as a nurse (see Chapter 3).

BROWNELL, Kady (Mrs. Robert S). [†] Enlisted with her husband in the 1st Rhode Island Infantry and 5th Rhode Island Infantry/Heavy Artillery. She was a color bearer at First Bull Run, where she was slightly wounded in the leg. Daughter of the Regiment in the 5th Rhode Island and in action at New Bern, North Carolina (see Chapter 2 and Appendix B).

BUCKLIN, Sophronia E. (given as Brecklin in some sources). Served as a hospital nurse in Washington, D.C., at Point Lookout, Maryland, at a Gettysburg field hospital, and at White House Landing, Virginia, sharing the hardships of military life.[6]

BUCKNER, Louisa. [P] Confederate smuggler, arrested and found to have more than 100 ounces of quinine sewed in her skirt, some Confederate mail intended for Richmond, and a letter in secret cipher concealed in her petticoat. She was incarcerated in Old Capitol Prison in Washington, D.C. (Massey 1966, 105–106; *Peoria Morning Mail,* Illinois, November 6, 1862, attributed to the *New York Times* special correspondent in Washington, D.C.).

BUDWIN, Florena. [p†] Served in male disguise with her husband in a Pennsylvania regiment until captured and imprisoned with him in Andersonville, where he died. She became ill and later died in another prison (see Chapter 7).

BURGHARDT, Caroline A. From Massachusetts, she served as an army nurse for more than four years. She was among the caregivers at Antietam and Gettysburg. She also served in field hospitals at Fortress Monroe and Winchester, Virginia. After the war she received a "Testimony of Hospital Services" signed by Dorothea L. Dix, Superintendent of Women Nurses. She studied medicine and established a practice in Washington, D.C. (Schultz 2004, 175).

BURNS, Mary ("John Burns"). Enlisted in the 7th Michigan Cavalry to be with her sweetheart. She was discovered in about two weeks and sent home (Massey 1966, 80; Milbrook 1963, 33).

BYRNE, Mrs. ___. A spy apparently throughout the war, active in Missouri during 1864, and personally known to Captain W. T. Leeper, 3rd Missouri State Militia Cavalry. Leeper implied that she had engaged in very dangerous work: "Our good, loyal friend Mrs. Byrne has been a regular spy since the commencement of the war.... [If she] was a man, and guilty of the crimes that she is, he would not live here 24 hours" (Leonard 1999, 230; *Official Records,* Series 1, Vol. 34/2, letter February 1, 1864).

CAMPBELL, Mrs. Anna. A Union heroine and military courier in northern Alabama. She once rode seventy miles in thirty-six hours to deliver information to a Union general (Massey 1966, 104).

CHADICK, Mrs. Mary Cook. Wife of a chaplain in the 4th Alabama Infantry, she lived under military occupation in Huntsville in 1862, where she pitched in to help wounded Confederate soldiers on a hospital train captured by Union troops. Her group of volunteer nurses also cared for prisoners of war and patients in Union-operated hospitals in a war zone, until all civilians were prohibited from the hospitals. She also sent information about Union military forces to her husband in the field and occasionally smuggled food and supplies to him through Union lines (Sterkx 1962, 13–24).

CHAMBERLAIN, Mary E. (later Mrs. Mary Perkins). Enlisted as a regimental nurse in the 11th Maine Infantry and traveled with the regiment to Virginia, where she served in the brigade hospital. Later worked in Hygeia Hospital at Hampton, Virginia. Also cared for wounded soldiers on hospital ships during the Peninsula Campaign in 1862, and after that in the field hospital near Fortress Monroe. In October 1862 she left the army to go home and care for her only brother, who had been disabled during army service (Holland 1897, 323–325; Sudlow 2000, 77–78).

CHILDERS, Mrs. M. J. Performed secret service work for the Union army in May 1862, for which she was paid $150 (Leonard 1999, 232).

CLAPP, Mrs. Anna L. A former teacher, she served in the Ladies Aid Society of St. Louis visiting hospitals to minister to the needs of soldiers. She delivered medical supplies to the field on a hospital boat after the Battles of Shiloh and Vicksburg and helped care for the wounded on board during the return trip (Brockett and Vaughan 1867, 633–636).

CLAPP, Sarah C. Served openly as a commissioned nurse and assistant surgeon with the 7th Illinois Cavalry for nine months. Long after the war she applied for and received a small pension after obtaining testimony confirming her medical work (see Chapter 4).

CLARK, Jerema. See Munday, Sue.

CLARK, Mary Ann (a.k.a. Amy Clarke, Anna Clark, Mrs. Walter Clark; aliases "Richard Anderson," "Henry Clark"). † ᴾ Enlisted in a Confederate Louisiana cavalry unit and later in the 11th Tennessee Infantry in Braxton Bragg's command. She was severely wounded in action, captured, imprisoned, and later exchanged. Attained the rank of lieutenant (see Chapters 6 and 9 and Appendix B).

CLEMENTS, Mrs. Mary E. Served as a Union secret service agent in Atlanta and in March 1865 applied for payment for services rendered. (Leonard 1999, 233).

COLBURN, Amanda (Mrs. Amanda Farnham). She served as matron of the regiment in her brother's 3rd Vermont Infantry in July 1861. Later appointed a regular army nurse, she continued in service until the end of the war. During the 1862 Peninsula Campaign she marched with the soldiers in the Vermont Brigade, and she was also at Antietam, Chancellorsville, and Gettysburg.[7]

COLLIER, ___. ᴾ A female Union prisoner from East Tennessee identified only as Mrs. Collier was discovered disguised as a man at Belle Island Prison, Virginia, on December 23, 1864 (see Chapter 7).

COLLINS, Sarah. Enlisted with her brother, Mason, in a Wisconsin regiment but was detected in camp and sent home (see Chapter 6).

COLLIS, Septima M. (wife of General Charles H. T. Collis). An officer's wife who followed her husband into the army and participated extensively in camp life in the field under hardship conditions. Her husband enrolled as a captain in 1861, became colonel of the 114th Pennsylvania in 1862, was awarded the Medal of Honor for his actions at Fredericksburg in December 1862, and by war's end had been breveted a major general (Collis 1889; Civil War Database regimental roster).

COMPTON, Lizzie (Elizabeth). † Enlisted in one regiment after another and was repeatedly discovered but persisted and saw a lot of action. She was wounded by shrapnel at Fredericksburg in 1862. In spring 1863 she was arrested in Louisville while serving in a Minnesota regiment. She also served in the 11th Kentucky Cavalry and the 125th Michigan Cavalry and received a shoulder wound that led again to her discovery (see Chapters 6 and 9 and Appendix B).

COOK, Mrs. Betsey A. Joined her husband's 2nd Illinois Cavalry regiment as a nurse in 1861 and served in the field, living in tents and sharing the hardships of camp life. Also worked in a hospital on Island No. 10 in 1862 and 1863 (Holland 1897, 357–359).

COOK, Lizzie. Iowa girl who tried to enlist at St. Louis to join her brother in the army, but her mannerisms gave her away. She admitted to a Missouri newspaper that her decision to join the army was largely due to the monotony of a woman's life; that is, she sought some adventure (see Chapter 6).

COOK, Mary A. (♀ Discovered in the ranks of the 2nd Kentucky Cavalry, she was reported to have enlisted in the army along with three other women, two of whom were serving together in an infantry regiment.[8]

CORBIN, Mary. Discovered in uniform in the 89th Ohio Infantry and discharged (see Chapter 6).

COX, Lucy Ann. Vivandiere and nurse in the 13th Virginia Infantry, where she served along with her husband. She marched with the soldiers, including their two invasions of Maryland in Lee's army, and nursed wounded soldiers during combat. After the war she was buried with military honors (see Chapter 2).

COX, Susan. A regimental nurse with the 83rd Illinois Infantry, she served at Fort Donelson where the regiment was engaged in almost daily skirmishes with the enemy. She was exposed to enemy fire and the hardships of camp life while caring for sick and wounded soldiers. When on one occasion the fort was attacked, "the Northern women were ordered on board a boat that was to drop down the river. While on the way to the landing the shot and shell were flying all around us, and I saw one of our boys lying dead, having been fearfully mangled" (Holland 1897, 313).

CRYDER, Sophia. Enlisted in Company A of the 11th Pennsylvania Infantry in 1861 as a young teenager. Two men showed up at camp one day looking for her, apparently sent by her family. She was found on guard duty and discharged (see Chapter 9).

CUMMING, Kate. Born in 1835 in Scotland, she emigrated to Canada with her family as a child. The family then settled in Mobile, Alabama. Her brother enlisted in the 21st Alabama Infantry and she became a volunteer field nurse in 1862, traveling to battle areas to care for the wounded. Her conscientious work was accomplished under extreme hardship conditions, including sometimes sleeping on floors and subsisting on army food. She persisted in service to the end of the war (see Chapter 1).

CURTIS, Sallie. After serving for twenty months in an Indiana regiment, she was discovered and summarily discharged. She reenlisted in the Union 2nd Kentucky Heavy Artillery, but was discovered after one week and again discharged (see Chapter 6).

CUSHMAN, Pauline. [†] [p] Well-known actress who became famous as a Federal spy, scout, and courier, sometimes dressed in male clothing. Twice imprisoned by Confederates in 1863, she managed to escape. She is reported to have been wounded twice while engaging in secret service missions. In consideration of her long and arduous duties for the Union, the army conferred upon her the rank and title of major.[9]

CUSTIS, Mrs. ____. A daughter of the regiment from Rochester, New York, who was captured wearing quasi-military attire and detained by Confederates in Richmond (see Chapter 7).

CUTTER, Carrie E. [†] Went to war from Warren, Massachusetts, as a nurse along with her father, Calvin Cutter, who was surgeon of the 21st Massachusetts Infantry. She died of unspecified causes while on duty with the regiment during the New Bern, North Carolina, campaign (online town history at http://www.samnet.net/esso/CWV.htm).

DABNEY, Mrs. A black couple by the name of Dabney served as spies for the Union (see Chapter 10).

DADA, Harriet A. [p] An army nurse from New York State, she served in military hospitals around Washington, D.C., in 1861, in field hospitals throughout Virginia in 1862 and 1863, at Gettysburg after the battle in July 1863, and in the Tennessee campaigns in 1864 (see Chapter 2).

DAME, Harriet P. She went to war with the 2nd New Hampshire Infantry and served throughout the war as a field nurse while traveling with the regiment. She also served in field hospitals at First Bull Run in 1861; Fair Oaks, Virginia, in 1862; and Gettysburg in 1863. She was once captured during a battle, but promptly released (see Chapter 2).

DARLING, Mrs. Mary E. Became a regimental nurse in her husband's Missouri Home Guard unit that was mustered into U.S. service in December 1861. She traveled with the regiment and cared for soldiers in tents and field hospitals and in the division hospital near the Shiloh battleground.[10]

DAVIDSON, Catherine E. † Enlisted in the 28th Ohio Infantry in male disguise, she was severely wounded at Antietam in September 1862 and her arm was amputated (see Chapter 9 and Appendix B).

DAY, Frances (alias "Frank Mayne"). † Enlisted in the 126th Pennsylvania infantry to be with her sweetheart but deserted after he died. Later she reenlisted and was discovered when mortally wounded in a western battle. Attained the rank of sergeant (see Chapter 7).

DEMING, Mrs. L. L. Daughter of the Regiment and nurse for the 10th Michigan Infantry, she served along with her husband from the time the regiment was formed until he resigned in late 1862. She wore a uniform in camp, including a haversack, canteen, and belt with revolvers (see Chapter 2).

DENNIS, Mary. She was reported to have been commissioned lieutenant in a Minnesota regiment in 1861 and performed brief service.[11]

DIVERS (DEAVERS/DEVAN/DEVENS), Bridget. She served in the 1864–1865 Virginia campaigns as a battlefield nurse with Sheridan's cavalry, at times participating in battles (see Chapter 2).

DUNBAR, Lois H. Dennett. Cared for the wounded from the battle at Fort Donelson. She also served in a military hospital in Indiana and as a hospital ship nurse on the Ohio and Mississippi Rivers, assisting physicians in many amputations. She was under enemy fire while aboard hospital transport ships (Holland 1897, 295–297).

DUVALL, Betty. Confederate courier for Rose O'Neal Greenhow, she carried cipher messages braided into her hair, including advance warning of General McDowell's advance toward Manassas in July 1861 (Kane 1954, 32–33; Markle 1994, 19, 160).

EATON, Harriet H. A. A widow from Maine, she went into the field to care for soldiers from Maine under extreme hardship conditions, very near the front in the Army of the Potomac. She worked closely with Isabella Fogg, first at Antietam then in Virginia, where she was exposed to enemy fire while caring for wounded soldiers.[12]

EDMONDS, Sarah Emma (alias "Franklin Thompson"). Served for two years in the 2nd Michigan Infantry as soldier, spy, and nurse. After the war when she applied for a pension, her former comrades confirmed her service and she also was admitted to membership in the Grand Army of the Republic (see Chapters 3 and 6).

EDMONDSON, Isabella (Belle; alias "Brodie West"). Confederate agent who engaged in courier work, spying, and smuggling of contraband goods and supplies through the lines in West Tennessee. She openly admitted her smuggling activities in her wartime diary (see Chapter 5).

ELLIS, Mrs. Mary A. Helped her husband raise the 1st Missouri Cavalry regiment (Union) in 1861. She wore quasi-military uniform on occasion while acting as a courier and a detective. Mostly she served as a battlefield nurse, assisting with surgical operations in the field.[13]

EPPING, Mrs. Lewis. Enlisted in male disguise along with her husband in Company G of the Union 2nd Maryland Infantry (see Chapter 3).

ETHERIDGE, Anna (nee Anna Blair). Enlisted as daughter of the regiment in the 2nd Michigan Infantry in the Army of the Potomac, later transferring to the 3rd and 5th Michigan Infantry regiments. She became a battlefield nurse, was under fire on several occasions, and was awarded the Kearny Cross for gallantry. Etheridge continued in service for more than three years (see Chapter 2)

EWBANK, Hannah. () Served as a vivandiere in the 7th Wisconsin Infantry while in camp, but it is uncertain whether she experienced duty in the field (see Chapter 2).

FALES, Almira (Mrs. J. I.). Became a Union field nurse at the outbreak of the war and cared for wounded soldiers both in the eastern and western theaters of war. At Corinth, Pittsburg Landing, and elsewhere in the west she cared for the wounded on the battlefield. She also served on hospital ships during the 1862 Virginia Peninsula campaign, coming under enemy fire, and as a battlefield nurse during several major battles in Virginia (Brockett and Vaughan 1867, 279–283).

FARNHAM, Mrs. Amanda. See Colburn, Amanda.

FAY, Mrs. Delia Bartlett. Served as a regimental nurse in the 118th New York Infantry, where her husband, Willie, had enlisted in Company C. During the Virginia Peninsula Campaign in 1862, she marched with the regiment carrying her own supplies, and at one point acted as a scout to locate the position of Confederate forces.[14]

FEATHERSTONE, Jane. An operative in Ulysses S. Grant's western spy network during the Vicksburg Campaign (Feis 2002, 167).

FERGUSON, Mrs. Jane (alias "John F. Findsley"). P A teenage Confederate girl who enlisted in the 13th Kentucky Cavalry (Union). She was arrested as a suspected spy, and tried in Louisville on November 25, 1863. She admitted to the provost marshal that her husband was a Confederate soldier and was sentenced to be hanged, but the sentence was later reversed (see Chapter 3).

FICKLE, Annie E. P A supporter of William C. Quantrill's Partisan Rangers (guerrillas) in Missouri at age eighteen or nineteen, she was arrested when found in company with one of them but later rescued. She made a battle flag for the guerrillas that they carried into battle. Later she was incarcerated at

Gratiot Prison in St. Louis, sentenced to ten years for her guerrilla activities, and sent to the penitentiary at Jefferson City. She was pardoned by President Abraham Lincoln on January 30, 1865 (Gratiot Prisoner Notes online at http://www.civilwarstlouis.com/Gratiot/; http://www.rulen.com/moflag/).

FIFIELD, Almira. Field nurse with the 9th Indiana Infantry. Schuyler Colfax, congressman from Indiana, is reported to have recommended her to Dorothea Dix in 1861 (Schultz 2004, 126).

FINNERN, Elizabeth. Enlisted with her husband in the 81st Ohio Infantry. After being discovered, she stayed on with the regiment as a nurse, physician's assistant, and general helper, marching with the regiment in the field for three years (see Chapter 3).

FLOYD, Olivia. [P] While her brother served in the Confederate army, Olivia and her mother lived in the Washington area, and she was an active spy transmitting messages and papers to Confederate authorities. A letter implicating her as "engaged in all sorts of disloyal practices" was intercepted by Federal authorities, and she was ordered to be arrested and imprisoned (Larson 1993, 57–58; Leonard 1999, 67–68; *Official Records*, Series 2, Vol. 4, 1862).

FOGG, Isabella M. [†] Cared for wounded in the field after the battles of Fredericksburg, Chancellorsville, Gettysburg (on July 4, one day after the battle ended), and on the Virginia Peninsula, while exposed to frequent hardships and dangers. She came under enemy fire at Chancellorsville and suffered a crippling injury in a fall on a hospital ship (see Chapter 2).

FORD, Antonia J. [P] An aristocratic young woman of Fairfax, Virginia, she served as a Confederate intelligence operative and a collaborator and guide for John Singleton Mosby in 1863. When a Union general was captured by surprise in his quarters, she was implicated in the plot and was arrested and confined in the Old Capitol Prison in Washington, D.C. At that time she was discovered to be carrying $1,000 in Confederate money (see Chapter 5).

FOSTER, Augusta M. Served as a battlefield nurse while nominally a Daughter of the Regiment, probably for the 5th Maine Infantry in which her husband, Charles, served. She had her horse shot out from under her at First Bull Run and continued as a field nurse after the battle (Young 1959, 125; Sudlow 2000, 104–106).

FOSTER, Harriet. After the battle at Corinth, Mississippi, Harriet Foster of Florence, Alabama, gathered a supply of bandages and other medical supplies and left for the front. She found a hospital for the wounded Confederates at Iuka, and volunteered as a nurse, spending three months caring for the soldiers (*Savannah Republican,* Georgia, March 5, 1863, report from Columbia, Tennessee, February 27, 1863).

FOWLE, Mrs. Elida Rumsey. See Rumsey, Elida B.

FRANCES, Eliza (alias "Frank Glenn"). Arrested in camp of 1st West Virginia Cavalry at Harpers Ferry in soldier uniform (see Chapter 4).

FRANCES, Kate (alias "James Johnson"). Arrested along with Eliza Frances in 1st West Virginia Cavalry (see Chapter 4).

FRUSH, Mrs. Mary Alice. See Smith, Mary Alice.

FYFE, Jennie. A U.S. Sanitary Commission nurse from Michigan, she was stationed at a hospital in Paducah, Kentucky, where battles were raging around her and contingency plans were made for the possibility of Confederate capture of the hospital. Nathan Bedford Forrest's guerrillas once plundered the hospital supplies.[15]

GALLOWAY, Mary. † Female soldier in male disguise wounded in the chest during the Battle of Antietam at Sharpsburg, Maryland, in September 1862. A physician trying to treat her wound suspected that the soldier was female and referred her to Clara Barton, who confirmed his suspicions and took the young woman under her wing (see Chapter 7).

GATES, Edmonia. Enlisted in the 121st New York Infantry, where she served both as a teamster and as a drummer boy (see Chapter 3).

GEARY, Elizabeth. Free black woman in Georgia who took risks to help Union soldiers (see Chapter 10).

GEORGE, Mrs. Eliza E. † A nurse from Fort Wayne, Indiana, she first worked in a Memphis, Tennessee, hospital in spring 1863. Then she followed the army to Chattanooga and was present during Sherman's spring 1864 campaign into Georgia. "During the battle of Jonesboro, she was dressing the wounded in a tent so near the front as to be in range of the enemy's guns." Later she succumbed to typhoid fever acquired during her army labors.[16]

GIBSON. A mother and daughter pair, Mrs. and Miss Gibson were arrested by Union cavalry near Cassville, Missouri, in 1864 while attempting to cut the Federal telegraph wires (see Chapter 5).

GIBSON, Elizabeth O. Worked as a nurse in military hospitals in several states and cared for wounded at the battlefields of Shiloh and Vicksburg. While evacuating wounded from Vicksburg, the hospital ship she was serving on came under fire, but the passengers and crew escaped unharmed (Holland 1897, 387–388).

GIBSON, Ella H. Elected as chaplain of the 1st Wisconsin Heavy Artillery in 1864 and served in that position for nine months. Mary Massey refers to her as Ella Hobart and reports that after the war she lectured in the North and in September 1865 addressed a large audience at the Cooper Union in New York City, the famous venue of an early address by Abraham Lincoln (Wiley 1952, 337, from National Archives records; Massey 1966, 86).

GILSON, Helen L. Worked as a Hospital Transport Service nurse under the auspices of the Sanitary Commission on the Virginia Peninsula in June 1862. Arrived at Antietam within a few hours after the battle in September and also served as a nurse in camps and hospitals at Fredericksburg in December. Then in the following spring she cared for the wounded from the Battle of Chancellorsville and at Gettysburg a few hours after the last day's fighting there.

GODDARD, Mrs. Abba A. Went into the field in 1861 with the 10th Maine Infantry and served as a nurse in the regimental hospital. She was active in procuring supplies for the sick and wounded soldiers. At Harpers Ferry she was forced to flee when Confederate cavalry attacked. Later she acted as a nurse at Virginia and Pennsylvania field hospitals (Sudlow 2000, 109–115).

GOLDSBOROUGH, Euphemia ("Effie") M. A small, slender Baltimore girl, she served as a volunteer field nurse following the Battles of Antietam and Gettysburg. A Federal inspection of her house in November 1863 disclosed supplies and correspondence intended for Confederates; she was arrested, questioned, and then banished to the South for the duration of the war. During her trip to Richmond she managed to carry several confidential dispatches to Confederate headquarters (Davis 1968).

GRAHAM, Catherine (Mrs. Michael). She was employed along with her husband by General Robert Milroy as a Union spy in Virginia. An 1863 incident in which she traveled with and exposed two Confederate female spies was reported in a contemporary newspaper (Fishel 1996, 304; *Spectator,* Staunton, Virginia, July 7, 1863).

GRAVES, Nellie. See Wilson, Fanny.

GRAY, Martha. Served with the 54th Massachusetts Infantry, the famous "Glory" regiment of black soldiers: "I consider myself a worn out soldier of the U.S. I was all around the South with the regiment administering to the wants of the sick and wounded and did have the name of the Mother of the Regiment" (*Journal of the Afro-American Historical and Genealogical Society,* Spring/Summer 1991: 33).

GREEN, Marian. Enlisted in male disguise in the 1st Michigan Engineers and Mechanics along with a male friend. When he became ill, she took care of him in the hospital but was exposed and sent home. Later they were married (see Chapter 3).

GREEN, Mary Jane. ᴾ Served as a spy for Confederate guerrillas and as a saboteur in male disguise. She was arrested at least seven times, then incarcerated at Old Capitol Prison in Washington, D.C., for the duration of the war (see Chapter 7).

GREENHOW, Rose O'Neal. ᴾ Operated an extensive, sophisticated, and successful Confederate spy ring in Washington, D.C., mainly in support of the Army of Northern Virginia. She was arrested and incarcerated at Old Capitol Prison and deported to the South in 1862 (see Chapter 5).

GREGG, Jennie R. () According to discharge papers in a private collection, Sergeant Jennie R. Gregg, 128th Ohio Infantry, was discharged at Johnson's Island prison camp where members of the regiment were guards. The discharge paper says she was twenty-two, four feet ten inches tall, dark complexion, black eyes, auburn hair. Her civilian occupation is given as "Lady."[17]

GUERIN, Elsa J. (alias "Charles Hatfield"). ✝() Reportedly served in an Iowa cavalry regiment, was an orderly and occasional spy. She was once wounded and captured during a cavalry charge but later released and promoted to lieutenant (see Chapter 4).

HALL, Maria M. C. A native of Washington, D.C., she was too young to meet Dorothea Dix's requirements for army nurses and so volunteered independently for hospital work. She served on a hospital transport ship on the Virginia Peninsula and assisted a surgeon at Antietam in caring for wounded Confederate soldiers for more than a week. Despite her youth, she was later appointed superintendent of a hospital at Annapolis, Maryland, where emaciated soldiers released from Andersonville Prison were nursed back to health (Moore 1866, 397–408; Sifakis, *Who Was Who in the Union*, 1988, 171; Schultz 2004, 221–223).

HANCOCK, Cornelia. A young Quaker woman, she served as a volunteer nurse in field hospitals and on battlefields and "soldiered" with the men even in winter quarters. She was one of the first nurses to arrive at the Gettysburg and Fredericksburg battlefields. She slept in a tent, was exposed to the elements, and subsisted on army food (Jaquette 1956; Brockett 1867, 284–286; Greenbie 1944, 172–173; Culpepper 1991, 23–24, 329–330).

HANES, Althea F. ᴾ Union spy arrested in Columbia, S.C., and sent to Castle Thunder prison, Richmond, Va., in July 1864 (*Richmond Sentinel*, July 20, 1864).

HANSON, Katie. Joined an Ohio regiment in 1861. She had lived as a man prior to the war and worked on a Great Lakes steamboat. In the army she rose to the rank of sergeant. When discovered, she was discharged and became a nurse (Blanton and Cook 2002, 39, 43, 72, 118).

HARKIN, Mrs. M. V. Went to war in 1862 as a nurse with the 17th Wisconsin Infantry along with her mother, Mrs. Sarah A. M. Kenna. They traveled by steamer to Pittsburg Landing and helped care for the wounded from the Battle of Shiloh. The steamer was used as a hospital, and tents were pitched in the field. Mrs. Harkin once barely avoided capture by the enemy in the vicinity of Corinth. She also served in various other field hospitals (see Chapter 2).

HARRIS, Eliza A. (Mrs. John Harris). Wife of a physician, she risked her life and health repeatedly while caring for soldiers in dangerous circumstances on or near the battlefields and on Hospital Transport Service ships. Arriving the day after the battle at Antietam, she cared for the wounded there for over a month. She also served in field hospitals at other major battle sites. Though not a robust person herself, she gave yeoman service in the army, assisting physicians with amputations and pitching in to care for the most morbidly ill soldiers (Moore 1866, 176–212; Brockett and Vaughan 1867, 149–160; Greenbie 1944, 132–133, 159–161).

HARRIS, Fanny. A girl from Indiana who, according to a newspaper story, served as a drummer boy and was said to have been in close to a dozen battles. When discovered in fall 1864, she was discharged and sent home (Blanton and Cook 2002, 71, 113).

HART, Jennie D. Orderly sergeant of Company D, Jenkins's Cavalry (probably a Virginia regiment); according to a newspaper story, she was discovered to be a woman and arrested about April 1, 1863, in Fayetteville, Virginia.[18]

HART, Nancy. ᴾ A young Virginia girl who served as a guide for Stonewall Jackson's cavalry. In 1861 and 1862 she led soldiers in raids on Federal outposts. The Union offered a reward for her capture, and in July 1862 she was captured. But she quickly escaped and later led Confederate soldiers in a raid during which the Union colonel who had captured her was, in turn, seized and imprisoned (see Chapter 5).

HARVEY, Mrs. Cordelia A. P. When her husband, the governor of Wisconsin, was killed in an accident while visiting the soldiers at the front in 1862, she determined to go into hospital service. She first worked in hospitals at St. Louis and Cape Girardeau, Missouri, then at many field hospitals along the Mississippi River and at Wisconsin regimental hospitals. She was instrumental in establishing a military hospital in Madison, Wisconsin, and in providing aid to soldiers' orphans after the war (Brockett and Vaughan 1867, 260–268).

HAYS, Molly. See Mary Ann Pitman.

HENRY, Margaret. ᴾ Captured by Federal troops near the end of the war along with another female soldier in Confederate uniform, she was imprisoned at Nashville (see Chapter 7).

HENSLEY, Mary Jane. She was hired as a Union army spy in Springfield, Missouri, in August 1864, and given a horse for her personal use. The government paid her $5 per day (Leonard 1999, 232).

HEWITT, Ada M. See Morris, Augusta H.

HIGGINS, Bridget. ᴾ Went into military service with her husband in a Confederate artillery company and was taken prisoner with him in April 1862 after the battle for Island No. 10 (see Chapter 7).

HILL, Mary S. Followed her brother to war in an unnamed Confederate regiment and served as a vivandiere. She later became a hospital matron for Louisiana soldiers during the Seven Days Battles around Richmond, Virginia, in 1862. Confederate President Jefferson Davis once sent her to Europe on a diplomatic mission (Lonn 2002, 375, 378, 380).

HINSDALE, Jane. ᴾ Enlisted as a regimental nurse in the 2nd Michigan Infantry along with her husband, Hiram H. Hinsdale, and was captured by Confederate forces at the Battle of First Bull Run. She escaped and continued as a nurse for the duration of the war (see Chapter 2).

HOBART, Ella. See Gibson, Ella H.

HOBBS, Clarissa (Clara) Gear. According to an online article about Nebraska women in the Civil War, she joined the 12th Iowa Infantry with the knowledge of the colonel; her husband was a private. He was later appointed hospital steward, and she became an army nurse. She was buried with military honors in 1923.[19]

HOBSON, Clara. ᴾ The arrest in Wheeling, Virginia, "a few days ago" of a young woman in military uniform was reported by the *New Orleans Daily Picayune,* January 18, 1865. She gave her name as Clara Hobson and said she was from Jeffersonville, Indiana, and had served in the army for two years without being detected. "The straight-laced magistrate," said the newspaper, "cruelly sent her to jail for thirty days."

HODGE, Lizzie. Arrested in Bowling Green, Kentucky, in army uniform and brought before the provost marshal in Nashville (see Chapter 7).

HODGERS, Jennie (alias "Albert Cashier"). An Irish immigrant, she served a complete three-year term of enlistment in the 95th Illinois Infantry disguised as a man, participating in considerable campaigning and combat. Her male disguise remained intact until long after the war when an accidental injury caused her to be exposed (see Chapter 3).

HOFFMAN, Lizzie. Arrested at Alexandria, Virginia, in uniform while boarding a steamer with other members of the 45th U.S. Infantry (Colored). She was a black woman from Winchester, Virginia (see Chapter 10).

HOFFMAN, Louisa. Using the name "John Hoffman," she reportedly enlisted (or tried to) in all three branches of the Union army at different times. Initially she is said to have served in the 1st Virginia Cavalry at First Bull Run and through August 1862, then as a cook in the three-months 1st Ohio Infantry, and finally was arrested after enlisting in Battery C of the 1st Tennessee Light Artillery (Union) in 1864 (see Chapter 6).

HOGE, Jane Currie (Mrs. A. H). An agent for the U.S. Sanitary Commission and close associate of Mary Livermore, she arranged for medical and other supplies to reach the field hospitals, often touring the field hospital circuit. She once helped to improvise a hospital for wounded soldiers on a steamship. At Vicksburg a tugboat was placed at Mrs. Hoge's disposal to visit outlying camps and hospitals. She witnessed combat at Vicksburg and came under enemy fire while visiting Missouri soldiers in a rifle pit at the front (Moore 1866, 346–372; Brockett and Vaughan 1867, 562–576, 610; Faust 1986, 364).

HOLSTEIN, Anna. Saw extensive service along with her husband, William H. Holstein, as a battlefield nurse. They cared for the wounded after the battles at Antietam, Gettysburg, and the later Virginia campaigns, including the Battle of the Wilderness in 1864 (see Chapter 2).

HOOK, Frances (aliases "Frank Martin," "Frank Miller," "Harry Miller," "Frank Henderson," "Frank Fuller," "Harry Fuller"). † Enlisted in six or more infantry and cavalry regiments, mostly from Illinois, joining a new unit each time she was discovered in a previous one. She was wounded in action two or more times (see Chapter 9 and Appendix B).

HOPE, Charlotte (alias "Charlie Hopper").† An account in an 1898 book says that a woman of this name joined the Confederate 1st Virginia Cavalry in the summer of 1861 using the name "Charlie Hopper." She is said to have enlisted to avenge her sweetheart's death in the army. She looked like a young boy, but the captain reportedly knew she was a woman. "Hopper" was reported to have been killed in a raid.[20]

HOPKINS, Juliet Ann. † Wife of an Alabama judge, she served as a nurse for soldiers from her state and established frontline hospitals in Virginia. While aiding wounded Confederate soldiers on the battlefield of Seven Pines (or Fair Oaks) on May 31–June 1, 1862, she was wounded twice.[21]

HORNE, Lucinda. Followed her husband and son into the war from a German settlement in Edgefield County and served as a vivandiere in Company K of the 14th South Carolina Infantry regiment. She was with the regiment during the Virginia Peninsula Campaign in 1862, and at Second Bull Run, Antietam, Fredericksburg, and Petersburg. She stayed with the company throughout the war and was made an honorary member (Lonn 2002, 380; Schultz 2004, 57, 180).

HOWARD, Mrs. Key. P A descendant of Francis Scott Key, she was a Confederate courier who was arrested in 1864 and incarcerated in Old Capitol Prison (H. B. Smith 1911, 92–94).

HOWLAND, Eliza Woolsey. See Woolsey, Eliza N.

HUNT, Satronia Smith. Enlisted in an Iowa regiment with her first husband, who died of wounds. When she was discovered, the captain allowed her to remain with the regiment as a battlefield nurse (Blanton 1993, 28; Blanton and Cook 2002, 117).

HUSBAND, Mrs. Mary Morris. Served as a nurse on Hospital Transport Service ships during the 1862 Virginia Peninsula Campaign. She came under fire when a ship was shelled by Confederate forces. Another time she helped evacuate seriously wounded soldiers north as superintendent of a hospital ship. Later she cared for wounded soldiers from the Antietam battlefield at a field hospital, living in a tent, and at Gettysburg where she arrived on July 4 (Moore 1866, 313–332; Brockett 1867, 287–298).

HYATT, Elizabeth. A nurse who worked in the field with the 4th Wisconsin Infantry, where she was deputized to drive a horse-drawn ambulance (Schultz 2004, 39).

HYDE, Mollie. Major Thomas Hendrickson, commandant of the Union military prison at Alton, Illinois, sent a letter to the Commissary-General of Prisoners in Washington, D.C., on May 20, 1863: "Colonel, I have the honor to report that another female prisoner, a Miss Mollie Hyde, of Nashville, Tenn., has been sent to this prison 'for spying and other misdeeds.' to be confined during the war or until released by competent authority. She was sent here by the order of General Rosecrans." By implication, she was not the first or only female prisoner there (*Official Records,* Series 2, Vol. 5, No. 118).

IBECKER, Elvira (alias "Charles D. Fuller"). Enlisted in Company D, 46th Pennsylvania Infantry, and served for about a month before being discovered. She was known to drink whiskey and chew tobacco. She was discharged early in October of 1861 (see Chapter 3).

IRVIN, Mrs. (alias "Charley Green"). † P An apparently reliable newspaper story in September 1863 reported that a female Confederate soldier using the name "Charley Green" had fought in 13 battles and was wounded once and imprisoned at Alton, Illinois. The story states that she had resumed female apparel and planned to serve as a nurse.[22]

JAMES, Fanny C. ᴾ Arrested as a Confederate spy, she was incarcerated in the Baltimore jail. A letter to her that implicated her in smuggling activities was intercepted by Federal authorities (see Chapter 5).

JAMIESON, Frances (alias "Frank Abel"). ᴾ Served with her husband in a Union cavalry regiment until he was killed at First Bull Run. Then she became a nurse and physician's assistant. Later she acted as a spy for General Banks, at times in male disguise, and was captured on October 1, 1862, by Confederate cavalry and imprisoned in Richmond (see Chapter 5).

JENKINS, Mary Owen (a.k.a. Mary Stevens Jenkins, Mary Owens; alias "John Evans"). ⁺ Although there is confusion about her exact name, all the stories apparently refer to the same person. She reportedly served eighteen months in a Pennsylvania regiment with her husband; she was wounded twice and her husband killed in the same battle. She was discovered to be a woman while in the hospital (see Chapter 9).

JOHNSON, Estelle S. Enlisted as a nurse, along with her sister, Lydia A. Wood, in the 4th Vermont Infantry in 1861 to be with her husband. Traveled with the regiment and lived in tents around Washington, D.C., while exposed to the hardships of camp life. She became matron of a hospital set up in a deserted house where she took care of soldiers of the Vermont Brigade, remaining until March 1862. While there her sister died of typhoid fever, and her husband became severely ill but survived.[23]

JOHNSON, Mrs. Jane Claudia. Assisted her husband in raising, arming, and equipping a company of the 1st Maryland Infantry (Confederate) in 1861. She traveled with the company and served as a nurse in the field until the regiment was disbanded in 1862. When her husband later assumed a new command, she spent another winter with the army as a nurse and helpmeet (Leonard 1999, 148–150).

JOHNSON, Mary Jane. ᴾ Served in the 11th Kentucky Cavalry (Union) for about a year until captured during a battle. While a prisoner of war at Belle Isle Prison, Richmond, Virginia, in 1863, she was discovered to be a woman (see Chapter 7).

JONES, Annie E. ᴾ () Alleged consort of Custer and other Union officers in Washington, D.C., area camps, she was said to have served as a scout and spy, but this is uncertain. She was captured by Federal detectives and incarcerated at Old Capitol Prison, Washington, D.C. (see Chapter 5).

JUDD, Mrs. Clara. ᴾ The widow of an Episcopal clergyman, she served successfully as a Confederate spy and smuggler of medicines in Tennessee early in the war. Eventually she was fooled by a Union counterspy who pretended to be a Confederate agent and was arrested and sent to the Federal prison in Alton, Illinois, arriving there January 23, 1863.[24]

KAISER, Lucy L. Campbell. Volunteered as a Union army nurse in Missouri and Tennessee. She served on a hospital ship carrying soldiers to Pittsburg Landing and in a field hospital tent at Shiloh, where she was exposed to enemy fire. After the battle she helped to evacuate wounded soldiers and cared for them in the field for several days. Later she helped to evacuate wounded soldiers from Vicksburg on a hospital ship (Young 1959, 168–170; Holland 1897, 175–187).

KAMOO, Mrs. Abrev (aliases "Tommy Kamoo," "Thomas H. Kamouse"). Born in Tunis in 1815, she came to the United States in 1862 after having attended the University of Heidelberg and enlisted in the Union army in male disguise. She served as a nurse and drummer and was slightly wounded in the nose at the Battle of Gettysburg. Her female identity was not discovered. She died in Boston in 1904 at age eighty-nine (see Chapter 3).

KELLY, Georgianna. Free black woman in Georgia who aided Union prisoners at great personal risk (see Chapter 10).

KENNA, Mrs. Sarah A. M. See Harkin, Mrs. M. V.

KINSEY, Emma A. B. After the war a man claimed that his ex-wife had been a lieutenant-colonel in the 40th New Jersey Infantry, but the National Archives told him they could find no record of her. Historical evidence suggests the claim may well have been true.[25]

KIRBY, Mrs. William. † ᴾ Smuggled weapons through Federal lines at Baton Rouge, Louisiana. She was caught, convicted as a spy, and imprisoned on Ship Island, where she died near the end of the war. Her son was killed at Gettysburg, but her husband survived the war (see Chapter 5).

KNEELAND, Mary ("Molly"). A widow from Maine living in East Tennessee, she sheltered escaped Union prisoners, acted as a courier, and after a battle in 1864 served as a volunteer nurse caring for wounded Union soldiers (Sudlow 2000, 128–131).

KNOX, Mrs. H. L. ᴾ A story from the *Richmond Whig* stated: "Female Spy.— Mrs. H. L. Knox, of Mobile, Ala., was brought to this city [Richmond] yesterday under arrest, and committed to Castle Thunder as a spy." A follow-up story in April from the *Richmond Dispatch* said that she had subsequently been released on parole and was being kept under surveillance in a hotel pending an examination (*Mobile Register and Advertiser,* March 17, 1864).

LAWTON, Mrs. Hattie. ᴾ An Allan Pinkerton operative (as was her husband, Hugh), she engaged in dangerous spying missions at Richmond. She worked closely with famous Union spy Timothy Webster early in the war, and was arrested and imprisoned with Webster in Richmond in 1862. Webster was hanged as a spy, but Lawton was exchanged and obtained her freedom.[26]

LEE, Fannie. A young woman from Cleveland, she was discovered in male disguise in Washington, D.C., while serving with the 6th Ohio Cavalry in 1864. She asked to be assigned as a nurse to one of the area hospitals, but her request was denied by the irate provost marshal, who sent her home.[27]

LEE, Mrs. Mary W. An immigrant from Great Britain as a child, she had a son in the Union army. At first she worked in a Philadelphia hospital, then went into the field in Virginia and labored on a Hospital Transport Service ship along with Mrs. Eliza Harris. She was among the first on the field after the Battle of Antietam in September 1862 caring for the wounded, and later at Fredericksburg. In 1863 she was at Gettysburg "as soon as the cannon smoke had cleared away" and continued in field hospital service to the end of the war (Moore 1866, 148–169).

LEONARD, Margaret (Mrs. Newton). ᴾ Went to war with her husband as a laundress in the 2nd Massachusetts Heavy Artillery. When their unit was overrun by Confederate forces, she was captured and imprisoned at Andersonville and later at Castle Thunder in Richmond (see Chapter 7).

LEVASAY, Ellen. ᴾ A female soldier with the Confederate 3rd Missouri Cavalry, she was discovered among the troops who surrendered to Ulysses S. Grant's army at Vicksburg, Mississippi, on July 4, 1863. She was held in prison for almost a year (see Chapter 4).

LEWIS, Maria. A black woman who passed for a white male while serving eighteen months in the 8th New York Cavalry, she joined forces with abolitionists in Alexandria, Virginia, in 1865 to assist freed slaves (see Chapter 10).

LILLYBRIDGE, Annie. † Enlisted in the 21st Michigan Infantry to be with her sweetheart. She was wounded in the arm while on picket duty and taken to a hospital in Louisville, Kentucky, where she was discharged by the surgeon due to disability (see Chapter 9 and Appendix B).

LINDLEY, Martha P. (alias "Jim Smith"). Enlisted with her husband in the 6th U.S. Cavalry in 1861, attaining the rank of sergeant. They were in combat together during the Virginia Peninsula Campaign in May–June 1862 (see Chapter 4).

LOCKWOOD, Jenny. Reported to have served in male disguise in the 2nd Michigan Infantry, the same regiment that Sarah Edmonds, Jane Hinsdale, and Annie Etheridge served in. She remained in Washington, D.C., after the war but was poor and in ill health. In October 1866 Lockwood went to authorities for help and her story was reported.[28]

LOOMIS, Mary A. (Mrs. G. W. Van Pelt). Went to war with her husband as a volunteer nurse with the 1st Michigan Light Artillery regiment in May 1861. She served about a year in hospitals in Alabama and Tennessee, and "the remainder of the time I was in camp or on the march with my husband." Captain George W. Van Pelt, her husband, enlisted as a private but was quickly promoted up through the ranks.[29]

LUCAS, Mrs. Elizabeth. Enlisted as a nurse with the 4th Michigan Cavalry, initially to care for her husband who was ill. She went with the regiment to the front, then served in a hospital. While aboard a steamship carrying soldiers from Cincinnati to Louisville, Confederate guerrillas opened fire on the ship from the shore, "breaking windows and frightening everyone generally." The soldiers returned fire and they escaped to safety down river.[30]

MAGRUDER, Mrs. E. J. Wife of a Confederate captain, she worked as a nurse at the First Battle of Bull Run, Virginia (see Chapter 2).

MAINARD, Mary. [P] An operative in Ulysses S. Grant's western spy network, she was arrested and held in a Confederate prison until the end of the war (see Chapter 5).

MALONE, Mary. An operative in Ulysses S. Grant's western spy network during the Vicksburg Campaign (Feis 2002, 167).

MARCUM, Julia. According to notes by historian Ida Tarbell in the National Archives, Record Group 94, Julia Marcum was a female soldier from Kentucky. No details reported.

MARTIN, Annie B. [P] Imprisoned at Alton, Illinois, October 2, 1864. Transferred to Gratiot Prison, St. Louis, Missouri, February 27, 1865, for banishment to the south (provost marshal prisoner roster, Gratiot Prison, St. Louis, Missouri).

MASON, Emily. Helped to establish a Confederate field hospital near Fredericksburg, Virginia, during the Battle of the Wilderness in 1864. She served as a nurse at field hospitals and in private homes (Schultz 2004, 33, 50, 108).

MAYHEW, Mrs. Ruth S. A native of Maine, she served in Union field hospitals caring for sick and wounded soldiers from Maine after the Battle of Gettysburg in July 1863 and at Brandy Station and City Point, Virginia, in 1864. Experiencing all the hardships of field military life, she continued in nursing service near Petersburg, Virginia, until the end of the war (Sudlow 2000, 137–142).

MCCARTY, Mrs. L. A. (alias "John Barton"). [P] Arrested in male disguise in March 1862 while en route to the South carrying contraband ordnance and medicine, she was imprisoned in Washington, D.C. (Leonard 1999, 200–201; Markle 1994, 206; Axelrod 1992, 103).

MCCRERY, Mary (previously reported as "McCreary"). Enlisted as a private with her husband in Company H, 21st Ohio Infantry. After several months she "found herself in a delicate condition," obtained leave from the colonel, went home, and never returned. She was among the numerous female soldiers whose careers were ended by pregnancy.[31]

MCDONALD, Mrs. ___. A newspaper story early in 1862 reported that a young widow named Mrs. McDonald was found in Colonel Boone's regiment (28th Kentucky Infantry, CSA) in male disguise and was discharged. She was said to have enlisted several times previously (see Chapter 6).

MCKAY, Mrs. Charlotte. A widow from Massachusetts, she served in III Corps Hospital, in Falmouth, Virginia, and at field hospitals following the battles of Fredericksburg and Gettysburg. Arriving at the division hospital in Gettysburg on July 7, 1863, she remained almost two months caring for the wounded soldiers. In 1864 she joined many other famous nurses at Belle Plains and City Point, Virginia. She received the Kearny Cross for valor and continued in service after the war in the care and instruction of freed slaves (McKay 1876; Moore 1866, 278–306; Brockett and Vaughan 1867, 514–516; Sudlow 2000, 142–144).

MCKENZIE, Marian (alias "Harry Fitzallen"). [p] When arrested in West Virginia in December 1862, she said that she had served in the 23rd Kentucky Infantry regiment (Union) at the start of the war, and in several other regiments, one of which was said to have been the Confederate 5th Virginia Infantry (see Chapter 7 and Appendix B).

MCLANE, Eliza. Worked as a nurse in Confederate field hospitals in Alabama, Georgia, and Mississippi. An excellent horsewoman, early in 1864 she made a solo trip across Mississippi to central Alabama to obtain badly needed hospital supplies, which she carried back to the hospital in saddlebags through the combat zone. She was present during the Battle of West Point, Mississippi. Later she rode alone 200 miles to her home in Alabama, avoiding Federal soldiers who then were raiding that section of Alabama (Sterkx 1962, 48–52).

MCLELLAN, Emeline. [p] An army nurse from Maine, she served in a field hospital at Winchester, Virginia, in 1862. Taken prisoner during the Battle of Winchester, she was rescued a week later. Afterwards she worked as a nurse at Point Lookout, Maryland, and Washington, D.C. In 1865 she married one of her former patients (see Chapter 2).

MCLURE, Margaret. A resident of St. Louis, Missouri, she used her home on Natural Bridge Road as a rendezvous for Confederate spies and couriers who penetrated Union lines. In May 1863 she was banished from the city by Union authorities (Gerteis 2001, 179).

MCMAHON, Mrs. Anna. † Died of measles contracted while serving as a field nurse at Pittsburg Landing, Tennessee, along with Mrs. M. V. Harkin. She was buried in the field (see Mrs. M. V. Harkin, Chapter 2).

MERRILL, Harriet (aliases "Frederick Woods," "Charles Johnson"). Discovered in Company G, 59th New York Infantry, where she was implicated with an officer in a court martial (see Introduction).

MILLER, Charley (alias "Edward O. Hamilton"). Reported to have served as a drummer boy in the 18th New York Infantry. According to a newspaper story, "From childhood she had chosen to unsex herself and lead a masquerady [sic] life in male garb."[32]

MITCHELL, Sarah E. (alias "Charles Wilson"). P A sixteen-year-old Virginia girl who served as a Confederate soldier and spy, she was captured and incarcerated at Old Capitol Prison, Washington, D.C. (see Chapter 4).

MOON, Charlotte. See Moon, Virginia.

MOON, Virginia ("Miss Ginger," "Ginnie"). P Along with her sister, Charlotte ("Lottie"), she became a Confederate nurse and spy in Memphis, Tennessee, and also acted as a courier and smuggler. She was once arrested and imprisoned in Virginia. Acting as *femmes fatales,* the sisters courted and became engaged to numerous Union soldiers from whom they extracted military information (see Chapter 5).

MOONEY, Molly. A married woman, she was reported to have enlisted in male disguise in the 7th Iowa Infantry. She served for almost six months before being recognized in St. Louis by someone who knew her before the war.[33]

MOORE, Jane Boswell. A young woman from Baltimore, she was a field hospital nurse following the battles of Antietam, Chancellorsville, Gettysburg, and Petersburg, among others. Her memoirs clearly depict the horror and pathos of what battlefield nurses experienced (see Chapter 2 and Appendix B).

MOORE, Mary E. Became a hospital matron for the 58th Illinois Infantry in 1861, sharing the hardships and dangers of the regiment. At Fort Donelson, Tennessee, she "helped to care for the sick and wounded during the battle, and afterwards on a hospital steamer.... At one time [while at Fort Donelson] all the sleep I had for three nights was on the bare floor, between my husband and a sick soldier, and with my husband's arm for a pillow" (Holland 1897, 293).

MORRIS, Augusta (alias "Ada M. Hewitt"). P A paid spy for the Confederacy, she was arrested in Washington on February 7, 1862, for supplying military information about Washington defenses to the Confederacy, and confined in Old Capitol Prison. A fellow prisoner was Rose Greenhow, with whom she had a rivalry. While in prison she wrote to a friend on February 24, 1862, "They arrested a woman in men's clothes and brought her here." Morris suspected she was either a Yankee spy or a plant "to degrade us" (see Chapter 7).

MORRIS, Louisa (alias "William Morris"). A woman named Lou Morris enlisted in two Union Missouri regiments using the name "William Morris." She first served in a cavalry regiment for nine months. Then she enlisted with Jane Short ("Charley Davis") in a Missouri infantry regiment and was not detected until August 1864 (see Chapter 4).

MORRISON, Isadora. ᴾ Reported as "female spy" on provost marshal list of prisoners at Gratiot Prison, St. Louis, Missouri, as of July 12, 1862.

MUNDAY, Sue (alias "Lieutenant Flowers"; a.k.a. Jerema Clark). () A woman in Berry's Confederate guerrilla gang who dressed in male attire in full Confederate uniform. She led the guerrillas in robbing stagecoaches, banks, mail carriers, and toll-keepers. In 1865 her real name was reported to be Jerema Clark. On the other hand, the memoirs of a Confederate Tennessee soldier published online state that "Sue Munday" was a man (*Official Records*, Series 1, Vol. 49/1, No. 103; Kirkland 1867, 596–597; Andrews 1920, 116–119).[34]

MURPHY, Margaret Catherine. () She was reported to have enlisted in the 98th Ohio Infantry with her father, who was the orderly sergeant of the company. She served for six months, attaining the rank of corporal, but was exposed while drunk and arrested in Wheeling, West Virginia, on suspicion of being a Confederate spy. She was shunted from jail to jail, and once was sent south and jailed in Petersburg, Virginia; she was finally incarcerated in Fitchburg, Massachusetts, in December 1863. Her alleged service in the 98th Ohio, or that of her father, could not be confirmed and seems questionable.[35]

MURPHY, Mary Ann (alias "Samuel Hill"; a.k.a. Mrs. Peter Johnson). () Claimed to have served in Company B, 53rd Massachusetts Infantry, with her brother Tom. Her story cannot be confirmed.[36]

MYERS, Mrs. Hester A. Official records show that she was compensated by the Union government on several occasions from April through June 1863 for detective work (Leonard 1999, 232).

NEWSOM, Ella King. A well-to-do widow of a physician, she helped to organize Confederate hospitals in Tennessee and Kentucky in 1861. She then volunteered as a nurse in the field and helped to evacuate and care for wounded soldiers fleeing from Nashville. Newsom also cared for wounded soldiers from the battlefields in field hospitals in Tennessee, Mississippi, and Georgia for several years.[37]

NICHOLS, Elizabeth B. When her husband was captured, then exchanged and was ill, she became a volunteer nurse with his Illinois regiment to take care of him. She then continued on as a field nurse with the regiment, sharing its hardships until her husband was discharged (Holland 1897, 95–98).

NILES, Mrs. Elizabeth A. Previously believed to have fought alongside her husband, Martin, in the 4th New Jersey Infantry, participating in many engagements, and never discovered. She died at age ninety-two. More recently, definitive evidence has been found that she and her husband served in the 14th Vermont Infantry (see Chapter 3).

NUTT, Laetitia LaFon Ashmore. When her husband enlisted in the Confederate army, she followed him around in the field with their three daughters, recording her travels in a diary. Often close to battlefield areas, they experienced the hardships of field life and had several narrow escapes (Culpepper 1991, 277–278).

O'CONNELL, Mary (Sister Anthony). Born in Ireland, educated in Massachusetts, she joined the Catholic Sisters of Charity and was assigned to Cincinnati. Sister Anthony became involved in hospital work, and served in the camps and on the battlefields throughout the war wherever Ohio soldiers were engaged (Sifakis, *Who Was Who in the Union,* 1988, 8–9).

OSTRANDER, Mrs. R. C. Served with her husband in the 1st Michigan Cavalry in 1861, refusing to leave camp. The officers allowed her to remain as a vivandiere (see Chapter 4).

OWENS, Mary (alias "John Evans"). See Jenkins, Mary Owen.

PARSONS, Emily E. Studied to become a nurse in a Massachusetts hospital and in 1862 practiced at Fort Schuyler Hospital, Long Island. She was sent by the U.S. Sanitary Commission to St. Louis as a hospital nurse. There she was placed in charge of the hospital ship *City of Alton* and sent to Vicksburg to pick up 400 sick and wounded soldiers. She became superintendent of nurses at Benton Barracks Hospital, St. Louis (Brockett and Vaughan 1867, 273–278, 382, 489, 502).

PEPPERCORN, Melverina Elverina. One of three sisters in rural Mississippi, with a brother in the Confederate army, who enlisted and saw combat (see Chapter 3).

PERKINS, Sarah Jane. ᴾ While a Confederate prisoner at Point Lookout, Maryland, Federal prison in 1864, she was discovered to be a woman. She was captured on May 27, 1864, while serving with a Virginia artillery unit at Hanover Junction (see Chapter 7 and Appendix B).

PETERMAN, Rebecca (a.k.a. Georgianna). Enlisted in the 7th Wisconsin Infantry as a drummer boy for the first year, then as a soldier and scout. She saw combat at Antietam in 1862. Her "return from the army" to Ellenboro, Wisconsin, in 1864 in "soldier clothes" was reported in the *Platteville Witness,* March 1864. After being discharged she was arrested and hounded by the press while traveling home through Chicago early in 1865.[38]

PETERSON, Belle. () In a postwar (1910) letter, a woman in Ellenboro, Wisconsin, reported that a neighborhood girl by the name of Belle Peterson had enlisted in the army about 1862 and "served in the army for some time, possibly as a spy or scout" (Hurn 1911, 103). This may have been faulty memory with reference to Rebecca Peterman of Ellenboro (see previous entry).

PHELPS, Mary Whitney (Mrs. John S.). A Union loyalist in Missouri, she went into the field with her husband's six-months militia regiment, the Greene Home Guard, late in 1861. After the Battle of Wilson's Creek, in which General Nathaniel Lyon was killed, she protected his body and helped the family arrange to have it shipped home. Her husband, Colonel Phelps, led his regiment into battle at Pea Ridge, Arkansas, on March, 8, 1862. She cared for the wounded while the Battle of Pea Ridge was still going on, tearing up her own clothes to make bandages. Colonel Phelps, a lawyer-politician, became governor of Missouri after the war.[39]

PHILIPS, Bettie Taylor (Mrs. W. S.). She went to war with her husband in the Confederate 4th Kentucky Infantry, experiencing all the hardships of field life and caring for wounded soldiers on the battlefield. Once she was arrested and held as a spy in Nashville (see Chapter 2).

PHILLIPS, Lucinda (Mrs. William). She and her husband jointly performed detective work for the Union in 1864, for which they were compensated (Leonard 1999, 232).

PIGOTT, Emeline. A Confederate nurse and smuggler in North Carolina, she became a courier for the secret service. In 1865 she was arrested at New Bern, North Carolina, but managed to obtain her release (see Chapter 5).

PITMAN, Mary Ann (alias Lt. "Rawley"; a.k.a. "Molly Hays"). Enlisted in a Confederate Tennessee regiment and later as First Lieutenant Rawley in Forrest's cavalry command. She also served as a secret agent and gun runner using the name Molly Hays (see Chapters 4, 5, and 9).

PITT, Mary. [P] A woman from Isle of Wight County, Virginia, she was arrested and sent to Castle Thunder Prison in Richmond, Virginia, in October 1864. The charge: "Being a spy and a suspicious character. She had upon her person several Yankee passes" (*Richmond Whig,* October 31, 1864).

PLUMMER, Judith. She and her sister, Susan, volunteered as army nurses from Maine in 1862, serving in Washington, D.C., Virginia, and at a Gettysburg field hospital in 1863. At the Patent Office hospital in Washington she contracted serious throat problems from sleeping on a stone floor with only a thin blanket for cover, but continued in service until November 1864 (Sudlow 2000, 159–160).

POND, Harriet Stinson. [+] A field nurse from Maine, she was once captured by Confederate forces. While removing wounded soldiers from the battlefield at Antietam in September 1862, she suffered a disabling leg injury in a wagon accident. After the war she received a somewhat larger than typical government pension (Schultz 2004, 189).

POOLE, Ella (Ellie) M. [P] She was arrested in West Virginia on October 6, 1861, as a Confederate spy while carrying concealed documents. A January 1862 Arkansas newspaper reported that she probably would be released from Old Capitol Prison in Washington, D.C., "the government having nothing particular against her, except being a dangerous woman at large. She has conducted herself very quietly and properly since her arrest" (Larson 1993, 63; Axelrod 1992, 64–65, 71; *Daily State Journal,* Little Rock, Arkansas, January 18, 1862).

PORTER, Eliza C. (Mrs. Jeremiah). Her husband was chaplain of the 1st Illinois Light Artillery, and she was a nurse in field hospitals following the Battle of Shiloh and at the hospital of her husband's regiment at Fort Pickering. She organized a school for escaped slaves and their families in Memphis, Tennessee, in 1863, and continued working as a nurse in field hospitals in 1864 and until the end of the war.[40]

PORTER, Sarah L. Volunteered as an army nurse from Bath, New Hampshire, and served from December 1862 until July 6, 1865, at field hospitals in New York, Virginia, and Maryland. She was among the nurses to care for wounded soldiers from the Battle of the Wilderness in May 1864 at Fredericksburg, Virginia (Sudlow 2000, 161).

PRATER, Mary Jane. [P] Arrested in the Kanawha Valley early in 1863 while wearing a Union cavalry uniform, she was sent to jail in Wheeling, West Virginia, under suspicion of being a Confederate spy, but later released without charges and sent to Pennsylvania. Prater returned to West Virginia dressed in male attire and was again arrested, found to be pregnant (March 1863), and sent back to Wheeling. There she had an altercation with a colonel and was jailed for thirty days (Larson 1992, 42; Middleton 1993, 124–125; Blanton and Cook 2002, 120, 122).

PRICE, Elizabeth. A female soldier about twenty-one years old, she was arrested in Louisville, Kentucky, in March 1864, wearing a Union uniform and was taken before the provost marshal. She claimed to be from Cincinnati and to have served two years in the field with an Ohio regiment.[41]

QUINN, Ellen. [P] According to a Recorder's Court case reported in the *Nashville Dispatch*, August 29, 1862, a young woman named Ellen Quinn was arrested on August 27 for being "drunk and disorderly," and two female witnesses were testifying against her. She had been arrested "some months ago" in male attire after having served in male disguise for some months in an Ohio regiment before she was discovered. She had left the army, then reenlisted in another Ohio regiment. In April she was again exposed, arrested, and placed in the workhouse. She remained there until about six weeks before the court session.

RATCLIFFE, Laura. Her home in Fairfax, Virginia, was sometimes used as a headquarters by Colonel John Singleton Mosby of the famous "Mosby's Raiders." Early in the war she is said to have discovered a plan to capture Mosby and alerted him so that he could avoid it. She also is reported to have concealed money and supplies for Mosby and to have used a hiding place in a rock near her home to convey messages and money to him. She also knew and interacted with Confederate Maj. Gen. "Jeb" Stuart, famous cavalry commander (http://womenshistory.about.com).

RENO, Ella. Enlisted in the 5th Kentucky Cavalry (Union) and later labored as a teamster in General Phil Sheridan's army where her sex was discovered. She also served in the 8th Michigan Infantry (see Chapter 9 and Appendix B).

REYNOLDS, Anna. [P] She was arrested and imprisoned in Missouri in 1864 for alleged involvement with a group of Confederate bushwhackers. Her brother, Hedgeman, was a bushwhacker and former Confederate soldier (Missouri State Archives, Provost Marshal Papers, Microfilm Roll F1257; cited on Missouri Secretary of State web site).

REYNOLDS, Mrs. Belle (nee Arabella Macomber). Reynolds enlisted with her husband in the 17th Illinois Infantry, traveling with the regiment. She was under fire at Shiloh, where she performed heroic hospital service as a nurse. The governor of Illinois awarded her the honorary rank of major. She became a doctor after the war.[42]

RHODEN, Charlotte. She was employed as an official Union army detective in Huntsville, Alabama, receiving pay for espionage work in March 1865 on the order of the provost marshal (Leonard 1999, 231).

RICKETTS, Fanny L. (Mrs. James B.). [P] After her husband, a captain, was severely wounded and captured at First Bull Run, she made her way through Confederate lines to join him. Both were confined in Libby Prison at Richmond, where she served as a nurse for the Union prisoners. After they were released she converted her Washington, D.C., home into a hospital and managed the wards until the end of the war (Brockett and Vaughan 1867, 517–519; Kirkland 1867, 536; Dannett and Jones 1963, 14; Parker 1990, 5).

ROGERS, Mrs. Matilda. Received substantial payments from the Union government in March 1864 for secret service activities (Leonard 1999, 232).

ROONEY, Mrs. Rose K. Enlisted in Company K, the "Crescent City Blues," of the 15th Louisiana Infantry as a battlefield nurse and as a hospital matron in New Orleans. The regiment was organized in Richmond, July 25, 1862, from preexisting units. She served throughout the war, remaining with her company until the surrender at Appomattox in 1865 (Beers 1888, 217–220; Simkins and Patton 1936, 75; Jones 1987, 13–14).

ROWELL, Emma C. From Burlington, Iowa, she worked as a Union secret service detective in Memphis, Tennessee, starting in July 1864 (Leonard 1999, 233–234).

RUMSEY, Elida B. (Mrs. Elida Fowle). Too young and attractive to meet Dorothea Dix's standards for army nurses, she volunteered as a hospital worker in Washington, D.C., area hospitals in November 1861. She used her strong singing voice to entertain the soldiers and gave concerts to help raise money for a library and other services. She cared for wounded soldiers in a makeshift hospital near Manassas after the Second Battle of Bull Run and in hospitals in and around Washington, D.C., for three years (Holland 1897, 66–78).

SAFFORD, Mary Jane. One of the earliest volunteer nurses in the west who worked with Mary Ann Bickerdyke in Illinois, caring for wounded soldiers from the Battles of Belmont and Fort Donelson. She searched out wounded soldiers on the battlefield under a personal flag of truce. Safford also worked as a nurse on hospital transport ships and in field hospitals in Tennessee. After the war she graduated from a medical college and opened a medical practice (see Chapter 2).

SAMPSON, Sarah Smith (Mrs. Charles A.L.). She went to war as a nurse with her husband's Company D of the 3rd Maine Infantry regiment, moving from camp to camp with the soldiers. Sampson served in field hospitals and on hospital transport ships in Virginia during the 1862 Peninsula Campaign, at Gettysburg in 1863, and in Fredericksburg after the Battle of the Wilderness in 1864. She is buried in Arlington National Cemetery (MacCaskill and Novak 1996, 51–80; Sudlow 2000, 175–180).

SANCHEZ, Lola. With her brother serving in a Confederate unit and her father imprisoned at St. Augustine on suspicion of spying, Floridian Lola Sanchez spied on visiting Union soldiers and carried vital information to the Confederate camp (Larson 1992, 51; Middleton 1993, 131).

SAWYER, Mrs. Mary E. ᴾ A Confederate spy from Baltimore, Maryland, she was convicted by a military commission of sending letters and contraband through the lines and imprisoned for the duration of the war (*New Orleans Daily Picayune,* August 11, 1864).

SCABERRY, Mary Y. (alias "Charles Freeman"). She was reported to have enlisted as a private in Company F of the 52nd Ohio Infantry at age seventeen. After being hospitalized with fever on November 7, 1862, in Lebanon, Kentucky, hospital personnel discovered she was a woman. She was transferred to a general hospital in Louisville and discharged on December 13, 1862.[43]

SCOTT, Harriet M. Went into the field as a volunteer nurse initially to be with her husband in the 3rd Vermont Infantry. Commissioned as an army nurse by Dorothea L. Dix, she served in hospitals, then as a hospital ship nurse on the Virginia Peninsula, where she was exposed to the threat of enemy sharpshooter fire. In winter 1863 she used an ambulance to take food and drink to wounded soldiers in the field and to pick up the wounded for transport to the ship. One night was spent in the ambulance on the battlefield near the enemy lines (Holland 1897, 563–567).

SHELL, Eleanora. Compensated by the Union government in February 1864 for "special services" ordered by General William T. Sherman (Leonard 1999, 232).

SHORT, Jane (alias "Charley Davis"). † She enlisted in the 6th Illinois Cavalry seeking adventure and was slightly wounded in the hand at Shiloh, April 6–7, 1862. Later she enlisted in the band of a Missouri Union infantry regiment (see Chapter 4).

SIEZGLE (or SEIZGLE), Mary. She was reported to have served as a field nurse, then as a soldier in male disguise in a New York Infantry regiment along with her husband (see Chapter 3).

SIMPSON, Mary (a.k.a. Mary Timms). ᴾ Confederate spy, courier, and smuggler in the vicinity of Fort Pillow, Tennessee. She was arrested and imprisoned when found to be carrying Confederate papers ("The Black-Eyed Smuggler," *Harper's Weekly,* May 14, 1864, reproduced online at http://www.civilwarliterature.com; Frazier 1867, 487–488).

SINNOTTE, Mrs. Ruth H. Served as a nurse on hospital ships on the Mississippi River and as a regimental nurse with the 113th Illinois Infantry, which she accompanied in the field (Holland 1897, 125–130).

SLATER (or SLATOR), Mrs. Sarah (a.k.a. "Kate Brown," "Kate Thompson"). A French-speaking Confederate spy and courier who was acquainted with the Lincoln assassination conspirators, she carried dispatches and money to and from the North and into Canada. At the end of the war she disappeared, very possibly to Europe.[44]

SMALL, Mrs. Jerusha R. [†] Enlisted with her husband in the 12th Iowa Infantry as regimental and battlefield nurse. At Shiloh she succumbed to fatigue and exposure and died at home. She was buried with military honors (see Chapter 2).

SMITH, Adelaide W. At first a hospital nurse in New York, she transferred to field hospital work in July 1864. She worked in hospital tents at Point of Rocks on the Appomattox River, then at City Point Depot Field Hospital for a year, living in tents and subsisting on army food. In November 1864 the tents had floors made with broken boxes and were infested by mice. At times she was exposed to enemy fire and to capture. Her postwar reminiscences contain detailed descriptions of army and hospital life (A. W. Smith 1911).

SMITH, Diana. [P] Soldiered with the 3rd Virginia State Line and Company A (the "Moccasin Rangers") of the 19th Virginia Cavalry, participating in several battles. She was captured five times but escaped from guards each time (see Chapter 4 and Appendix B).

SMITH, Katie (Mrs. Emma Smith Porch). [P] A scout, dispatch carrier, and spy for the Union in late 1864, she later received a government pension. Smith was imprisoned more than once in a period of three months while in the service of the Union Department of the Missouri (Leonard 1999, 235–237).

SMITH, Mary. She enlisted in the 41st Ohio Infantry ("McClellan Zouaves") to avenge the death of her only brother at Bull Run. While at Camp Wood, Ohio, she was found out to be a woman by her mannerisms (see Chapter 6).

SMITH, Mary Alice (Mrs. M. L. Frush). From Greencastle, Pennsylvania; beginning at age eighteen she served for three years as a volunteer nurse in army hospitals and on the battlefields of Antietam and Gettysburg. In December 1864 she married Sergeant M. L. Frush of Company B, 6th Virginia Cavalry.[45]

SMITH, Sarah Jane. A smuggler and saboteur for the Confederacy in Missouri starting at age fourteen, from 1862 to 1864, she once cut four miles of Union telegraph lines. Arrested in 1864, she was sentenced to hang, but General Rosecrans commuted the sentence to imprisonment for the duration of the war (Massey 1966, 105).

SMITH, Sarah Perry (Mrs. Hillman Smith). Enlisted with her officer husband in Company K of the 8th Maine Infantry. She came under enemy artillery fire in South Carolina during the siege of Morris Island in 1863. Mrs. Smith lived in camp with her husband near the front lines and twice encountered Confederate pickets, once having to flee from them on horseback. The commanding general finally ordered her away from camp (Sudlow 2000, 181–183).

SOUDER, Mrs. Emily Bliss. Initially worked at a canteen for soldiers in Philadelphia, then went to Gettysburg as a nurse following the battle in July 1863. There she experienced the horrors of the battlefield and cared for severely wounded soldiers. She wrote numerous letters home, which were later compiled into a volume describing the aftermath of the battle (Sudlow 2000, 183–187).

SPENCER, Henrietta. She was discovered in uniform in the camp of the 10th Ohio Cavalry and discharged (see Chapter 6).

SPENCER, Jennie M. ᴾ Arrested January 2, 1865, in Boone County, Missouri, and made a prisoner of war at Gratiot Prison, St. Louis, Missouri (see Chapter 7).

STEIN, Mrs. E. H. She and her husband both were on Allan Pinkerton's payroll as spies, conducting information-gathering missions in Virginia and elsewhere (Fishel 1996, 56, 85–86, 100, 131–132, 148).

STEVENS, Melvina. Served as a Union scout and spy at about age sixteen or seventeen, helping to guide Union prisoner escapees through the mountains of East Tennessee to safety (see Chapter 5).

STINEBAUGH-BRADFORD, Mary. From Galion, Ohio, she became matron of a Union hospital at Milliken's Bend, near Vicksburg, Mississippi. When the hospital came under threat of attack by Confederate guerrillas, she was forced to take refuge in the canebrake for three days. When a group of the hospital refugees then started to recross the river and their boat was caught up in the current and out of control, she and a companion jumped overboard and waded to shore, followed by the others. Later in 1864, at Natchez, her hospital came under attack by Confederate forces but the assault was repelled (Holland 1897, 243–253).

STREETER, Mrs. Elizabeth M. A founder of the Ladies' Relief Association of Baltimore, she helped care for wounded soldiers on the battlefield at Antietam in 1862. She continued in military hospital work thereafter and also helped care for destitute female refugees (Brockett 1867, 659–663).

STREIGHT, Lovina (Mrs. Abel D.). Early in the war she followed her husband's 51st Indiana Infantry regiment from Indianapolis south where it was engaged in battles in Alabama, Kentucky, and Tennessee, including Stones River and Murfreesboro, Tennessee. She acquired the title of "Mother of 5000 Soldiers." Her portrait hangs in the Indiana Statehouse. Colonel Streight was breveted brigadier general March 13, 1865 (http://www.iupui.edu/~geni/lsort/hoosierwomen.html, "Thumbnail Sketches of Women of the Civil War Era").

SULLIVAN, Betsy (Mrs. John C). Served as a battlefield nurse at Shiloh and Corinth, while accompanying her husband, John Sullivan, in Company K, Confederate 1st Tennessee Infantry. She shared all the hardships of army life with the regiment (see Chapter 2).

SWARTZ, Mrs. Charles (alias "Mrs. C. Wilson"). A spy reported by a field officer to be formally employed by the Union government in 1863, briefly acknowledged in the *Official Records* (Leonard 1999, 230; *Official Records, Series* 1, Vol. 29, No. 49*).

TABOR, Serina. Arrested as a spy at the front in Georgia wearing a full Confederate uniform in early September 1863, she was brought under guard to Nashville, Tennessee, where she was questioned by military authorities. After an inquiry she was confined to the workhouse until further notice. The newspaper reporter thought her to be of "unsound mind, although occasionally she talks quite sensibly" (*Nashville Dispatch,* Tennessee, September 15, 1863).

TALLY, Susan Archer. P A Confederate spy and smuggler. In 1861 she attempted to take a coffin full of percussion caps through Union lines into Richmond, claiming that the coffin contained her brother's body. She was later imprisoned at Fort McHenry for spying until June 28, 1862. She was said to be about thirty years old and a good artist (*Austin State Gazette,* Texas, October 8, 1862, from special correspondent of the *Philadelphia Press* at Fort McHenry).

TAYLOR, Sarah ("Sallie"). P At age eighteen she served as Daughter of the Regiment for the 1st Tennessee Infantry (Union). She carried a sword and pistols and traveled with the men, mounted on a horse (see Chapter 2 and Appendix B).

TAYLOR, Susie King. Mother of the Regiment for the Union 1st South Carolina Infantry, the first black regiment. She served with her husband and was on the payroll as laundress, but she also functioned as a nurse, taught soldiers, practiced shooting, and handled and cleaned rifles (see Chapter 10).

TEPE, Marie ("French Mary"). † She soldiered in the 27th Pennsylvania Infantry and in the 114th Pennsylvania Infantry, originally with her husband. On the Fredericksburg battlefield she was wounded in the ankle. For courageous service at Chancellorsville she was awarded the Kearny Cross (see Chapter 2).

THOMAS, Mary F. A practicing doctor in Fort Wayne, Indiana, along with her husband before the Civil War, she lived after that in Richmond, Indiana. During the war she worked with the U.S. Sanitary Commission, carried supplies to the front by steamer, and treated soldiers wounded at the Battle of Vicksburg. Thomas later served as an assistant physician with her husband, an army contract surgeon, in Nashville, Tennessee. She also was a women's rights activist.[46]

THOMPSON, Adelaide E. From New York City, she first became an army nurse in Washington, D.C., early in the war, then after an illness entered the secret service for the provost marshal. In that capacity she discovered female soldiers in male disguise (see Chapter 2).

THOMPSON, Ellen P. L. She served in the 139th Illinois Infantry late in the war in male disguise.[47]

THOMPSON, Kate. See Slater (or Slator), Mrs. Sarah.

THOMPSON, Lucy Matilda (alias "Bill Thompson"). [+] Enlisted with her husband in the 18th North Carolina Infantry and was twice wounded in action (see Chapter 9).

THOMPSON, Mrs. Sarah Lane. She worked along with her husband, an army recruiter, among Union sympathizers in a predominantly Confederate area near Greeneville, Tennessee. Early in 1864 her husband was ambushed and killed by a Confederate soldier. Thompson continued working for the Union as a courier and spy, once alerting Union forces to John Hunt Morgan's presence in Greeneville. Morgan was killed in the resulting Union raid. Later she served as an army nurse in Tennessee and Ohio.[48]

THOMPSON, Sophia.() She reportedly served in the 59th Ohio Infantry along with a sister who, apparently, used the name "Joseph Thompson." When discovered at Cincinnati, the sisters were eighteen and twenty years old. One said her father died at her side at Chickamauga. Sophia had served for two years before being discovered.[49]

THORNBURG, Mary A. Joined the Union Army in male disguise from Randolph County, Indiana. She was discovered when she contracted smallpox (see Chapter 6).

TRADER, Mrs. Ella K. See Newsom, Ella King.

TRUTH, Sojourner (nee Isabella Baumfree). Free black woman from New York who spoke eloquently for abolition of slavery and at personal risk encouraged and supported army enlistment of black men (see Chapter 10).

TUBMAN, Harriet. After serving as the "Moses" of her people in the Underground Railroad prior to the war, leading slaves to freedom in the North, Tubman during the Civil War commanded scouts and river pilots for Union forces in South Carolina, 1862–1865. She also conducted spying missions and led black troops in raids, carrying a musket (see Chapter 10).

TURCHIN, Nadine (wife of General John B.). She accompanied her husband in the 19th Illinois Infantry, which he commanded. Once when her husband became ill, she assumed command of the regiment and the soldiers accepted her leadership. She also served as a battlefield nurse and was frequently under fire (see Chapter 2).

UNDERWOOD, Margaret. [P] Enlisted in her sweetheart's Confederate regiment to be with him. Eventually she was discovered and imprisoned for about six months in Castle Thunder, Richmond, under suspicion of being a Union spy (see Chapter 7).

USHER, Rebecca R. One of the first Maine women to enter military nursing service, she worked at a Philadelphia hospital in 1862 and 1863. In late 1864 and early 1865 she cared for soldiers from Maine in a field hospital near Petersburg, Virginia, and then served at City Point, Virginia, living and working in a crude log stockade with canvas roof during the winter. She continued in hospital work to the end of the war (Moore 1866, 453–464; Sudlow 2000, 200–208).

VAN LEW, Elizabeth (aliases "Babcock," "Romona"). Conducted a Union spying ring and courier network in Richmond; her home was a "safe house" for Union couriers and escaped prisoners. Van Lew cultivated informants among prominent people. She also visited and carried supplies to imprisoned Union soldiers and obtained valuable information from them which she transmitted to Union officials.[50]

VELAZQUEZ, Loreta Janeta (a.k.a. Alice Williams, Laura J. Williams, Mrs. S. T. Williams, Mrs. Arnold; alias "Harry Buford"). [†][P] Served as a lieutenant in the Confederate army and as a spy and counterspy. She was wounded at Shiloh and imprisoned on several occasions (see Chapters 5 and 9 and Appendix B).

WAKEMAN, Sarah Rosetta (aliases "Lyons Wakeman," "Edwin R. Wakeman"). [†] Enlisted as a private in the 153rd New York Infantry and fought in the Red River campaign in April 1864. She died of chronic diarrhea in 1864 and is buried in Chalmette National Cemetery, Metairie, Louisiana (see Chapter 7).

WALKER, Mary. [P] Worked as a Union army nurse for three years and thereafter as an army surgeon. She apparently also served as a spy while attached to the 52nd Ohio Infantry. Once captured in Georgia while treating a Confederate soldier on the battlefield, she was imprisoned for four months in Richmond. Walker was awarded the Congressional Medal of Honor for her wartime services (see Chapter 7).

WARNE, Mrs. Kate. A spy for the Union who worked with Allan Pinkerton, disguising herself to obtain important information from secessionist groups in the North (see Chapter 5).

WATKINS, Mrs. Wesley. She enlisted in male disguise along with her husband in Company G, 2nd Maryland Infantry (Union) (see Chapter 3).

WEBSTER, Nannie. A young Maryland woman who smuggled letters, medicine, and other supplies to Richmond concealed in her clothing (see Chapter 5).

WEED, Mrs. Margaret A. Edgar. She was employed as an army nurse in Jefferson, Missouri, and Paducah, Kentucky. On March 25, 1864, Confederate forces attacked and took over the Paducah hospital to use as a site for sharpshooters. She and another nurse were led by the enemy into an open field between the lines, where they came under fire. She escaped and fled into Illinois. Returning next day she found the hospital burned down. Weed continued in service until the end of the war (Holland 1897, 345–349).

WELLMAN, Louisa. * She saw action in an early Iowa regiment at Fort Donelson and Pittsburg Landing, where she was wounded in the collarbone and discovered by the surgeon to be a woman (see Chapter 3).

WEST, Brodie. See Edmondson, Belle.

WEST, Mary Ann. Twice tried to enlist in Illinois regiments, once in the 66th Infantry and once in the 124th Infantry, but was detected each time (see Chapter 6).

WESTON, Mrs. Modenia McColl. She became Mother of the Regiment and a nurse for the 3rd Iowa Infantry and helped establish a field hospital in Missouri. Weston was with the regiment at the Battle of Shiloh and also cared for the wounded on board a steamship after the battle (Holland 1897, 163–164).

WHETTEN, Harriet Douglas. She served as a U.S. Sanitary Commission nurse in field hospitals and on Hospital Transport Service ships on the Virginia peninsula. Once in 1862 she discovered a pregnant female soldier among the patients under her care (see Chapter 1).

WHITE, Lilly. * Early in 1862 a railroad accident near Atlanta, Georgia, crushed the legs of a Confederate soldier who turned out to be female. Her legs had to be amputated. The soldier, who gave her name as Lilly White, said that she had enlisted in male disguise to avenge herself against a lover who had deceived her. She did not survive the amputations (*Southern Confederacy*, Atlanta, Georgia, March 6, 1862).

WHITE, V. A. Enlisted in the 1st Michigan Mechanics to leave a life of prostitution and mustered out with the men in 1865 (see Chapter 3).

WILLETS, Georgiana. A New Jersey woman who worked as a nurse under dangerous conditions in 1864. She cared for the wounded from the Battle of the Wilderness and on board hospital transport ships; she also participated in the evacuation of patients from Fredericksburg under emergency conditions (see Chapter 2).

WILLIAMS, Nellie (alias "Charles H. Williams"). Reported to have served in the 2nd Iowa Infantry for three months before being arrested in Louisville during August 1861 and discovered to be a woman (see Chapter 9).

WILLIAMS, Sarah (alias "John Williams"). ᴾ According to a newspaper report, a private in the 2nd Kentucky Cavalry (Union) was discovered in October 1864 to be a woman and imprisoned after serving in the ranks for three years (see Chapter 6).

WILSON, Eliza. () Daughter of the Regiment for the 5th Wisconsin Infantry, she reportedly lived and marched with the soldiers in camp and helped to care for them. It is not clear whether she went into the field with the regiment (see Chapter 2).

WILSON, Fanny (or Fannie). () She is reported to have served for two years in the 24th New Jersey Infantry along with a friend, Nellie Graves, before being discovered and discharged. Later when reenlisted, in the 3rd Illinois Cavalry, she was discovered again and sent home (see Chapter 9 and Appendix B).

WILSON, Maggie (alias "Charles Marshall"). Reported to have served in the 13th New York Infantry in 1861 and when discovered, stayed on as a vivandiere.[51]

WINDER, Nora. Performed spying activities for General William T. Sherman in 1864–1865 in Georgia and South Carolina, particularly monitoring the activities of Confederate General John B. Hood's Army of Tennessee (see Chapter 5).

WITHERELL, Mrs. E. C. † A hospital nurse in St. Louis, Missouri, she contracted a fever while working aboard the hospital ship *Empress* and died July 10, 1862 (http://missouricivilwarmuseum.org/sanitaryfair.htm).

WITTENMYER, Annie Turner. During her pioneering work in developing diet kitchens for wounded soldiers at field hospitals, she was exposed to enemy gunfire on several occasions as she traveled around the country to camp and battlefield areas.[52]

WOOLSEY, Eliza N. (Mrs. Eliza Woolsey Howland). The seven Woolsey sisters, from a well-to-do family in New York City, all served in some capacity during the war. Eliza was a nurse in the U.S. Sanitary Commission Hospital Transport Service with her sister Georgeanna during the 1862 Virginia Peninsula Campaign (see next entry).

WOOLSEY, Georgeanna M. A Hospital Transport Service nurse in 1862 in Virginia, she also cared for wounded soldiers in field hospitals and as a battlefield nurse at Chancellorsville and Gettysburg in 1863. She continued as a nurse in Virginia during Grant's campaign in 1864 (see Chapter 1).

WORMELEY, Katharine Prescott. One of the earliest Hospital Transport Service nurses in 1862, she cared for large numbers of severely wounded soldiers on board ships, newly arrived from the Virginia battlefields (see Chapter 1).

WRIGHT, Mary. [P] Arrested in Confederate uniform and imprisoned in Nashville with another female soldier, Margaret Henry, near the end of the war (see Chapter 7).

Unidentified Female Soldiers

1861

LOUISIANA. A Confederate private soldier using the name "William Bradley" in the Louisiana Miles's Legion served for two months before being discovered to be female. A year later a Mrs. Bradley, wife of a sergeant in Miles's Legion, received a leg wound from a shell, the leg was amputated, and she died (Leonard 1999, 221; Blanton and Cook 2002, 116).

KENTUCKY (UNION). A woman using the name "John Thompson" enlisted as a private in the 1st Kentucky Infantry (Union) on May 28, 1861, and served for two months. She was discovered to be a woman, and suspected of being a Confederate spy at that time. Later she was caught with incriminating evidence and confessed (see Chapter 7).

PENNSYLVANIA. A woman is reported to have served in the three-months 7th Pennsylvania Infantry regiment, which was in the field from late April to late July 1861 (see Chapter 3).

ILLINOIS. Nurse Mary Livermore, while visiting the camp of the 19th Illinois, had a soldier pointed out to her by a captain, and she confirmed his suspicions that the soldier was female (see Chapter 6).

LOUISIANA. The *Arkansas True Democrat,* Little Rock, October 10, 1861, reported: "A Female Warrior.—The *Memphis Avalanche* of September 12, says: One of the Louisiana companies in the battle of Manassas [First Bull Run] lost its captain. The company then unanimously elected the wife of the deceased to fill his place, and the lady, in uniform, passed through the city [Memphis] yesterday, on her way to assume command of her company."

NEW JERSEY. The *New York Herald,* October 14, 1861, reported that a New Jersey girl donned male disguise and tried to join her sweetheart in the "Garibaldi Guard," 39th New York Volunteers, but was soon discovered and sent home. She then tried to commit suicide by taking arsenic but was saved and put under watch.

1862

KENTUCKY (CONFEDERATE). A story in a South Carolina newspaper reported that a young widow named McDonald in the Confederate 28th Kentucky Infantry had been detected and discharged. She was said to have been discharged from one or more Confederate regiments previously (see Chapter 6).

OHIO. A female soldier using the name "Frank Deming" saw action in the 17th Ohio Infantry. She was in battle at Mill Springs, Kentucky, January 19, 1862. She was discovered to be a woman and discharged "for disability" on May 18, 1862.[53]

MARYLAND. According to a contemporary Pennsylvania newspaper story in March 1862, "Two Maryland girls, 18 and 20 years old respectively, were arrested in Washington on Wednesday, in soldier's uniform. They said that they had been in the army some time, and one of them was at the battle of [First] Bull Run. They were admonished by Gen. Wadsworth and sent to their homes in Hagerstown, Maryland."[54]

UNION SOLDIER. The remains of a female soldier who had been killed in the Battle of Shiloh, April 6–7, 1862, were found over seventy years later (see Chapter 7).

IOWA. In April 1862, the lieutenant of an Iowa regiment stationed in the Washington, D.C., area was found to be a woman and was arraigned before a military tribunal. She was apparently engaged to the captain of the company (*Dubuque Herald,* Iowa, April 13, 1862, from the *Troy Budget,* Iowa).

UNION SPY. The *Memphis Daily Appeal* for April 12, 1862, reported that an unnamed female Union spy who had been under observation was arrested and transported to Corinth, Mississippi, where she was allowed to retire to a room unsearched. Shortly afterwards a guard proceeded to the room to search her but smelled burned paper and realized that she had managed to destroy the evidence that she had been carrying.

KENTUCKY (UNION). Early in May 1862 in Detroit, an intoxicated soldier was found on the street unconscious and was arrested. When examined in the jail, the soldier was found to be a woman. When she awoke, she said that she had moved from western Canada to Kentucky before the war and enlisted in the army there. She had been in battle. Eventually she had tired of military life and had made her sex known. The authorities had immediately discharged her and she had arrived in Detroit a few days previously (*Chicago Daily Tribune,* May 6, 1862, from the *Detroit Advertiser*).

CONFEDERATE SOLDIERS. Two Confederate soldiers, one a woman in uniform, arrived in Rome, Georgia, in early May 1862, and were arrested on suspicion of spying. They were released after telling a plausible story of being in pursuit of a spy, but were arrested again in Chattanooga, Tennessee, and were being held in custody (*Southern Confederacy,* Atlanta, Georgia, May 23, 1862, from Rome, Georgia, dateline May 15).

OHIO. The *Nashville Dispatch,* May 31, 1862, reported that a teamster with an Ohio regiment who had been hospitalized for several days with measles was discovered to be a woman. She said she was from the vicinity of Gallapolis, Ohio, and had previously joined the regular army, but had been discovered and discharged (see Chapter 7).

NEW YORK/PENNSYLVANIA. The July 19, 1862, issue of *Frank Leslie's Illustrated Newspaper* reported that a woman from Chenango County, New York, had been discovered posing as a man in a Pennsylvania regiment. She had previously served as a nurse in the 61st New York Infantry along with her husband, but had become separated from that regiment (see Chapter 7).

UNION SOLDIERS. Two slight soldiers in uniform were questioned by the Washington, D.C., provost marshal early in August 1862. They admitted that they were females and had been serving as privates in Pope's army for months. "They were furnished with proper apparel and sent northward" (*Chicago Times,* August 14, 1862).

UNION VIVANDIERE. In the Virginia Shenandoah Valley during August 1862, a Confederate cannoneer saw a group of Union prisoners on horseback, one of them a woman wearing a red dress (see Chapter 4).

UNION SOLDIER. On August 21, 1862, Union nurse Harriet Whetten recorded in her diary that she had found a pregnant female soldier among the patients under her care (Leonard 1999, 219).

MARYLAND (UNION). In August 1862, two privates in the 2nd Maryland Cavalry (Union) were discovered to be female while in camp near Harpers Ferry, Virginia (Blanton and Cook 2002, 113).

NORTH CAROLINA. During the week of August 10–16, 1862, a female soldier was discovered in the ranks during a roll call of an unnamed North Carolina regiment in training at Raleigh. The young woman said she had joined to accompany her friends and to avenge the death of a brother who was killed in battle near Richmond (*Weekly Columbus Enquirer,* Georgia, August 19, 1862).

UNION SOLDIER. On August 22, 1862, a Union soldier captured by Confederates at Catlett Station, Virginia, confessed to being a woman and asked to be released. She said she had joined the army to be with her sweetheart. She was turned over to authorities in Richmond (Blanton and Cook 2002, 80–81).

UNION SOLDIER. According to an 1864 newspaper story, a Union soldier named Margaret, reported to be a color sergeant who carried the unit flag in battle, was killed at Second Bull Run in late August 1862 (Blanton and Cook 2002, 72).

CONFEDERATE SOLDIER. At the Battle of Perryville, Kentucky, October 8, 1862, a wounded Confederate soldier was found to be a woman. She was about twenty years old, and her name was reported only as "Mrs. Stone" in the newspaper. She had been serving with her husband, who also was captured. After agreeing to take the oath of allegiance to the Union they were released and moved to New York City (Blanton and Cook 2002, 82, 152).

CONFEDERATE SMUGGLER. The Chambersburg, Pennsylvania, *Valley Spirit* for November 26, 1862, reported that a woman by the name of "Sloan" was arrested on November 21 in Chambersburg after arousing suspicion by making extensive purchases of drugs and medicines and was found to have a large quantity of them in her possession that she apparently planned to smuggle to the South (see Appendix B, Unidentified Women).

UNION SOLDIER. A squad of men arrived at Fort Snelling, Minnesota, late in 1862 to join the 1st Minnesota Cavalry, "Mounted Rangers." A newspaper reported: "The Orderly in charge was very boyish looking, but of singularly neat and soldier-like appearance." The colonel suspected that the young orderly was an underage boy who had run away from home. The father of the soldier showed up in camp one day and reclaimed his runaway daughter (*Peoria Morning Mail,* Illinois, January 4, 1863, from the *Saint Paul Press,* Minnesota).

1863

ILLINOIS. Early in 1863 a soldier in the 116th Illinois Infantry wrote a letter home reporting the presence of a soldier named "Kate" in the regiment, wearing men's clothes. "She has been with the regiment ever since we left Memphis."[55]

INDIANA. (Uncertain date, but probably 1863). A female soldier in an Indiana regiment, after serving for two years, apparently tired of military life, informed her colonel, donned female attire, and headed for home, leaving the officers and men dumbfounded. According to the story she had done her duty, fought bravely, and had been wounded two times in battle, but had remained undiscovered. She said that she had joined to be near her lover but had become disgusted when he proved to be a coward (Kirkland 1867, 524–535).

INDIANA. On February 23, 1863, Trooper Joseph F. Shelly of the 2nd Indiana Cavalry wrote in a letter to his wife from Louisville, Kentucky: "We discovered last week a soldier who turned out to be a girl. She had already been in service for 21 months and was twice wounded. Maybe she would have remained undiscovered for a long time, if she hadn't fainted. She was given a warm bath which gave the secret away" (Anderson 1948, 186). Except for the reported means of discovery, this account bears a striking resemblance to the Kirkland reference above and most likely it is the same female soldier.

NEW JERSEY. In early April 1863, while the Union army was in camp along the Rappahannock River in Virginia, soldiers wrote a flurry of letters home reporting that a corporal in a New Jersey regiment had given birth to a baby. The event caused a sensation throughout the army. An Indiana soldier in a letter to his girlfriend from Pratts Point, Virginia, dated April 19, 1863, said: "The 'lady soldier' has been sent home to her folks. Her man remains in the army. Sorry for the girl—forced to leave him at last & in much worse condition. I understand [a] contribution fund has been established in the Army to give her boy a military education. I hope it is so. I have a mite to cast for such a purpose."[56]

OHIO. A sergeant in the 74th Ohio Infantry in XX Corps stationed at Murfreesboro, Tennessee, gave birth to a baby on April 17, 1863. She had been in service for about two years. General Rosecrans (April 17, 1863) termed it "a flagrant outrage...in violation of all military law and of the army regulations" (see Appendix B).[57]

CONFEDERATE SOLDIER. A Confederate female soldier, an orderly sergeant in the cavalry, was captured at Chancellorsville early in May 1863 (Blanton and Cook 2002, 72).

CONFEDERATE SOLDIER. The *Montgomery Weekly Advertiser,* May 13, 1863, reported that a young woman of about seventeen in military uniform was arrested in Augusta, Georgia, on May 5. She said that she was a married woman from Mississippi and was a member of a Confederate company in Charleston, South Carolina.

LOUISIANA. While traveling by train between Chattanooga, Tennessee, and Atlanta, Georgia, on June 5, 1863, British officer Arthur Freemantle's companions pointed out to him a female army private who they said had served in a Louisiana regiment and had been in two battles. They told him that she had recently been "turned out...for her bad and immoral conduct," and that she was not the only woman in the Confederate army. "When I saw her," Freemantle noted, "she wore a soldier's hat and coat, but had resumed her petticoats." Conceivably this could have been Loreta Janeta Velazquez (Freemantle 1863, 174).

CONFEDERATE SOLDIER. Unidentified female soldier killed at Gettysburg, July 3–4, 1863 (see Chapter 7).

CONFEDERATE SOLDIER. Unidentified female soldier lost a leg at Gettysburg, July 3–4, 1863 (see Chapter 7).

UNION SCOUT. Brigadier General Thomas A. Davies in a letter from Rolla, Missouri, dated July 14, 1863, reported to his commanding general relaying information from "my woman scout" about the disposition of the enemy. Davies was a West Point graduate and colonel of the 16th New York Infantry, then brigade commander, and served with distinction throughout the war. He was breveted major general of volunteers at the end of the war (*Official Records*, Series 1, Vol. 22/2, No. 33).

OHIO. According to an 1887 book a girl using the name "Joseph Davidson" went to war as a private in an Ohio regiment with her father. The father was killed at Chickamauga (September 19–20, 1863), and she stayed on and served for three years. (This could not have been Catherine Davidson, 28th Ohio, a separate female soldier. See page 234.)[58]

UNION SOLDIER. In September 1863, a Union female lieutenant was discovered among about 300 prisoners held in Atlanta, Georgia (Blanton and Cook 2002, 81).

UNION SOLDIER. After the Battle of Chickamauga, Tennessee, September 19–20, 1863, a captured Union soldier was returned through the lines with the following note: "As the Confederates do not use women in war, this woman, wounded in battle, is returned to you" (see Chapter 7).

UNION SOLDIER. In the fall of 1863 a young soldier named "Charles Martin" was found to be a girl when she was admitted to a Philadelphia hospital for treatment of typhoid fever (see Chapter 3 and Appendix B).

CONFEDERATE SOLDIER'S WIFE. During the Union artillery bombardment of Charleston, South Carolina, in fall of 1863, the wife of an unidentified Confederate officer was with him in the earthworks of one of the artillery batteries defending the city. She remained for sixty days, sleeping among the soldiers, and was in the midst of an artillery duel with shells bursting all around them, killing or injuring many soldiers. Her food consisted of "the wormy bread and half-cured pork" that the soldiers ate, "and her drink was brackish water from the ditch that surrounded the earth-work." Eventually the garrison had to be evacuated at night, and four of the soldiers carried her into the city in an ambulance (Fowler 1877, 423–425).

UNION SOLDIER. The *Nashville Dispatch*, November 14, 1863, reported that at Barracks No. 1 in Louisville, Kentucky, there was a very pretty young lady of about seventeen who had served in the army for two years. "She was recently mustered out of the service, and is now waiting for five months' pay due her from Uncle Sam."

ILLINOIS. A Union soldier in camp at Pulaski, Tennessee, wrote to a friend on November 21, 1863, reporting the presence of "a splendid new recruit [in] his company [who] turned out to be a woman" and had to be discharged. Presumably the soldier was in an Illinois regiment, since his letter is archived by the Chicago Historical Society (Culpepper 1991, 115, from William F. Hertzog Letters, Archives and Manuscripts, Chicago Historical Society).

ILLINOIS. An Illinois woman was one of eighteen scouts sent out to reconnoiter General Braxton Bragg's position at the Battle of Lookout Mountain, Tennessee, November 24, 1863. She served as an attaché in General Francis P. Blair, Jr.'s, XVII Corps during operations into Georgia, North Carolina, and South Carolina (see Chapter 4 and Appendix B, "Soldier Tom").

UNION SOLDIER. According to a St. Louis newspaper article, September 24, 1864, a female soldier died of disease in Overton Hospital, Memphis, Tennessee, some time in 1863. Her sex was not discovered until shortly before her death. She was reported to have enlisted at the start of the war to follow her lover, then reenlisted for a second term (Blanton and Cook 2002, 100).

1864

UNION SOLDIERS. Two women in army uniform were arrested in Louisville, Kentucky, in early January 1864 and turned over to civilian authorities. The *Nashville Dispatch,* January 6, 1864, reported: "Two others who had served in the Federal army upwards of one year, were sent away from Barracks No. 1."

CONFEDERATE SOLDIER. The *New Orleans Daily Picayune,* February 12, 1864, reported that a group of eight to ten Confederate soldiers had been captured in Virginia and taken to Harpers Ferry. There a guard suspected that one of the prisoners was a young woman, and it proved to be true. She was removed, given female clothes, and set free. It was learned that she came from a wealthy family in the vicinity of Harpers Ferry and had followed her sweetheart into the army, serving in the same company with him.

CONFEDERATE SOLDIERS. The late Lee Middleton reported a promising case, which in its entirety said: "From Camp Neal on March 6, 1864, Sgt. Major Fitzpatrick mentions in a letter home to his family that two women discovered in uniform with the 49th Georgia were refused permission to cross the Shenandoah River with General Thomas and his troops."[59]

CONFEDERATE SPY. A daring female Confederate spy was captured near Chattanooga, Tennessee, in March, thanks to a rigorous system of safeguards established by the Federal commander. The *New Orleans Daily Picayune,* March 27, 1864, attributing the story to the Chattanooga correspondent of the *Cincinnati Commercial,* reported that the guards had been instructed to keep a close watch on pedestrians and examine all passes carefully. As a result, the Confederate spy was discovered wearing the uniform of a Union artillery captain.

UNION SOLDIER. The *Mobile Register and Advertiser* for April 28, 1864, reported the arrest of a female soldier in Green Bay, Wisconsin. "[She] sports a light mustache, speaks two or three languages, circulates counterfeit money, and does not like her husband well enough to live with him."

INDIANA. A female soldier associated with the 34th Indiana Infantry was arrested on April 28 by the military conductor on the Louisville and Nashville Railroad on suspicion of being a Confederate spy. She was dressed in full uniform and bore the insignia of an orderly sergeant. The conductor took her to the provost marshal in Nashville. The *Press* (not further identified) reported on May 2 that she had shown her documents and credentials to the provost marshal and was immediately released (*Nashville Dispatch*, May 1, 1864, and May 3, 1864).

CONFEDERATE SOLDIER. In April 1864 a Confederate prisoner at Rock Island Prison, Illinois, gave birth to a baby boy (Blanton and Cook 2002, 84).

UNION SOLDIER. After the Battle of the Wilderness (May 5–7, 1864), Catholic Sister Margaret Hamilton at the U.S. Military Hospital in Philadelphia reported discovering a Union female lieutenant who had been wounded in the battle (see Chapter 7).

UNION SOLDIER. When some bodies were being removed from the May 13–14, 1864, Resaca, Georgia, battle site in 1886 for reburial in a national cemetery, the remains of a soldier identified by a wooden grave marker as Private "Charles Johehous[e]" of the 6th Missouri Infantry were recognized as those of a woman. She was in full uniform and had been shot through the head. The name identification clearly is mistaken, but the basic story apparently is true: a female soldier was killed in the battle.[60]

CONFEDERATE SOLDIER. In a diary entry for May 26, 1864, a soldier in the 104th New York Infantry noted that a female Confederate cavalry trooper was taken prisoner that morning during the North Anna campaign and presumed to be a spy. An army engineer writing to a friend from the Army of the Potomac on May 29, 1864, reported the female cavalry soldier among the prisoners brought in. "She was mounted just like a man . . . wore her hair long and did not like to have our men looking at her." She had been captured five days earlier along the North Anna River in Virginia and reacted angrily when a curious crowd gaped at her while she was being held at Baldwin's Mill. O. B. Curtis of the 24th Michigan reported the same incident. She was taken as a prisoner to White House Landing under suspicion of being a spy.[61]

CONFEDERATE SOLDIERS. On May 26, 1864, Union sergeant Robert Ardry of the 111th Illinois Infantry, during a battle at Dallas, Georgia, observed female soldiers in the Confederate forces opposing them, who, along with the male soldiers, "fought like demons." After the battle he "saw 3 or 4 dead women soldiers in the heap of bodies [who had been shot down] during the final rebel charge upon our works" (Campbell and Rice 1996, 92–93).

CONFEDERATE SOLDIER. A female Confederate artillery sergeant (not Sarah Jane Perkins) was captured while manning a gun during the Battle of Cold Harbor, Virginia (June 1–3, 1864), and taken to White House Landing (Blanton 2001, 107–108).

UNION SCOUT. Brigadier General John B. Sanborn, in a letter to Major General Rosecrans from Springfield, Missouri, September 24, 1864, lauded "the woman scout" in his service, saying, "She has spied a good deal for us from Neosho and has always been reliable and correct" (Official Records, Series 1, Vol. 41/3, No. 85).

MISSISSIPPI. The Lynchburg Virginian for October 6, 1864, reported a story from the Charlotte Times, North Carolina, that on Friday, September 30, a female Confederate captain passed through Charlotte on a train headed to Richmond. "She wore a black belt with a chain attached. She is said to be from Mississippi, and has participated in several hard fought battles, and was promoted on the field for distinguished gallantry. She wore a straw cap, set jauntily on her head, adorned with two rows of miniature gilt buttons." She was in the company of an army major.

UNION SOLDIERS. A Massachusetts soldier on provost guard duty in Baltimore recorded in his diary for October 13 and 14, 1864, the arrival of two Union women prisoners who had been serving in male disguise. They were jailed overnight, then sent away in the morning. In November he reported the arrival of two more Union female soldiers "sent here to be discharged" (Blanton and Cook 2002, 113).

CONFEDERATE SOLDIER. In December 1864 a Confederate officer incarcerated in Johnson's Island Prison on Lake Erie gave birth to a baby boy (Sandusky Register, Ohio, December 12, 1864).

1865

UNION SPY. A Union officer in official correspondence dated February 11, 1865, referred to a female spy in his employment (see Appendix B, page 317–318).

UNION SOLDIER. On February 28, 1865, a female Union soldier from New England "who has served three years creditably, and received three wounds" was sent into Washington, D.C., from camp. The *New Orleans Daily Pica-yune,* March 5, 1865 (taking the story from a Washington paper), reported that she was discharged from the army and forced to adopt "the appropriate garb of her sex."

CONNECTICUT. A woman was in the ranks of the 29th Connecticut Infantry (Colored), at the siege of Petersburg, Virginia. She was with the regiment in the trenches from August 1864 until, on February 28, 1865, she gave birth to a baby. On March 2, 1865, a sergeant wrote a letter home to his wife reporting the event and stating that the woman was then in the hospital (see Chapter 10).[62]

NEW YORK. On March 6, 1865, a corporal in the 6th New York Heavy Artillery, stationed at Bermuda Hundred, Virginia, went into labor while on picket duty. Taken to the division hospital, she gave birth to a baby boy.[63]

UNION SOLDIER. In spring 1865, according to a newspaper story, a young female Union soldier in hospital at Tullahoma, Tennessee, confided in the surgeon shortly before she died. The doctor kept the secret for seventeen years (Blanton and Cook 2002, 100–101).

APPENDIX B

Contemporary Documents

A cross-section of documents and newspaper reports relating to women who served in the armies or as spies during the Civil War are reproduced as originally reported or partly paraphrased. Editorial notes appear in brackets. The documents are arranged alphabetically by last name. Unidentified women are grouped at the end chronologically by date of the document.

MRS. C. V. BAXLEY
Official Records of the Union and Confederate Armies, Series II, Vol. 2, 1862.
Suspected and Disloyal Persons
Cases of Mrs. C. V. Baxley and Septimus Brown

Mrs. Baxley was arrested in Baltimore about the 30th of December, 1861, by Deputy Provost-Marshal McPhail and committed to the Greenhow *Prison* [*sic*] in Washington and from thence to the Old Capitol. She was charged with being a spy and with having lately been to Richmond, Va., with letters to Jefferson Davis and others. When arrested concealed upon her person were found numerous letters which she brought from Richmond; also a commission appointing a Doctor Brown, of Baltimore, a surgeon in the rebel army. John L. Brown writing from headquarters of General Franklin's division, near Alexandria, Va., January 2, 1862, says of Mrs. Baxley: "This woman is the strongest kind of a secessionist. She made her brags to me some five months ago that she had sent some 200 guns to the Southern army."

In numerous letters addressed by Mrs. Baxley to the Secretary of State since her imprisonment she admits having carried the letters above referred to to Jefferson Davis, and refers to the communications with General Winder, Mr. Benjamin and other leading rebel authorities, and admits having procured the commission for Doctor Brown by personal application, and as a consideration or reward for the safe conveyance of letters, &c., to the chief of the rebel Government. The said Mrs. C.V. Baxley remained in custody at the Old Capitol in Washington February 15, 1862, when she was transferred to the charge of the War Department.—*From Record Book, State Department, "Arrests for Disloyalty."*

SARAH E. BRADBURY
Nashville Dispatch, Tennessee, March 11, 1863.
The Romantic Story of the Female Soldiers

[After a brief introduction, the article reports excerpts from the statement given under oath by Miss Bradbury before the Judge Advocate; see Chapter 9.]

I am eighteen years old, was born in Wilson county, Tennessee, and moved from there to this county about one year ago. I was raised by a step-father, my mother having died when I was seven years old. I have no recollection of having ever seen my father. I lived seven miles from Nashville, on the old Chicken road that leads from Nashville to Lebanon.

I have been in the service six months. I first went into the 7th Illinois cavalry, in company C. This company was the body guard of Gen. [John M.] Palmer [later Governor of Illinois and a U.S. Senator]. I was induced to go into the service by my friend, Mr. H., who, by his frequent visits and manifestations of love, won my heart. I dressed myself in men's clothing and determined to follow him. I served in this company two months, making a faithful and attentive soldier; while there I became Orderly for my General, and flatter myself that I made him a good officer. During all this time my sex was never discovered. Unfortunately, my friend [Mr. H.] was captured by the rebels while out scouting the day after I went into his company, and I have never heard of him since.

Despairing of seeing him again, and becoming attached to a young man in the 22d Illinois infantry, I joined his regiment [implying desertion from the 7th Cavalry] in order that I might be the more with him. I was with him constantly, and we have passed many pleasant hours together. One day, while taking a walk with him, and thinking that I had gained his confidence, I gave him my history and disclosed my sex. This he was surprised to hear, for he had taken me for a boy, and was disposed to doubt me. Since that time he has made me frequent proposals of marriage. Circumstances proved to me that I was mistaken in my man, for I soon became satisfied that he was not a gentleman. Thus losing confidence in him, I made up my mind to return to my home. When I thought of having left home without the consent of my friends,

I instantly abandoned the thought and determined to remain in the army. Camp life agreed with me, and I never enjoyed better health in my life.

Afterward I became a member of General Sheridan's escort, company L, 2d Kentucky cavalry. One day Colonel Barret sent me as bearer of dispatches to Col. Libott, a distance of six miles. On my return, one of my brother orderlies betrayed me to the Colonel, he becoming jealous of my reputation as an orderly, and having found out my sex a few days previous. My sex thus exposed, I was arrested and sent to Col. Truesdail in irons. May I never fall into worse hands, for I found him a gentleman in every sense of the word.

I have made a good and faithful soldier, have learned a good deal of human nature, and had some aspirations as a soldier, and thought at the time of my arrest that my chances were good for promotion. I will try to profit by the lessons I have learned.

KADY C. BROWNELL

Saturday Globe, Utica, New York, December 21, 1895.
Honor Is Her Due
Mrs. Brownell, Heroine of Bull Run and Newbern

The Park Board of the city of New York has appointed as matron at the Park Department house in Mount Morris Park, Mrs. Kady Brownell, the only woman on record as having regularly enlisted in the civil war. There is no particular significance in this fact except as it brings to public notice a woman with a record to be proud of. Mrs. Brownell was an English girl. She was the daughter of Col. Southwell, of the British army, and from him she inherited unbounded pluck and spirit and a love of things military. Father and daughter came to America when the girl was quite young, and settled in Rhode Island.

Just before Sumter was fired upon Kady Southwell became Mrs. Robert S. Brownell. When the war broke out the young husband enlisted in the First Rhode Island Volunteers. Determined not to be left behind, Mrs. Brownell insisted upon going too, and she enlisted in a company known as the Carbineers [sic]. She was made its color bearer. The colonel of her regiment is authority for the statement that she became a skillful shot and that no soldier in the regiment was her equal at a slashing saber stroke. She marched beside her husband in the ranks, asking no favors or consideration on account of her sex, and always wearing the accoutrements of a soldier.

At the first battle of Bull Run Mrs. Brownell stood unflinchingly beside her husband as long as the regiment stood, and when the First Rhode Island was swept back in the common repulse Kady retired in good order.

During the disastrous retreat she was slightly wounded in the leg by a piece of a spent shell, but she pluckly [*sic*] tied up the wound and tramped along in the stampede back to Washington.

When their term of enlistment, three months, had expired, Mr. and Mrs. Brownell returned to Rhode Island. There Mr. Brownell organized a regiment and returned to the army a colonel. [This is incorrect. He became a sergeant in the 5th Rhode Island Heavy Artillery.] Again his brave wife went with him. At the battle of Newbern, N.C., the "Daughter of the Regiment," as Mrs. Brownell had come to be called, performed her greatest warlike exploit. The color company, to which she had attached herself, was charging a battery of Confederate guns, and had about succeeded in driving the gunners from their posts, when another command of the Union forces, coming up on the flank of the Rhode Island boys, mistook them, in the smoke of battle, for the enemy.

A galling cross fire was begun before the error was discovered, and the boys in blue were beginning to drop around Mrs. Brownell. Without a moment's pause she seized the colors from the color sergeant, who had not dropped them, and rushed forward into the fire of the advancing command. Seeing the stars and stripes borne aloft by the fair hands of the Daughter of the Regiment, the soldiers ceased firing and the color company was saved.

Mr. Brownell is still living, but he is in poor health and out of work and so the position to which his gallant wife has been appointed will be very acceptable.

Saturday Globe, Utica, New York, January 16, 1915.
Woman Veteran of Civil War

Mrs. Kady C. Brownell, Who Died in Oxford Recently, Fought in the Rebellion and Was the only Female Admitted to Full Membership in the G.A.R. [Grand Army of the Republic]

Norwich, Jan. 15.—The recent death of Mrs. Kady C. Brownell which occurred at the W.R.C. Home in Oxford, reveals a remarkable life history which, it is said, can be proven by records. Mrs. Brownell was born 72 years ago near Caffara on the south coast of Africa, on a battlefield of the first Boer war with Great Britain. In the extraordinary excitement of a visit to the battle scene the mother gave premature birth to the child and marked her for a military career. She was named after Sir George Kady, a chaplain in the English army and an intimate friend of her father.

She was still in her teens when she married Robert Brownell just at the outbreak of the civil war. Her husband enlisted and left his girl-bride to go to the front. Undaunted she designed and donned a special uniform and followed her husband's regiment to Washington. Armed with a letter she sought out the colonel and prevailed upon him to permit her to join her husband in the service, becoming a member of the same company with him, a special order being issued in her case, the only one of the kind during the war. She was in the first Bull Run battle, accompanied Burnside's expedition and participated in the battles of Newburn [sic] and Roanoke Island, receiving a special medal for bravery at Newburn.

After the war she was placed on the pension roll and drew a pension as a survivor and the only woman who saw service in the ranks. . . . For a number of years she was custodian of the Jumel mansion in New York city.

On account of age and infirmities and failing health Mr. and Mrs. Brownell were admitted to the W.R.C. Home in Oxford. During their brief residence there they had endeared themselves to the other veterans and their wives and deep sympathy is shown for the bereaved husband, besides whom Mrs. Brownell is survived by a son, Eugene Brownell, of Crescent, Iowa; by 17 grandchildren and by 13 great-grandchildren. Funeral services were held at the W.R.C. Home, the remains being taken to Providence, R.I., for interment.

[The Jumel mansion is a historic house in New York City that served as George Washington's headquarters during the American Revolution. After the war it became a popular tavern and it is now a museum. The W.R.C. home in Oxford was a veterans' home established by the Women's Relief Corps in the 1890s.]

MARY ANN (AMY) CLARK
Cairo City Weekly News, Illinois, Dec. 25, 1862.
A Confederate Romance—History of Mrs. Anna Clark
A Cairo correspondent of the *Philadelphia Inquirer* writes:

Among the prisoners brought here is a young person wearing the uniform of a private in the Confederate army. Not above medium height, rather slight in build, features effeminate but eye full of resolution and spirit, the party is not disagreeable to look upon. The descriptive roll calls him Richard Anderson. A note to Gen. Tuttle, however, from the Provost Marshal at another point, explained that, for once, "Richard was not himself," but another personage altogether. In fact, that Richard Anderson was no less a personage than Mrs. Anna Clark, wife of the late Walter [sic] Clark. When requested to tell her story, she revealed the following incidents in her history. They may be true or untrue, but the relator appeared perfectly truthful and candid in her recital.

Mrs. Clark is a native of Iuka, Tennessee. Early in the war her husband joined a regiment, and left her at home to manage as best she could. She did not manage as a prudent wife should. She fell in love with a gallant hussar, belonging to a Louisiana regiment. She determined to follow this love. She dressed as a trooper, procured a horse, and enlisted in his company. For four months she remained attached to the cavalry service of the Confederate army, but the fatigues of that department were more than she could bear, and after one or two narrow escapes from serious fits of sickness, she resolved to leave the mounted service and enter the infantry branch, for which, she argued, she was by nature better fitted.

Her exchange was effected. She left her trooper's command and joined a company of the 11th Tennessee infantry. In this regiment she served under the name of Richard Anderson, until the battle of Richmond, Kentucky, where she with others was made prisoner. Her husband [name unknown] was killed at Shiloh or Donelson, she never knew which. At the former battle, Mrs. Clark, according to her own story, performed prodigies of valor, frequently having to stand upon the dead body of a comrade to obtain a sight of the enemy, upon whom she continually emptied the contents of her musket.

Thus, for over 10 months, as cavalry, and then as infantryman, then as prisoner of war, this woman endured the brunt war [sic]. The latter sphere she found irksome enough, and she desired nothing better than to be sent to Vicksburg, there to be returned to her friends, promising that she had had enough of this latter life, and would there again assume her apparel and the condition of her sex. Some benevolent ladies and gentlemen contributed to her purchase of a dress and other suitable clothing, and yesterday she was a woman once more. She was sent to the department of the Provost Marshal, and Gen. Tuttle will undoubtedly forward her to Vicksburg with the next batch of prisoners.

Mrs. Clark is not yet 30 years of age, and dressed in the costume of a lady is not by any means an unpresentable woman. She is well informed upon politics, literature, and other general topics, and has less of the rowdy in her conversation and air than one would expect from her late associations.

Jackson Mississippian, December 30, 1862.
A Female Soldier

Among the strange, heroic and self-sacrificing acts of woman in this struggle for our independence, we have heard of none which exceeds the bravery displayed and hardships endured by the subject of this notice, Mrs.

Amy Clarke. Mrs. Clarke volunteered with her husband as a private, fought through the battles of Shiloh, where Mr. Clarke was killed—she performing the rites of burial with her own hands. She then continued with Bragg's army in Kentucky, fighting in the ranks as a common soldier, until she was twice wounded—once in the ankle and then in the breast, when she fell a prisoner into the hands of the Yankees. Her sex was discovered by the Federals, and she was regularly paroled as a prisoner of war, but they did not permit her to return until she had donned female apparel. Mrs. C was in our city on Sunday last [December 27], en route for Bragg's command. [As cited in *Southern Women of the Second American Revolution*, by Henry Jackson, Atlanta, Georgia, 1863. The identical story also was reproduced in the *Charleston Mercury*, South Carolina, January 8, 1863, and the *Southern Confederacy*, Atlanta, January 11, 1863.]

Natchez Daily Courier, Mississippi, February 13, 1863.
The Woman Soldier
[This story apparently refers to Mary Ann Clark.]

The editor of the *Winchester (Tenn.) Bulletin* was lately in Atlanta, where, among other "novelties," he met with Mrs.——, dressed up *a la militaire*, who had a furlough to visit Atlanta. This woman soldier is a member of the Louisiana cavalry, and "in for the war." She is about twenty years of age, rather small, and tolerably good looking.—Her husband was killed at Shiloh, and she forthwith took his place in the ranks. She has twice been wounded in battle and in one of the battles was taken prisoner, and regularly exchanged. We mention these facts as a part of the history of this war, let what may be said of the propriety of such conduct in woman.

FRANCES LOUISA CLAYTON
Nashville Dispatch, Tennessee, May 22, 1863.

The *Louisville Journal* of yesterday says: A female soldier, who has been in service twenty-two months, reported at headquarters yesterday, for transportation to Minnesota, where she resides. She was in the battles of Shiloh and Stone River, and twice wounded severely. She enlisted in the same company with her husband, and was with him up to the time of his death, which occurred at Murfreesboro, when she concluded to leave the army and return to her friends.

Nashville Dispatch, Tennessee, October 7, 1863.
Adventures of a Soldier Woman,
From the *Grand Rapids* (Mich.) *Eagle*

Mrs. Frances Louisa Clayton called at the Provost Marshal's office, in this
city [Grand Rapids], Thursday, with letters from officers, to procure a pass to
her home in Minnesota. Mrs. Clayton enlisted as a private, with her husband,
in a Minnesota regiment, some two years since. She was in Rosecrans' army,
and did full duty as a soldier nearly a year before her sex was discovered.
While in the army, the better to conceal her sex, she learned to drink, smoke,
chew and swear with the best or worst of the soldiers. She stood guard, went
on picket duty, in rain and storm, and fought on the field with the rest, and
was considered a good fighting man.

At the battle of Stone River, while making a charge, her husband was instantly killed by a ball, just five paces in front of her, in the front rank. She
charged over his body with the rear line, driving the rebels with the bayonet,
but was soon struck with a ball in the hip, and conveyed to the hospital,
where her sex was, of course, discovered. On recovering sufficiently to travel
she was discharged, on the 3rd of January last, and sent North. On the
way between Nashville and Louisville a guerrilla party attacked the train and
robbed her of her papers, money, etc.

After reaching home and recovering from her wound, Mrs. Clayton started
for the army again, to recover the papers belonging to her husband, but was
turned back at Louisville, and ordered home. By mistake her pass carried
her to Kalamazoo instead of Chicago, and she was compelled to apply to the
Provost Marshal there, who sent her through this way.

She is a very tall, masculine looking woman, bronzed by exposure to the
weather, and attracted universal attention by her masculine stride in walking,
erect and soldierly carriage, and generally *outre* appearance. Some soldiers
following her rather too familiarly, Thursday evening, she drew a revolver and
promptly scattered the crowd. She was recognized as an old acquaintance by
the keeper of an eating house on Monroe street, who knew her before her
marriage, and knew of her disappearance when her husband enlisted, and
who provided food and shelter for her Thursday night [see Chapter 8].

ELIZABETH COMPTON

Frazar Kirkland, *Pictorial Book of Anecdotes and Incidents of the War of
the Rebellion*, 1867, 605.
Young Feminine Spoiling for Fight

Lizzie Compton, a smart young Miss of sixteen, presented herself one day at Louisville, for the purpose of being mustered out of the service, she having been for some months a member of the Eleventh Kentucky cavalry. She had served in seven different regiments, and participated in several battles. At Fredericksburg she was seriously wounded, but recovered and followed the fortunes of war, which cast her from the Army of the Potomac to the Army of the Cumberland. She fought in the battles of Green River bridge, on the 4th of July, receiving a wound which disabled her for a short time. Seven or eight times she was discovered and mustered out of service, but immediately re-enlisted in another regiment. She stated that her home was in London, Canada West, that being the place of her parents' residence.

[This fairly typical example of newspaper style reporting, in fact probably quoted verbatim from a Kentucky newspaper, illustrates the distortions that occur in this medium. The report makes it sound as if all of the events described happened while she was in the 11th Kentucky Cavalry, which clearly could not have been the case. If she did in fact muster out with this regiment, that would have been in July 1865 at the conclusion of the war, and it would have been the last regiment in which she served. In any event, adventures that happened in more than one regiment quite apparently have been telescoped in this highly condensed report. The gist of the story apparently is true.]

Roxbury City Gazette, Massachusetts, May 14, 1863 (quoted from the
    Louisville Journal).
Soldier Girl

Lieut. Garraty brought to our office last evening a young girl in Federal uniform, who was arrested by Sergeant Murray of the patrol Guard yesterday. Her name is Lizzie Compton; her parents died when she was an infant in Anderson County, Tenn., and strangers brought her up. She fared well until the rebellion broke out, when she was living with Elijah Schermerhorn, a furious Secessionist, who has joined the Confederate army. Lizzie, true to the Union, with female determination on all occasions asserted her loyalty, until the man attempted to punish her for her fidelity, when she found her way to a Federal regiment, the Second Minnesota, we think.

For six months Lizzie has been known as Jack, and although not more than sixteen years old, has gone through a great deal of service. Colonel Mundy, commanding this post, proposed to her to resume the habiliments of her sex and take a position as hospital attendant, but she refused and reiterates her determination 'to die before she wears anything else but Uncle Sam's uniform, until the war is over.' In this resolve she seems inflexible and says she can die but once. She has a pleasant face, intelligent eyes and dimpled cheeks, and is at present domiciled at the Park Barracks. Her conduct, as far as we can learn, has been irreproachable.

CATHERINE E. DAVIDSON

Frank Moore, *The Civil War in Song and Story,* 1889, 451–452.
[Essentially the same story was reported by L. P. Brockett, *Battle-Field and Hospital,* 1888, 358–360.]
A Romantic Incident

While in Philadelphia, Gov. Curtin of Pennsylvania was introduced to a young woman who expressed joy at seeing him and kissed him on the forehead. She reminded him that after the battle of Antietam he had helped care for the wounded and dying. One was a soldier of the 28th Ohio who had been badly wounded in the arm. As Curtin had helped lift the soldier into an ambulance, the grateful soldier had given him a ring with the initials C.E.D. engraved on the interior. She pointed at the ring he was wearing on his little finger. Gov. Curtin removed the ring and saw the initials C.E.D.

"The finger that used to wear that ring will never wear it anymore," she said. "The hand is dead, but the soldier lives still." Gov. Curtin inquired whether that soldier had been her lover or a relative. She replied, "That soldier who placed that little ring upon your finger stands before you now." The girl was Catharine E. Davidson of Sheffield, Ohio. She had followed her lover into service, in a different regiment. "He was killed in the same battle where she fell wounded." She was the soldier who, in gratitude for his care on the battlefield, had placed the ring on his finger.

EMILY OF BROOKLYN

Frank Moore, *Women of the War: Their Heroism and Self-Sacrifice,* 1866, 529–532.
Women as Soldiers

In the early part of the year 1863, when the national fortunes were darkest, and victory perched continually on the standards of the rebellion, this young lady, then fresh from school, and scarce nineteen years of age, conceived the idea that Providence had destined her, as an American Joan of Arc, to marshal our discouraged forces, rally them to new efforts, and inspire them with a fresh and glowing enthusiasm....

Her parents at first treated this fancy of hers as a harmless day-dream, produced by excessive study, and by hearing of the constant reverses of the Union arms. At length more active means were employed to disabuse her mind of an impression so idle, and to dissuade her from a plan of action so utterly impracticable; but in vain.

An eminent physician was consulted, her pastor called to converse with her, and her former associates at school brought to her, that by their united influence she might see the folly of her dream; but none of their representations could dissuade her from a determination that was every day becoming more fixed.

Finally in a family meeting, it was held the most judicious course to take her to Michigan; and a maiden aunt became the companion and custodian of the enthusiastic girl. But she was not improved by the change, for only the positive command of her aunt prevented her from going to Washington to seek an interview with the good president, and ask the command of the national forces. At length it was found necessary to deprive her to some extent of her liberty; but this made her quite unmanageable, and she determined to enlist at all hazards. Escaping from her aunt, she disguised herself as a boy, and joined the drum corps of a Michigan regiment. All efforts to trace her were unavailing; and after some weeks of search, she was mourned by her parents as dead, and was believed to have committed suicide.

The regiment to which she was attached being ordered to reinforce General Rosecrans, she went with it to Tennessee, and marched under that accomplished strategist in all those skilful movements by which the rebel general Bragg was forced across the Cumberland Mountains [Tullahoma Campaign]....Then followed the hard struggle for Chattanooga. Her regiment was in Van Cleve's division, and in the sharp but indecisive engagements of Saturday she was unhurt. But on the disastrous day which followed, as the fair young soldier was standing unterrified under a deadly fire, a minie ball pierced her side, and she fell. On being carried to the surgeon's tent, an examination of her wound revealed her sex. The surgeon told her that she could not live, and advised her to disclose her name. This she was unwilling to do.

But the colonel of the regiment, though suffering from a painful wound, at length prevailed upon her to inform her family of her situation; and just before she died she dictated the following telegraphic despatch which was sent to her father:

"Mr. ____, No. __ Willoughby Street, Brooklyn. Forgive your dying daughter. I have but a few moments to live. My native soil drinks my blood. I expected to deliver my country, but the Fates would not have it so. I am content to die. Pray, pa, forgive me. Tell ma to kiss my daguerreotype. Emily. P.S. Give my old watch to little Eph."

The gentle enthusiast was buried under the shadow of the cloud-capped mountain [Lookout Mountain], which a few weeks after echoed from base to summit with the victorious cheers of out triumphant host, and the broad blue Tennessee murmurs for her a requiem soft and sad. A grave more glorious or more fitting she could not have chosen.

Frazar Kirkland, *Pictorial Book of Anecdotes and Incidents of the War of the Rebellion,* 1867, 520.

[Kirkland reports a condensed version of the story, including the information that the girl's aunt lived in Ann Arbor, Michigan, and the following passage:]

Military Monomania of a Brooklyn Girl

The regiment to which she was attached had a place in the division of the gallant Van Cleve, and during the bloody battle of Lookout Mountain, the fair girl fell, pierced in the left side by a Minie ball, and when borne to the surgeon's tent her sex was discovered.

ANNIE ETHERIDGE
National Tribune, April 17, 1890.
A Genuine Heroine; Gentle Annie Etheredge [*sic*], of the 5th Mich.

[In answer to an inquiry in the newspaper about the presence of women in battle, Sergeant F. O. Talbot, formerly with Company K, 1st Maine Heavy Artillery, reported the following incident.]

On June 22, 1864, we of the Second Corps [in the vicinity of Petersburg, Virginia] were suddenly attacked on the left flank and in rear, and . . . we ran back a few rods to a small breastwork, where we turned about, and after an hour or two of hot work drove the Johnnies. . . . Well, we broke and ran, as I say, and being in the thick woods, we became "mixed up."

When I jumped down behind the low breastwork, where, as fast as we arrived, we halted and turned about, I landed right beside a good-looking young woman. Can you imagine my astonishment? She stood with her head and shoulders above the works, watching us as we emerged from the thicket and came over the breastwork, to which she paid not the slightest attention, but stood calmly watching, and when she saw a wounded man coming, she lifted up her voice and called and beckoned to him. If he heard or saw her he came to her. I stood close beside her and watched her. As the wounded men came to her, they would hold up an arm, or tear away the cloth from a leg or side, or hold the head patiently, while she would bind some kind of cloth around the wound, and they would then proceed to the rear or take a place in line, if not too severely hurt, while she looked for the next one.

I was afraid she would get hit. I got nervous and wanted to make her get down out of danger, but did not do so. I just stood and watched her and said nothing.

Our line was very thin, and the Johnnies were coming with their familiar yell, and I wanted a Second Corps battery to come to our assistance. Finally one came—four guns, with four horses to a gun. They came on the gallop from the rear, went in battery close beside us, and in a short time silenced the rebel battery, and the fight was over.

I at once began to make inquiries of the men around me, none of whom I knew, as we were separated from our regiment, and all "mixed up." None of them had ever seen or heard of her, until I found a man who said:

"She belongs to the 5th Mich.; she's been with it from the first; she's been in mor'n a thousand battles; she's got a horse and tent of her own, and follows that regiment all the time. I tell you, it don't do for anybody to say any harm of her 'fore one of them 5th Mich. Fellows. They'd have his life in a minute. I don't know what her name is, but they call her 'Gentle Annie.'" I afterwards learned that her name was Annie Etheredge [sic].

There probably are some survivors of that splendid regiment who knew and saw her in battle, and we may hear from them. She was the only woman I saw before or afterwards anywhere near a battle, and she was on the front line, exposed to bullet and shell for at least two hours.—F.O. Talbot, Co. K, 1st Me. H.A., Alma, N.B [New Brunswick]

KATE FRANCES and ELIZA FRANCES
[Harpers Ferry provost marshal letter concerning two female prisoners
    (Credit: Virginia Historical Society.)]
OFFICE PROVOST MARSHAL
Military District of Harper's Ferry
Harper's Ferry, Va., Sept. 12th 1864
Lt. Col. John Wooley
Prov. Mar., Mid. Dept., 8th A.l.c.

Colonel,
I have the honor to forward to you, under guard, two (2) female prisoners, bogus soldiers, entitled

Kate alias James Johnson, and

Eliza Frances alias Frank Glenn.

They were arrested for loitering about the camps dressed in the U.S. uniform, & claiming to belong to Co. "K," 1st W. Va. Cav. It is reported that they have another companion, if not several, of the same "persuasion" who will be "gobbled" as speedily as possible by the military authorities. I would respectfully recommend that you make a levy in some of the generous feminine of Baltimore for a proper suit of wearing apparel, for the benefit of these wayward damsels.

Very Respectfully,

Your Obdt. Servt.

Alonzo D. Pratt,

Capt. & Prov. Marshal

[The cover sheet with this letter, signed only by the initials W.H.W., gives a somewhat different and interesting slant on this incident. The annotation says: "This is one of the *queer* features of war. These women were arrested in camp, while in uniform, and while doing regular duty as enlisted men."]

ELLEN GOODRIDGE

Frank Moore, *Women of the War: Their Heroism and Self-Sacrifice,*
    1866, 532–533.

Equally romantic, and more sad if possible, is the story of the Wisconsin girl, who, with a devotion of which only woman is capable, followed her soldier-lover through four years of active service, and at last closed his eyes in death in a Washington hospital a few days after Lee's surrender.

Her name is Ellen Goodridge, and the brave boy she loved so truly was James Hendrick. He volunteered for three months when the war broke out in 1861, and was at the first battle of Bull Run. Receiving a lieutenant's commission, he enlisted for three years, and wrote to that effect to his parents, and also to Ellen. When she told her parents that she had made up her mind to go with her lover and share the fortunes of war by his side, they were so incensed at what they considered her folly, that they turned her from their doors, and bade her never return. Going to Washington, she found young Hendrick's regiment, and obtained permission to remain at the Colonel's headquarters and look after the cooking.

They were in every great battle that was fought in Virginia, and in the intervals she often went with him in skirmishes and raids, on one such occasion receiving a painful wound in her arm from a minie ball. His health remained good till after the fall of Richmond. Then he became very sick, and was taken to Washington, where she watched over his couch, bathed his hot forehead, read to him, wrote for him, and showed the most painful anxiety for his recovery; but all in vain.

A day or two before he died, their marriage was solemnized by an Episcopal clergyman. The occasion was inexpressibly sad, he writhing in the grasp of a fatal disease, having survived all the great battles of the war only to die, and leave the noble girl, who had been so true to him, broken-hearted and a widow, and she almost wild with the terrible thought that, after giving up so much, to be near him, death would leave her only his name, and a bleeding heart.

FRANCES HOOK

Gettysburg Star & Sentinel, Pennsylvania, June 19, 1863.
Female Soldier—An Unusual Story

[T]here is no doubt but the following statement of the bravery and patriotism displayed by a young Pennsylvania girls eclipses all others.

The girl in question has been serving in the army for near a year, under the assumed name of Frank Martin, and is still retained though her disguise has been detected a second time, and is, at present, said to be on duty at Louisville. She was born near Bristol, Pa. [New Bristol, Conn., according to another version; see below], and her parents reside in Allegheny city, where she was raised. They are highly respectable people, and in very good circumstances. She was sent to the convent in Wheeling, Virginia, at the age of twelve years... [See 25th Michigan Infantry history excerpt below].

[She] accompanied the Army of the Cumberland [having enlisted in the 2nd East Tennessee Cavalry] to Nashville. She was in the thickest of the fight at Mufreesboro, and was severely wounded in the shoulder, but fought gallantly and waded Stone's River on the memorable Sunday on which our forces were driven back. She had her wound dressed, and here her sex was disclosed....

She left the Army of the Cumberland resolved to enlist in the first regiment she met. When she arrived at Bowling Green she found the 8th Michigan there, and enlisted, since which time she has been and is now connected with it. She is represented as an excellent horseman, and has been honored with the posting of regimental bugler in the regiment.

Frazar Kirkland, *Pictorial Book of Anecdotes and Incidents of the War of the Rebellion,* 1867, 173–174.

Career of Frank Henderson

The war produced many heroines... The following case of triple enlistment [by a woman] shows a military penchant quite rare and remarkable....

While our army was at Chattanooga, Colonel Burke, of the Tenth Ohio, went out to Graysville, Georgia, under flag of truce, with authority of General Thomas to exchange twenty-seven prisoners in our hands for an equal number in the hands of the rebels, the preliminaries of which had been previously arranged. Among the number in the hands of the enemy was a member of the Nineteenth Illinois, who may be called Frank Henderson.

Frank's history was briefly this: On the breaking out of the rebellion she had an only brother, the only relative, living in Chicago, Illinois. The brother enlisted in the Eleventh Illinois Infantry, and being left alone in the world she resolved to enlist in the service in order to be near her brother. She enlisted in the Eleventh, participated in its engagements, and on the mustering out of the regiment for the three months' service she was discharged, without her sex having been discovered.

She next enlisted in the Third Illinois regiment, and served for several months, during which time she managed to retain her secret, and by her staid habits won the universal esteem of the officers.

Wounded in one of the battles in which she participated, she was discharged. But Frank's love for the service did not permit her long to pursue the inert life incident to home, and the organization of the Ninetieth Illinois regiment offered her an opportunity to gratify her love for a military life. She enlisted as a private in Colonel O'Mara's regiment, and proved herself an excellent soldier. She served in all the battles of that regiment, and was present at the capture of Holly Springs by the rebels—denounced by her as a disgraceful proceeding on the part of our forces, who could have held the place.

In the latter part of the summer [1864], while the regiment was marching through Florence, Alabama, she asked and obtained permission of her Colonel to enter a house in search of something to eat; her regiment moved on, and while waiting for the supper to be prepared in the house where she was, two rebels crawled out from under a bed, and presenting themselves before her, ordered her to surrender.

Thus in their power, she was forced to yield herself a prisoner, and was taken to Atlanta, Georgia, and there placed in duress. In a few weeks after her arrival, Frank made a desperate attempt to escape, and when ordered to halt by the guard, paid not the least attention to the demand, and was fired upon. The ball took effect in her leg, and she continued to suffer from the wound. Colonel Burke, while out with the flag of truce, effected her exchange, among others, and she became an inmate of the hospital, where in due time she happily recovered from her wounds.

From the time of her first enlistment, which was in June, 1861, until some weeks after her capture, she kept her sex a secret from everybody, nor was there ever any suspicion excited in regard to her not being of the sex whose attire she wore.

In personal appearance she was prepossessing, and her whole demeanor was such as would have done no discredit to the best man in the ranks.

Frazar Kirkland, *Pictorial Book of Anecdotes and Incidents,* 1867, 567.
Girl-Boy Soldier in the Ninetieth Illinois

Frances Hook's parents died when she was only three years old, and left her, with a brother, in Chicago, Illinois. Soon after the war commenced, she and her brother enlisted in the Sixty-Fifth "Home Guards." Frances assumed the name of "Frank Miller." She served three months and was mustered out, without the slightest suspicion of her sex having arisen.

She then enlisted in the Ninetieth Illinois, and was taken prisoner in a battle near Chattanooga. She attempted to escape and was shot through the calf of one of her limbs while said limbs were doing their duty in the attempt. The rebels searched her person for papers and discovered her sex. The rascals respected her person as a woman, and gave her a separate room while in prison at Atlanta, Ga.

During her captivity she received a letter from Jeff. Davis, offering her a Lieutenant's commission if she would enlist in their army. She had no home and no relatives, but said she preferred to fight as a private soldier for the stars and stripes rather than be honored with a commission from the "rebs." At last she was exchanged. The insurgents tried to extort from her a promise that she would go home, and not enter the service again.

"Go home;" she said, "my only brother was killed at Pittsburg Landing [Shiloh], and I have no home—no friends!" Frank is described as of about medium height, with dark hazel eyes, dark brown hair, rounded features, and feminine voice and appearance.

[The following appears as an unattributed quote in the history of the 25th Michigan Infantry in John I. Robertson, *Michigan in the War,* 1880.]

In 1863, a Captain, accompanied by a young soldier apparently about seventeen, arrived in Louisville in charge of some rebel prisoners. The soldier attracted the attention of Colonel Mundy, at that time commanding officer of the post, by his intelligence and sprightly appearance. The Colonel detailed him for duty at Barracks No. 1, with the Twenty-fifth Michigan, then garrisoning Louisville. He soon won the esteem of his officers, and became a general favorite with all. Soon, however, the startling secret was disclosed, and whispering went thick and fast, the young soldier was a *lady*; the fact was reported and established by a soldier who was raised in the same town with her and knew her parents. She begged to be retained; having been in service ten months, she desired to serve during the war [i.e., for the duration]; her wish was granted, and she was continued on duty in the hospital.

Her name then was *Frank Martin;* her proper name [Frances Hook] she refused to give. She was born in New Bristol, Conn., but was raised in Alleghany City, Penn.; her parents were very respectable people. At the age of twelve she was sent to a convent at [Virginia], where she remained until the outbreaking of the war, and was well educated and accomplished. She left the convent, enlisted in an East Tennessee cavalry regiment, and went with the army of the Cumberland to Nashville. She was in the engagement at Stone[s] River, and severely wounded. Her sex was then discovered, and she was mustered out, although entreating earnestly with tears in her eyes to be continued in service.

Determined to enlist again, it is reported that she joined the Eighth Michigan Infantry, and is supposed to have belonged to it when she came to Louisville with the Captain and prisoners. Frank was quite small, a beautiful figure, auburn hair, large blue eyes beaming with brightness and intelligence; her complexion naturally very fair, though bronzed by exposure. She was exceedingly pretty and very amiable. She was very patriotic and determined to see the war out. [Immediately following this passage, the 25th Michigan history goes on to say that when the regiment left Louisville to join the Atlanta campaign in spring of 1864, "...she remained there, and of her whereabouts since nothing is known by the members of the regiment."]

Peoria Morning Mail, Illinois, May 16, 1863.
Female Soldiers

A Pennsylvania girl, who has been serving as a soldier in the Army of the West [*sic*] for 10 months, says that she has discovered a great many females among the soldiers, one of whom is now a Lieutenant. She has assisted in burying three female soldiers at different times, whose sex was unknown to any one but herself.

[Although she is not named, the content indicates that the girl was Frances Hook.]

MRS. CLARA JUDD

Official Records of the Union and Confederate Armies, Series 2, Vol. 5,
   No. 118.
OFFICE CHIEF OF POLICE, FOURTEENTH ARMY CORPS
Nashville, January 13, 1863
Capt. WILLIAM M. WILES
Provost-Marshal-General, Fourteenth Army Corps

SIR: The following is the substance of the testimony elicited in the case
of Mrs. Clara Judd, arrested by the army police on charge of attempting to
carry through the lines articles contraband of war such as quinine, morphine,
nitrate of silver, besides other goods, and one knitting-machine carried as
a pattern, which articles were found and have been purchased by her and
brought within these army lines upon a pass obtained under false pretenses.

Mrs. Judd is the widow of an Episcopal clergyman who resides in Winchester, Tenn. He died some two years since leaving a large family of some
seven children. Mrs. Judd passed through our lines with permission to take
her three youngest children to Minnesota, from whence the family originally
came. She took them, leaving them with a sister, she herself returning and
passing through our lines to the rebel army. [Mrs. Judd obtained funds from
various people to purchase articles in the north.] Having thus provided herself she came through our lines and was, under her representations that she
wished to go to her children in Minnesota, granted a pass North. . . .

It is respectfully submitted that she is a dangerous person to remain in
these lines; that she is probably a spy as well as a smuggler; that cases of this
kind being of frequent occurrence by females examples should be made; and
that there is at present no proper tribunal for her especial trial or proper
place of imprisonment at Nashville she be commited to the military prison at
Alton, in the State of Illinois, for trial. . . .

Very respectfully, JOHN FITCH, Provost-Judge

ANNIE LILLYBRIDGE

John Truesdale, *The Blue Coats, and How They Lived, Fought, and
   Died for the Union,* 1867, 442–443; Frazar Kirkland, *Pictorial Book*

of Anecdotes and Incidents, 1867, 621–622. [Substantially the same
account appeared previously in the *Nashville Dispatch,* July 11, 1863,
attributed to the *Chicago Post.*]
Annie Lillybridge and Lieutenant W.

Annie Lillybridge, of Detroit, was for 'Union,' and in favor of the hardships
and dangers of war, if need be, to secure that end. She courted, rather than
shrank from, those hardships, and bared her breast to rebel bullets.

According to Annie's account, her parents resided in Hamilton, Canada
West. In the spring of 1862, she was employed in a dry goods store in Detroit,
where she became acquainted with Lieutenant W—, of one of the Michigan
regiments, and an intimacy immediately sprang up between them. They cor-
responded for some time, and became much attached to each other. But during the ensuing summer season, Lieutenant W— was appointed to a position
in the twenty-first Michigan infantry, then rendezvousing in Ionia county.

The thought of parting from the gay lieutenant nearly drove Annie mad,
and she resolved to share his dangers and be near him. No sooner had she
resolved upon this course than she proceeded to act. Purchasing male attire
she visited Ionia, and enlisted in Captain Kavanagh's company, twenty-first
regiment. While in camp she managed to keep her secret from all; not even
the object of her attachment who met her every day, was aware of her presence so near him.

Annie left with her regiment for Kentucky, passed through all the dangers
and temptations of a camp-life, endured long marches, and slept on the cold
ground—all without a murmur. At last, before the battle of Pea Ridge, in
which her regiment took part, her sex was curiously discovered by a member
of her company, upon whom she laid the injunction of secrecy, after relating
to him her previous history.

On the following day [the expression "on the following day" appears in
both the 1863 and 1867 versions, but since it is referenced to Pea Ridge or
Prairie Grove it cannot be correct; the regiment was not present at either
battle] she was under fire, and from a letter in her possession, it appears she
behaved with marked gallantry, and by her own hand shot a rebel captain
who was in the act of firing upon Lieutenant W—. But the fear of revealing her
sex continually haunted her.

After the battle, she was sent out with others to collect the wounded, and
one of the first corpses found by her was the soldier who had discovered her
sex. Days and weeks passed on, and she became a universal favorite with the

regiment; so much so that her colonel, Stephens, frequently detailed her as regimental clerk—a position that brought her in close contact with her lover, who, at this time, was major, or adjutant, of the regiment.

A few weeks subsequently she was out on picket duty, when she received a shot in the arm that disabled her, and notwithstanding the efforts of the surgeon, her wound grew worse from day to day. She was sent to the hospital at Louisville, where she remained several months, when she was discharged by the post surgeon, as her arm was stiffened and useless.

Annie implored to be permitted to return to her regiment, but the surgeon was unyielding, and discharged her. Annie immediately hurried toward home. At Cincinnati she told her secret to a benevolent lady, and was supplied with female attire. She declared she would enlist in her old regiment again, if there was a recruiting officer for the twenty-first in Michigan. She still clung to the lieutenant—said she must be near him if he fell, or was taken down sick—that where he went she would go—and when he died, she would end her life by her own hands.

CHARLES MARTIN
Frazar Kirkland, *Pictorial Book of Anecdotes and Incidents of the War of the Rebellion,* 1867, 206.
Girl-Boy Drummer

A fair and sprightly girl, of but twelve dimpled summers, and giving the name of Charles Martin, enlisted in one of the Pennsylvania regiments, in the early period of the war, as a drummer boy. She had evidently enjoyed the advantage of education, could write a good hand, and even composed very well. She made herself useful to officers of the regiment in the capacity of a clerk; and though involved in the scenes and chances of no less than five battles, she escaped unwounded and unharmed. The officers never dreamed of any hitch as to her sex.

After a while, she was taken down sick with the typhoid fever, a disease then quite prevalent in Philadelphia, and was removed to Pennsylvania Hospital. It was while there that the worthy matron of the institution discovered the drummer boy, who had passed through so many fatigues, perils and rough experiences, to be no more nor less than a girl not yet in her teens.

MARIAN McKENZIE
Chicago Daily Tribune, April 18, 1862.
A Romantic Female

On Sunday evening [April 13] as an officer of the North Division was patrolling his beat at a late hour of the night, his attention was called to a woman found standing at the corner of Chicago Avenue and Clark streets, having a small bundle in her arms. He accosted her, learned that she had no place to stay and kindly took her to the station house, where she was transferred to the Police Court, told her story, and was discharged, there being no testimony adduced that she was other than a poor but honest girl.

Yesterday forenoon the same policeman, as he was passing along Rush street, near the bridge, had his curiosity considerably excited by something peculiar in the appearance of a man dressed in soldier's uniform, walking ahead of him. He followed the person into a saloon and there recognized the quasi soldier as the girl he had taken to the station on Sunday night. Of course he arrested her, charging that she was a woman in man's attire, which was at first stoutly denied, but afterwards confessed.

Yesterday afternoon she was again brought to the Armory and upon being questioned, gave her name as Mary Fitzallan [sic], said she was 18 years of age, unmarried, a native of Kentucky, and had under the title of Harry Fitzallan worn male habiliments for the past 7 months, four of which she had passed as a Union volunteer in the 23rd Kentucky regiment, and previously working as a hired hand on a farm near Newport, Kentucky. When asked as to her former history and what made her dress in clothes unbecoming her sex, she refused to be communicative, but answered that she had her peculiar reasons, and that her history would be of no avail to the Court.

She is a girl of medium size, rather *embonpoint* [plump, chubby], with heavy and not wholly unhandsome face, her features being more masculine than otherwise, and hair black, cut short in the present style, and parted on one side. Her eyes are blue. Her hands betray evidences of manual labor. She stood in the presence of the Magistrate with not a bold but confident air, answered the few questions she wished to respond to deliberately, and apparently truthfully, betraying but little of the modesty and shrinking nature we have been [in] the habit of attributing to the share of the gentler sex.

Justice Akin, after giving the young woman some sound advice, fined her $20, under the ordinance, but suspended execution to allow her to get out of the city, and she made her exit from the court room in her male attire, and deliberately walked down into the street. Whether she will take her departure for Canada, or remain here, hunting up a friend—or lover—and again get arrested, remains for the future to solve.

Official Records of the Union and Confederate Armies, Series 2, Vol. 5,
   No. 118.
OFFICE PROVOST-MARSHAL-GENERAL
Wheeling [Virginia], December 24, 1862
Col. W. Hoffman, Commissary-General of Prisoners.

SIR: I have the honor specially to report the receipt of a prisoner of war
sent here by Brigadier-General Crook in the shape of a female wearing male
apparel charged as a spy for the rebels, arrested in the streets of Charleston, Va. Her statements are contradictory, at one time asserting she was in
the rebel army, at another time affirming she served with the Twenty-third
Kentucky Volunteer Infantry, U.S. Army. She is a coarse-looking creature,
scarcely answering the description of *la fille du regiment*. I have placed her in
the Ohio County jail for the present, ordered clothes for her suitable to her
sex, and await your order regarding her.
   Very respectfully, Jos. Darr, Jr.
   Major and Provost-Marshal General.
   [Indorsement.]
   Respectfully referred to Colonel Doster, provost-marshal, to know if he
can provide for the within-named woman in the Old Capitol Prison if she is
ordered to this city. Please return this letter.
   W. Hoffman
   Colonel Third Infantry, Commissary-General of Prisoners.
   [Inclosure]

A FEMALE SOLDIER IN CUSTODY—AN EVENTFUL CAREER
[Unidentified newspaper report]

Among the prisoners brought up yesterday on the steamer Bostona, No. 2,
was the somewhat famous female soldier, Harry Fitzallen, of whom our readers have doubtless heard something through the Cincinnati papers. Harry,
who was dressed in a tight-fitting cavalry uniform, was taken to jail yesterday
soon after his arrival, when the provost-marshal, Major Darr, with a view of
ascertaining if possible the truth in relation to the charge that has been made
against Harry of being a rebel spy, held an interview with her.
   During the conversation she said her name was Marian McKenzie. She
was born in Glasgow, Scotland. Her mother died when she was an infant and
her father removed with her to this country when she was only four years
old. Her father dying a short time after reaching New York Marian was left
alone upon the world and managed to make her living in various ways, as

she expressed it. She educated herself and studied for the stage but finding the profession of an actress not exactly suited to her taste she traveled about from place to place engaging in divers employments.

Shortly after the breaking out of the war she enlisted in a Kentucky regiment at Newport and served two months. Upon her sex being discovered she had to quit. She enlisted several times after this in as many different regiments and was several times arrested. The last time she was arrested in Charleston, Kanawha County, in men's apparel by the provost-marshal.

She says that she has brothers and sisters residing in Canada. Upon being asked what part of Canada her relations inhabited she declined to answer, saying:

"This sensation will have publicity enough if it has not already and I do not wish the innocent to suffer for the guilty."

When told that she would be detained until her statements could be corroborated she said: "Very well, I cannot help it. The only way in which I have violated the law is in assuming men's apparel. The injury that I have done is principally to myself."

She speaks fluently and uses the best of language, and is evidently an educated woman, well skilled in the iniquities of the world. She visited this city about three years ago under the name of Miss Fitzallen and in the character of a prostitute. She says she went into the army for the love of excitement and from no motive in connection with the war, one way or another.

She is about twenty-five years of age, very short and very thick. She has heretofore acknowledged that she has been engaged in the rebel service but now denies the soft impeachment. As there are several suspicious circumstances connected with the case Harry will be furnished with appropriate clothing and detained until all doubts are removed.

Official Records of the Union and Confederate Armies, Series 2, Vol. 5, No. 118.

OFFICE COMMISSARY-GENERAL OF PRISONERS
Washington, D.C., January 9, 1863.
Maj. JOSEPH DARR, Jr.
Provost-Marshal-General, Wheeling, Va.

MAJOR: Your letters of 24th and 25th ultimo in relation to Marian McKenzie were answered on the 30th ultimo but my letter was missent and I therefore rewrite it and inclose it herewith, but do not release her until you have referred her case again with such charges as may be presented against her. I approve of your suggestion that Mary Jane Green should be placed in a house of refuge, and if there is one within reach where she will be received the Government paying for her board you are authorized to send her there, and you may make the same disposition of Marian McKenzie if she cannot be brought to trial as a spy and her character is like that of Mary Jane Green. Should you be unable to have them received at a house of refuge what are your means for holding them at Wheeling? I approve of your action in paroling Kate Brown.

Very respectfully, your obedient servant,

W. HOFFMAN,

Colonel Third Infantry, Commissary-General of Prisoners.

JANE BOSWELL MOORE

[Battlefield nurse, Baltimore, Maryland, who served in the field along with her mother.]

Frank Moore, *Women of the War: Their Heroism and Self-Sacrifice,* 1866, 554–570, quotes extensively from her memoirs. Following are some excerpts.

It is not often I allow myself to dwell on the fearful realties of the past, as they now rise before me;—from the first hospital, or barracks thrown open in Baltimore, after the battles of Bull Run and Williamsburg, in the closing scenes of the great struggle.... By the light of a dimly-rising moon we rode over the burial trenches of Antietam to Smoketown Hospital, through whose scattered grove of trees the roaring of the December wind sounded like the notes of some great funeral organ. Our tent was daily visited by an ever coming and going throng of the maimed and sick. How humble their thanks for paper, ink, books, and little delicacies made us!...

A picture of desolate grandeur was Harper's Ferry, with its rude hospitals, its dead on the hill-side, whose march was over.... We hurried away from here to the wounded of Chancellorsville, those of a single corps covering a large plain at Brook Station. Our tents (for store-room, kitchen, and sleeping) were in a secluded ravine, overhung with laurel. We had sad music—the bands on the hill-side with their mournful 'dead march,' by open graves, and the plaintive cry of the whippoorwill, when our busy day was done.

The hurried falling back, and Gettysburg with all its horrors, among whose dead and dying we passed a month, and then found ourselves encamped along the Rappahannock.... A deserted cabin formed our next quarters at Point of Rocks, close to the swamps of the Appomattox, where we saw the opening bombardment of Petersburg. . . . Half an hour after they were wounded, many of the victims of the fatal mine explosion [Battle of the Crater, July 30, 1864] were under our care, for, by a special order from General Grant, we were allowed to remove to the 'front,' something over a mile and a half from Petersburg. Our tent, which stood in the midst of a group of pines, was shaded with boughs, and the earth strewn with a carpet of pine needles, the dull, monotonous, awful sound of continued musketry firing being ever in our ears. The soul sickens with the horror of the scenes in those woods on and after July 30. What noble letters those brave, crippled, colored soldiers dictated, through us, to friends they were never to see! . . .

Colored citizens of Baltimore cried to us to give them 'only one cracker,' and our hearts melted when the appeal was enforced by their directing attention to the stump of an amputated arm or leg. . . .

SARAH JANE PERKINS

[Enlisted in the Confederate army with her brother and was captured in spring of 1864.]

Official Records of the Union and Confederate Armies, Series 2, Vol. 7, No. 120.

Union & Confederate Correspondence, Orders, Etc., Relating to Prisoners of War and State from April 1, 1864, to December 31, 1864. -#18

WASHINGTON, D.C., July 9, 1864.

Col. W. HOFFMAN, U.S. Army

Commissary-General of Prisoners of War, Washington, D.C.

COLONEL: Inclosed I have the honor to transmit report of inspection made at Point Lookout, Md., July 1, 1864, complying with instructions received, dated Washington, June 19, 1864.

I am, sir, very respectfully, your obedient servant,

C.T. ALEXANDER

Surgeon, U.S. Army.

...

COLONEL: I deem it proper to call your attention especially to the following points: First, the water, being brackish and scanty, is causing a large increase of disease. This should be remedied at once by a sufficient supply of fresh water being furnished by boats until condensers suitable for the purpose are obtained. Second. The misunderstanding in reference to the construction of a hospital. At present material has been purchased only sufficient to erect one ward, this being understood as your order on the subject. A necessity exists for the building as soon as practicable at least six wards, with laundry, mess-room, kitchen, and sinks. Third. An extra issue of anti-scorbutics to correct the scurvy and tendency thereto now existing. If it could be so arranged that the Baltimore and Fortress Monroe daily boat could touch at this point it would be a great convenience. Among the prisoners is a woman, Sarah Jane Perkins, whose removal is desirable.

C.T. ALEXANDER
Surgeon, U.S. Army
Acting Medical Inspector, U.S. Army

MARY ANN PITMAN

Official Records of the Union and Confederate Armies, Series 2, Vol. 7,
    No. 120; Annex Z 10.
Examination of Mary Ann Pitman by Col. J.P Sanderson, provost-
    marshal-general, Department of the Missouri.
SAINT LOUIS, June 20, 1864
[Deposition of Mary Ann Pitman.]

I resided near Chestnut Bluff, Tenn., and went into the Confederate service on the breaking out of the rebellion. Myself and Lieutenant Craig went around and got together enough volunteers to make up a company, which we took into Freeman's regiment. I was second lieutenant in the infantry. After the battle of Shiloh I commanded the company. I took my company then and joined Forrest's command, as first lieutenant, and acted as such under the name of Lieutenant Rawley. While with Forrest's command I was, a large portion of the time, occupied on special service. Much of which was of a secret character and in the performance of which I passed in the character of a female. Whilst so employed I was detailed to procure ordnance and ammunition, and came to Saint Louis as Mary Hays.

[Describes contacts with John Beauvais at the Everett House and purchase of munitions from him.] At three different interviews I made known to Mr. Beauvais that these things were for Forrest's command. The first time he said to me that they were talking of conscripting, and he told me that if they did he was going South; if they did not, he would not go, for he could be of more service to the Confederacy here [in St. Louis] than in the South; but if they conscripted he was going, for he never would fight for the Federal Government; that he was a Southern man in principle and always had been....

I went to this store the last time under the advice of a Memphis detective with a view to see if he would continue the sale after he was arrested. I landed, on the last trip, at Randolph. When I got there I was not going to Forrest; I was going to send him those things, which I did, by one of his officers, Captain Wright, and was not going. I was going back to Saint Louis. I had sent him a letter stating that I had procured a large quantity of caps, powder, ammunition, &c; that I had employed Mr. Williams to bring them down. I was waiting for an order from Forrest to say where he wanted them sent to. There was a large quantity, quite a wagonload. I was not going to Forrest myself at all, but when I got there, the next day after I had sent them as many as Captain Wright and his brother and a negro boy, which he owned, could carry, I sent word to Forrest I intended to go right back to Saint Louis as soon as I could arrange the business there.

I received a dispatch from Forrest ordering me to report at his headquarters, about ten miles from Fort Pillow. He wanted me to take my position in the field, as he said he would rather detail ten of his best officers for this business than lose my services at that time. So I started on a mule and was captured. Somebody told on me. They had something in the papers about my being captured—taking an officer's horse away and threatening to shoot him—which was all false. I was taken from the place where I was captured to Fort Pillow. I was captured about five or six miles from Fort Pillow at the house of Mr. Green, a Southern man. I was there, three days; two or three, I am not certain which. . . .

Before my capture my mind and feeling had undergone a very material change from what they were when I started out in the war as to the character of the Northern people and soldiers and the merits of the controversy involved. I started out with the most intense feelings of prejudice against the Northern people. I regarded all I had heard as to their views, character, and purposes to be true, but my intercourse with such as came into our possession during my service in the Confederate Army, and especially my trip to Saint Louis, convinced me of my error in this respect. I found the Union officers and soldiers not to be the desperadoes which I had been taught to believe them to be. . . .

This was the condition of my mind when I was captured, and I accordingly immediately resolved to perform an honorable part and do nothing to discredit or disgrace my name. While satisfied that I had been performing services which placed my life at the mercy and disposal of the Federal Government, I felt it to be my duty to tell the truth and do what I could to atone for the past, and resolved to throw myself upon the [mercy of the?] Government. I resolved, be the result with me personally what it might, never to return to the Confederate service and continue my former career. I accordingly, immediately on my arrival at Fort Pillow, gave such information as I could to vindicate my personal integrity and show the authorities my determination to act in good faith....

[Annex Z 10 concludes with a transcript of questions by Colonel Sanderson and Pitman's answers, focusing on her knowledge of and participation in the secret society known as the Order of American Knights, which had chapters in the North and worked covertly to undermine the Union and advance the Confederate cause.]

MARY JANE PRATER

Official Records of the Union and Confederate Armies, Series 2, Vol. 5, No. 118.

OFFICE PROVOST-MARSHAL-GENERAL

Wheeling [Virginia], March 9, 1863

Col. W. HOFFMAN, Commissary-General of Prisoners [Washington, D.C.]

SIR: I have to apologize for an unintentional error in my late report of the female prisoner Mary Jane Prater. I set her down as one, but it now appears she is two. The jailer informs me that she has been *enceinte* [pregnant] about five months. This complicates the matter somewhat. I presume I will soon receive final instructions from you concerning this one and Marian McKenzie, both arrested on same charge, wearing soldiers' apparel and frequenting our camps in that garb.

Very respectfully,

JOS. DARR, JR.,

Major and Provost-Marshal-General.

DIANA SMITH

Frank Moore, *The Civil War in Song and Story,* 1889, 223–224.

[The same story appears in the *Washington Telegraph,* Arkansas, December 24, 1862, and the *Dallas Herald,* Texas, January 7, 1863, one or both of which probably were Moore's "Southern paper."]

Diana Smith: The Heroine of the Northwest

She was born and raised in the county of Jackson, Virginia. Her father is a consistent member of the Methodist Episcopal Church, and was leading a quiet, peaceful, and useful life, until his country was invaded, when he called his countrymen to arms, and raised the first company of guerrillas, which he commanded until last fall, when, by fraud and treachery, he was captured, and ever since has been confined in a loathsome dungeon at Camp Chase, Ohio, without hope of delivery, unless our government should interpose and procure his release.

Diana, his only daughter, a beautiful girl, has been tenderly raised and well educated. She is also a member of the Methodist Episcopal Church and has always been regarded as very pious and exemplary. She is descended from a race of unflinching nerve, and satisfied with nothing less than freedom, as unrestrained as the pure air of their mountain home.

Her devotion to the cause of Southern rights, in which her father had nobly engaged, has caused her, too, to feel the oppressor's power. Although a tender and delicate flower, upon whose cheek the bloom of sixteen summers yet lingers, she has been five times captured by the Yankees, and marched sometimes on foot, in *manacles*, a prisoner; once a considerable distance into Ohio, at which time she made her escape. She was never released, but in each instance managed to escape from her guard. She, too, has seen service; she was in several battles in which her father engaged the enemy. She has seen blood flow like water. Her trusty rifle has made more than one of the vile Yankees bite the dust. She left her home in company with the Moccasin Rangers, Captain Kelser, and came through the enemy's lines in safety, and is now at Blue Sulphur Springs.

She was accompanied by Miss Duskie, who has also earned the proud distinction of a heroine. On one occasion this fearless girl, surrounded by fifty Yankees and Union men, rushed through their ranks with a daring that struck terror to their craven hearts. With her rifle lashed across her shoulders, she swam the west fork of the Kanawha River, and made her way to the Mountain Rangers, preferring to trust her safety to those brave spirits, well knowing that her sex would entitle her to protection from these brave mountaineers. These young ladies have lain in the mountains for a month, with no bed but the earth, and no covering but the canopy of heaven. They have shared the soldier's rough fare, his dangers, his hopes, and his joys.

The great crime with which these daring young ladies are charged by the enemy, is cooking, washing, mending and making clothes, and buying powder for the soldiers. We are informed that they are both ladies of the first rank at home, and are every way worthy of the highest place in any society where virtue, integrity, and sterling principle give position. —Southern paper.

"SOLDIER TOM"

Emporia News, Illinois, May 13, 1870; from the *St. Louis Times.*
A Degenerate Female Soldier

During the investigation of city cases, yesterday, a tall specimen of the demimonde, clad in unimpeachable black, and with a countenance beaming with smiles, appeared in the lobby. This lady is an historical character, having served over two years in the Federal army during the war—fifteen months as a private in the Illinois cavalry, and over nine months as a teamster in the noted Lead Mine Regiment [45th Illinois Infantry], which was raised in Washburn's District, from the counties of Jo Davis and Carroll. She was at the siege of Corinth, and was on duty during most of the campaign against Vicksburg. At Lookout Mountain she formed one of a party of eighteen selected to make a scout and report the position of [Confederate] Gen. Bragg's forces. She was an attache of Gen. Blair's 17th corps during most of the campaign of the Army of the Tennessee, and did good service in the reconnoitering operations around the Chattahoochie River, at which time she was connected with Gen. Davis' 14th corps.

The girl, who is now 22 years of age, but who looks much younger, went through her army life under the cognomen "Soldier Tom," by which name she will be recognized by many who served in the Department of the West. Her business in the police court was in the capacity of a witness in the case of a courtesan named Julia Roberts, who pleaded guilty to the charge of disturbing the peace at Mozart Hall a few nights ago.

SARAH TAYLOR

Savannah Republican, Georgia, June 27, 1862.
A Female Prisoner

Some excitement was created on Thursday [June 26] by the arrival of a female prisoner, in the uniform of a *Fille du Regiment.* She is said to have been for some months following the Third Regiment of East Tennessee Renegades in Kentucky. Her name we learn is Sallie Taylor; she is from Anderson County, where she has respectable relations. She was captured somewhere in the neighborhood of Jacksonboro. An examination before the Provost Marshal, we understand, elicited some valuable information from this romantic damsel, in regard to the movement of the enemy. (*Knoxville Register.*)

Memphis Daily Appeal, Atlanta, Georgia, July 18, 1863.
Sallie Taylor, *Le Fille du Regiment*

This notorious (beautiful, though, she was) woman arrested, as our readers will remember, some months ago, and discharged upon her parole, has kept herself quiet recently, when, as we are informed, she so far captivated, if not captured, a private in Cobb's battery stationed at Clinton, as to induce him to steal the horse of one of the lieutenants of his company and to escape with her into Kentucky, where she may resume in *propria personnae*, her *nom de plume* of "Daughter of the 1st (Bird's) Tennessee regiment. (*Knoxville Register.*)

Frazar Kirkland, *Pictorial Book of Anecdotes and Incidents of the War of the Rebellion*, 1867, 544–545.

Miss Captain Taylor, of the First Tennessee

One of the features of the First Tennessee Regiment, was a brave and accomplished young lady of but eighteen summers, and of prepossessing appearances, named Sarah Taylor, of East Tennessee, the step-daughter of Captain Dowden, of the First Tennessee Regiment. Miss Taylor was an exile from home, having joined the fortunes of her step-father and her wandering campaigns, accompanying them in their perilous and dreary flight from their hearths and homesteads.

She formed the determination to share with her late companions the dangers and fatigues of a military campaign; and to this end, she donned a neat blue chapeau, beneath which her long hair was fantastically arranged, bearing at her side a highly finished regulation sword, and silver-mounted pistols in her belt, all of which gave her a very neat appearance. She became quite the idol of the Tennessee boys, who looked upon her as a second Joan of Arc, believing that victory and glory would perch upon the standards borne in the ranks favored by her presence.

Miss Captain Taylor was, indeed, all courage and skill. Having become an adept in the sword exercise, and a sure shot with a pistol, she determined to lead in the van of the march—to return her exiled countrymen to their homes, if it cost the sacrifice of her own life's blood. [The order came to reinforce Col. Garrard, and excitement prevailed in camp] . . . the persecuted Tennesseans looked upon the daring girl who followed their fortunes through sunshine and shadow, with the tenderest feeling of veneration, and each would willingly have offered his life in her defence.

There was but little sleep in the camp on Saturday night, so great was the joy of the men at the prospect of meeting the foe, and at a very early hour in the morning they filed away jubilantly, with their Joan of Arc in the van. . . .

LORETA JANETA VELAZQUEZ

[See Chapter 9 for discussion of the accuracy and credibility of the
    following newspaper reports.]

Spectator, Staunton, Virginia, June 30, 1863, from Jackson, Mississippi,
    June 6, 1863.

[Several slightly different versions of this story appeared in other
    newspapers in June and July, apparently all taken from the *Jackson
    Mississippian*.]

Adventures of a Young Lady in the Army

Among the registered enemies of the United States government who have
been recently sent across the lines, from New Orleans, there is now in this
city a lady whose adventures place her in the ranks of the Molly Pitchers of
the present revolution.

At the breaking out of the war, Mrs. Laura J. [Mrs. James J. In one paper]
Williams (the lady to whom we allude,) was a resident of Arkansas. Like
most of the women of the South, her whole soul was enlisted in the struggle
for independence. Her husband was a Northern man by birth and education,
and a strong Union man. After Arkansas seceded from the Union, he went to
Connecticut, he said, to see his relations and settle upon some business. Mrs.
Williams suspected his purpose, and finally she received information that he
had joined the Yankee army.

Possessing little of the characteristic weakness of her sex, either in body or
mind, Mrs. W. Vowed to offer her life upon the altar of her country. Disguising herself in a Confederate uniform, and adopting the name of "Henry Benford," she proceeded to Texas where she raised and equipped an independent
company, and went to Virginia with it as 1st Lieutenant. She was in the battle
of Leesburg and several skirmishes; but, finally, her sex having ben discovered by the surgeon of the regiment—the 5th Texas Volunteers, to which the
company had been attached—she returned to her home in Arkansas.

After remaining there a short time, she proceeded to Corinth, and was in
the battle of Shiloh, where she displayed great coolness and courage. She saw
her father on the field, but, of course, he did not recognize her, and she did
not make herself known to him. In the second day's fighting she was wounded
in the head, and was ordered to the rear. She wrote to her father, and then
came on down to Grenada, where she waited for some time, but never saw
or heard from him.

She then visited New Orleans, was taken sick, and while sick the city was
captured. On recovery, she retired to the coast, where she employed herself

in carrying communications, assisting parties to run the blockade with drugs and cloths for uniforms. She was informed on by a negro and arrested and brought before general Butler. She made her appearance before Gen. Butler in a Southern homespun dress. She refused to take the oath, told him she gloried in being a rebel—had fought side by side with Southern men for Southern rights, and if she ever lived to see "Dixie" she would do it again.

Butler denounced her as the most incorrigible she rebel he had ever met with. By order of the Beast she was placed in confinement, where she remained three months. Some time after her release, she was arrested again for carrying on "contraband correspondence," and kept in a dungeon fourteen days on bread and water at the expiration of which time she was placed in the State prison as a dangerous enemy.

Her husband, it so happened, was a lieutenant in the 18th [13th] Connecticut regiment, and on duty as Provost Guard in the city. He accidentally found her out and asked if she wanted to see him. She sent him word she never wanted to see him as long as he wore the Yankee uniform. But he forced himself upon her, tried to persuade her to take the oath, get a release, when he said he would resign to take her to his relations in Connecticut. She indignantly spurned his proposition, and he left her to her fate. When Gen. Banks assumed command he released a great many prisoners, but kept her in confinement until the 17th of May last, when she was sent across the lines to Meadesville with the registered enemies.

An article was recently published in the New York "World" in relation to the part Mrs. Williams has played in this war, but the above is, we are assured, a true account of her remarkable career. We understand she has attached herself to the medical staff of a brigade now in this city, and will render all assistance in her power to our wounded in the approaching struggle for possession of the great Valley of the Mississippi. Jackson, Miss., June 6, 1863.

Savannah Republican, Georgia, July 15, 1863.
The Female Lieutenant

"Lieutenant Buford," the female Lieutenant from the South, arrived in this city [Richmond], and sent to Castle Thunder, has been released by General Winder. The charge of being a Yankee spy was never alleged against her, and she is indignant that such a thing was ever insinuated. She persists in sporting her military costume, and it was this that got her into trouble with the Richmond authorities.

Her real name is Mrs. S.T. Williams, and her husband is a 1st Lieutenant in Company E, 13th Connecticut regiment, under Banks in Louisiana. Her father is Major J.S. Roche, of Mississippi, but she was born in the West Indies. Her people were wealthy, and her annual income before the war was $20,000, most of which she spent in getting medicines for the Confederate Government. Her penchant was to follow the army in a private ambulance with medicines, bandages, and servant, and apply herself to the relief of the wounded, though she was known to lend a helping hand with the musket at several battles in which she participated. —*Richmond Examiner.*

Spectator, Staunton, Virginia, September 22, 1863.
Weekly Columbus Enquirer, Georgia, October 6, 1863.
[Identical story taken from the *Richmond Examiner.*]
The Female Lieutenant

The public will remember the numerous paragraphs published concerning one "Lieut. Harry Buford," nee Mrs. Williams, with a history romantic in war as that of Joan of Arc. Last summer the Lieutenant got into Castle Thunder, her sex not corresponding with the dashing uniform she wore. She was released, and went from Richmond to Chattanooga, where she joined Gen'l Bragg's army, got upon the staff of General A.P. Stewart, and for a time was employed in the secret service, effecting important arrests of spies, and doing some very daring things.

The other day she visited Richmond again, not as the gay Lieutenant, but in the garments more becoming her sex, and bearing the name of Mrs. Jeruth DeCaulp, she having, in the interval, married an officer of the Confederate States Provisional army of that name, first obtaining a divorce from her first husband, Williams, who is in the army of Gen. Grant.

In consideration of her services, the Confederate Government has commissioned Mrs. DeCaulp with the rank of Captain, and, since her arrival in Richmond, she has drawn $1,600 back pay. —She is now at the Ballard House, en route for Georgia, and the home of her new husband.

The heroine of this sketch is a native of Mississippi, and a devoted Southern woman. —*Richmond Examiner.*

Official Records of the Union and Confederate Armies, Series 1, Vol. 32/3.
Confederate Correspondence, Orders, and Returns Relating to Operations in Kentucky, Southwest Virginia, Tennessee, Mississippi, Alabama, and

North Georgia from March 1, 1864, to April 30, 1864. #3

[This correspondence in the *Official Records* in all probability refers to Loreta Janeta Velazquez. The date and circumstances described fit exactly with the account in her memoirs of her spying activities at this time.]

March 15, 1864

H. Winslow to Maj. J.C. Denis, Provost-Marshal-General, Mobile, Alabama

Major,

I have the honor to report that in compliance with instructions received from your office, I proceeded as near the enemy's lines as was necessary and completed such arrangements as will secure to the general commanding information from time to time of the forces, designs, and movements of the enemy, as well as other information of general use to the Confederacy. I have also placed within the lines a person who will within the next few weeks traverse a large part of the West and North, gathering all the general movements of the enemy, their strength, and future plans as far as an individual can. This person is a highly intelligent and observant lady, and one who from her connections has access to influential and popular leaders of different political parties. She proposes to be in Richmond during the month of April. Letters by flag of truce, chemically prepared, will be sent me at Fort Valley, Ga., as that was the best point I could arrange for the present, and I respectfully suggest that I be sent there for a time at least. These agents will be named to the department commander or yourself if deemed prudent.

Bellville Countryman, Texas, April 13, 1866

Carroll Record, Carroll Parish, Louisiana, June 23, 1866

Romance of the War. Thrilling Adventures of a Young and Beautiful Woman.

Among the many thrilling events of the late war (says the St. Louis Republican of the 7th), none can exceed the adventures of Mrs. Loretta De Camp [*sic*], the subject of this sketch. Mrs. DeCamp, whose maiden name was Roach, was born in the West Indies, in 1838, and is now about twenty-eight years of age. At an early period her parents moved to the United States and settled in the parish of St. James, Louisiana. [At the outbreak of the war she donned male attire and became a soldier.] Raising a company of cavalry, and equipping it at her own expense, she proceeded to Virginia, and there served for eight months on the Peninsula, under the command of the celebrated Colonel Dreux, before her sex was discovered.

When this occurred she was at once, mustered out and ordered home. Instead of obeying the order, she proceeded to Columbus, Ky., and was serving with General Polk at the evacuation of that place. She proceeded to Island No. 10, but not being satisfied with the manner in which affairs were conducted there, she left and went to Fort Pillow, where she was elected first lieutenant in Captain Phillips's company of Independent Tennessee Cavalry. With her company she proceeded to Corinth, and reported to General A.S. Johnston.

At the battle of Shiloh Captain Phillips fell mortally wounded, and the command then devolved upon her. While gallantly leading her company in a charge, she was twice wounded and carried from the field. After the retreat from Corinth she was taken to New Orleans for surgical treatment, and when the city fell into Federal hands she was among those taken prisoner. After a confinement of several months she was paroled, and soon after exchanged.

Proceeding at once to Richmond, the disguised female soldier was commissioned first lieutenant in the Adjutant General's department, and ordered to report to General Marcus J. Wright, commanding the district of Atlanta. Upon reporting, she was assigned to duty with the Provost Marshal, as chief of detectives and military conductor. Serving for several months in this capacity, she met Major De Camp [sic], of the Third Arkansas Cavalry, to whom she was engaged to be married previous to the war. The ceremony was then performed at Atlanta, and from the dashing Lieutenant Looch [sic] she was transformed to the sober Mrs. Major DeCamp.

From this time her services ceased as an officer in the field, and she was engaged in secret service—sometimes in the Confederacy, again in England, and then in Canada. In 1864 she spent several months traveling in the United States, and even went as far as the Sioux country in Minnesota. Her husband who was taken prisoner in the fall of 1863, while serving with his regiment in Georgia, was carried to New York. After a long and arduous siege she at length succeeded in getting him paroled in January, 1865, but he lived only eight days after his release from prison. Subsequent to the death of her husband she proceeded to Columbus, Ohio, to watch over the interests of the Confederate prisoners confined at Camp Chase.

After the final collapse of the Confederacy, Mrs. De Camp remained in the North until January, when she returned home to Louisiana; but remaining there only a few days, she proceeded to Memphis, and purchased a stock of goods, which were shipped on the ill-fated steamer Miami, which was blown up on the Arkansas [River] in February. She was one of the two ladies who were saved, but with the sacrifice of all her baggage and goods. By an unfortunate oversight on the part of her merchants, her goods were not insured, and consequently, she lost her all.

Mrs. De Camp is now in this city [St. Louis], and sojourning at the Southern Hotel. Many who served in the Confederate army will remember the dashing Lieutenant Roach, of whom so much was said in Mobile and Selma [Alabama] in 1863. Our space will not permit a full recital of her adventures.

James Longstreet, 1888 letter about Loreta Janeta Velazquez.
From the Rare Book, Manuscript, and Special Collections Library, Duke
    University, Durham, N.C.
[Some words in the handwritten letter are difficult to interpret. Portions
    in doubt are indicated by brackets.]
Gainesville, Ga.
18th June 1888
Miss [Emmy? Emily?] W. Park
Dorchester, Mass,

Dear Lady,
Your favor of the 15th instant is received and noted.

There was a woman in the ranks with us who became Lieutenant and called her name Buford, though I did not know her till some years after the war. Her enterprise after the war was a trip to the Rocky Mountains, with a party of men in her disguise as Lieutenant Buford. The party had much trouble with the Indians, lost their horses and had to travel afoot a great distance when she gave out and her comrades had to assist her. In that way she became known. Afterwards she had success in gold speculations, and became a [filer] of course in Nevada. She referred her suitors to me, but I had not known of her in the ranks, nor as Lieutenant, and could only attest of points she gave for identification. She was married out west, and passed through New Orleans when I was there and there I met her, the only time of my life. I cannot now recall her maiden name, nor her name after marriage. Her adventures as she gave them and as they were given by her western suitors were remarkable.

Most Respectfully Yours,
James Longstreet

FANNY WILSON

Frank Moore, *The Civil War in Song and Story,* 1889, 413–414.
[The story of Fanny Wilson as related by a "Western journalist" is
    entirely in quotation marks, suggesting that Moore is quoting it
    verbatim from an unidentified source. Mostly paraphrased here.]
Adventure of a Long Island Girl

Miss Fanny Wilson was a native of Williamsburg, Long Island. About a
year before the war (1860) she came West to visit a relative living in LaFayette, Indiana. While there she wrote regularly to her fiance in New Jersey.
Stayed for about a year. As war was imminent she learned that her fiance had
enlisted. She started home in company of Miss Nelly Graves whose boyfriend
had enlisted in the same regiment. En route home they conceived the idea of
enlisting in disguise to follow their lovers in the service.

They cut their hair, acquired appropriate clothes, and enlisted in a different company of the same regiment, the 24th New Jersey. Although they saw
their lovers and drilled along with them, they maintained their disguise. The
24th New Jersey served in the early West Virginia campaign, and later were
ordered to Vicksburg. There Fanny's lover was wounded and she nursed him,
but he died. She and Nelly were hospitalized, sick and exhausted. They were
sent to Cairo, Illinois, along with other sick and wounded, and there hospital
attendants discovered that they were women. When she recovered, Fanny
was dismissed from service. But Nelly's illness became more serious and she
was detained in the hospital, so the two parted. No more is known of Nelly.

At Cairo, Fanny danced in the ballet for a short while, then joined the 3rd
Illinois Cavalry as a private. While serving in Memphis, Tenn., about two
weeks later, while riding with a fellow soldier, "she is stopped by a guard,
and arrested for being 'a woman in men's clothing.'" She was questioned
by detectives on suspicion of being a spy, but was released. "An appropriate
wardrobe is procured her, and her word is given that she will not again attempt a disguise." At this point she was 19, fair but somewhat tanned, "of a
rather masculine voice," and well educated.

Frazar Kirkland, *Pictorial Book of Anecdotes and Incidents of the War of
    the Rebellion,* 1867, 170–171; *New York Herald,* August 12, 1864.
Fannie [Wilson] and Nellie of the Twenty-fourth New Jersey:

[Fanny, a native of Williamsburg, Long Island, and her friend Nellie Graves
conspired to enlist in male disguise in the 24th New Jersey Infantry, where

both had sweethearts.] In just another company from their own were their patriotic lovers. . . . On parade, in the drill, they were together; they obeyed the same command.

[The regiment first campaigned in West Virginia, then were stationed near Vicksburg, Mississippi, where Fanny's lover was wounded. She nursed him faithfully, but he died of the wounds. Fanny and Nellie then fell ill and were sent with other wounded and ill soldiers to Cairo, Illinois. At the hospital there they were found out and dismissed from the service after recuperating. Fanny recovered more quickly than Nellie and departed first, and their histories were no longer linked.]

Having again entered society as a member of her real sex, Fanny was next heard of on the stage of a theatre at Cairo, serving an engagement as a ballet girl. But this was only for a few days. She turns up in Memphis, even as a soldier again! But she had changed her branch of the military service, having become a private in the Third Illinois *cavalry*. Only two weeks, however, had she enlisted in this capacity, when, to her utter surprise, she was stopped by a guard and arrested for being a woman in men's clothing. She was taken to the office of the detective police and questioned until no doubt remained as to her identity, not proving herself, as was suspected, a rebel spy, but a Federal soldier. An appropriate wardrobe was procured her, and her word given that she would not again attempt a disguise.

A brief description of Fanny would be that of a young lady of about nineteen years, of a fair but somewhat tanned face, rather masculine voice, sprightly and somewhat educated mind—being very easily able to pass herself off for a boy of about seventeen or eighteen years.

[Fanny was stationed in Memphis, Tennessee, when her sex was discovered again. Various companies of the 3rd Illinois Cavalry regiment served in the Department of Tennessee between February and April 1864, and again between June and November 1864. A Nashville newspaper, without naming the regiment, reports her arrest as occurring about August 23, 1864, and that she was an actress at the Memphis Theater.]

TWO FEMALE SOLDIERS IN SHERIDAN'S COMMAND
Philip H. Sheridan, *Personal Memoirs*, Vol. 1, 1888, 253–255.
[General Sheridan reported the discovery of two female soldiers in his
command during a foraging expedition early in 1863 in Tennessee.
Colonel Joseph Conrad of the 15th Missouri reported to Sheridan
upon return from the expedition, as follows:]

[He] informed me that he got through without much difficulty; in fact, that everything had gone all right and been eminently satisfactory, except that in returning he had been mortified greatly by the conduct of *the two females belonging to the detachment and division train at my headquarters.* These women, he said, had given much annoyance by getting drunk, and to some extent demoralizing his men. To say that I was astonished by his statement would be a mild way of putting it, and had I not known him to be a most upright man and of sound sense, I should have doubted not only his veracity, but his sanity.

Inquiring who they were and for further details, I was informed that there certainly were in the command two females, that in some mysterious manner had attached themselves to the service as soldiers; that one, an East Tennessee woman, was a teamster in the division wagon-train and the other a private soldier in a cavalry company temporarily attached to my headquarters for escort duty.

While out on the foraging expedition these Amazons had secured a supply of "apple-jack" by some means, got very drunk, and on the return had fallen into Stone River and been nearly drowned. After they had been fished from the water, in the process of resuscitation their sex was disclosed, though up to this time it appeared to be known only to each other. The story was straight and the circumstance clear, so, convinced of Conrad's continued sanity, I directed the provost-marshal to bring in arrest to my headquarters the two disturber's of Conrad's peace of mind.

After some little search the East Tennessee woman was found in camp, somewhat the worse for the experiences of the day before, but awaiting her fate contentedly smoking a cob-pipe. She was brought to me, and put in duress under charge of the division surgeon until her companion could be secured. To the doctor she related that the year before [1862] she had "refugeed" from East Tennessee, and on arriving in Louisville assumed man's apparel and sought and obtained employment as a teamster in the quartermaster's department. Her features were very large, and so coarse and masculine was her general appearance that she would readily have passed as a man, and in her case the deception was no doubt easily practiced.

Next day the "she dragoon" was caught, and proved to be a rather prepossessing young woman, and though necessarily bronzed and hardened by exposure, I doubt if, even with these marks of campaigning, she could have deceived as readily as did her companion. How the two got acquainted I never learned, and though they had joined the army independently of each other, yet an intimacy had sprung up between them long before the mishaps of the foraging expedition. They both were forwarded to army headquarters, and, when provided with clothing suited to their sex, sent back to Nashville, and thence beyond our lines to Louisville.

[Blanton and Cook (2002) report that the "she dragoon" was Sarah Bradbury, alias "Frank Morton," and the teamster was Ella Reno.]

UNIDENTIFIED WOMEN
The Valley Spirit, Chambersburg, Pa., November 26, 1862.
A Secesh Female in the Drug Trade

On Friday morning last [November 21] a somewhat singular looking specimen of the feminine gender made her appearance in town, by way of the Western turnpike, mounted on a grey steed of venerable appearance, bearing evidence of hard service and a short allowance of provender. The lady, from her dress, general appearance and "getting up" [get-up?] was evidently a stranger in this section of the country. On alighting and securing her gallant grey to an awning post on Main Street, she proceeded to several of our Drug Stores and engaged extensively in the purchase of Quinine, Morphine, Opium, &c. Suspicion being excited that she was purchasing these articles for the use of Uncle Sam's enemies in the land of Dixie, she was arrested by order of Capt. Ashmead, A.Q.M., and on being searched, several hundred dollars worth of these Drugs were found concealed in secret recesses of her dress. The previous night she passed at the tavern of Mr. Josiah Allen, three miles west of this place, where she stated that she was in search of several Horses, taken by the Rebels from her father in Virginia, and having heard that a number had been turned loose by Stuart's Cavalry, in this section she thought that she might possibly find her fathers among them. She had in her possession a Pass from general Banks dated about a year ago. We are informed by a citizen, who recognized her, that her name is Sloan, and that she resides near Winchester, Virginia. For the present, she occupies apartments in "Fort Brandt" and the Philistines across the border will *shake* considerable before they get *that* quinine.

Rosecran's Orderly Sergeant Delivered of a Baby in Camp
Frazar Kirkland, *Pictorial Book of Anecdotes and Incidents of the War of the Rebellion,* 1867, 554–555.

The following order, as unique in its way as any that the war gave rise to, can be best explained—if any further explanation be needed—by Major-General Rosecrans:

HEAD-QUARTERS DEPARTMENT OF THE CUMBERLAND, April 17th, 1863. GEN-
ERAL:—The general commanding directs me to call your attention to a flagrant
outrage committed in your command,—a person having been admitted inside
your lines, without a pass and in violation of orders. The case is one which
calls for your personal attention, and the general commanding directs that
you deal with the offending party or parties according to law.

The medical director reports that an orderly-sergeant in Brigadier-General
_____'s division *was to-day delivered of a baby*,—which is in violation of all
military law and of the army regulations. No such case has been known since
the days of Jupiter.

You will apply the proper punishment in this case, and a remedy to prevent a repetition of the act.

Official Records of the Union and Confederate Armies, Series 1, Vol.
　34/4, No. 64.
Correspondence Trans-Mississippi States
Headquarters District of Southwest Missouri
Springfield, Mo., May 28, 1864
Majors Melton and Moore
Berryville, via Cassville, Mo.

Send out women spies or scouts and ascertain, if possible, what the enemy's force is and what he intends to do and who is in command. If the enemy
designs to attack you at once, and has largely superior forces and artillery,
retreat to Cassville; otherwise hold your position and fight the enemy when
he comes to you.... I think you are safe enough if the enemy has no artillery.
In an emergency exercise your own judgment and do what you deem best for
the Government and it will be approved. I will send you re-enforcements just
as soon as the troops ordered to Cassville reach there.

John B. Sanborn
Brigadier-General Commanding.

Poughkeepsie Telegraph, New York, August 27, 1864.
A Female Veteran

We saw this morning in the recruiting office of J. N. Pardee, a woman who
under the guise of a soldier's uniform has served an honorable membership
in the great south-western army and has participated in all the memorable

engagements of those gallant troops. She enlisted in St. Louis in January 1861 as a private in a cavalry regiment; the recruits at that time did not have to pass examination, which accounts for her sex not being discovered. Her husband was also a member of the same regiment. When the regiment marched to the seat of war she left with it, and shared the toils and fatigues of the march and in camp as well as the best of them. She was frequently detailed with members of her regiment to catch deserters and break up guerrilla bands, and well did she perform her part.

Her sex remained undiscovered until the battle of Stones River where she received a wound in the knee which rendered it impossible for her to longer conceal her secret and she disclosed herself. So complete had the deception been that on disclosing the true facts her comrades would not believe her and told her it would not do to try to sell them in that manner. Her husband also fell in this engagement, a shell tearing his left side away and instantly killing him.

In appearance she is decidedly masculine looking and dressed in the garb of a man with false mustache and whiskers which she wore in the army would pass for an able-bodied recruit. She is quite talkative and takes delight in recounting her adventures and wild camp life. She considers herself able to take care of herself and threatens with dire vengeance any one that molests her. She brags of having deprived more than one reb of his life with her trusty steel, and wears several rings taken from fallen foes as trophies of her prowess. She seems to be about jagged out by long marches and little rest, and we understand that she has been taken in and kindly cared for by a benevolent person of this city.

[This story, which cannot be traced further at present, was submitted by Joel Craig. who maintains a Civil War web site. Some elements of it resemble the original story of Frances Clayton (see Chapter 8), but there are insufficient clues to verify any of it. However, it is a good example of contemporary newspaper reporting of the war in its dramatic style, obvious exaggerations, and essentially vague content insofar as providing identifying details is concerned. Accurate reporting seems to have taken a back seat to telling a "good story" even 140 years ago.]

Official Records of the Union and Confederate Armies, Series 1, Vol. 48/1, No 101.

Operations in Louisiana and Trans-Mississippi States.

Cassville, Missouri, February 11, 1865.

Brigadier-General Sanborn:

I have received information from a female spy that I had employed that the rebels are concentrating their forces, 500 strong, on the Dry Fork of Osage, in Arkansas. Please give me a sufficient number of men to dislodge them, or instructions what course I shall pursue. If I receive no instructions I shall leave in the morning.

Jas. M. Moore, Major, Commanding

NOTES

Introduction

1. Mary Elizabeth Massey, *Bonnet Brigades* (New York: Alfred A. Knopf, 1966), 3.
2. Lori A. Ginzberg, *Women in Antebellum Reform* (Wheeling, Ill: Harlan Davidson, 2000), 113.
3. Ibid., 54–56.
4. Ibid., 67.
5. Ibid., 91.
6. A Library of Congress web page that contains links to contemporary news stories about the convention and a list of the signatories to the "Declaration of Sentiments" may be found at http://www.loc.gov/exhibits/treasures/trr040.html.
7. Nancy A. Hewitt, *Women's Activism and Social Change: Rochester, New York, 1822–1872* (Ithaca, N.Y.: Cornell University Press, 1984), 18–19.
8. From detailed newspaper interviews reported in the *Lansing State Republican*, Michigan, June 19–26, 1900. See also Richard Hall, *Patriots in Disguise: Women Warriors of the Civil War* (New York: Paragon House, 1993), 74–82; in regard to Edmonds's youth, prewar life, and use of male disguise, see Philip P. Mason and Paul J. Pentecost, *From Bull Run to Appomattox: Michigan's Role in the Civil War* (Detroit: Wayne State University, 1961), 39–42, who give her birth date as 1839.
9. Drew Gilpin Faust, *Mothers of Invention: Women of the Slaveholding South in the American Civil War* (Chapel Hill: University of North Carolina Press, 1996), 10–11.
10. Ibid., 13.
11. See also George C. Rable, *Civil Wars: Women and the Crisis of Southern Nationalism* (Urbana: University of Illinois Press, 1989), 112–113.
12. *National Democrat*, Little Rock, Arkansas, October 20, 1863.
13. U. R. Brooks, *Stories of the Confederacy* (Camden, S.C.: J. J. Fox, 1991; reprint edition).
14. Elizabeth D. Leonard, *All the Daring of the Soldier: Women of the Civil War Armies* (New York: W.W. Norton, 1999), 99–200; DeAnne Blanton and Lauren M. Cook, *They Fought like Demons: Women Soldiers in the American Civil War* (Baton Rouge: Louisiana State University Press, 2002), 126; Faust, *Mothers of Invention*, 204.
15. *Charleston Mercury*, South Carolina, April 8, 1861, reported that Chickasaw County "has a regularly officered and drilled company of young ladies...in the event that the men are called into service, to protect their homes and families during their absence...."; Hall, *Patriots in Disguise*, 104–105; Faust, *Mothers of Invention*, 203–204; Anne J. Bailey, "The Defenders," in *Confederate Women*, ed. Mauriel Phillips Joslyn (Gretna, La.: Pelican Publish-

ing, 2004), 43–61; C. Kay Larson, "Bonny Yank and Ginny Reb Revisited," *Minerva* 10, 2 (Summer 1992): 52; Ella Lonn, *Foreigners in the Confederacy* (Chapel Hill: University of North Carolina Press, 1940), 380.

16. Marilyn Mayer Culpepper, *Trials and Triumphs: The Women of the American Civil War* (East Lansing: Michigan State University Press, 1991), 315–323. Newton Martin Curtis, *From Bull Run to Chancellorsville: The Story of the Sixteenth New York Infantry together with Personal Reminiscences* (New York: G.P. Putnam's Sons, 1906), 287, notes that "women nurses, during our Civil War, were pioneers in a new field in our military policy."

17. Lynda L. Sudlow, *A Vast Army of Women: Maine's Uncounted Forces in the American Civil War* (Gettysburg, Pa.: Thomas Publications, 2000), 42–43.

18. Agatha Young, *The Women and the Crisis: Women of the North in the Civil War* (New York: McDowell, Obolensky, 1959), 55–63, 98–109, 193–196; Culpepper, *Trials and Triumphs*, 323–325. See also Richard Hall, "Women in Battle in the Civil War," in *American History, Volume I: Pre-Colonial through Reconstruction*, ed. Robert James Maddox (Guilford, Conn.: Dushkin Publishing Group, 1995), 197–200.

19. Culpepper, *Trials and Triumphs*, 328.

20. Thomas P. Lowry, *The Story the Soldiers Wouldn't Tell: Sex in the Civil War* (Mechanicsburg, Pa.: Stackpole Books, 1994), chapters 6 and 7. See also Thomas P. Lowry, "The Army's Licensed Prostitutes," *Civil War Times Illustrated* 41, 4 (2002): 30–35.

21. Bell I. Wiley, *The Life of Billy Yank: The Common Soldier of the Union* (Baton Rouge: Louisiana State University Press, 1978), 338.

22. *Civil War Times Illustrated* 22, 9 (1984): 31, from *Detroit Advertiser and Tribune*, August 27, 1863; Blanton and Cook, *They Fought like Demons*, 14, 67, 112, 156.

23. Frazar Kirkland, *Pictorial Book of Anecdotes and Incidents of the War of the Rebellion* (Hartford, Conn.: Hartford Publishing,1867), 193. The 12th Rhode Island was a nine-months regiment organized in October 1862. After being heavily engaged at the Battle of Fredericksburg, Virginia, in December 1862, the regiment was transferred to the western army and was stationed in Kentucky during April 1863 when Tommy enlisted. Thereafter it was only lightly engaged in skirmishes with guerrillas, and on July 29, 1863, was mustered out of service.

24. Lee Middleton, *Hearts of Fire: Soldier Women of the Civil War* (Torch, Ohio: privately published, 1993),111–112, from *History of the 141st Pennsylvania Volunteers, 1862–1865*, as reported by Chaplain David Craft. The regiment served from August 29, 1862, to May 28, 1865, and was at Chancellorsville. No one by the name of Norton appears in the roster of Company E. There was a Captain Joseph B. Reeve (instead of Reeves) in Company E, but he resigned in 1862. The captain of Company I was Charles Mercur.

25. Blanton and Cook, *They Fought like Demons*, 28, 36, 125, 199; Leonard, *All the Daring of the Soldier*, 246–247, from court-martial records, National Archives. The 59th was in service from October 1, 1861, to June 30, 1865. Jerome B. Taft first served in Company B (not Company G) as a second lieu-

tenant, then attained the captaincy of Company E officially on October 30, 1861. He was dismissed from service shortly after the court martial proceedings. A James Miller served in Company D as a private, but that was in 1864; there was no officer by that name.

No Frederick Woods (or Wood) appears on the regimental roster. A Charles E. Johnson served in Company G (also Companies A and B at different times), but his military record indicates promotion to sergeant in 1863, being wounded in the Battle of the Wilderness in 1864, and being mustered out June 30, 1865—thus he could not have been Harriet Merrill.

26. Francis A. Lord, *They Fought for the Union* (New York: Bonanza Books, 1960), 325–327, provides a discussion of the estimated numbers that fought on each side. See also "Numbers Engaged," in *Historical Times Illustrated Encyclopedia of the Civil War,* ed. Patricia L. Faust (New York: Harper & Row, 1986), 540.
27. Ginzberg, *Women in Antebellum Reform,* 118–119.

Chapter 1. War on a Colossal Scale

1. Sarah Emma Edmonds ("Frank Thompson") served in male disguise in the ranks of the 2nd Michigan Infantry; Jane Hinsdale and Anna Etheridge served as nurses. See Richard Hall, *Patriots in Disguise: Women Warriors of the Civil War* (New York: Paragon House, 1993), 46–97.
2. Robert W. Hodge, ed., *The Civil War Letters of Perry Mayo* (East Lansing: Michigan State University, 1967).
3. Ethel Alice Hurn, *Wisconsin Women in the War between the States,* Original Papers No. 6 (Wisconsin History Commission, 1911), 11–13.
4. Bell I. Wiley, *The Life of Johnny Reb: The Common Soldier of the Confederacy* (Baton Rouge: Louisiana State University Press, 1978), 22–23.
5. Terry L. Jones, *Lee's Tigers: The Louisiana Infantry in the Army of Northern Virginia* (Baton Rouge: Louisiana State University Press, 1987), 13.
6. Robert W. Johannsen, "Mexican War," in *The Reader's Companion to American History,* ed. Eric Foner and John A. Garraty (Boston: Houghton Mifflin, 1991), 722–724.
7. Russell F. Weigley, "Armed Forces," in Foner and Garraty, *Reader's Companion,* 47–50.
8. "Lincoln's Call for Troops," War Department, Washington, April 15, 1861, *Official Records of the Union and Confederate Armies [The War of the Rebellion: A Compilation of the Official Records of the Union and Confederate Armies],* Series 3, Vol. 1, No. 122 (Washington, D.C.: Government Printing Office, 1884).
9. George C. Rable, *Civil Wars: Women and the Crisis of Southern Nationalism* (Urbana: University of Illinois Press, 1989), 75–90.
10. Francis A. Lord, *They Fought for the Union* (New York: Bonanza Books, 1960), 4–7.
11. John Whiteclay Chambers II, "Conscription," in Foner and Garraty, *Reader's Companion,* 216–217.

12. Marjorie Barstow Greenbie, *Lincoln's Daughters of Mercy* (New York: G. P. Putnam's Sons, 1944), 41. Although Greenbie garbles some of the information about vivandieres and Daughters of the Regiment, she provides valuable contextual information and contributes insightful comments about the roles of women throughout the war.

13. Ibid., 42–43. With regard to sanitation and diet, see also Harold Elk Straubing, comp., *In Hospital and Camp: The Civil War through the Eyes of Its Doctors and Nurses* (Harrisburg, Pa.: Stackpole Books, 1993), 4–5.

14. Gordon W. Jones, "Sanitation in the Civil War," *Civil War Times Illustrated* 5 (1966): 12–18.

15. Gordon W. Jones, "Wartime Surgery," *Civil War Times Illustrated* 2 (1963): 7–9, 28–30. See also Richard Vickery, "On the Duties of a Surgeon in Action," *Civil War Times Illustrated* 17, 3 (1978): 12–23. An excellent internet site on all aspects of Civil War medicine is http://www.library.vcu.edu/tml/bibs/cwmed.html.

16. Marilyn Mayer Culpepper, *Trials and Triumphs: The Women of the American Civil War* (East Lansing: Michigan State University Press, 1991), 335; Earl J. Hess, *The Union Soldier in Battle: Enduring the Ordeal of Combat* (Lawrence: University Press of Kansas, 1997), 33–34.

17. Jones, *Lee's Tigers,* 192.

18. Newton Martin Curtis, *From Bull Run to Chancellorsville: The Story of the Sixteenth New York Infantry together with Personal Reminiscences* (New York: G. P. Putnam's Sons, 1906), 275.

19. Ibid., 276.

20. George R. Lee, "Scene Aboard Ship Loaded with Wounded," *Civil War Times Illustrated* 5, 3 (1966): 48–49.

21. Peter Josyph, ed., *The Wounded River: The Civil War Letters of John Vance Lauderdale, M.D.* (East Lansing: Michigan State University Press, 1993), 126.

22. For a detailed account of the state of medicine during the Civil War, see C. Keith Wilbur, M.D., *Civil War Medicine, 1861–1865* (Old Saybrook, Conn.: Globe Pequot Press, 1998). Horace H. Cunningham, *Field Medical Services at the Battles of Manassas (Bull Run)* (Athens: University of Georgia Press, 1968), provides a well-researched monograph on field ambulance services early in the war, including detailed information about the overwhelming scope and atrocious nature of battlefield wounds that posed an insoluble problem for understaffed and poorly supplied medical service personnel. See also Thomas P. Lowry, *The Story the Soldiers Wouldn't Tell: Sex in the Civil War* (Mechanicsburg, Pa.: Stackpole Books, 1994), 99–102, about the general state of medical knowledge.

23. Culpepper, *Trials and Triumphs,* 316; "Sanitary Commission," in Foner and Garraty, *Reader's Companion,* 964.

24. L. P. Brockett and Mary C. Vaughan, *Woman's Work in the Civil War: A Record of Heroism, Patriotism and Patience* (Philadelphia: Zeigler, McCurdy, 1867), 97–108; Jean Getman O'Brien and Robert D. Hoffsommer, "Dorothea Dix: A Personality Profile," *Civil War Times Illustrated* 4, 5 (1965): 39–44;

Lynda L. Sudlow, *A Vast Army of Women: Maine's Uncounted Forces in the American Civil War* (Gettysburg, Pa.: Thomas Publications, 2000), 81–84.

25. Report of Surgeon Charles S. Tripler, *Official Records,* Series 1, Vol. 5, No. 5.

26. Brockett and Vaughan, *Woman's Work in the Civil War,* 299–315; Katharine Prescott Wormeley, *The Other Side of War: On the Hospital Transports with the Army of the Potomac* (Gansevoort, N.Y.: Corner House Historical Publications, 1998 reprint edition); Diane Cobb Cashman, "The Hospital Transports," in *Headstrong: The Biography of Amy Morris Bradley, 1823–1904* (Wilmington, N.C.: Broadfoot Publishing Co., 1990), 111; Greenbie, *Lincoln's Daughters of Mercy,* 127–131, 137–141; Frederick Law Olmstead, "Hospital Transports," in Straubing, *In Hospital and Camp,* 132–147.

27. For more information about Georgeanna Woolsey, see Agatha Young, *The Women and the Crisis: Women of the North in the Civil War* (New York: McDowell, Obolensky, 1959), 381–382; "The Misses Woolsey," in Brockett and Vaughan, *Woman's Work in the Civil War,* 324–342; Curtis, *From Bull Run to Chancellorsville,* 280–282.

    Helen Gilson references: Brockett and Vaughan, *Woman's Work in the Civil War,* 133–148; Mary A. Gardner Holland, *Our Army Nurses* (Boston: Lounsbery, Nichols & Worth, 1897), 535–544. The description of her work in the latter book notes, "Through scorching heat and pinching cold, in the tent or upon the open field, in the ambulance or on the saddle, through rain and snow, amid unseen perils of the enemy, under fire upon the field, or in the more insidious dangers of contagion, she worked quietly on."

    Katharine Wormeley references: Brockett and Vaughan, *Woman's Work in the Civil War,* 318–323; Wormeley, *Other Side of War,* letters from hospital ships during the 1862 Virginia Peninsula Campaign; Young, *Women and the Crisis,* 382–383; Culpepper, *Trials and Triumphs,* 331–333.

28. Jane E. Schultz, *Women at the Front: Hospital Workers in Civil War America* (Chapel Hill: University of North Carolina Press, 2004), 53–54.

29. Drew Gilpin Faust, *Mothers of Invention: Women of the Slaveholding South in the American Civil War* (Chapel Hill: University of North Carolina Press, 1996), 92.

30. Ibid., 93–97, 102–108; H. E. Sterkx, *Some Notable Alabama Women during the Civil War* (University, Ala.: Alabama Civil War Centennial Commission, 1962), 37; Rable, *Civil Wars,* 125.

31. Rable, *Civil Wars,* 121–128.

32. Katharine M. Jones, ed., *Heroines of Dixie: Confederate Women Tell Their Story of the War* (Indianapolis: Bobbs-Merrill, 1955), 107–117, 325–329; Sterkx, *Some Notable Alabama Women,* 25–33; Stuart Sifakis, *Who Was Who in the Confederacy* (New York: Facts on File, 1988), 68–69.

Chapter 2. In the Field and on the March

1. William W. Fowler, *Woman on the American Frontier* (Hartford, Conn.: S. S. Scranton, 1877), 396.

2. Ibid., 420.

3. *St. Louis Daily Democrat*, Missouri, September 12, 1862; Richard Dobbins, Historical Data Systems online *American Civil War Research Database*, Duxbury, Massachusetts (http://www.civilwardata.com); hereafter Civil War Database army service information.

4. Ethel Alice Hurn, *Wisconsin Women in the War between the States*, Original Papers No. 6 (Wisconsin History Commission, 1911), 100–102; Elizabeth D. Leonard, *All the Daring of the Soldier: Women of the Civil War Armies* (New York: W. W. Norton, 1999), 151–152.

5. Hurn, *Wisconsin Women in the War*, 102; H. Sinclair Mills, Jr., *The Vivandiere: History, Tradition, Uniform and Service* (Collinswood, N.J.: C. W. Historicals, 1988), 15–16; Frazar Kirkland, *Pictorial Book of Anecdotes and Incidents of the War of the Rebellion* (Hartford, Conn.: Hartford Publishing, 1867), 535–536; Leonard, *All the Daring of the Soldier*, 144. The three-months 6th Massachusetts Infantry roster includes a Sergeant Timothy A. Crowley, thirty, from Lowell, Massachusetts.

6. For a summary of Anna Etheridge's military activities, see Richard Hall, *Patriots in Disguise: Women Warriors of the Civil War* (New York: Paragon House, 1993), 33–45. Primary sources include Frank Moore, *Women of the War: Their Heroism and Self-Sacrifice* (Hartford, Conn.: Scranton,1866), 513; L. P. Brockett and Mary C. Vaughan, *Woman's Work in the Civil War: A Record of Heroism, Patriotism and Patience* (Philadelphia: Zeigler, McCurdy, 1867), 747–153; Mary A. Gardner Holland, *Our Army Nurses* (Boston: Lounsbery, Nichols & Worth, 1897), 597–600; Minnie D. Millbrook, "Michigan Women Who Went to War," in *Michigan Women in the Civil War* (Michigan Civil War Centennial Observance Commission, 1963), 22–26; *Official Records of the Union and Confederate Armies*, Series 1, Vol. 51 (Washington, D.C.: Government Printing Office, 1884), includes the order authorizing Mrs. Anna Etheridge, 5th Michigan Volunteers, to receive the Kearny Cross.

7. See Hall, *Patriots in Disguise*, 4–6, based on contemporary sources. A statement obtained from the Rhode Island State Archives includes the following: "The 1st Rhode Island [Infantry] was a short term regiment and Robert Brownell was mustered out, re-enlisted, also appointed 1st Sergeant of Co. A, 5th Rhode Island Heavy Artillery; was wounded in action at New Berne [sic], N.C., March 14, 1862, and was on furlough until December 8th of that year, when he was discharged for disability owing to his wound." The Civil War Database notes that the unit was converted from infantry to heavy artillery on May 27, 1863, which would have been after Robert was wounded and discharged. See also Moore, *Women of the War*, 54–64; Leonard, *All the Daring of the Soldier*, 113–121. C. Kay Larson, "Bonny Yank and Ginny Reb Revisited," *Minerva* 10, 2 (Summer 1992): 37, reports on Kady Brownell's postwar life and cites details of her exploits at New Bern, North Carolina, based in part on a *New York Times* article, February 16, 1913.

8. For a summary of her activities, see Hall, *Patriots in Disguise*, 6–8. See also Leonard, *All the Daring of the Soldier*, 150–151, and Patricia L. Faust, ed., *Historical Times Illustrated Encyclopedia of the Civil War* (New York: Harper

& Row, 1986), 744–745. *Official Records*, Series I, Vol. 51, contains the order authorizing Tepe to receive the Kearny Cross. There she is listed as Mrs. Mary Tepe, but in many other references as Tebe.

9. Online article at http://cwnurses.tripod.com/mtepe.html.

10. Strong anecdotal evidence from a number of well-known nurses indicates that Divers did serve as a battlefield nurse and occasional soldier with the Michigan cavalry late in the war. See Moore, *Women of the War*, 109–112; Frank Moore, *The Civil War in Song and Story* (New York: P. F. Collier, 1889), 461–62, 533–535; Brockett and Vaughan, *Woman's Work in the Civil War*, 771–773; Charlotte E. McKay, *Stories of Hospital and Camp* (Philadelphia: Claxton, Remsen & Haffelfinger, 1876), 124–126. Mary A. Livermore, *My Story of the War* (Hartford, Conn.:. A.D. Worthington, 1887), 116–119, gives her name as Devens. Mary Elizabeth Massey, *Bonnet Brigades* (New York: Alfred A. Knopf, 1966), 78, reports that Divers was honored by the Grand Army of the Republic. Marjorie Barstow Greenbie, *Lincoln's Daughters of Mercy* (New York: G. P. Putnam's Sons, 1944), 135–136, refers to her as "Bridget Devan, an illiterate, tough, brown little Irishwoman whose husband was a non-commissioned officer." For a summary of her exploits, see Hall, *Patriots in Disguise*, 28–32.

11. Kirkland, *Pictorial Book of Anecdotes and Incidents*, 544–545; Susan Lyons Hughes, "The Daughter of the Regiment: A Brief History of *Vivandieres* and *Cantinieres* in the American Civil War," online at http://www.civilwarweb. com/articles/05-00/vivandieres.htm, from the *Memphis Daily Appeal*, July 18, 1863. No officer by the name of Dowden was found on the roster of Byrd's Union 1st (East) Tennessee Infantry. There was a Captain James A. Doughty, and also a Major Benjamin F. Taylor. Ezra J. Warner, *Generals in Blue: Lives of the Union Commanders* (Baton Rouge: Louisiana State University Press, 1989), provides a biography of Colonel (later Brigadier General) Theophilus T. Garrard.

12. "Tennessee and the Civil War," online at http://www.tngenweb.org/civilwar.

13. Edmund J. Raus, Jr., *Ministering Angel: The Reminiscences of Harriet A. Dada, a Union Army Nurse in the Civil War* (Gettysburg, Pa.: Thomas Publications, 2004); Lynda L. Sudlow, *A Vast Army of Women: Maine's Uncounted Forces in the American Civil War* (Gettysburg, Pa.: Thomas Publications, 2000), 145.

14. Moore, *Women of the War*, 522–528.

15. Fannie A. Beers, *Memories: A Record of Personal Experience and Adventure during Four Years of War* (Philadelphia: J. B. Lippincott, 1888); Francis Butler Simkins and James Welch Patton, *The Women of the Confederacy* (Richmond, Va.: Garrett and Massie, 1936), 75. The regiment she served in was organized in Richmond July 25, 1862, from pre-existing units.

16. Ibid., 109–112.

17. Ibid., 152–157.

18. Matthew Page Andrews, *Women of the South in War Times* (Baltimore: Norman, Remington,1920), 112–115; Ella Lonn, *Foreigners in the Confederacy* (Chapel Hill: University of North Carolina Press, 1940), 380. More than

one unit was known as the 1st Tennessee Infantry (Confederate). An online history and roster of the 1st (Feild's) Tennessee Infantry fits the reported military experiences of the Sullivans, and John Sullivan is listed as a private in Company K. What happened to Mrs. Sullivan's husband, the lieutenant, and herself after being captured is not reported.

19. Andrews, *Women of the South in War Times,* 120–126. Her name originally was reported as Mrs. W. D. Philips, with one "l." A roster check of the 4th Kentucky Infantry (C.S.A.) shows a lieutenant and quartermaster named William S. (Rather than "D.") Phillips.

20. Online databases for the 8th Georgia Infantry show that E. J. Magruder was captain of Company A, the Rome Light Guards.

21. "Charlotte S. Branch, 'The Mother of the Oglethorpe Light Infantry,'" in *Confederate Women,* ed. Mauriel Phillips Joslyn (Gretna, La.: Pelican Publishing, 2004), 13–24.

22. Brockett and Vaughan, *Woman's Work in the Civil War,* 493–494; Agatha Young, *The Women and the Crisis: Women of the North in the Civil War* (New York: McDowell, Obolensky, 1959), 167. The roster of the 12th Iowa Infantry indicates that Henry J. F. Small was 1st sergeant, Company F, November 2, 1861; 2d lieutenant, November 29, 1862; 1st lieutenant, August 9, 1863. He mustered out on December 1, 1864. The record notes that he was wounded at Shiloh in 1862.

23. Jane E. Schultz, *Women at the Front: Hospital Workers in Civil War America* (Chapel Hill: University of North Carolina Press, 2004), 38.

24. Holland, *Our Army Nurses,* 552–556. See also New Hampshire state web site (http://www.state.nh.us/nhdhr/warheroes/dameh.html) and Appleton's Cyclopedia of American Biography entry (http://www.famousamericans.net/harrietpatiencedame/). The encyclopedia entry quotes the colonel of the 2nd New Hampshire, Gilman Marston: "Wherever the regiment went she went, often going on foot, and sometimes camping on the field without tent. . . . She was truly an angel of mercy, the bravest woman I ever knew. I have seen her face a battery without flinching."

25. Moore, *Women of the War,* 113–126; Libby MacCaskill and David Novak, *Ladies on the Field: Two Civil War Nurses from Maine on the Battlefields of Virginia* (Livermore, Maine: Signal Tree Publications, 1996), 13–50; Sudlow, *Vast Army of Women,* 18–19, 92–100. Greenbie, *Lincoln's Daughters of Mercy,* 141, reports that during the Peninsula Campaign of 1862, Isabella Fogg managed an advanced field station for the Sanitary Commission two miles behind the front lines. When McClellan's army retreated, she kept it open until the last minute and then retreated with the army.

26. Sylvia G. L. Dannett and Katharine M. Jones, *Our Women of the Sixties* (Washington, D.C.: U.S. Civil War Centennial Commission, 1963), 11.

27. Holland, *Our Army Nurses,* 487–494.

28. Brockett and Vaughan, *Woman's Work in the Civil War,* 357–361; Faust, *Historical Times Illustrated Encyclopedia,* 650–651; Schultz, *Women at the Front,* 176.

29. Pension and military record files from U.S. National Archives.

30. Moore, *Women of the War,* 254–277; Brockett and Vaughan, *Woman's Work in the Civil War,* 791; Kirkland, *Pictorial Book of Anecdotes and Incidents,* 558–559; Young, *Women and the Crisis,* 376, citing Illinois State Historical Society; Leonard, *All the Daring of the Soldier,* 125–131; *Chicago Times,* May 19, 1862. The 17th Illinois served in Missouri, Tennessee, Mississippi, and Arkansas.

31. Brockett and Vaughan, *Woman's Work in the Civil War,* 770–771; Peter Cozzens, *This Terrible Sound: The Battle of Chickamauga* (Urbana: University of Illinois Press, 1992), 176–178; Leonard, *All the Daring of the Soldier,* 131–141. The railroad accident testimonial is reported in the *Leavenworth Daily Times,* Kansas, October 30, 1861, from the *Chicago Times.*

32. Mrs. John A. Logan, *The Part Taken by Women in American History* (Wilmington, Del.: Perry-Nalle Publishing, 1912), 492; Massey, *Bonnet Brigades,* 85; Leonard, *All the Daring of the Soldier,* 146. The 13th Virginia fought in almost every major eastern battle. The rosters of several companies in the regiment have been reconstructed from many sources in a regimental history by David F. Riggs, *13th Virginia Infantry* (Lynchburg, Va.: H. E. Howard, 1988). Although this is a very thoroughly researched regimental history and contains numerous interesting and amusing anecdotes, there is no mention of Lucy Ann Cox.

33. This and the following information and quotes are taken primarily from Sylvia G. L. Dannett, *Noble Women of the North* (New York: Thomas Yoseloff, 1959), 257–259, 291–301. See also Brockett and Vaughan, *Woman's Work in the Civil War,* 251–259; and Young, *Women and the Crisis,* 210–213, 257–259, 291–295, 320–326. The roster of the 17th Pennsylvania Militia Infantry shows William Holstein's enlistment on September 17, 1862, on the day of the Battle of Antietam. The unit was mustered out eleven days later.

34. John Y. Foster, "Four Days at Gettysburg," *Civil War Times Illustrated* 11, 1 (1972): 19–23; reprinted from *Harper's New Monthly Magazine* 28 (Feb. 1864): 381–388.

35. For insight into the conditions at City Point, Virginia, for military nurses in 1864, see Jeanne Christie, "'No Place for a Woman': City Point, Virginia, 1864–1865," *Journal of Women's Civil War History* 1 (2001): 26–38. In the last two years of the war, City Point became a congregating place for many of the most famous Civil War nurses, including Sophronia Bucklin, Annie Etheridge, Amanda Farnham, Helen Gilson, Cornelia Hancock, and Anna Holstein.

36. Dannett, *Noble Women of the North,* 320–326.

37. George Barton, *Angels of the Battlefield: A History of the Labors of the Catholic Sisterhoods in the Late Civil War* (Philadelphia: Catholic Art Publishing, 1898); Ellen Ryan Jolly, *Nuns of the Battlefield* (Providence, R.I.: Providence Visitor Press, 1927); Culpepper, *Trials and Triumphs,* 317–318; Sister Mary Denis Maher, *To Bind Up the Wounds: Catholic Sister Nurses in the U.S. Civil War* (Baton Rouge: Louisiana State University Press, 1989); Schultz, *Women at the Front,* 21, 79. See also Michael F. Fitzpatrick, "The Mercy Brigade: Roman Catholic Nuns in the Civil War," *Civil War Times Il-*

lustrated 36, 5 (1997): 34–40. The so-called battlefield nuns were called by the soldiers, generically, Sisters of Mercy or Sisters of Charity, but in fact included many other orders such as the Sisters of St. Joseph and the Sisters of the Holy Cross.

38. A cross-section of nurses in the war with biographical sketches is contained in Mary A. Holland, *Our Army Nurses* (Boston: Lounsbery, Nichols & Worth, 1897), which is now available in a reprint edition.

39. James A. Buttimer, "Servants of God and Man: The Sisters of Mercy," in Joslyn, *Confederate Women,* 155, 160–161.

40. Peter Josyph, ed., *The Wounded River: The Civil War Letters of John Vance Lauderdale, M.D.* (East Lansing: Michigan State University Press, 1993), 128.

41. William A. Fletcher, *Rebel Private: Front and Rear: Memoirs of a Confederate Soldier* (New York: Meridian Books, 1995), 103–106.

42. Ibid., 220.

43. Maher, *To Bind Up the Wounds,* 100–124; female soldiers, pp. 115–116. See also "Sisters of Charity in the Civil War," http://members.tripod.com/Setonspath/civilwar.html.

44. Holland, *Our Army Nurses,* 455–465.

Chapter 3. Foot Soldiers North and South

1. *Louisville Daily Journal,* Kentucky, August 24, 1861; *New York Tribune,* September 1, 1861. The latter source identifies the unit as the 2nd Iowa; as of May 6, 1861, Hugh P. Cox was captain of Company I. The 2nd Iowa was organized at Keokuk and mustered in May 27, 1861. It was a three-year regiment. The Louisville article is dated almost exactly three months after the muster-in date of the 2nd Iowa. However, the regiment didn't muster out until July 1865. The story would make more sense if the unit in question were a three-month regiment, but the 1st Iowa is the only one from that state. No Capt. Cox appears on the roster of the 1st Iowa and no "Charles H. Williams" appears on the roster of either regiment.

2. *Valley Spirit,* Franklin County, Pennsylvania, September 5, 1861. The three-months 7th Pennsylvania Infantry regiment served from April 23 to July 29, 1861. Among the 781 soldiers listed in the regimental roster, all served the full three months and there is no clue as to which may have been a woman.

3. William W. Fowler, *Women on the American Frontier* (Hartford, Conn.: S. S. Scranton, 1877), 420–422.

4. The Civil War Database indicates that Charles Cline, age eighteen, of Anamosa, Iowa, enlisted in Company H of the 14th Iowa Infantry on December 31, 1861. The entry indicates that he (she?) was wounded at Shiloh on April 6, 1862. No description of the position and type of the wound is provided, though it often is for regimental casualty data in the more completely recorded regiments. The entry further states that Cline was discharged (reason not given) on April 18, 1862. A wounded soldier normally would not be

quickly discharged. As in some other cases, genealogical research may be able to disconfirm this hypothetical identification.

5. For a detailed discussion of what motivated women to serve as soldiers or spies, see Elizabeth D. Leonard, *All the Daring of the Soldier: Women of the Civil War Armies* (New York: W. W. Norton, 1999), 227–272.

6. Francis A. Lord, *They Fought for the Union* (New York: Bonanza Books, 1960), 244; Richard Hall, *Patriots in Disguise: Women Warriors of the Civil War* (New York: Paragon House, 1993).

7. Rebecca D. Larson, *Blue and Gray Roses of Intrigue* (Gettysburg, Pa.: Thomas Publications, 1993), 63; DeAnne Blanton and Lauren M. Cook, *They Fought like Demons: Women Soldiers in the American Civil War* (Baton Rouge: Louisiana State University Press, 2002), 125–126; Donald E. Markle, *Spies and Spymasters of the Civil War* (New York: Hippocrene Books, 1994), 200.

8. Blanton and Cook, *They Fought like Demons*, 36–164. The roster of the 1st Michigan Engineers and Mechanics on the Civil War Database indicates that the regiment was organized in Marshall, Michigan, and served from October 29,1861, to September 22, 1865. Eleven soldiers by the name of White served in the regiment, but none in Company D or with the initials V.A. The Company D roster includes 246 names but insufficient clues to identify a female soldier using a male alias.

9. L. P. Brockett and Mary C. Vaughan, *Woman's Work in the Civil War: A Record of Heroism, Patriotism and Patience* (Philadelphia: Zeigler, McCurdy, 1867), 770. Mary Elizabeth Massey, *Bonnet Brigades* (New York: Alfred A. Knopf, 1966), 78–79, observed: "Many a romantic girl dreamed of being a second Joan of Arc, but those who actually entered the ranks by posing as men were usually viewed by contemporaries as mentally unbalanced or immoral."

10. Bell I. Wiley, *The Life of Billy Yank: The Common Soldier of the Union* (Baton Rouge: Louisiana State University Press, 1978), 296–302.

11. *Maysville Dollar Bulletin,* November 12, 1863, from *Philadelphia Press;* Frazar Kirkland, *Pictorial Book of Anecdotes and Incidents of the War of the Rebellion* (Hartford, Conn.: Hartford Publishing, 1867), 206; Blanton and Cook, *They Fought like Demons*, 35, 67, 71, 102; Leonard, *All the Daring of the Soldier*, 212, citing *Frank Leslie's Illustrated Newspaper*, October 1863, which stated that the girl was "recently detected." The other somewhat less likely candidate, Charles Martins, saw service in the 107th Pennsylvania Infantry from August 22, 1862, to February 13, 1863, and the 132nd Pennsylvania Infantry from August 11, 1862, to January 6, 1863.

12. Blanton and Cook, *They Fought like Demons*, 71, 121, 124.

13. Gregory A. Coco, *On the Bloodstained Field* (Hollidaysburg, Pa.: Wheatfield Press, 1987), 47; from the *Lancaster Examiner*, Pennsylvania, March 2, 1904.

14. *Plattville Witness*, Wisconsin, March 1864; Mary Livermore, *My Story of the War* (Hartford, Conn.: A. D. Worthington, 1887), 119; Agatha Young, *The Women and the Crisis: Women of the North in the Civil War* (New York: McDowell, Obolensky, 1959), 95; Blanton and Cook, *They Fought like*

Demons, 14, 33, 44, 51, 65, 97–98, 156. A note in the latter also cites stories about Rebecca Peterman in the Plattville, Wisconsin, *Grant County Witness,* February 16, 1865, and March 30, 1865. Two other soldiers by the name of Haney also served in the 7th Wisconsin Infantry regiment, but their histories do not fit that of Peterman.

15. Ira B. Gardner, *Recollections of a Boy Member of Co. I, Fourteenth Maine Volunteers, 1861–1865* (Lewiston, Maine: Lewiston Journal, 1902). A roster check confirms that Gardner was a sergeant in Company I, later promoted to captain in 1863. The 14th Maine was organized in Augusta and mustered in December 31, 1861. Its service record includes New Orleans Campaign, 1862; Department of the Gulf to July 1864; Virginia, Sheridan's Valley Campaign, August–November, 1864; Battle of Winchester, September 19, 1864; Battle of Cedar Creek, October 19, 1864. Mustered out January 13, 1865, at the end of 3 years. Some veterans and recruits volunteered for further duty and were consolidated into a battalion of four companies, serving in Georgia. They were mustered out August 28, 1865.

16. An interesting web site that specializes in documenting cases of underage Civil War soldiers is http://www.denniskeesee.com. Dennis Keesee is also author of *Too Young to Die: Boy Soldiers of the Union Army 1861–1865* (Huntington, W.Va.: Blue Acorn Press, 2001). Keesee reports on the web site that of the 200,000 or more boy soldiers aged seventeen or under, "most served as drummer boys, musicians and orderlies."

17. Leonard, *All the Daring of the Soldier,* 201–206.

18. Hall, *Patriots in Disguise,* 91–92.

19. *The Republican,* Pittsfield, Illinois, May 14, 1913.

20. For a detailed summary of her exploits, see Hall, *Patriots in Disguise,* 46–97. Primary sources include Sylvia Dannett, *She Rode with the Generals: The True and Incredible Story of Sarah Emma Seelye, Alias Franklin Thompson* (New York: Thomas Nelson & Sons, 1960); S. Emma E. Edmonds, *Nurse and Spy in the Union Army: Comprising the Adventures and Experiences of a Woman in Hospitals, Camps, and Battle-Field* (Hartford, Conn.: W. S. Williams, 1864); Betty Fladeland, "Alias Franklin Thompson," *Michigan History* 42 (1958): 435, 438–439; Betty Fladeland, "New Light on Sarah Emma Edmonds, Alias Franklin Thompson," *Michigan History* 47 (1963): 357–362; House Report No. 820, U.S. Congress, March 18, 1884; *State Republican,* Lansing, Michigan, May 20, June 20–21, June 26, 1900. Leonard, *All the Daring of the Soldier,* 170–185, supplies important new details about her relationships, based primarily on the diary of Jerome Robbins.

21. Blanton and Cook, *They Fought like Demons,* 54–55, 116. The 2nd Maryland was a three-year regiment, serving from June 1, 1861, through July 17, 1865. The roster of Company G shows one soldier by the name of Watkins, Wesley Watkins, who enlisted on August 16, 1861, as a private. He was discharged sometime in 1862 for disability. A soldier named Lewis Epping, the only one by that name, enlisted in Company G on August 9, 1861 (a week before Watkins). Although he is reported to have served also in Battery E, U.S. 4th Light Artillery, at some point, apparently on temporary duty, a

roster check of that regiment does not show his name. He mustered out of the 2nd Maryland on August 9, 1864.

22. Ibid., 30–32, 116–117, 144, 165–166. The Civil War Database shows a John Finern (one "n") enlisting as a private in Company I of the 15th Ohio at thirty-eight years old, serving from May 15, 1861, to August 28, 1861. The roster for the 81st Ohio Infantry shows a John *Finan,* thirty-six, mustering into Company D on September 23, 1861, and serving through September 26, 1864. No clues could be found as to another soldier in Company D or any other company who could have been Elizabeth. Lee Middleton, *Hearts of Fire: Soldier Women of the Civil War* (Torch, Ohio, privately published, 1993), 60, notes that the *National Tribune,* Washington, D.C., July 25, 1907, made reference to an obituary from the *Indianapolis News* reporting that Elizabeth Cain *Finnan* had been a vivandiere and also took part in some battles dressed in male attire. The couple's gravestone in Indiana, pictured by Blanton and Cook on page 144, shows the spelling as Finnern. These variant spellings are not unusual for the period.

23. Blanton and Cook, *They Fought like Demons,* 31, 164–165, 166, based in part on files in Record Group 94, National Archives. In her 1993 article in the National Archives magazine *Prologue,* Blanton reproduces a newspaper clipping on Elizabeth Niles's death.

24. Francis Butler Simkins and James Welch Patton, *The Women of the Confederacy* (Richmond, Va.: Garrett and Massie, 1936), 80; C. Kay Larson, "Bonnie Yank and Ginnie Reb," *Minerva* 8 (Spring 1990): 41; National Archives military service records; Peter F. Stevens, *Rebels in Blue: The Story of Keith and Malinda Blalock* (Dallas, Tex.: Taylor Publishing, 2000). Malinda Blalock's discovery and discharge from the army was reported in the *Daily Chronicle & Sentinel,* Augusta, Georgia, May 15, 1862, from the *Richmond Whig,* with the headline "A North Carolina Amazon." Their name is there reported as Blaylow. The story that they fought together in three battles for the South is contradicted by the regimental history, since the regiment was not in three battles during the period of their service from March 14 to April 20, 1862. They were mustered in on the day of the Battle of New Bern and possibly were in action there, but no other battle is indicated in the records. Also, the North Carolina Archives records note that Keith was discharged by reason of "hernia" and "poison from sumac" and no mention is made of Malinda being wounded. Instead, it is implied that she simply announced to the captain and colonel that she was a woman.

25. Lynda L. Sudlow, *A Vast Army of Women: Maine's Uncounted Forces in the American Civil War* (Gettysburg, Pa.: Thomas Publications, 2000), 71–74; Blanton and Cook, *They Fought like Demons,* 30, 34, 117. The Civil War Database indicates that the regiment served from April 1, 1864, to July 15, 1865. The regiment contained twenty-one soldiers named Brown. None of them fits the profile to have been Mary Brown, and if she served for a time in male disguise, she probably used some other name.

26. Blanton and Cook, *They Fought like Demons,* 15, 26. Leonard, *All the Daring of the Soldier,* 223–224, reports the regiment to be the 44th New

York Infantry. Middleton, *Hearts of Fire*, 139, reports her name as Seizgle and identifies the regiment as the 41st New York Infantry. Rosters in the Civil War Database show that the 41st New York Infantry was composed of Germans, organized in New York City in June of 1861, and served for three years. The regiment was engaged at Gettysburg, where it suffered seventy-five casualties. The regimental roster does not show any soldier by the name of Siezgle or Seizgle, but it does show a Heinrich Siegle. He enlisted at age thirty-two as a private in Company I and mustered out with the regiment in June 1864. No Seizgle, Siezgle, or other variant name appears on the roster of the 44th New York Infantry.

27. Blanton and Cook, *They Fought like Demons*, 17–18; "December 12–14, 1863.—Expedition from Williamsburg to Charles City Court-House, Va., and Skirmish," December 14, 1863, *Official Records of the Union and Confederate Armies [The War of the Rebellion: A Compilation of the Official Records of the Union and Confederate Armies]*, Series 1, Vol. 29/1, No. 48 (Washington, D.C.: Government Printing Office, 1884). The Civil War Database, regrettably, does not contain a history or roster of the 42nd Battalion, Virginia Cavalry; such rosters often include prisoner of war information.

28. Simkins and Patton, *Women of the Confederacy*, 81; from Ross's *A Visit to the Cities and Camps of the Confederate States* (London, 1863), 132; *Lynchburg Virginian*, October 6, 1864 (female captain on train to Richmond); B. A. Botkin, ed., *A Civil War Treasury of Tales, Legends, and Folklore* (Secaucus, N.J.: Blue & Gray Press, 1985), 396–400; from David P. Conyngham, *Sherman's March through the South* (New York: Sheldon, 1865), 194–197 (female major at Atlanta). C. E. Dornbusch, *Military Bibliography of the Civil War*, Vol. 3 (New York Public Library, 1972), 164, identifies Conyngham as a war correspondent in Sherman's command.

29. Elizabeth Avery Meriwether, *Recollections of 92 Years* (McLean, Va.: EPM Publications, 1994 reprint edition), 95–97, 149–150. The Civil War Database Personnel Directory shows one A. Peppercorn ("residence not listed") who enlisted as a private in Company F, 5th Texas Cavalry. No further information is provided as to dates of service or personal history. The regiment served in the Southwest as part of the Army of New Mexico in 1862. No regimental roster could be found.

30. J. L. Scott, *36th Virginia Infantry* (Lynchburg, Va.: H. E. Howard, 1987), 46, 57; *Richmond Daily Dispatch*, October 31, 1864; *Richmond Sentinel*, October 31, 1864; Massey, *Bonnet Brigades*, 84–85. The *Richmond Daily Examiner*, October 31, 1864, also reports that the two women were confined in Castle Thunder prison, but reports Molly's alias as Bob Martin (rather than Morgan). "Molly is seventeen and good looking. Mary is twenty-four and scrawny. . . ." The story goes on to say that the captain of their company "asserts that the women were common camp followers, and that they have been the means of demoralizing several hundred men in his command. They adopted the disguise of soldiers the better to follow the army and hide their iniquity." Thomas P. Lowry, *The Story the Soldiers Wouldn't Tell: Sex in the Civil War* (Mechanicsburg, Pa,: Stackpole Books, 1994), 33, apparently

accepts the "camp followers" story. Leonard, *All the Daring of the Soldier*, 243–245, provides additional details and pertinent commentary about the "camp followers" allegation, which she disputes.

31. Kirkland, *Pictorial Book of Anecdotes and Incidents*, 159–160. The story was reported in the *Detroit Tribune*, November 18, 1864, and picked up from there by the *Nashville Dispatch*, December 4, 1864; Blanton and Cook, *They Fought like Demons*, 111. The 1st Michigan Engineers and Mechanics was formed on October 29, 1861, and served through September 22, 1865.

32. Blanton and Cook, *They Fought like Demons*, 53, 62, 112; military service records, National Archives; unit history from Civil War Database.

33. Pennsylvania newspaper story on "Joel Craig's Bivouac" web site (http://www.valstar.net˜jcraig/). The same story was reported in the *Nashville Dispatch*, June 7, 1863, quoting a letter from a soldier in Lake Providence, Louisiana. Blanton and Cook, *They Fought like Demons*, 10, 48, 72, 99–100. See also Dee Brown, "Wilson's Creek," *Civil War Times Illustrated* 1 (1972): 8–18. Brown provides background and context for the battle and discusses the units involved and casualty rates and notes: "Lack of distinguishable uniforms caused more confusion at Wilson's Creek than in any other Civil War battle." Troops on both sides wore mixed blue and gray uniforms, or no uniforms at all.

34. For a summary of Jennie Hodgers's life and military career, see Hall, *Patriots in Disguise*, 20–26. Primary sources include Rodney O. Davis, "Private Albert Cashier as Regarded by His/Her Comrades," *Journal of the Illinois State Historical Society* 82, 2 (Summer 1988): 108–112; Gerhard P. Clausius, "The Little Soldier of the 95th: Albert D. J. Cashier," *Journal of the Illinois State Historical Society* 51, 4 (Winter 1958): 380–387; *The Republican*, Pittsfield, Illinois, May 14, 1913; Albert Cashier pension files, National Archives; Illinois Veterans' Home administrative papers and correspondence. Leonard, *All the Daring of the Soldier*, 185–191, also provides a cogent summary of the story of Jennie Hodgers.

35. *Louisville Daily Journal*, Kentucky, May 23, 1864; from *Nashville Press*, Tennessee. The 101st Ohio was organized August 30, 1862. It participated in the battle of Perryville, October 8, 1862, and the Murfreesboro/Stones River campaign, December 26–31, 1862. It had continued service in Tennessee and Georgia through 1865, including battles around Atlanta and Nashville, mustering out June 12, 1865.

36. John Ransom, *John Ransom's Andersonville Diary* (New York: Berkley Books, 1988), 21–22. Re: Sarah Emma Edmonds anecdote, see Hall, *Patriots in Disguise*, 67–68.

Chapter 4. Horse Soldiers and "She Dragoons"

1. John E. Stanchak, "Horse Artillery," in *Historical Times Illustrated Encyclopedia of the Civil War*, ed. Patricia L. Faust (New York: Harper & Row, 1986), 370.

2. Bell I. Wiley, *The Life of Billy Yank: The Common Soldier of the Union* (Baton Rouge: Louisiana State University Press, 1978), 319.

3. Edward G. Longacre, "Boots and Saddles, Part I: The Eastern Theater: A Short History of the Cavalry during the Civil War," *Civil War Times Illustrated* 31, 1 (1992): 35–40.

4. Francis A. Lord, *They Fought for the Union* (New York: Bonanza Books, 1960), 73–77.

5. Wiley, *Life of Billy Yank*, 221–223.

6. Lord, *They Fought for the Union*, 31, 43, 49, 73–77, 108.

7. *The Book of Humour, Wit and Wisdom: A Manual of Table-Talk* (New York: Lee and Shepard, 1874); cited on the Making of America web site (http://moa.umdl.umich.edu/). See also DeAnne Blanton and Lauren M. Cook, *They Fought like Demons: Women Soldiers in the American Civil War* (Baton Rouge: Louisiana State University Press, 2002), 10, 38, 71, 99, 111. No records could be found to verify that Short's 6th Illinois Cavalry or any of its elements was at Shiloh (the companies were scattered mostly through Tennessee and Kentucky at the time). A Charles Davis does appear on the roster of Company E, but with no information on term of service or time and circumstances of discharge. Company C of the 7th Illinois Cavalry was an escort company, which fits the story, but the roster does not show a Charles Davis.

8. Wiley, *Life of Billy Yank*, 337; Jane E. Schultz, *Women at the Front: Hospital Workers in Civil War America* (Chapel Hill: University of North Carolina Press, 2004), 194–195. Although both cite National Archives pension records as their source, Wiley gives Clapp's middle initial as "E."

9. *Book of Humour, Wit and Wisdom*; Blanton and Cook, *They Fought like Demons*, 41, 50, 111. Morris's reported service in Company G of the 10th Missouri Cavalry could not be confirmed. The only Morris on the regimental roster is a William Morris, quartermaster sergeant in Company K. However, Captain John Rice did command the Company G "Red Rovers." One problem with verifications for women who served in several different regiments is that they may not have used the same alias every time, and newspapers often condensed the stories in such a way as to garble the details. The story reported in the 1874 book cited here in all probability was based on one or more newspaper reports, and it bears the hallmarks of being essentially true.

10. Blanton and Cook, *They Fought like Demons*, 113. The New York soldier who apparently reported this occurrence seems to have misidentified the regiment. The 2nd Maryland Cavalry did not begin forming until June 1863. However, the 1st Maryland Cavalry was operating in Virginia at the time in question, and Companies H and I were part of the garrison at Harpers Ferry.

11. David Lindsey, "Tennessee," in Faust, *Historical Times Illustrated Encyclopedia,* 745.

12. Blanton and Cook, *They Fought like Demons,* 17, 83–84. Blanton and Cook report that another soldier from the same regiment whose name was William Levasay, very possibly a relative, arrived at Camp Morton prison on the same day as Ellen Levasay. The 3rd Missouri Cavalry was among the garrison at Vicksburg. The National Park Service online "Civil War Soldiers and Sailors System" contains a roster for the 3rd Missouri Cavalry and several

other similarly named units with "State Militia" or "Cavalry Battalion" in their names, but no one by the name of Levasay was found in any of these units.

13. Confederate regiments from Tennessee often have convoluted histories because of constant reorganizations, mergers, and changes in designation. Several of Vaughn's brigade served as mounted infantry at various times. See Tennessee Civil War Centennial Commission, *Tennesseans in the Civil War: A Military History of Confederate and Union Units with Available Rosters of Personnel*, Part 1 (Nashville, Tenn., 1964).

14. Sgt. Eastham Tarrant, *Wild Riders of the First Kentucky Cavalry*, cited by Gerald D. Hodge, Jr., at http://www.geocities.com/Pentagon/Quarters/8558/other/woman2.html. The 45th Ohio was part of Wolford's Independent Cavalry along with the 1st Kentucky Cavalry.

15. Lee Middleton, *Hearts of Fire: Soldier Women of the Civil War* (Torch, Ohio: privately published, 1993), 84; Blanton and Cook, *They Fought like Demons*, 78–79. Lynda L. Sudlow, *A Vast Army of Women: Maine's Uncounted Forces in the American Civil War* (Gettysburg, Pa.: Thomas Publications, 2000), 124–125, states that Mary Jane Johnson's discovery at Belle Isle was reported in a Maine newspaper on January 5, 1864, copied from the *Richmond Whig* newspaper. See also "Women of Achievement and Herstory" online at http://holysmoke.org/fem/fem0509.htm. Although we don't know what male alias she was using, no one by the name of Johnson was among the captured soldiers. Among the prisoners who were taken to Richmond that day, five stand out as possible candidates to have been Johnson. Four of them died in prison, and the fifth was Samuel McAfee, whose military history reports enlistment July 19, 1862, at Louisville, Kentucky, as a private. "He was discharged on 11/15/1863 at Richmond, Virginia." For a Union soldier to be discharged from service in the Confederate capital seems most unlikely unless there were special circumstances. S[he] would have served a year and three months at the time of capture, and the timing fits the story. Genealogical research might be able to settle the question.

   The *Nashville Dispatch*, December 29, 1863, reports the discovery of a female prisoner by the name of Mary Jane Johnson at Belle Isle Prison but states that she was a member of the 16th Maine Infantry (no doubt an error). At this date she was said to be imprisoned in Castle Thunder, Richmond. The *Nashville Dispatch* for January 4, 1865, reported that Johnson was transferred to a female prison at Fitchburg, Massachusetts, on March 24, 1864.

16. C. Kay Larson, "Bonny Yank and Ginny Reb," *Minerva* 8, 1 (Spring 1990): 41; letter dated November 20, 1863, from Colonel W. Grose, commanding Third Brigade, Whiteside's, Tenn., to Colonel Starling, Assistant Adjutant-General.

17. Edward G. Longacre, *Custer and His Wolverines: The Michigan Cavalry Brigade, 1861–1865* (Conshohocken, Pa.: Combined Publishing, 1997), 23–24. The Civil War Database reports that Richard Ostrander was dishonorably discharged "(date not stated)." Nor were the reasons stated.

18. Fred M. Mazzula and William Kostka, *Mountain Charlie or the Adventures of Mrs. E. J. Guerin, Who Was Thirteen Years in Male Attire*

(Norman: University of Oklahoma Press, 1968); for a summary of the story, see Richard Hall, *Patriots in Disguise: Women Warriors of the Civil War* (New York: Paragon House, 1993), 167–177.

19. Searches were conducted on the Civil War Database, the online National Park Service Soldier and Sailor System, the *Official Records* CD-ROM, the Iowa 3rd Cavalry web site at http://www.iowa3rdcavalry.com, and Google searches for individual names and records. Chapman S. Charlot initially served as a lieutenant-colonel of Missouri militia from October 7, 1862, through March 19, 1863. A year later, on March 8, 1864, he was commissioned in the regular army as a major and assistant adjutant-general in the Adjutant-General Department, serving on the staff of Major General Samuel R. Curtis.

20. Blanton and Cook, *They Fought like Demons*, 13, 77, 160. A search of the Civil War Database found five candidate "1st New York Cavalry" regiments, based on New York State Adjutant General Office records. Two of these units served on the Virginia Peninsula in 1862 and only one was at Savages Station: the "Lincoln Cavalry." In this three-year regiment, Private Benjamin F. Fish, Company F, forty-two at enlistment on July, 18, 1861, is listed as a prisoner of war (POW) and is a strong candidate to be the husband in question. However, he is the only POW listed from Company F. After being paroled on August 5, 1862, he rejoined the regiment early in 1863 and was discharged for disability on June 25, 1863, at Washington, D.C.

Another Lincoln Cavalry soldier by the name of John Hirlinger, a private in Company G, is also listed as a POW earlier in June 1862, captured at an unspecified location during the Peninsula Campaign. Hirlinger enlisted in the regiment at age twenty-two in New York City about a month after Fish. He (or she) was paroled on September 13, 1862, and deserted on June 27, 1863, at Bloody Run, Pennsylvania, two days after Fish's discharge. The timing is very suggestive. Although the differing dates of capture and parole indicate possible discrepancies, these dates often are estimates rather than hard-and-fast facts. Other elements of the records suggest that Hirlinger may well have been Mrs. Fish.

21. Blanton and Cook, *They Fought like Demons*, 12, 30–31, 40, 65–66, 75–76, 129, 164, from National Archives muster rolls and other records. The Civil War Database shows a William D. Lindly (no "e") in Company D, but no information on date of enlistment or discharge. A Private James Smith also served in Company D; no other information.

22. *Washington Telegraph*, Arkansas, December 24, 1862, and *Dallas Herald*, Texas, January 7, 1863. See Appendix B.

23. Jeffry D. Wert, *From Winchester to Cedar Creek: The Shenandoah Campaign of 1864* (Carlisle, Pa.: South Mountain Press, 1987), 104–105, 164–165, 249.

24. Blanton and Cook, *They Fought like Demons*, 121–122.

25. John E. Stanchak, "Field Artillery," in Faust, *Historical Times Illustrated Encyclopedia*, 258; Lord, *They Fought for the Union*, 77–81; Edward A. Moore, *The Story of a Cannoneer under Stonewall Jackson* (New York:

Neale Publishing, 1907); Les D. Jensen, "Grape Shot; Canister," in Faust, *Historical Times Illustrated Encyclopedia*, 321.

26. Ashley Halsey, ed., *A Yankee Private's Civil War* (Chicago: Henry Regnery, 1961), 36–38. For a memoir of life in the Confederate Washington Artillery of New Orleans, see Charles W. Squires, "My Artillery Fire Was Very Destructive," *Civil War Times Illustrated* 14, 3 (1975): 18–29.

27. Moore, *Story of a Cannoneer*, 53–54.

Chapter 5. The Secret Service

1. Francis A. Lord, *They Fought for the Union* (New York: Bonanza Books, 1960), 132–135; Rhodri Jeffreys-Jones, "Espionage," in *The Reader's Companion to American History*, ed. Eric Foner and John A. Garraty (Boston: Houghton Mifflin, 1991), 357–358.

2. Donald E. Markle, *Spies and Spymasters of the Civil War* (New York: Hippocrene Books, 1994), 96–97, 155–189. The author includes summaries of the activities of well-known female spies Belle Boyd, Rose O'Neal Greenhow, Pauline Cushman, Sarah Emma Edmonds, Elizabeth Van Lew, and a number of lesser-known female spies. His final chapter contains a useful "Listing of All Known Civil War Spies"; Jeffry D. Wert, "Scout," in *Historical Times Illustrated Encyclopedia of the Civil War*, ed. Patricia L. Faust (New York: Harper & Row, 1986), 663.

3. Correspondence from Colonel William A. Phillips to General James G. Blunt, September 5, 1862. *Official Records of the Union and Confederate Armies [The War of the Rebellion: A Compilation of the Official Records of the Union and Confederate Armies]*, Series 1, Vol. 13, No.19 (Washington, D.C.: Government Printing Office, 1884); William B. Feis, *Grant's Secret Service: The Intelligence War from Belmont to Appomattox* (Lincoln: University of Nebraska Press, 2002), 125–138, 166–167.

4. *Official Records*, Series 1, Vol. 24/1, No. 61.

5. *Official Records*, Series 1, Vol. 47/2, No. 99; the Missouri letter is from *Official Records*, Series 1, Vol. 48/1, No. 101. Elizabeth D. Leonard, *All the Daring of the Soldier: Women of the Civil War Armies* (New York: W. W. Norton, 1999), 230–237, provides numerous examples of government-paid spies mentioned in the *Official Records* and in National Archives Adjutant General Office records.

6. *Memphis Daily Appeal*, June 7, 1861, from the Harpers Ferry correspondent of the *Louisville Courier*, May 30; *Memphis Daily Appeal*, December 19, 1861, from the Richmond correspondent of the *Nashville Union*.

7. C. Kay Larson, "Bonny Yank and Ginny Reb Revisited," *Minerva* 10, 2 (Summer 1992): 50, from Lucy London Anderson, *North Carolina Women of the Confederacy*, Fayetteville, N.C., 1926; Women's History web site (http:/womenshistory.about.com.

8. Harnett T. Kane, *Spies for the Blue and Gray* (New York: Doubleday, 1954), 263–281. Kane devotes an informative chapter to the "Sister Act."

9. Marilyn Mayer Culpepper, *Trials and Triumphs: The Women of the American Civil War* (East Lansing: Michigan State University Press, 1991), 41–42; Markle, *Spies and Spymasters,* 169–170; "Confederate Sister Act–The Moon Sister Spies," http://userpages.aug.com/captbarb/moon.html.

10. H. B. Smith, *Between the Lines: Secret Service Stories Told Fifty Years After* (New York: Booz Brothers, 1911), 97.

11. Charles E. Taylor, *The Signal and Secret Service of the Confederate States* (Harmans, Md.: Toomey Press, 1986), vi.

12. Allan Pinkerton, *The Spy of the Rebellion: Being a True History of the Spy System of the United States Army during the Late Rebellion* (Hartford, Conn.: M. A. Winter & Hatch, 1883), 74–75, 79–80, 93, 543–544;.William A. Tidwell, *Come Retribution: The Confederate Secret Service and the Assassination of Lincoln* (Jackson: University Press of Mississippi), 229–232.

13. Alan Axelrod, *The War between the Spies: A History of Espionage during the American Civil War* (New York: Atlantic Monthly Press, 1992), 175–176; Lafayette C. Baker entry in *Appleton's Cyclopedia of American Biography,* online at http://www.famousamericans.net/lafayettecbaker/.

14. *Savannah Republican,* Georgia, May 21 and 22, 1863.

15. Kane, *Spies for the Blue and Gray,* 11–67; Katharine M. Jones, ed., *Heroines of Dixie* (Indianapolis: Bobbs-Merrill, 1955), 61–66, 74–75, 249–254; Pinkerton, *Spy of the Rebellion,* 252–270; Axelrod, *War between the Spies,* 43–70; William G. Beymer, *On Hazardous Service: Scouts and Spies of the North and South* (New York: Harper & Brothers, 1912), 179–210; William A. Tidwell, *Confederate Covert Action in the American Civil War: April '65* (Kent, Ohio: Kent State University Press, 1995), 32, 36–37, 53–54, 57–59.

16. Lafayette C. Baker, *Spies, Traitors and Conspirators of the Late Civil War* (Philadelphia: John E. Potter, 1894), 146–147; see also Kane, *Spies for the Blue and Gray,* 169–75.

17. The quotes and the information that follows are from the Antonia Ford chapter, Children of the Confederacy web site, "Who Was Antonia Ford?" (http://users.erols.com/kfraser/fairfax/antonia.html).

18. Larson, "Bonny Yank and Ginny Reb Revisited," 50–51; Leonard, *All the Daring of the Soldier,* 44–50; Markle, *Spies and Spymasters,* 167–168; Stewart Sifakis, *Who Was Who in the Confederacy* (New York: Facts on File, 1988), 94. A story reported in the *Southern Confederacy,* Atlanta, Georgia, on April 2, 1863, and in the *Weekly Columbus Enquirer,* Georgia, April 7, 1863, both attributed to the *Baltimore Clipper,* states that Ford "was the principal spy and guide for Captain Mosby in his recent raid on Fairfax Court House." The article quotes a commission given to her by J.E.B. Stuart in October 1861 as his Honorable Aide de Camp.

19. DeAnne Blanton and Lauren M. Cook, *They Fought like Demons: Women Soldiers in the American Civil War* (Baton Rouge: Louisiana State University Press, 2002), 66, 78, 118–119, 199; Markle, *Spies and Spymasters,* 187, reports her name as "Mrs. Frances Abel."

20. John E. McDowell, "Nathaniel Banks; Fighting Politico," *Civil War Times Illustrated* 11, 9 (1973): 4–9, 44–47.

21. Leonard, *All the Daring of the Soldier,* 231–232. Jamieson and her husband almost certainly served in a regular army (U.S.) Cavalry regiment, since there were only about six companies of Union cavalry present at First Bull Run altogether, all from the 1st U.S. Cavalry and 2nd U.S. Cavalry. The rosters of these very early cavalry units are not very complete. A Private James Jamieson was enlisted in Company F of the 1st Cavalry. However, according to the best information available, only Companies A and E were present at First Bull Run.

   Again with the caution that the rosters are not necessarily complete, no officers by the name of Jamieson were found in the Civil War Database Personnel Directory for the entire Union army. Several officers were found by the name of Abel, but all of them survived the war.

22. "Who Was Antonia Ford?" (http://users.erols.com/kfraser/fairfax./antonia.html).

23. Blanton and Cook, *They Fought like Demons,* 119, 199.

24. Record Group 107, National Archives, Office of Secretary of War special file of papers; *Nashville Dispatch,* September 22, 1863; The *Nashville Dispatch* for January 4, 1865, reports that Jones was imprisoned at Fitchburg, Massachusetts, on March 24, 1864. She is described in the story as a "camp follower" suspected of being a Confederate spy; Evan J. Albright, "Custer's Cape Cod Mistress," Cape Cod Confidential, November 16, 2004, http://www.capecodconfidential.com/cccanniejones011230.shtml.

25. Baker, *Spies, Traitors and Conspirators,* 239–240. See also Thomas P. Lowry, *The Story the Soldiers Wouldn't Tell: Sex in the Civil War* (Mechanicsburg, Pa.: Stackpole Books, 1994), 154–155.

26. Ezra J. Warner, *Generals in Blue: Lives of the Union Commanders* (Baton Rouge: Louisiana State University Press, 1989), 482.

27. D. A. Kinsley, *Custer: Favor the Bold: A Soldier's Story* (New York: Promontory Press, 1988), 159–164.

28. Ibid., 192–199.

29. Ibid., 195.

30. C. J. Worthington, ed., *The Woman in Battle* (Hartford, Conn.: T. Belknap, 1876).

31. For example, see Kane, *Spies for the Blue and Gray,* 129–155.

32. Marilyn Mayer Culpepper, *Trials and Triumphs,* 40–41; Axelrod, *War between the Spies,* 71–83; Leonard, *All the Daring of the Soldier,* 25–35. Boyd's capture at sea and subsequent marriage to one of the sailors on the U.S. vessel, and his eventual arrest, were reported in the *Washington Star,* December 7, 1864, as quoted in the *National Democrat,* Little Rock, Arkansas, December 31, 1864.

33. William Galbraith and Loretta Galbraith, *A Lost Heroine of the Confederacy: The Diaries and Letters of Belle Edmondson* (Jackson: University Press of Mississippi, 1990); Leonard, *All the Daring of the Soldier,* 74–75; Markle, *Spies and Spymasters,* 167; Culpepper, *Trials and Triumphs,* 43; Jones, *Heroines of Dixie,* 270–275.

34. Matthew Page Andrews, *Women of the South in War Times* (Baltimore: Norman, Remington, 1920), 116–119.

35. L. P. Brockett, *Battle-Field and Hospital; Or, Lights and Shadows of the Great Rebellion* (Philadelphia: Hubbard Brothers, 1888), 365–366. Larson, "Bonny Yank and Ginny Reb Revisited," 54–55. See also "Captain Daniel Ellis: A Biographical Sketch" (http://www.nku.edu/~ellisa/danielellis/biography.html).

36. Francis Butler Simkins and James Welch Patton, *The Women of the Confederacy* (Richmond, Va.: Garrett and Massie, 1936), 77; Boyd B. Stutler, "Nancy Hart, Lady Bushwhacker," *Civil War Times Illustrated* 1, 9 (1960): 7; Leonard, *All the Daring of the Soldier,* 91; "Nancy Hart: Confederate Spy: A Young Girl" (http://www.nkclifton.com/nancy.html); Markle, *Spies and Spymasters,* 96–97, 155–189. The author includes summaries of the activities of well-known female spies Belle Boyd, Rose O'Neal Greenhow, Pauline Cushman, Sarah Emma Edmonds, and Elizabeth Van Lew, and a number of lesser-known female spies.

Chapter 6. They Were Determined to Serve.

1. Frazar Kirkland, *Pictorial Book of Anecdotes and Incidents of the War of the Rebellion* (Hartford, Conn.: Hartford Publishing, 1867), 204. No roster could be found for the 5th Kansas or for the 1st Missouri State Militia Cavalry. The latter, according to other records, served from April 1862 through July 1865 and was engaged at Walnut Creek, August 8, 1862. DeAnne Blanton and Lauren M. Cook, *They Fought like Demons: Women Soldiers in the American Civil War* (Baton Rouge: Louisiana State University Press, 2002), 41, cite an 1863 newspaper story quoting Cook to the effect that her motivation was largely boredom with the monotony of a woman's life. That is, she was seeking some excitement or adventure. Elizabeth D. Leonard, *All the Daring of the Soldier: Women of the Civil War Armies* (New York: W. W. Norton, 1999), 209, reports that when Cook tried to enlist at St. Louis, she gave herself away by her mannerisms.

2. Kirkland, *Pictorial Book of Anecdotes and Incidents,* 168. The Civil War Database regimental roster shows that Sergeant Lewis B. White enlisted in Company H on August 27, 1861, at Rochester, New York. As each company was organized, it was sent to the front in Virginia, where the regiment was officially organized as a unit on September 9, 1861.

3. Lee Middleton, *Hearts of Fire: Soldier Women of the Civil War* (Torch, Ohio: privately published, 1993), 111–112, from *History of the 141st Pennsylvania Volunteers, 1862–1865,* as reported by Chaplain David Craft. The regiment served from August 29, 1862, to May 28, 1865, and was at Chancellorsville. No one by the name of Norton appears in the roster of Company E. There was a Captain Joseph B. Reeve (instead of Reeves) in Company E, but he resigned in 1862. The captain of Company I was Charles Mercur.

4. Ethel Alice Hurn, *Wisconsin Women in the War between the States,* Original Papers No. 6 (Wisconsin History Commission, 1911), 103; Mary

Elizabeth Massey, *Bonnet Brigades* (New York: Alfred A. Knopf, 1966), 80. A search of the rosters of the 1st through 7th Wisconsin Infantry regiments found no Mason Collins. No roster was found for the 4th Infantry. A William M. Collins was found in the 5th Infantry, no residence listed. Conceivably, the middle initial "M" might stand for Mason. The regiment was formed in Madison, about twenty-eight miles west of Lake Mills where Mason and Sarah were reported to have lived.

5. *Maysville Dollar Weekly Bulletin*, Kentucky, November 27, 1862; Albert D. Richardson, *The Secret Service, the Field, the Dungeon, and the Escape* (Hartford, Conn.: American Publishing, 1865), 175; Blanton and Cook, *They Fought like Demons*, 40, 51, 122. The *Daily Chronicle & Sentinel*, Augusta, Georgia, August 7, 1861 (from the *Cincinnati Commercial*), states that the young woman in the 1st Kentucky Infantry was from Georgia and enlisted at Cincinnati. The regiment was formed in Pendleton, Ohio, during April and May of 1861.

6. Kirkland, *Pictorial Book of Anecdotes and Incidents*, 580; *Cairo City Weekly News*, Illinois, June 13, 1861. The three-months 3rd Ohio Infantry regiment (April 27, 1861, to August 15, 1861) was organized at Camp Jackson, near Columbus. Its colonel was Isaac H. Marrow. The unit history states: "On April 28 [1861] a part of the regiment was sent to Camp Dennison to prepare a suitable camping place for the regiment, where it was joined by the remainder two days later."

Although no record could be found of a soldier who was dismissed early on, the roster does contain one suspicious entry. A twenty-two-year-old private by the name of Ashabel Blivin, who is recorded as having enlisted in Company B on April 19, 1861, is indicated to have been "sent home" with no exact date or circumstances being specified. However, the roster also includes quite a few other soldiers' names for whom only the enlistment date is given, with no further record. Only the unelaborated expression "sent home" stands out.

7. Blanton and Cook, *They Fought like Demons*, 43, 114.

8. Culpepper, *Trials and Triumphs*, 115; from "Letters of William F. Hertzog," Archives and manuscripts, Chicago Historical Society (the letter date is two days before the battle of Chattanooga); 63rd Illinois soldier from Record Group 94, National Archives; Garold L. Cole, *Civil War Eyewitnesses: An Annotated Bibliography of Books and Articles, 1955–1986* (Columbia: University of South Carolina Press, 1988), 14; from "Civil War Letters of Henry C. Bear," *Lincoln Herald*, 1960–1961; Lowry, *The Story the Soldiers Wouldn't Tell: Sex in the Civil War* (Mechanicsburg, Pa.: Stackpole Books), 33; Blanton and Cook, *They Fought like Demons*, 128.

9. Blanton and Cook, *They Fought like Demons*, 114–115, 148. Leonard, *All the Daring of the Soldier*, 222, cites the *Richmond Daily Examiner*, September 3, 1864, in regard to Louisa Hoffman. The *Nashville Dispatch*, Tennessee, August 18, 1864, reported her arrest on August 16, 1864, and mentions her alleged other services. No record could be found of any Union Virginia cavalry. There was a 1st West Virginia Union cavalry regiment, but it was not at First Bull Run. No regimental rosters were found for the 1st Ten-

nessee Artillery, either light or heavy artillery. The roster of the Confederate 1st Virginia Cavalry shows a John F. Hoffman in Company H, but he was still serving in 1864 and could not be the same person.

10. *Valley Spirit,* Franklin County, Pennsylvania, September 5, 1861. The three-months regiment served from April 23, 1861, to July 29, 1861. Among the 781 soldiers listed in the regimental roster, all served the full three months and there is no clue as to which may have been a woman.

11. Leonard, *All the Daring of the Soldier,* 221; DeAnne Blanton, "Women Soldiers of the Civil War," *Prologue: Quarterly of the National Archives* 25, 1 (Spring 1993): 28; Record Group 94, National Archives. Both Leonard, *All the Daring of the Soldier,* 221, and Blanton and Cook, *They Fought like Demons,* 112, report that the service record of "John Williams" reads "Discharged (Proved to be a Woman)." The regimental roster on the Civil War Database lists a Private John Williams in Company H but has no dates or locations of enlistment or discharge.

12. *Cincinnati Daily Press,* January 6, 1862.

13. Leonard, *All the Daring of the Soldier,* 221.

14. Record Group 94, National Archives; Blanton and Cook, *They Fought like Demons,* 118.

15. Middleton, *Hearts of Fire,* 40–42, from Colonel Caleb Carleton Papers, 89th Ohio, Manuscript Division, Library of Congress.

16. *Cleveland Plain Dealer,* September 10, 1861; *The Standard,* Clarksville, Texas, October 5, 1861; Record Group 94, National Archives; Blanton and Cook, *They Fought like Demons,* 41–42, 109. Blanton and Cook cite an 1863 newspaper story quoting Mary Smith to the effect that her motivation was due largely to being bored with the monotony of her customary life.

17. *Charleston Mercury,* South Carolina, January 16, 1862. A Civil War Database search for a Colonel Boone established that Col. William P. Boone was in charge of the Confederate 28th Kentucky Infantry at that time. The *Austin State Gazette,* February 22, 1862, attributing the information to the *Arkansas True Democrat,* reported that "a widow McDonald has been detected in several regiments and discharged as many times."

18. *Owensboro Monitor,* Kentucky, August 10, 1862. Although the regiment served from August 19, 1862, to June 3, 1865, Captain John W. Gerard, Company I, was commander only during August and September of 1862, when he "was dismissed...for drunkenness." The newspaper story dates the incident as "yesterday afternoon," which would have been August 9, 1862. The troubled regiment had an extraordinary number of desertions in 1862, including two on August 21 and three on September 1, immediately prior to Gerard's dismissal on September 10.

   A search of the Company I roster turned up no direct evidence of a soldier being discharged under unusual circumstances at this time. It did turn up seven deserters, a rubric that could conceal the release of a female soldier.

19. Mary A. Livermore, *My Story of the War* (Hartford, Conn: A. D. Worthington, 1887), 113–114. The 1861 date is inferred from the fact that the regiment left Camp Douglas by July 12, 1861.

20. *Unconditional Union,* Little Rock, Arkansas, March 18, 1864, from the *Monmouth Atlas,* Illinois.
21. Richard Hall, *Patriots in Disguise: Women Warriors of the Civil War* (New York: Paragon House, 1993), 126.
22. *Semi-Weekly Dispatch,* Franklin County, Pennsylvania, April 1, 1862. Jackson A. Brand was captain of Company K, 107th Pennsylvania Infantry, from February 24, 1862, until his resignation on November 24, 1862.
23. Hall, *Patriots in Disguise,* 28.
24. Kirkland, *Pictorial Book of Anecdotes and Incidents,* 524–525.
25. A search of the 14th Iowa Infantry roster on the Civil War Database turned up no reference to a soldier who committed suicide or died in camp. Blanton and Cook, *They Fought like Demons,* 155–156, cite a newspaper report that said the girl was using the name "Charlie" and was serving with her boyfriend, a captain. When rumors began circulating, she apparently feared that she would be separated from her lover and took her own life. The authors note that the newspaper may not have recorded the regimental number correctly. One candidate to have been the female soldier, if it was the 14th Iowa, is Daniel Hallmark, twenty, of Columbus, Kentucky, who enlisted as a private in Company H on October 31, 1861. The entry states simply, "He died (date not stated)." This soldier was also reported to have been born in Tennessee. The entry is based on "Roster and Record of Iowa Soldiers in the War of Rebellion."
26. Thornburg Newsletter, Issue No. 3, formerly posted at http://www.indy. net. The newsletter suggests that the unidentified female soldier arrested in Indianapolis and sent home to Winchester, Indiana, may have been Mary Thornburg since Winchester is the county seat of Randolph County where Mary lived.
27. *Maysville Dollar Bulletin,* Kentucky, November 12, 1863, from *Philadelphia Press;* Kirkland, *Pictorial Book of Anecdotes and Incidents,* 206.
28. Gregory A. Coco, *On the Bloodstained Field* (Hollidaysburg, Pa.: Wheatfield Press, 1987), 40, from Letter of Thomas Read, Company E, 5th Michigan Infantry, dated August 20, 1863.
29. Mary A. Gardner Holland, *Our Army Nurses* (Boston: Lounsbery, Nichols & Worth, 1897), 341.
30. Leonard, *All the Daring of the Soldier,* 219; from "A Volunteer Nurse in the Civil War: The Diary of Harriet Douglas Whetten," *Wisconsin Magazine of History* 48 (Winter 1964–1965): 217. Newton Martin Curtis, *From Bull Run to Chancellorsville: The Story of the Sixteenth New York Infantry together with Personal Reminiscences* (New York: G.P. Putnam's Sons, 1906), 280, mentions Whetten among the U.S. Sanitary Commission doctors and nurses who were on duty aboard the hospital ship *Wilson Small* in May 1862 when he was a patient.
31. See Appendix A, "Unidentified Female Soldiers" for 1863; "An Indiana Soldier in Love and War: The Civil War Letters of John V. Hadley," ed. James I. Robertson, Jr., *Indiana Magazine of History* 59, 3 (September 1963): 238; Bell I. Wiley, *Confederate Women* (Westport, Conn.: Greenwood Press,

1975), 142, from *Sandusky Register,* Ohio, December 12, 1864; Massey, *Bonnet Brigades,* 84; *National Democrat,* Little Rock, Arkansas, January 7, 1865.

Chapter 7. Casualties of War

1. *Official Records of the Union and Confederate Armies [The War of the Rebellion: A Compilation of the Official Records of the Union and Confederate Armies]* (Washington, D.C.: Government Printing Office, 1884), Series 1, Vol. 10, Part 2, 374–376, 390, 402.
2. Louis Fisher, *Military Tribunals and Presidential Power: American Revolution to the War on Terrorism* (Lawrence: University Press of Kansas, 2005), 41–70.
3. Peggy Robbins, "Prisoners," in *Historical Times Illustrated Encyclopedia of the Civil War,* ed. Patricia L. Faust (New York: Harper & Row, 1986), 603–604.
4. For additional information about Augusta H. Morris, see *Official Records,* Series 2, Vol. 2, No. 115, 1862; Harnett T. Kane, *Spies for the Blue and Gray* (New York: Doubleday, 1954), 61–62; Elizabeth D. Leonard, *All the Daring of the Soldier: Women of the Civil War Armies* (New York: W.W. Norton, 1999), 234–235; Donald E. Markle, *Spies and Spymasters of the Civil War* (New York: Hippocrene Books, 1994), 169; Alan Axelrod, *The War between the Spies: A History of Espionage during the American Civil War* (New York: Atlantic Monthly Press, 1992), 71–73; William A. Tidwell, *Confederate Covert Action in the American Civil War: April '65* (Kent, Ohio: Kent State University Press, 1995), 40, 60. For additional information about Mrs. Catherine V. Baxley, see Leonard, *All the Daring of the Soldier,* 237–238; Tidwell, *Confederate Covert Action,* 36–37, 40; *Daily State Journal,* Little Rock, Arkansas, January 18, 1862.
5. "Gratiot Street Prison" (http://www.civilwarstlouis.com/Gratiot/Listwomen.htm).
6. Louis S. Gerteis, *Civil War St. Louis* (Lawrence: University Press of Kansas, 2001), 170–201.
7. John Moore Hammond, comp., *South Carolina and the Southern Claims Commission, 1871–1880* (South Carolina Historical Society, 1982). Bound photocopies arranged alphabetically by county, courtesy of Grace Fleming, Winder, Georgia.
8. Jeanne M. Christie, "The Prisoner: The Incarceration of Mrs. Mary M. Stockton Terry," in *Confederate Women,* ed. Mauriel Phillips Joslyn (Gretna, La.: Pelican Publishing, 2004), 118–119. For a discussion of the refugee phenomenon in the South, see George C. Rable, *Civil Wars: Women and the Crisis of Southern Nationalism* (Urbana: University of Illinois Press, 1989), 181–201.
9. *Bellville Countryman,* Texas, September 27, 1864.
10. Albert D. Richardson, *The Secret Service, the Field, the Dungeon, and the Escape* (Hartford, Conn.: American Publishing, 1865), 175; DeAnne Blanton and Lauren M. Cook, *They Fought like Demons: Women Soldiers in the American Civil War* (Baton Rouge: Louisiana State University Press,

2002), 40, 122, document the male name and spying charge of "John Thompson." A soldier by that name enlisted in the three-year 1st Kentucky Infantry regiment (Union) on May 28, 1861, at Camp Clay, Ohio, and was mustered in to Company D on June 5, 1861. The soldier was discharged July 25, 1861, at Ravenswood, Virginia, "discovered to be a woman." (Civil War Database information from Report of Adjutant General of Kentucky.) An article in the *Daily Chronicle & Sentinel,* Augusta, Georgia, August 7, 1861, reports that the woman was from Georgia, enlisted at Cincinnati, and was caught transferring information to the enemy.

11. Agatha Young, *The Women and the Crisis: Women of the North in the Civil War* (New York: McDowell, Obolensky, 1959), 137. The *Savannah Republican,* Georgia, August 6, 1861, spells her name as Mrs. Curtis rather than Custis and reports that she had a brother in the Rochester 2nd New York regiment. The *Daily Chronicle & Sentinel,* Augusta, Georgia, August 4, 1861 (from the *Richmond Dispatch,* August 2), reports her arrival in Richmond as a prisoner of Captain Fremaux and William S. Read of the 8th Louisiana regiment.

    A roster check indicates that Leon J. Fremaux was captain of Company A, 8th Louisiana Infantry. No record could be found of a William S. Read. The wording in one newspaper story was: "She belongs, it appears, to the 2nd N.Y. Regiment"; in the other, she was said to have a brother in the "Rochester Regiment." The 2nd New York Infantry, known as the "Troy Regiment," was not at First Bull Run. The 8th New York Cavalry, which was known as the "Rochester Regiment," was not formed until after First Bull Run. However, the other "Rochester Regiment," the 13th New York Infantry, was heavily engaged at First Bull Run and in fact had seventeen soldiers taken prisoner.

12. Unsourced and undated reference on Joel Craig's Bivouac web site (http://www.valstar.net/~jcraig). When queried by e-mail, Craig replied that the stories on his site are taken from various Pennsylvania newspapers. General James S. Wadsworth was military governor of the District of Columbia in March 1862, and went on to field command later that year.

13. Blanton and Cook, *They Fought like Demons,* 82–83; C. Kay Larson, "Bonny Yank and Ginny Reb Revisited," *Minerva* 10, 2 (Summer 1992): 53; Lee Middleton, *Hearts of Fire: Soldier Women of the Civil War* (Torch, Ohio: privately published, 1993), 67; *Official Records,* Series 2, Vol. 5, No. 118.

14. *Louisville Daily Journal,* Kentucky, January 21, 1864; from *Wheeling Register,* West Virginia. Jeremiah Cutler Sullivan, a former Navy officer, was commanding the 1st Division, Department of West Virginia, December 1863 to April 1864. See Stewart Sifakis, *Who Was Who in the Union* (New York: Facts on File, 1988), 398.

15. *Nashville Dispatch,* Tennessee, August 26, 1864.

16. Annie Wittenmeyer, *Under the Guns: A Woman's Reminiscences of the Civil War* (Boston, 1895), 17–20; cited by Mary Elizabeth Massey, *Bonnet Brigades* (New York: Alfred A. Knopf, 1966), 84.

17. Wesley Thurman Leeper, *Rebels Valiant: Second Arkansas Mounted Rifles (Dismounted)* (Little Rock Ark.: Pioneer Press, 1964), 190–204, reports

the Battle of Chickamauga from the perspective of a Confederate regiment engaged in the battle.

18. C. Kay Larson, "Bonny Yank and Ginny Reb Revisited," 45.

19. Lauren Cook Burgess, ed., *An Uncommon Soldier: The Civil War Letters of Sarah Rosetta Wakeman* (Pasadena, Md.: Minerva Center, 1994), 44.

20. Sandra V. Parker, *Richmond's Civil War Prisons* (Lynchburg, Va.: H. E. Howard, 1990), 25–26. Parker reports that an estimated 100 women were imprisoned in Castle Thunder during the war, most of them arrested while wearing Confederate uniforms and suspected of treason or prostitution.

21. "Wild Riders of the First Kentucky Cavalry," by Sergeant Eastham Tarrant, Company A; cited by Gerald D. Hodge, Jr., Niota, Tennessee, at http://www. homestead.com/ohio45. The 45th Ohio was part of Wolford's Independent Cavalry along with the 1st Kentucky Cavalry. Hodge reports that the information about "Tommy" came from a fellow prisoner at Belle Isle, James E. King, Company A, 1st Kentucky Cavalry. King stated, "Early in February 1864, Tommy was taken very sick, and was compelled to disclose his sex. Tommy proved to be a female," who was then removed from prison, and her fate after that is not known.

22. Middleton, *Hearts of Fire,* 84. See "Women of Achievement and Herstory" at http://www.holysmoke.org/fem/fem0509.htm. The 11th Kentucky received the brunt of an attack October 20, 1863, at Philadelphia, Tennessee. About 100 soldiers were taken prisoner. Although we don't know what male alias Mary Jane Johnson was using, no one by the name of Johnson was among the captured soldiers. The Civil War Database casualty analysis does not list any captain who was a casualty that day; the only soldier killed was a private.

Among the prisoners that day who were taken to Richmond, five originally stood out as possible candidates to have been Mary Jane Johnson. Four of them died in prison, and the fifth was Samuel McAfee, whose military history reports enlistment July 19, 1862, at Louisville, Kentucky, as a private. "He was discharged on 11/15/1863 at Richmond, Virginia." For a Union soldier to be discharged from service in the Confederate capital seems most unlikely unless there were special circumstances. He would have served a year and three months at the time of capture, and the timing fits the story. However, the soldier diary dates her discovery at Belle Isle as occurring on December 9, 1863, which seems to rule out that identification.

23. Sefakis, *Who Was Who in the Union,* 52; Blanton and Cook, *They Fought like Demons,* 44, 79–80. Middleton, *Hearts of Fire,* 30, reports that Budwin is buried at Florence, South Carolina, National Cemetery, and this was verified using the cemetery's web site. There her name is given as Budwin "or Baduine," and her grave number is stated to be D-2480. A search was conducted in the rosters of the 1st through 6th Pennsylvania light and heavy artillery regiments. No one named Budwin or Baduine was found, but there was no data for some units. See also G. Wayne King, "Death Camp at Florence," *Civil War Times Illustrated* 12, 9 (1974): 34–42. King provides detailed information about the origins and history of the prison camp, its dimensions and physical conditions, numbers of prisoners, and mortality rates.

24. Young, *Women and the Crisis*, 380; Martha Thomas, "Amazing Mary," *Civil War Times Illustrated* 23, 1 (1984): 37–41; Robert Werlich, "Mary Walker: From Union Army Surgeon to Sideshow Freak," *Civil War Times Illustrated* 6, 3 (1967): 46–49. The *National Intelligencer,* Washington, D.C., April 19, 1864, reported a story in a Virginia newspaper from Dalton, Georgia, dated April 12: " Miss Mary E. Walker, surgeon of the 53d [*sic*] Ohio, was captured by our pickets and brought here yesterday."

25. See "Mary Edwards Walker: Civil War Doctor" (http://www.northnet. org/stlawrenceaauw/walker.htm); Faust, *Historical Times Illustrated Encyclopedia of the Civil War,* 798; Parker, *Richmond's Civil War Prisons,* 26; Captain Barbara A. Wilson's web site, "They Were There" (http://userpages. aug.com/captbarb/femvets2.html).

26. Blanton and Cook, *They Fought like Demons,* 78–79; December 23, 1863, diary entry concerning Mrs. Collier in John Ransom, *John Ransom's Andersonville Diary* (New York: Berkley Books, 1988), 22.

27. *Civil War Times Illustrated* 17, 5 (1978): 41; Blanton and Cook, *They Fought like Demons,* 52–53.

28. Massey, *Bonnet Brigades,* 81–82.

29. Thanks to Frank Rawlinson for alerting me to the fictionalized version of Mollie Bean in the book *Guns of the South,* by Harry Turtledove, based on a true story. See also Leonard, *All the Daring of the Soldier,* 222, citing the *Richmond Whig,* February 20, 1865, identifying the real historical Mollie Bean. No Melvin Bean appears on the regimental roster; however, John Houston Thorpe (with an "e") was captain of Company C. Her imprisonment at Castle Thunder also was reported by Priscilla Rhoades, "The Women of Castle Thunder," *Kudzu Monthly* (ezine), August 2002 (http://www.kudzu-monthly.com/kudzu/aug02/CastleThunder.html).

30. Mary A. Gardner Holland, *Our Army Nurses* (Boston: Lounsbery, Nichols & Worth, 1897), 42–64; L. P. Brockett and Mary C. Vaughan, *Woman's Work in the Civil War: A Record of Heroism, Patriotism and Patience* (Philadelphia: Zeigler, McCurdy, 1867), 111–132; Elizabeth Brown, *Clara Barton: Professional Angel* (Philadelphia: University of Pennsylvania Press, 1987), 99; Jean Getman O'Brien, "Clara Barton Brought Mercy to Antietam," *Civil War Times Illustrated* 1, 5 (1962): 38–40;. Blanton and Cook, *They Fought like Demons,* 29, 32, 94; Jane E. Schultz, *Women at the Front: Hospital Workers in Civil War America* (Chapel Hill: University of North Carolina Press, 2004), 82. Blanton and Cook report that Galloway received a neck wound, whereas Pryor specifically states that it was a chest wound, and O'Brien reports that the bullet entered the upper part of her chest and lodged just under the skin of her back.

31. Eileen F. Conklin, *Women at Gettysburg 1863* (Gettysburg, Pa.: Thomas Publications, 1993), 134. *Official Records,* Series 1, Vol. 27, Part 1, 38. Footnote 1 states: "This was a notation at the bottom of General William Hays' report on the burial of Confederate dead by his command." See also Herbert L. Grimm and Paul L. Roy, *Human Interest Stories of the Three Days' Battles at Gettysburg* (Gettysburg, Pa.: Gettysburg Times & News Publishing, 1927), 18.

32. Ted Alexander, ed., *The 126th Pennsylvania* (Shippensburg, Pa.: Beidel Printing House, 1984), 39–40, 88.

33. Fred Brooks, "Shiloh Mystery Woman," *Civil War Times Illustrated* 17, 5 (1978): 29.

34. *Official Records of the Union and Confederate Armies,* Series 2, Vol. 5, [S# 118]; Union Correspondence, Prisoners of War, from December 1, 1862, to June 10, 1863, letter from Major Joseph Darr, Jr., Provost-Marshal General, Wheeling, W.Va., to Colonel W. Hoffman, Commissary-General of Prisoners, Dec. 24, 1862 (#5); Blanton and Cook, *They Fought like Demons,* 36, 49. The Union 23rd Kentucky Infantry served from January 1, 1862, to December 27, 1865 (according to Frederick H. Dyer, *A Compendium of the War of the Rebellion* [New York: Thomas Yoseloff, 1959]), having apparently served in the west after the war as some regiments did. The regimental roster shows a Henry (rather than Harry) Fitzallen, very likely a typographical error in the online database since it is the right person. Fitzallen enlisted October 4, 1861, as a private at Camp King, Kentucky, and was mustered into Company B on December 8, 1861. He/she was discharged, according to the database, on December 15, 1861 ("Discharged after being discovered female"), but according to the National Archives records the date should be 1862. The source of the information in the Civil War Database is given as "Report of Adjutant General, State of Kentucky."

35. The three-year 5th Virginia Infantry roster shows no one by the name of Fitzallen. The most likely male alias candidates for Marian McKenzie are Enoch Clark, private, Company H, Winchester, Va., mustered in July 21, 1861, "no further records"; A. V. Foster, private, Company L, enlisted April 17, 1861, discharged June 15, 1861, no information on reasons; John W. Montgomery, eighteen, private, Company F, Winchester, Va., enlisted June 15, 1861, reported missing and "believed to have deserted" July 2, 1861; Samuel J. Radner, twenty-one, private, Company C, Harpers Ferry, Va., enlisted May 12, 1861, sick and discharged Aug. 1, 1861; and Martin Will, twenty-nine, private, Company G, Staunton, Va., enlisted April 28, 1861, listed as absent without leave on Sept. 15, 1861, no further information.

36. Parker, *Richmond's Civil War Prisons,* 26. Parker reports that an estimated 100 women were imprisoned in Castle Thunder during the war, most of them arrested while wearing Confederate uniforms and suspected of treason or prostitution.

37. Burgess, *Uncommon Soldier,* 44.

38. *Official Records of the Union and Confederate Armies,* Series 2, Vol. 7, [S# 120]; DeAnne Blanton, "Pvt. Jane Perkins, CSA," in *Journal of Women's Civil War History* 1 (2001): 106–111. The *Nashville Dispatch* for January 4, 1865, reports that Perkins was transferred to a female prison at Fitchburg, Massachusetts, on October 13, 1864; Christie, "The Prisoner," 126.

39. Larson, "Bonny Yank and Ginny Reb Revisited," 42, from *Diary of a Confederate Soldier: James E. Hall,* 1961; Blanton and Cook, *They Fought like Demons,* 76, 85, 86–87, 122

40. Christie, "The Prisoner," 126; Blanton and Cook, *They Fought like Demons,* 86.

Chapter 8. Myths and Apocryphal Stories

1. David S. Sparks, ed. *Inside Lincoln's Army: The Diary of Marsena Rudolph Patrick, Provost Marshal General, Army of the Potomac* (New York: Thomas Yoseloff, 1964), 459–460; DeAnne Blanton and Lauren M. Cook, *They Fought like Demons: Women Soldiers in the American Civil War* (Baton Rouge: Louisiana State University Press, 2002), 147. The regimental rosters were checked using the Civil War Database, the National Park Service Soldiers and Sailors System, and other online web sites.
2. William W. Fowler, *Woman on the American Frontier* (Hartford, Conn.: S. S. Scranton, 1877), 425–428.
3. Earl J. Hess, *The Union Soldier in Battle: Enduring the Ordeal of Combat* (Lawrence: University Press of Kansas, 1997), 160.
4. Blanton and Cook, *They Fought like Demons,* 184–186. The authors note that Howe's story cannot be authenticated and express doubts about it. They refer to the Stanhope story as a "romantic tale" and an example of a postwar story that could be fact, fiction, or a blend of the two.
5. Frank Moore, *Women of the War: Their Heroism and Self-Sacrifice* (Hartford, Conn.: Scranton, 1866), 529–530; Frank Moore, *The Civil War in Song and Story* (New York: P. F. Collier,1889), 158. The *Brooklyn News,* as quoted in the *Savannah Republican,* Georgia, October 30, 1863, about five weeks after the Battle of Chickamauga, reported the story and noted that "Emily" had enlisted in a Detroit regiment. Essentially the same story was reported by the *Detroit Tribune* and picked up by the *Daily Intelligencer,* Atlanta, November 5, 1863. This version reports her being mortally wounded at Lookout Mountain (November 23–25, 1863), rather than at Chickamauga.
6. *Wellsburg Herald,* West Virginia, October 9, 1863; *Cincinnati Gazette,* Ohio, October 2, 1863, from the *Grand Rapids Eagle,* Michigan. Minnesota fielded only eleven infantry regiments, and only one of them (the 8th) was involved in the Murfreesboro/Stones River campaign in December 1862. Some soldiers by the name of Clayton were found in other regiments, but not in units that were at Stones River.
7. Blanton and Cook, *They Fought like Demons,* 10–11, 48, 52, 55, 58, 75, 149–150.
8. Moore, *Women of the War,* 532–533, repeated in many other sources.
9. Lee Middleton, *Hearts of Fire: Soldier Women of the Civil War* (Torch, Ohio: privately published, 1993), 81, from *Military Images,* May–June 1991.
10. Middleton, *Hearts of Fire,* 105, from J. David Truby, *Women at War* (Boulder, Colo.: Paladin Press, 1977); Elizabeth D. Leonard, *All the Daring of the Soldier: Women of the Civil War Armies* (New York: W. W. Norton, 1999), 250–252, from *The Lady Lieutenant* (1862), an alleged autobiography. C. E. Dornbusch, *Military Bibliography of the Civil War,* Vol. 3 (New York Public Library, 1972), 26–27, says of this autobiography: "The reader may

rely on this narrative as being strictly authentic." Blanton and Cook, *They Fought like Demons*, 156, declare that the book is total fiction. Leonard, *All the Daring of the Soldier*, 248–252, discusses the book skeptically, in the context of fictional women in uniform represented in American literature, and suggests that it possibly belongs to the fiction genre.

11. Leonard, *All the Daring of the Soldier*, 223; from *Charlestown Farmer's Advocate*, West Virginia, July 30, 1898.

12. Mary Elizabeth Massey, *Bonnet Brigades* (New York: Alfred A. Knopf, 1966), 80, states that Wise served in "an Indiana regiment." The *New York Herald*, August 14, 1864, indicated the 34th Indiana Infantry. That regiment was not at Lookout Mountain, and there is no John Wise on its roster. Blanton and Cook, *They Fought like Demons*, 93–94, 150–151, 155, provide thorough coverage of the story and correctly report the discrepancies.

The *Nashville Daily Union*, June 16, 1864, reported a story from the *Pittsburg Commercial*, Pennsylvania, about a female soldier using the name "John Wise" who was wounded at Lookout Mountain while serving in an Indiana regiment. The name "Mary" is not mentioned. It is reported that she was in "this city" (presumably Pittsburgh, though it is spelled without the final "h") on June 11 headed for Louisville, Kentucky, to be a hospital nurse.

13. If there are Blankenship genealogists out there who can confirm this person as a male ancestor, this hypothetical identification of Mary Wise could be ruled out.

14. Blanton and Cook, *They Fought like Demons*, 150–151.

Chapter 9. Case Studies

1. DeAnne Blanton and Lauren M. Cook, *They Fought like Demons: Women Soldiers in the American Civil War* (Baton Rouge: Louisiana State University Press, 2002), 34–35, 81–82, 151–152.

2. *Cairo City Gazette*, Illinois, December 25, 1862; *Cairo City Weekly News*, December 25, 1862 (see Appendix B).

3. *Jackson Mississippian*, December 25, 1862, as reported in *Southern Women of the Second American Revolution*, by Henry Jackson (Atlanta, 1863). The *Montgomery Weekly Advertiser*, Alabama, January 7, 1863, reported essentially the same story.

4. Wesley Thurman Leeper, *Rebels Valiant: Second Arkansas Mounted Rifles (Dismounted)* (Little Rock, Ark.: Pioneer Press, 1964), 105–115, contains an account of the Battle of Richmond, Kentucky, from the perspective of that regiment.

5. Maury Darst, "Robert Hodges, Jr., Confederate Soldier," *East Texas Historical Journal* 9, 1 (1971): 37–38.

6. Blanton and Cook, *They Fought like Demons*, 115–116.

7. *Valley Spirit*, Franklin County, Pennsylvania, September 25, 1861, from the *Harrisburg Patriot;* Lee Middleton, *Hearts of Fire: Soldier Women of the Civil War* (Torch, Ohio: privately published,1993), 44; Blanton and Cook, *They Fought like Demons*, 38, 56, 111.

8. Blanton and Cook, *They Fought like Demons,* 44, 78, 96–97, 169–170. Four of the six members of the 11th Illinois who were wounded at Shiloh died within a week or so. They were privates Henry Corwin of LaSalle, Orlando Bridgman of Winnebago County, James Wertz of Stephenson County, and Colonel Byron Parkhurst of Marion County.

9. The only meager possible clues to Hook's male alias in the 3rd Illinois Cavalry are these: A Lucius Fuller enlisted in the regiment June 12, 1861, as a bugler (a position Hook was reported to have held in the 8th Michigan Infantry) and was discharged for disability December 15, 1861; a soldier by the name of Edwin Henderson enlisted in Company A as a private on August 2, 1861, and was discharged for disability on some unknown date ("date not stated" in Illinois records).

10. Tennessee Civil War Centennial Commission, *Tennesseans in the Civil War: A Military History of Confederate and Union Units with Available Rosters of Personnel,* Part 1 (Nashville, Tenn, 1964), 321–324.

11. Frazar Kirkland, *Pictorial Book of Anecdotes and Incidents of the War of the Rebellion* (Hartford, Conn.: Hartford Publishing, 1867), 622–623. The *Peoria Morning Mail,* Illinois, reported on May 16, 1863, that "a Pennsylvania woman" had served in the western army for ten months, during which time she discovered many other female soldiers, one of whom was now a lieutenant. She said that she had helped to bury three female soldiers at different times whose sex was not known to the other soldiers. The same story appeared in the *Montgomery Weekly Advertiser,* Alabama, June 10, 1863. The story is identical to that of Frances Hook.

12. Kirkland, *Pictorial Book of Anecdotes and Incidents,* 173.

13. In an obvious reference to Frances Hook, though no name is reported, the *Mobile Register & Advertiser,* February 20, 1864, reports that ninety Yankee prisoners reached Dalton, Georgia, on February 14. "One . . . is a woman, disguised in masculine habiliments, and moving on crutches. She belongs to the 19th Illinois, noted for its barbarities, and claims to have been wounded at Florence, Ala., but her companions, who call her Frank, say that a dog bit her in the calf of the leg."

14. Kirkland, *Pictorial Book of Anecdotes and Incidents,* 173–174.

15. Ibid., 567.

16. Blanton and Cook, *They Fought like Demons,* 169–170, from National Archives records.

17. Middleton, *Hearts of Fire,* 79.

18. Kirkland, *Pictorial Book of Anecdotes and Incidents,* 173–174, 567, 622–623; 25th Michigan Regimental History, John Robertson, comp., *Michigan in the War* (Lansing, Mich.: W. S. George, 1882).

19. Kirkland, *Pictorial Book of Anecdotes and Incidents,* 161–162. The same story without identifying details was reported in the *Nashville Dispatch,* April 16, 1863. See also Elizabeth D. Leonard, *All the Daring of the Soldier: Women of the Civil War Armies* (New York: W. W. Norton, 1999), 222–223, citing *New York Times,* April 4, 1915.

20. Mary Elizabeth Massey, *Bonnet Brigades* (New York: Alfred A. Knopf, 1966), 80, whose source citations sometimes are unclear and confusing; DeAnne Blanton, "Women Soldiers of the Civil War," *Prologue: Quarterly of the National Archives* 25, 1 (Spring 1993): 27; "Served by Her Lover's Side," *Evening Star,* Washington, D.C., July 7, 1896; "Women Soldiering as Men," *New York Sun,* February 10, 1901. Betty Ingraham, in "Masquerade of Mary Owen Jenkins," *Civil War Times* (June 1959): 7, reportedly describes a woman who impersonated a soldier and fought in the 9th Pennsylvania Cavalry. I have not been able to find this issue.

21. *Antique Week,* May 29, 1989, 12B, quoting from an 1863 article.

22. Blanton, "Women Soldiers of the Civil War," 28, from *Washington Evening Star,* July 7, 1896.

23. Kirkland, *Pictorial Book of Anecdotes and Incidents,* 621–622; an identical account appears in John Truesdale, *The Blue Coats, and How They Lived, Fought, and Died for the Union* (Philadelphia: Jones Brothers, 1867), 442; *Nashville Dispatch,* Tennessee, July 11, 1863. Other references found on the internet but not personally verified include *Worcester Spy,* Massachusetts, June 21, 1863, and *Little Rock National Democrat,* Arkansas, October 20, 1863.

24. Massey, *Bonnet Brigades,* 79; C. Kay Larson, "Bonny Yank and Ginny Reb," *Minerva* 8, 1 (Spring 1990): 41, from Ferdinand Sarmiento, *Life of Pauline Cushman* (Philadelphia, 1865), 368–370.

25. Larson, "Bonny Yank and Ginny Reb Revisited," 41–42; Middleton, *Hearts of Fire,* 122. Blanton and Cook, *They Fought like Demons,* 10–11, 68–71, 87–90, 97–98, report her as using the alias "Molly Hays," possibly a confusion with the Mary Hays known as "Molly Pitcher" of Revolutionary War fame.

26. *Official Records of the Union and Confederate Armies [The War of the Rebellion: A Compilation of the Official Records of the Union and Confederate Armies].* (Washington, D.C.: Government Printing Office, 1884), Series 1, Vol. 16/1, No. 22, report from Headquarters Second Cavalry Brigade, McMinnville, Tennessee, July 24, 1862.

27. Blanton and Cook, *They Fought like Demons,* 70–71, 87–90.

28. Middleton, *Hearts of Fire,* 100–101, from journal of Daniel Reed Larned, General Ambrose Burnside's private secretary, May 14–15, 1863, entries, and William Marvel, *Burnside* (Chapel Hill: University of North Carolina Press, 1991); Blanton and Cook, *They Fought like Demons,* 48–49, 53, 59, 66, 108–109, 115, 117, 200–201. Middleton speculates that the soldiers known as Ella Reno and Frances Hook may have been one and the same since Hook is also said to have used the male alias "Frank Martin" and served in the 8th Michigan Infantry.

Larned's journal entries for May 14 and May 15, 1863, as reported, are contradictory as to which unit Reno was serving in when discovered. He first says she was brought in as "a cavalryman . . . [who] had been serving for 18 months in a Kentucky Cavalry regiment. . . ."

The next day he states that she had served four months in the 5th Kentucky Cavalry and then "transferred by her own request to the 8th Michigan Infantry." Larned continues that Reno was given a position at the hospital in Louisville, which fits the story of "Frank Martin," who elsewhere has been identified as Frances Hook. However, Blanton and Cook, *They Fought like Demons,* 48, report that Reno was a niece of Brigadier General Jesse Reno. They also identify Reno as one of the two female soldiers unmasked in General Sheridan's army (see Appendix B).

29. My source was John Mull, "Profile of a Woman Veteran: The Life of Private Bill Thompson, Confederate States of America," *National Women's Military Museum Newsletter* 1,1 (Spring 1989), which he, in turn, had taken from a book.

30. Scottsville, Virginia, is a small town on the James River in central Virginia, about sixty miles west of Richmond. During the Civil War four buildings in Scottsville were used as hospitals for Confederate soldiers. Today the town has a monument to Confederate soldiers who died there. However, Bryant Gause's body was reportedly shipped back to North Carolina for burial.

31. Richard Hall, *Patriots in Disguise: Women Warriors of the Civil War* (New York: Paragon House, 1993), 189–194, 207–211.

32. In her memoirs Velazquez reports marrying Captain DeCaulp in Atlanta, where he was in the hospital, during the summer of 1863 (see Hall, *Patriots in Disguise,* 126–135).

33. No Confederate soldier by the name of DeCaulp was found in the Personnel Directory of the Civil War Database.

34. Bromfield L. Ridley, *Battles and Sketches of the Army of the Tennessee* (Mexico, Mo.: Missouri Printing and Publishing, 1906), 495.

35. *Official Records,* Series 2, Vol. 8, 936. Although Conover was later charged with perjury and in faking witness testimony in regard to Jefferson Davis, this letter further confirms the reputation of Velazquez shortly after the war and her use of the alias "Alice Williams."

36. Alfred Jackson Hanna and Kathryn Abbey Hanna, *Confederate Exiles in Venezuela,* Confederate Centennial Studies No. 15 (Tuscaloosa, Ala.: Confederate Publishing, 1960).

37. St. James Parish, somewhat west of New Orleans and about midway between New Orleans and Baton Rouge, straddling the Mississippi River, was a flourishing plantation area by the mid-1850s, with crops such as tobacco and sugar. This location would fit the "Louisiana planter" description. Further, an internet site containing information about parish Civil War records makes it clear that both Roche and LaRoche were very common names in this area, and Roach even more so.

38. Jacob Mogelever, *Death to Traitors: The Story of Lafayette C. Baker, Lincoln's Forgotten Secret Service Chief* (Garden City, N.Y.: Doubleday, 1960), 196–201.

39. Blanton and Cook, *They Fought like Demons,* 38, 110, 124, 200.

40. Ibid., 32, 51, 102, 114; *Nashville Dispatch,* August 26, 1864.

41. Frederick H. Dyer, *A Compendium of the War of the Rebellion,* Vol. 3, Regimental Histories (New York: Thomas Yoseloff, 1959), 1363.

Chapter 10. African American Women at War

1. Minutes of the Vigilance Committee, January 4, 1860, Ravenel Family Documents, MS 12/316, Folder 16, South Carolina Historical Society.
2. Ibid.
3. John Hammond Moore, *South Carolina and the Southern Claims Commission, 1871–1880*, 1982, MS 3/542, South Carolina Historical Society, Charleston, South Carolina, testimony of Harry Quick and Joseph Rosier.
4. DeAnne Blanton and Lauren M. Cook, *They Fought like Demons: Women Soldiers in the American Civil War* (Baton Rouge: Louisiana State University Press, 2002), 67, 105–164. Three 8th New York Cavalry soldiers by the name of Lewis mustered out of the regiment on June 27, 1865, at Alexandria, Virginia. One served for only four months and the other two for three years.
5. Lisa Y. King, "In Search of Women of African Descent Who Served in the Civil War Union Navy," *Journal of Negro History* 84 (1998): 302–309.
6. Tonya Bolden, "Mary Elizabeth Bowser b. 1839–?)," *The Book of African-American Women* (Holbrook, Mass.: Adams Media, 1996), 75. Although the activities of Mary Elizabeth Bowser have been well documented, there does seem to be some confusion among historians stemming from her use of pseudonyms. For the story of Mary Elizabeth Bowser posing as Ellen Bond, see Ella Forbes, *African American Women during the Civil War* (New York: Garland Publishing: 1998), 41.
7. The term "contraband" was used initially in reference to refugee slaves or those who were set free by Union officers traveling through the South. The term was later replaced with "freedmen." See Forbes, *African American Women during the Civil War*, 9–10.
8. "The Clothes-line Telegraph," in *Anecdotes, Poetry and Incidents of the War: North and South, 1860–1865*, ed. Frank Moore (New York: Bible House, 1867), 263–264.
9. Scott J. Lucas, "High Expectations: African Americans in Civil War Kentucky," *Negro History Bulletin* 1 (January 2001): 19–22.
10. Noralee Frankel, *Freedom's Women: Black Women and Families in Civil War Era Mississippi* (Bloomington: Indiana University Press, 1999), 50.
11. As quoted in Forbes, *African American Women during the Civil War*, 151.
12. Olive Gilbert, *Narrative of Sojourner Truth: A Bondswoman of Olden Time, with a History of her Labors and Correspondence, Drawn from Her Book of Life* (New York: Penguin Books, 1998), 215.
13. Ibid., 120.
14. As quoted in Forbes, *African American Women during the Civil War*, 151.
15. Susie King Taylor, *A Black Woman's Civil War Memoirs: Reminiscences of My Life in Camp with the 33rd U.S. Colored Troops, Late 1st South Carolina Volunteers,* ed. Patricia W. Romero and Willie Lee Rose (Princeton, N.J.: Markus Wiener Publishers, 1997), 29. See also Virginia Mescher, "Military Laundresses in the Civil War," *Journal of Women's Civil War History* 1 (2001): 39–56; Jane E. Schultz, *Women at the Front: Hospital Workers in Civil War America* (Chapel Hill: University of North Carolina Press, 2004), 56–57.
16. Taylor, *Black Woman's Civil War Memoirs*, 48 n.

17. Ibid., 61.
18. Ibid., 57–61.
19. Ibid., 88.
20. Harriet's birth name was Araminta, but she changed her name sometime in her early teen years. The exact location of her birth, as well as the size of her family, are not known. See Catherine Clinton, *Harriet Tubman: The Road to Freedom* (New York: Little, Brown, 2004), 4–10.
21. "Southern Claims Commission Records," Georgia Historical Society, Manuscript Collections, MS. No. 1500, Box 2, Chatham County, testimony of Elizabeth Geary (testimony of William A. Geary for Elizabeth Geary), Georgia Historical Society Library, Savannah, Georgia. Microfilm from original National Archives Collection, U.S. Department of Treasury, Records of the Accounting Officers of the Department of the Treasury; Southern Claims Commission from the State of Georgia 1871–1880 (hereafter cited as "SCCR," Georgia).
22. Ibid. For a full account of the burning of the city of Darien, see Buddy Sullivan, *Early Days on the Georgia Tidewater: The Story of McIntosh County and Sapelo* (Darien, Ga.: McIntosh County Board of Commissioners, 1990); E. Merton Coulter, "Robert Gould Shaw and the Burning of Darien, Georgia," *Civil War History* 5 (1959): 363–373.
23. "SCCR," Georgia, Elizabeth Geary. The goal of the Southern Claims Commission was to reimburse Southern citizens who had remained loyal to the U.S. government for any losses they incurred from injurious acts committed by Union troops during the war. Mrs Geary gives a full account of the property she lost in the Darien fire in her testimony, which includes a large house, a grocery store, a large inventory of furniture, and "pots, kettles, ovens & crockery."
24. "SCCR," Georgia, Sarah Ann Black.
25. Ibid., Caroline DeWillis on loyalty for Sarah Ann Black.
26. Ibid., Edward Hornsby.
27. Ibid., Primus Wilson.
28. Ibid., Stephen Carter.
29. Allen O. Abbot, *Prison Life in the South at Richmond, Macon, Savannah, Charleston, Columbia, Charlotte, Raleigh, Goldsborough, and Andersonville, during the Years 1864 and 1865* (New York: Harper & Brothers, 1865), 87, 103.
30. "SCCR," Georgia, Peter Miller.
31. Ibid., Georgianna Kelly.
32. Ibid., J. P. Millege, witness for David Moses.
33. Taylor, *Black Woman's Civil War Memoirs*, 142.
34. "SCCR," Georgia, Georgianna Kelly.
35. This system explains in part the large free populations in cities like Savannah, as slaves often saved money toward purchasing their own freedom. For a study concerning the autonomy experienced by urban slaves, see Richard C. Wade, *Slavery in the Cities: The South, 1820–1860* (New York: Oxford University Press, 1964). For more on the system that enabled African American women to purchase property, see Loren Schweninger, "Property

Owning Free African-American Women in the South, 1800–1870," *Journal of Women's History* 1 (Winter 1990); also see Whittington B. Johnson, "Free African-American Women in Savannah: Affluence and Autonomy amid Adversity," *Georgia Historical Quarterly* 66 (1992): 260–283.

36. "SCCR," Georgia, Phoebe Rutledge.

37. Ibid., testimony of Judy Rose. One former slave from Savannah stated that "for twenty years, I hired my time [and] I was 'bleeged to pay him twelve dollars a month in advance." See Charles Carleton Coffin, *Four Years of Fighting* (Boston: Ticknor and Fields, 1866), 228. In 1822, city councilmen discussed meat sellers in the market who paid their guardians "the ordinary wages of three dollars per week." *Minutes of the Savannah City Council,* Georgia Historical Society Library, Savannah, July 1822, 42.

38. "SCCR," Georgia, Judy Rose.

39. Ibid., Rachel Bromfield.

40. Ibid.

41. Ibid., Francis Keaton.

42. Ibid., Larry Williams.

43. See Joseph T. Glatthaar, *The March to the Sea and Beyond: Sherman's Troops in the Savannah and Carolinas Campaigns* (New York: New York University Press, 1989), 58–63.

44. "SCCR," Georgia, Herb Strafford.

45. Ibid., Phoebe Rutledge.

46. Ibid., Peter Miller.

47. Ibid., Jerry Brown.

48. Ibid., Peter Miller.

49. As quoted in Taylor, *Black Woman's Civil War Memoirs*, 15.

50. "SCCR," Georgia, Phoebe Rutledge.

Appendix A

1. At the time of her death, her husband had risen to the rank of brigadier general, having been severely wounded twice and nursed back to health by her. A detailed article by Don Richard Lauter about the lives of Arabella Barlow and her husband appears in *Journal of Women's Civil War History* 1 (2001): 8–25.

2. Mary A. Holland, *Our Army Nurses* (Boston: Lounsbery, Nichols & Worth, 1897), 135–136. She does not identify the regiment, but states that she was sworn in by Captain S. M. Davis and served at Camp Reed initially, then in Baltimore and West Virginia. A Civil War Database search based on these clues identified Captain Davis's regiment as the 111th Pennsylvania Infantry, whose history matches that of her story.

3. L. P. Brockett and Mary C. Vaughan, *Woman's Work in the Civil War: A Record of Heroism, Patriotism and Patience* (Philadelphia: Zeigler, McCurdy, 1867), 172–186; Holland, *Our Army Nurses,* 517–533; Jean Getman O'Brien, "Mrs. Mary Ann (Mother) Bickerdyke: 'The Brigadier Commanding Hospitals,'" *Civil War Times Illustrated* 1, 9 (1963): 21–24; Diana Sauls,

"The Sunset Gun: The Story of Mary Ann Bickerdyke, Civil War Nurse," *Civil War: The Magazine of the Civil War Society* 21 (1989): 28–38.

4. Frank Moore, *Women of the War: Their Heroism and Self-Sacrifice* (Hartford, Conn.: Scranton, 1866), 75–90; Brockett and Vaughan, *Woman's Work in the Civil War,* 187–199; L. P. Brockett, *Battle-Field and Hospital; Or, Lights and Shadows of the Great Rebellion* (Philadelphia: Hubbard Brothers, 1888), 346–356.

5. Record Group 94, National Archives.

6. Holland, *Our Army Nurses,* 443–444; Sylvia G. L. Dannett, *Noble Women of the North* (New York: Thomas Yoseloff, 1959), 99–101, 168–173, 253–257, 348–350; Sylvia G. L. Dannett and Katharine M. Jones, *Our Women of the Sixties* (Washington, D.C.: U.S. Civil War Centennial Commission, 1963), 10–11; Harold Elk Straubing, comp., *In Hospital and Camp: The Civil War through the Eyes of Its Doctors and Nurses* (Harrisburg, Pa.: Stackpole Books, 1993), 94–107. The latter is an excerpt from Bucklin's postwar book. In it she describes some of the hardships and horrors of field hospital work.

7. Holland, *Our Army Nurses,* 283–290; Agatha Young, *The Women and the Crisis: Women of the North in the Civil War* (New York: McDowell, Obolensky, 1959), 186, 213; C. Kay Larson, "Bonny Yank and Ginny Reb Revisited, *Minerva* 10, 2 (Summer 1992): 44. The 3rd Vermont Infantry served from July 1, 1861, to July 11, 1865. Of the four soldiers by the name of Colburn who served in the regiment, Almon J. Colburn of Company B (who died of disease in 1864) and Henry H. Colburn of Company B (who served three years from July 1861 to July 1864) are the most likely candidates to have been her brother.

8. "A young lady named Mary Cook was lately discovered in soldier's attire in the 2nd Kentucky Cavalry, near Mumfordsville. She stated that she resided in Breckinridge County, Ky. Her father was a clergyman, and after his death she taught school in Hardin County, where she and three other young ladies agreed to adopt male attire and join the army. They divided two and two, but Mary's companion backed out and she went alone. One of the other girls, she says, is a lieutenant in a Kentucky infantry regiment, and takes good care of her companion, keeping her in her tent as a servant. She insists they were only influenced by a love of adventure." (Contributed from a Poughkeepsie, New York, newspaper by Joel Craig; see Joel Craig's Bivouac web site: http://www.valstar.net/~jcraig.)

9. Moore, *Women of the War,* 170–175; Brockett, *Battle-Field and Hospital,* 100–130; Harnett T. Kane, *Spies for the Blue and Gray* (New York: Doubleday, 1954), 177–191; Mary Elizabeth Massey, *Bonnet Brigades* (New York: Alfred A. Knopf, 1966), 102–103; Elizabeth D. Leonard, *All the Daring of the Soldier: Women of the Civil War Armies* (New York: W.W. Norton, 1999), 57–62. The *Savannah Republican,* Georgia, June 22, 1863, reported one of her arrests by Nathan Forrest's cavalry on suspicion of spying. She was found to be carrying drawings of Confederate fortifications and was placed under guard at Columbia. See also Irwin Richman, "Pauline Cushman,

She Was a Heroine but Not a Lady: A Personality Profile," *Civil War Times Illustrated* 7, 10 (1969): 38–44.

10. Holland, *Our Army Nurses,* 419–420. Regimental histories and rosters for early Missouri Union regiments are both incomplete and complex, due to the many short-term "Home Guard" or state militia units, some of which were mustered into Federal service.

11. DeAnne Blanton and Lauren M. Cook, *They Fought like Demons: Women Soldiers in the American Civil War* (Baton Rouge: Louisiana State University Press, 2002), 73, 111–112; *Savannah Republican,* Georgia, June 5, 1861. In a search of the Civil War Database a number of candidates were found in the 1st through 5th Infantry regiments who were commissioned as lieutenant in 1861 and served six months or less. However, there was no way to narrow it down any further.

12. Lynda L. Sudlow, *A Vast Army of Women: Maine's Uncounted Forces in the American Civil War* (Gettysburg, Pa.: Thomas Publications, 2000), 18–19, 86–91, 116–117. Sudlow includes quotes from diary entries and correspondence that provide graphic descriptions of the hardships and dangers of the field conditions that Eaton experienced. Jane E. Schultz, *Women at the Front: Hospital Workers in Civil War America* (Chapel Hill: University of North Carolina Press, 2004), 82, reports an incident in which Eaton at Chancellorsville was soaked to the skin by torrential rains and found refuge overnight sleeping in the corner of an attic, among wounded soldiers, in a house that had been pressed into service as an emergency hospital.

13. Holland, *Our Army Nurses,* 277–279; Larson, 43; Lee Middleton, *Hearts of Fire: Soldier Women of the Civil War* (Torch, Ohio: privately published, 1993), 53. Calvin A. Ellis was the first colonel of the 1st Missouri Cavalry, which served from August 6, 1861, to September 1, 1865.

14. Holland, *Our Army Nurses,* 477–480. Artemus W. Fay enlisted in Company C of the 118th New York Infantry on August 11, 1862, as a private at age twenty-seven. He was promoted to sergeant on April 15, 1863, and mustered out on June 13, 1865.

15. Schultz, *Women at the Front,* 83, 121–122, 301–302. The Bentley Library at the University of Michigan contains a collection of Fyfe's letters home from Paducah, Kentucky, describing conditions there.

16. Moore, *Women of the War,* 333–340. See also "Thumbnail Sketches of Women of the Civil War Era" (http://www.iupui.edu/~geni/lsort/hoosier-women.html).

17. Blanton and Cook, *They Fought like Demons,* 72. The date and circumstances of discharge are not reported. No soldier by the name of Gregg appears on the regimental roster in the Civil War Database. Since the only source is a document with no stated date in a private collection and it reportedly identified her as "Sergeant Jennie R. Gregg," some skepticism is justified about its authenticity. The 128th Ohio did serve primarily as guards at the Johnson's Island Prison.

18. *Nashville Dispatch,* May 18, 1863. The article reports that Company D of Jenkins's Cavalry was commanded by Captain White. Brigadier General Albert G.

Jenkins at that time commanded a cavalry brigade that included the 16th and 17th Virginia regiments. No rosters currently are available for these units.

19. Reported on a geocities.com web site in an article titled "Brief Biographies of Women Who Lived in Nebraska Who Had Served in the Civil War Most of Whom Were Civil War Nurses." The information about her, taken from her obituary in the *Morning World-Herald*, Omaha, Nebraska, January 23, 1923, states that she enlisted as a soldier with the approval of the colonel, and that her name was placed on the roster. However, her name was not on the roster after the war. The article states, "The impression is that women's names were generally later deleted from soldiers records."

Apparently she/they must have moved to Nebraska after the war. The Civil War Database, which confirms the service of James C. H. Hobbs as a private in Company A of the 12th Iowa Infantry as of October 17, 1861, records that he was from Joliet, Illinois, and that he afterwards was promoted to hospital steward. He was discharged April 2, 1862, at St. Louis, Missouri, for unstated reasons. The information is drawn from Iowa state records.

20. Ibid., 41–42, 51, 92, 126–127. No one by the name Hopper is listed in the roster of the 1st Virginia Cavalry, according to the Civil War Database.

21. H. E. Sterkx, *Some Notable Alabama Women during the Civil War* (University, Ala.: Alabama Civil War Centennial Commission, 1962), 34–47; Dannett and Jones, *Our Women of the Sixties*, 14; Drew Gilpin Faust, *Mothers of Invention: Women of the Slaveholding South in the American Civil War* (Chapel Hill: University of North Carolina Press, 1996), 94–95, 108; Schultz, *Women at the Front*, 85; Sterkx, "Juliet Ann Opie Hopkins—'The Angel of the South'" (http://www.mindspring.com/~redeagle/Oakwood/Hopkins.htm). Sterkx, Dannett and Jones, and Schultz all report that Hopkins was wounded by gunfire on the battlefield, but Faust reports that she "became a casualty when she broke her leg while lifting a wounded officer on the battlefield at Seven Pines." In either case, she was exposed to physical danger and was injured on the battlefield.

22. *Daily Intelligencer,* Atlanta, Georgia, September 18, 1863. No information is included about what regiment she served in or how she happened to be discovered.

23. Holland, *Our Army Nurses,* 206–213. Estelle's husband was Sergeant Judson R. Johnson of Company I, who was discharged for disability on April 3, 1862.

24. Rebecca Larson, *Blue and Gray Roses of Intrigue* (Gettysburg, Pa.: Thomas Publications, 1993), 39–40; *Official Records,* Series 2, Vol. 5, No. 118. See also Appendix B.

25. Leonard, *All the Daring of the Soldier,* 206–207. The 40th New Jersey Infantry was a late-war regiment that served from October 24, 1864, through July 13, 1865. The Civil War Database shows that a staff officer by the name of J. Warner Kinsey (rank not given) enlisted with the regiment as Quartermaster, "commissioned into Field & Staff" March 30, 1865, and mustered out with the regiment in July. Additional internet searches discovered that a J. Warner Kinsey, obviously the same person, had earlier served in the same

position in the 37th New Jersey Infantry, a one-hundred-days regiment, from June 24, 1864, through October 1, 1864. Unless family genealogical information indicates this person to have been male, "he" remains a likely candidate to have been Emma A. B. Kinsey.

26. Allan Pinkerton, *The Spy of the Rebellion: Being a True History of the Spy System of the United States Army during the Late Rebellion* (Hartford, Conn.: M.A. Winter & Hatch, 1883), 367–393, 478, 486–497, 502, 530–542, 548–560; Harnett T. Kane, *Spies for the Blue and Gray,* 100–108; Donald E. Markle, *Spies and Spymasters of the Civil War* (New York: Hippocrene Books, 1994), 187–188; William A. Tidwell, *Come Retribution: The Confederate Secret Service and the Assassination of Lincoln* (Jackson: University Press of Mississippi, 1988), 229; Edwin C. Fishel, *The Secret War for the Union: The Untold Story of Military Intelligence in the Civil War* (Boston: Houghton Mifflin, 1996), 131, 148. Pinkerton refers to her in one place as Carrie and in another as Hattie. All other sources consistently give her name as Hattie.

27. Blanton and Cook, *They Fought like Demons,* 117. A soldier by the name of Thomas Lee, age twenty-one, enlisted in Company I of the 6th Ohio Cavalry on February 16, 1864. The Civil War Database, based on State of Ohio records, reports "Date and method of discharge not given."

28. Ibid., 164, from a newspaper story dated October 8, 1866. The roster of the 2nd Michigan Infantry does not include a soldier by the name of Lockwood. However, it does list Edward (or Edwin) Lookwood, who enlisted in Company K at age nineteen as a drummer in 1861 and was transferred to the Veteran Reserve Corps at Washington, D.C., April 4, 1865. The author has done research in the records of the 2nd Michigan at the state archives in East Lansing and can report that consistency in spelling of names was not a strong feature in the Civil War years.

29. Holland, *Our Army Nurses,* 97. Loomis's husband, Captain George W. Van Pelt, was killed at Chickamauga on September 19, 1863. An interesting sidelight is that Battery A was known as "Loomis's Battery"; the colonel was Cyrus O. Loomis, age forty. It appears likely that Mary was related to him.

30. Ibid., 351–352. Lucas's husband, William Lucas, enlisted as a private in the 4th Michigan Cavalry at Spaulding, Michigan. He survived the war and was discharged on June 28, 1865.

31. Record Group 94, National Archives. The Civil War Database lists a Private John McCrery, age forty-one, who mustered in to Company H of the 21st Ohio Infantry on September 19, 1861, and served for two years before transferring to the Veteran Reserve Corps. A Private Mars McCrery, age twenty-four, mustered into the company on the same day but his (or more likely, her) date and method of discharge were not included in the *Official Roster of the Soldiers of the State of Ohio.*

32. *California News,* Missouri, February 1, 1862, taken from the *Rochester Democrat,* New York. The roster of the two-years (May 17, 1861, to May 28, 1863) 18th New York Infantry contained no one by the name of Hamilton. A thirty-days (June 18, 1863, to August 15, 1863) National Guard unit with the same designation is indicated, but no roster is available.

33. Blanton and Cook, *They Fought like Demons*, 34, 112, based on a May 4, 1863, newspaper story. A search was conducted on the Civil War Database. No soldiers by the name of Mooney were found on the regimental roster, but it is not known what male alias Molly Mooney used. Also, no record was found of any soldier in the regiment who was discharged or separated early in 1863.

34. The *National Intelligencer,* Washington, D.C., October 29, 1864, carried a story from Louisville, Kentucky, reporting the theft of hospital mail by guerrillas "under a notorious woman named Sue Munday" and the murder of the mail carrier. Four Confederate guerrillas in captivity were taken out and shot in retaliation for the murder. On March 16, 1865, the same paper reported a March 15 story from Louisville, Kentucky: "Jerema Clark, alias Sue Munday, the noted guerrilla, will be hanged this afternoon." The memoirs of a Confederate Tennessee soldier by the name of R. C. Carden published online (http://my.dmci.net/~bmacd/part2.htm) state that Munday was a boy with feminine features named Jerome Clark whom the soldiers used to call "Sissie." "They dressed him up one day and introduced him to Gen. Morgan as Miss Sue Munday. . . . after this he was known only as Sue Munday."

35. De Anne Blanton, "Pvt. Jane Perkins, CSA," *Journal of Women's Civil War History* 1 (2001): 106–111; Blanton and Cook, *They Fought like Demons*, 53, 121, 209. Jeanne M. Christie, "The Prisoner" (Gretna, La.: Pelican Publishing Co., 2004), 126, mentions her presence at the Fitchburg, Massachusetts, prison on July 28, 1864. A roster check in the Civil War Database shows no one by the name of Murphy in the entire regiment. The three-years 98th Ohio served from August 20, 1862, to June 1, 1865. Assuming that she may have given a false name to prison officials, I searched the roster of the 98th for a corporal or anyone regardless of rank who was arrested at Wheeling, West Virginia, or imprisoned in Fitchburg, Massachusetts. No such references were found. It is possible that the story of her military service is total fiction, but she was imprisoned for a long time and suspected of being a spy.

36. Blanton and Cook, *They Fought like Demons*, 190. As the authors report, the alleged service cannot be confirmed. According to the 53rd Massachusetts roster on the Civil War Database, no one by the name of Murphy served in Company B, nor did anyone named Samuel Hill. Several soldiers with the last name "Hill" served in other companies.

37. Matthew Page Andrews, *Women of the South in War Times* (Baltimore: Norman, Remington, 1920), 131–344; Stuart Sifakis, *Who Was Who in the Confederacy* (New York: Facts on File, 1988), 209; Barbara Duffey, "The Nurse: Ella K. Newsom Trader," in *Confederate Women,* ed. Mauriel Phillips Joslyn (Gretna, La.: Pelican Publishing, 2004), 95–116.

38. Mary Livermore, *My Story of the War* (Hartford, Conn.: A.D. Worthington, 1887), 119; Blanton and Cook, *They Fought like Demons,* 14, 59, 65, 71, 97, 152–153. Blanton and Cook provide excellent detail and also cite several other newspaper stories about Peterman.

39. Brockett and Vaughan, *Woman's Work in the Civil War,* 520–521; Sudlow, *Vast Army of Women,* 152–158; http://www.missouricivilwarmuseum .org; http://www.geocities.com/suvcamp66/.

40. Brockett and Vaughan, *Woman's Work in the Civil War,* 161–171. Mrs. Porter also had two sons in the army. One, James W. Porter, according to the regimental roster, served as a private in Battery B, 1st Illinois Light Artillery, then reenlisted and was transferred to Battery A, serving for three years. After the war Chaplain Porter continued service in the U.S. Army as a post chaplain until 1882.

41. *Nashville Dispatch,* Tennessee, March 29, 1864. Price said that she had followed her boyfriend into the army, but had no desire to continue in service. The same story appeared in the *Montgomery Weekly Advertiser,* Alabama, April 27, 1864, taken from the *Louisville Democrat.*

42. Frank Moore, *Women of the War,* 254–277; Richard Hall, *Patriots in Disguise: Women Warriors of the Civil War* (New York: Paragon House, 1993), 8–12; *Dubuque Herald,* Iowa, May 1, 1862, "A Woman Appointed Major," from the *Peoria Transcript; Chicago Times,* May 19, 1862.

43. Record Group 94, National Archives; Blanton and Cook, *They Fought like Demons,* 102; Leonard, *All the Daring of the Soldier,* 210. A roster check of the 52nd Ohio Infantry oddly shows no soldier by the name of "Charles Freeman" in Company F or in other companies. Since there appears to be no doubt that the story is true, perhaps Scaberry did not give her real male alias and/or unit designation when questioned, or perhaps the record has been expunged. The military hospital records cited by Blanton and Cook establish that a soldier using those names was referred for treatment for a fever.

44. Markle, *Spys and Spymasters,* 164–166; Tidwell, *Come Retribution,* 341, 407, 415–416. Christie, "The Prisoner," 118, reports her name as Antoinette Gilbert ("Nettie") Slator and that she was from New Bern, North Carolina. Her parole is reported in a January 1863 letter in the *Official Records.* See Appendix B, under Marian McKenzie, January 9, 1863.

45. Holland, *Our Army Nurses,* 101–102; Jane E. Schultz, *Women at the Front,* 193. Sergeant Marquis L. Frush served in Company B of the Union 6th West Virginia (as opposed to Virginia) Cavalry. The western counties of Virginia separated from the state during the war and formed the new state of West Virginia, which was accepted into the Union on June 19, 1863.

46. See "Thumbnail Sketches of Women of the Civil War Era," http://www.iupui.edu/~geni/lsort/hoosierwomen.html; "Dr. Mary F. Thomas (1816–1888)," http://www.mrl.lib.in.us/history/biography/thomasmf.htm.

47. Record Group 94, National Archives. The 139th Illinois was a 100-day regiment late in the war (June 1, 1864, to October 28, 1864). Ten soldiers by the name of Thompson served in it, all for the full term.

48. "Sarah E. Thompson Papers, 1859–1898: An On-line Archival Collection," Special Collections Library, Duke University, http://scriptorium.lib.duke.edu/thompson/#sarah.

49. *Louisville Daily Journal,* Kentucky, February 8, 1865; C. Kay Larson, "Bonny Yank and Ginny Reb," *Minerva* 8, 1 (Spring 1990): 40; from Susan B. Anthony, *History of Women's Suffrage;* Blanton and Cook, *They Fought like Demons,* 124. The 59th Ohio served from September 1861 through

October 1864 and was engaged at Chickamauga (September 19–20, 1863). Eight Thompsons served in the regiment, but the roster shows no Joseph. None of the Thompsons were casualties at Chickamauga. Only one, William C. Thompson, was killed in action in Tennessee, at Missionary Ridge, a month after Chickamauga. Since he was twenty-one years old at enlistment, he would be an unlikely candidate to be father of two soldier-aged children. Something is wrong with the story, but it may have a basis in fact.

50. Alan Axelrod, *The War between the Spies: A History of Espionage during the American Civil War* (New York: Atlantic Monthly Press, 1992), 104–107, 113–114; William G. Beymer, *On Hazardous Service: Scouts and Spies of the North and South* (New York: Harper & Brothers, 1912), 64–99; William B. Feis, *Grant's Secret Service: The Intelligence War from Belmont to Appomattox* (Lincoln: University of Nebraska Press, 2002), 237–241; Sandra V. Parker, *Richmond's Civil War Prisons* (Lynchburg, Va.: H.E. Howard, 1990), 5–7. General Ulysses S. Grant paid tribute to Van Lew, crediting her for the "most valuable information received from Richmond during the war." Beymer notes: "For four long years, without respite, she faced death to obtain that information; day after day suspected, spied upon, threatened, persecuted, she worked with a courage far higher than the excitement-mad valor of battlefields."

51. Middleton, *Hearts of Fire,* 182, apparently based on a newspaper story. There were four units designated as 13th New York Infantry, two of which served during 1861. The roster of the two-years 13th New York Infantry does not include a Charles Marshall. No roster was available for the three-months 13th New York State Militia Infantry.

52. Young, *Women and the Crisis,* 380–381; Marilyn Mayer Culpepper, *Trials and Triumphs: The Women of the American Civil War* (East Lansing: Michigan State University Press, 1991), 330–331, 339–340; Sudlow, *Vast Army of Women,* 46–47, 99. Her name often appears in the literature with the spellings "Wittenmeyer" or "Wittemeyer," but the correct spelling is Wittenmyer.

53. Blanton and Cook, *They Fought like Demons,* 10, 65, 107, provide documentation in for the label "disability" being used to disqualify a discovered female soldier from further service. This very likely occurred in other cases as well. Dyer's *Compendium of the War of the Rebellion* (1959) confirms that the regiment was engaged at Mill Springs. The Civil War Database regimental roster has a "Frank Demming" (two "m's") who enlisted in Company A as an eighteen-year-old private in August 1861 and confirms that he was discharged for "disability" on May 18, 1862.

54. Unsourced and undated reference on Joel Craig's Bivouac web site (http://www.valstar.net/~jcraig/). When queried by e-mail, Craig replied that the stories on his site were taken from various Pennsylvania newspapers. General James S. Wadsworth was military governor of the District of Columbia in March 1862 and went on to field command later that year.

55. Middleton, *Hearts of Fire,* 88, citing *Civil War Letters of Henry C. Bears,* Lincoln Memorial University Press (Harrogate, Tenn., 1961). The Memphis

reference would suggest that Kate was discovered early in 1863, since the regiment left that post during December 1862.

56. James I. Robertson, Jr., "An Indiana Soldier in Love and War: The Civil War Letters of John V. Hadley," *Indiana Magazine of History* 59, 3 (September 1963): 237–238; Blanton and Cook, *They Fought like Demons*, 103–104, 160. One of the other letters home about the incident was dated April 5, so the birth occurred either the first week of April or in late March 1863. Hadley was a lieutenant in the 7th Indiana Infantry in the Army of the Potomac. Although twice wounded and once captured and imprisoned, he survived the war, married his sweetheart, practiced law, served as a state senator, and became a district judge in Indiana.

57. Garold L. Cole, *Civil War Eyewitnesses: An Annotated Bibliography of Books and Articles, 1955–1986* (Columbia: University of South Carolina Press, 1988), 49; from Knox Mellon, Jr., ed., "Letters of James Greenalch," *Michigan History* 44 (June 1960): 188–240. Blanton and Cook, *They Fought like Demons*, 104–105. A search was conducted in the Civil War Database roster of the 74th Ohio Infantry for a sergeant discharged in April 1863 at Murfreesboro, Tennessee. The search yielded a single standout candidate to have been the male alias of the pregnant soldier: John W. James. James enlisted as a corporal in Company A on October 9, 1861, and was discharged at Murfreesboro April 16, 1863, after eighteen months service. No further details are reported. No other soldier in the regiment fits this profile.

58. Blanton and Cook, *They Fought like Demons*, 33. Since about forty-four Ohio regiments were involved in the Battle of Chickamauga, the roster search in the Civil War Database was difficult. A "Joseph Davidson" was found in the roster of Company D, 41st Ohio Infantry, who enlisted on October 29, 1861, at age twenty, was wounded at Missionary Ridge, Tennessee, on November 25, 1863, and was discharged on August 24, 1864, at Camp Dennison, Ohio. The regiment had thirteen killed at Chickamauga, but none of them was named Davidson and no obvious candidates were found to be the female soldier's father.

59. Middleton, *Hearts of Fire*, 61. Although it appears that the letter cited must have been in some repository collection, she neglected to identify it. However, a roster check of the 49th Georgia Infantry shows that there was no one by the name of Fitzpatrick (or possible variations such as Patrick) in the regiment. There were four soldiers by the name of Fitzgerald, but none was sergeant major and none fits the dates or circumstances of the story. Fitzpatrick may have been in some other regiment that was brigaded with the 49th Georgia.

60. "Women Fought and Died in the U.S. Civil War," in Women of Achievement and Herstory (accessed at undelete.org/woa07–04.html; printout of the article, which is no longer available online, is in the author's possession). Blanton and Cook (2002) give the name as Johehons and attribute the story to the *Austin Southern Intelligencer*, Texas, June 21, 1866. Another basic source of the story appears to have been a letter to the editor of the *National Tribune*, Washington, D.C., May 13, 1886. The letter read: "The enclosed

slip was handed to me recently by a comrade, and I would be very glad to find out if there is any truth in it. The name and date of the paper are not given: 'In disinterring the Federal dead near Resaca, Ga., a body was discovered which excited considerable attention from the smallness of the feet. On examination it was found to be that of a woman, shot through the head. The grave was marked Charles Johehous, private, 6th Mo.'–P. D. Davis, Co. I, 6th MO, Bushnell, Dak."

A roster check confirms that Phillip D. Davis was a sergeant in Company I of the 6th Missouri Infantry. Obviously he was curious to learn whether the story was true. Apparently it was not, or else something is badly garbled. No one by the name of Johehous or any variant spelling was found on the roster of the 6th Missouri Infantry.

The identity of "Charles Johehous" was said to be based on a decayed grave marker, which also could have been in error or its wording difficult to read. In any case, a further problem is that the 6th Missouri had no fatalities at Resaca so that the regimental identification clearly is wrong. Additionally, the Marietta National Cemetery in Georgia has an online grave registry compiled from a U.S. Department of Veterans Affairs database. It contains no Johehous or any similar name.

61. Julie Wheelwright, *Amazons and Military Maids: Women Who Dressed as Men in the Pursuit of Life, Liberty and Happiness* (London: Pandora Press, 1989), 27, 94, from correspondence in the collection of the William R. Perkins Library, Duke University, North Carolina; Blanton and Cook, *They Fought like Demons*, 22, 85; Blanton, "Pvt. Jane Perkins, CSA," 107; Middleton, *Hearts of Fire*, 110–111, from Noah Andre Trudeau, *Bloody Roads South*, (1989).

62. Blanton and Cook, *They Fought like Demons*, 23, 105. Sergeant Joseph O. Cross of Company H had told his wife that the female soldier was in Company F and was in the hospital on the date of his letter, March 2, 1865. These clues were sufficient to allow probable identification of the female soldier's male alias. A search was conducted in the Civil War Database roster of Company F for a soldier who was separated from the regiment shortly after this time. Only one fit the profile: Private William R. Webb, who was discharged for "disability" on March 9, 1865. This hypothetical identification will need further verification, since—as is suspected in some cases—the records may have been expunged, and the timing of Webb's discharge conceivably could be purely coincidental.

63. Ibid., 47, 105–106, from George W. Ward, *History of the Second Pennsylvania Heavy Artillery*, 1904, and Weiss family correspondence. Sergeant Herman Weiss of the 6th New York Heavy Artillery wrote a letter home to his wife dated March 25, 1865, saying that a woman had served in the ranks for almost three years. The Civil War Database indicates that Weiss enlisted in Company C as a private August 22, 1862, was promoted to corporal December 29, 1862, and to sergeant September 29, 1864. He mustered out June 28, 1865. Sergeant Weiss, who was said to be the sergeant of the female soldier ("her sergeant"), at the time served in Company I. A roster search of

Company I failed to identify a soldier who was discharged in March 1865. It is possible that she served in a different company. Since there were well over 4,000 members of the regiment throughout the course of the war, a search of the entire regimental roster was impractical.

There appears to be some confusion about the soldier's rank and unit iden- tification. *Civil War Times Illustrated* 17, 5 (1978): 41, also citing the Ward regimental history, gives the soldier's rank and unit as a sergeant (rather than corporal) in the 10th (rather than 6th) New York Heavy Artillery.

BIBLIOGRAPHY

Abbot, Allen O. *Prison Life in the South at Richmond, Macon, Savannah, Charleston, Columbia, Charlotte, Raleigh, Goldsborough, and Andersonville, during the Years 1864 and 1865*. New York: Harper & Brothers, 1865.

Alexander, Ted, ed. *The 126th Pennsylvania*. Shippensburg, Pa.: Beidel Printing House, 1984.

Anderson, Fanny J., ed. "The Shelly Papers." *Indiana Magazine of History* 44, 2 (1948): 186.

Andrews, Matthew Page. *Women of the South in War Times*. Baltimore: Norman, Remington, 1920.

Axelrod, Alan. *The War between the Spies: A History of Espionage during the American Civil War*. New York: Atlantic Monthly Press, 1992.

Baker, Lafayette C. *Spies, Traitors and Conspirators of the Late Civil War*. Philadelphia: John E. Potter, 1894.

Barton, George. *Angels of the Battlefield: A History of the Labors of the Catholic Sisterhoods in the Late Civil War*. Philadelphia: Catholic Art Publishing, 1898.

Beers, Fannie A. *Memories: A Record of Personal Experience and Adventure During Four Years of War*. Philadelphia: J.B. Lippincott, 1888. Time-Life reprint edition, 1985.

Bergeron, Arthur W., Jr. *Guide to Louisiana Confederate Military Units, 1861–1865*. Baton Rouge: Louisiana State University Press, 1989.

Beymer, William G. *On Hazardous Service: Scouts and Spies of the North and South*. New York: Harper & Brothers, 1912.

Blanton, DeAnne. "Women Soldiers of the Civil War." *Prologue: Quarterly of the National Archives* 25, 1 (Spring 1993): 26–33.

———. "Pvt. Jane Perkins, CSA." *Journal of Women's Civil War History* 1 (2001): 106–111.

Blanton, DeAnne, and Lauren M. Cook. *They Fought like Demons: Women Soldiers in the American Civil War*. Baton Rouge: Louisiana State University Press, 2002.

Bolden, Tonya. "Mary Elizabeth Bowser b. 1839–?." *The Book of African-American Women*. Holbrook, Mass.: Adams Media, 1996.

Botkin, B. A., ed. *A Civil War Treasury of Tales, Legends, and Folklore*. Secaucus, N.J.: Blue & Gray Press, 1985.

Brockett, L. P. *Battle-Field and Hospital; Or, Lights and Shadows of the Great Rebellion*. Philadelphia: Hubbard Brothers, 1888.

Brockett, L. P., and Mary C. Vaughan. *Woman's Work in the Civil War: A Record of Heroism, Patriotism and Patience*. Philadelphia: Zeigler, McCurdy, 1867.

Brooks, Fred. "Shiloh Mystery Woman." *Civil War Times Illustrated* 17, 5 (1978): 29.

Brooks, U. R. *Stories of the Confederacy*. Camden, S.C.: J. J. Fox, 1991. (Reprint of circa 1912 edition.)

Brown, Dee. "Wilson's Creek." *Civil War Times Illustrated* 1 (1972): 8–18.

Burgess, Lauren Cook, ed. *An Uncommon Soldier: The Civil War Letters of Sarah Rosetta Wakeman.* Pasadena, Md.: Minerva Center, 1994.

Campbell, Edward D. C., Jr., and Kym S. Rice, eds. *A Woman's War: Southern Women, Civil War, and the Confederate Legacy.* Richmond: Museum of the Confederacy and University Press of Virginia, Charlottesville, 1996.

Carroll, John M. *List of Field Officers, Regiments and Battalions in the Confederate States Army, 1861–1865.* Mattituck, N.Y.: J. M. Carroll, 1983.

Cashman, Diane Cobb. *Headstrong: The Biography of Amy Morris Bradley, 1823–1904: A Life of Noblest Usefulness.* Wilmington, N.C.: Broadfoot Publishing, 1990.

Christie, Jeanne. "'No Place for a Woman': City Point, Virginia, 1864–1865." *Journal of Women's Civil War History* 1 (2001): 26–38.

Clausius, Gerhard P. "The Little Soldier of the 95th: Albert D. J. Cashier." *Journal of the Illinois State Historical Society* 51, 4 (Winter 1958): 380–387.

Clinton, Catherine. *Harriet Tubman: The Road to Freedom.* New York: Little, Brown, 2004.

Coco, Gregory A. *On the Bloodstained Field.* Hollidaysburg, Pa.: Wheatfield Press, 1987.

Coffin, Charles Carleton. *Four Years of Fighting.* Boston: Ticknor and Fields, 1866.

Cole, Garold L. *Civil War Eyewitnesses: An Annotated Bibliography of Books and Articles, 1955–1986.* Columbia: University of South Carolina Press, 1988.

Collis, Septima M. *A Woman's War Record.* New York: G. P. Putnam's Sons, 1889.

Conklin, Eileen F. *Women at Gettysburg, 1863.* Gettysburg, Pa.: Thomas Publications, 1993.

Cozzens, Peter. *This Terrible Sound: The Battle of Chickamauga.* Urbana: University of Illinois Press, 1992.

Crute, Joseph H., Jr. *Confederate Staff Officers, 1861–1865.* Powhatan, Va.: Derwent Books, 1982.

———. *Units of the Confederate States Army.* Midlothian, Va.: Derwent Books, 1987.

Culpepper, Marilyn Mayer. *Trials and Triumphs: The Women of the American Civil War.* East Lansing: Michigan State University Press, 1991.

Cunningham, Horace H. *Field Medical Services at the Battles of Manassas (Bull Run).* Athens: University of Georgia Press, 1968.

Curtis, Newton Martin. *From Bull Run to Chancellorsville: The Story of the Sixteenth New York Infantry together with Personal Reminiscences.* New York: G. P. Putnam's Sons, 1906.

Dannett, Sylvia G. L. *She Rode with the Generals: The True and Incredible Story of Sarah Emma Seelye, Alias Franklin Thompson.* New York: Thomas Nelson and Sons, 1960.

———. *Noble Women of the North.* New York: Thomas Yoseloff, 1959.

Dannett, Sylvia G. L., and Katharine M. Jones. *Our Women of the Sixties.* Washington, D.C.: U.S. Civil War Centennial Commission, 1963.

Darst, Maury. "Robert Hodges, Jr., Confederate Soldier." *East Texas Historical Journal* 9, 1 (1971): 37–38.

Davis, Curtis Carroll. "Effie Goldsborough: Confederate Courier." *Civil War Times Illustrated* 7 (1968): 29–31.

Davis, Rodney O. "Private Albert Cashier as Regarded by His/Her Comrades." *Journal of the Illinois State Historical Society* 82, 2 (Summer 1989): 108–112.

Dornbusch, C. E. *Military Bibliography of the Civil War.* 3 vols. New York: New York Public Library, 1972.

Dyer, Frederick H. *A Compendium of the War of the Rebellion.* New York: Thomas Yoseloff, 1959. Vol. 1: Number and Organization of the Armies of the United States; Vol. 2: Chronological Record of the Campaigns, Battles, Engagements, Actions, Combats, Sieges, Etc., in the United States, 1861 to 1865; Vol. 3: Regimental Histories.

Edmonds, S. Emma E. *Nurse and Spy in the Union Army: Comprising the Adventures and Experiences of a Woman in Hospitals, Camps, and Battle-Fields.* Hartford, Conn.: W. S. Williams, 1864.

Faust, Drew Gilpin. *Mothers of Invention: Women of the Slaveholding South in the American Civil War.* Chapel Hill: University of North Carolina Press, 1996.

Faust, Patricia L., ed. *Historical Times Illustrated Encyclopedia of the Civil War.* New York: Harper & Row, 1986.

Feis, William B. *Grant's Secret Service: The Intelligence War from Belmont to Appomattox.* Lincoln: University of Nebraska Press, 2002.

Fishel, Edwin C. *The Secret War for the Union: The Untold Story of Military Intelligence in the Civil War.* Boston: Houghton Mifflin, 1996.

Fisher, Louis. *Military Tribunals and Presidential Power: American Revolution to the War on Terrorism.* Lawrence: University Press of Kansas, 2005.

Fitzpatrick, Michael F. "The Mercy Brigade: Roman Catholic Nuns in the Civil War." *Civil War Times Illustrated* 36, 5 (1997): 34–40.

Fladeland, Betty. "Alias Franklin Thompson." *Michigan History* 42 (1958): 435, 438–439.

——. "New Light on Sarah Emma Edmonds, Alias Franklin Thompson." *Michigan History* 47 (1963): 357–362.

Fletcher, William A. *Rebel Private: Front and Rear: Memoirs of a Confederate Soldier.* New York: Meridian Books, 1995.

Foner, Eric, and John A. Garraty, eds. *The Reader's Companion to American History.* Boston: Houghton Mifflin, 1991.

Forbes, Ella. *African American Women during the Civil War.* New York: Garland Publishing, 1998.

Foster, John Y. "Four Days at Gettysburg." *Civil War Times Illustrated* 11, 1 (1972): 19–23.

Fowler, William W. *Woman on the American Frontier.* Hartford, Conn.: S.S. Scranton, 1877.

Frankel, Noralee. *Freedom's Women: Black Women and Families in Civil War Era Mississippi.* Bloomington: Indiana University Press, 1999.

Freemantle, Arthur J. L. *Three Months in the Southern States.* London: William Blackwood & Sons, 1863.

Galbraith, William, and Loretta Galbraith, eds. *A Lost Heroine of the Confederacy: The Diaries and Letters of Belle Edmondson*. Jackson: University Press of Mississippi, 1990.

Gardner, Ira B. *Recollections of a Boy Member of Co. I, Fourteenth Maine Volunteers, 1861–1865*. Lewiston, Maine: Lewiston Journal, 1902.

Gerteis, Louis S. *Civil War St. Louis*. Lawrence: University Press of Kansas, 2001.

Gilbert, Olive. *Narrative of Sojourner Truth: A Bondswoman of Olden Time, With a History of Her Labors and Correspondence, Drawn from Her Book of Life*. New York: Penguin Books, 1998.

Ginzberg, Lori D. *Women in Antebellum Reform*. Wheeling, Ill.: Harlan Davidson, 2000.

Glatthaar, Joseph T. *The March to the Sea and Beyond: Sherman's Troops in the Savannah and Carolinas Campaigns*. New York: New York University Press, 1989.

Greenbie, Marjorie Barstow. *Lincoln's Daughters of Mercy*. New York: G.P. Putnam's Sons, 1944.

Grimm, Herbert L., and Paul L. Roy. *Human Interest Stories of the Three Days' Battles at Gettysburg*. Gettysburg, Pa.: Gettysburg Times & News Publishing, 1927.

Hall, Richard. *Patriots in Disguise: Women Warriors of the Civil War*. New York: Paragon House, 1993.

——. "Women in Battle in the Civil War." In *American History, Volume I: Pre-Colonial through Reconstruction*, ed. Robert James Maddox. University Park: Pennsylvania State University, 1995, 197–200.

——. "Loreta Janeta Velazquez: Civil War Soldier and Spy." In *Cubans in the Confederacy: Jose Agustin Quintero, Ambrosio Jose Gonzales, and Loreta Janeta Velazquez*, ed. Phillip Thomas Tucker. Jefferson, N.C.: McFarland, 2002, 225–239.

Halsey, Ashley, ed. *A Yankee Private's Civil War*. Chicago: Henry Regnery, 1961.

Hanna, Alfred Jackson, and Kathryn Abbey Hanna. *Confederate Exiles in Venezuela*. Confederate Centennial Studies No. 15. Tuscaloosa, Ala.: Confederate Publishing, 1960.

Hess, Earl J. *The Union Soldier in Battle: Enduring the Ordeal of Combat*. Lawrence: University Press of Kansas, 1997.

Hewitt, Nancy A. *Women's Activism and Social Change: Rochester, New York, 1822–1872*. Ithaca, N.Y.: Cornell University Press, 1984.

Hodge, Robert W., ed. *The Civil War Letters of Perry Mayo*. East Lansing: Michigan State University, 1967.

Holland, Mary A. Gardner. *Our Army Nurses*. Boston: Lounsbery, Nichols & Worth, 1897.

Horan, James D. *Confederate Agent: A Discovery in History*. New York: Crown Publishers, 1954.

Hughes, Susan Lyons. "The Daughter of the Regiment: A Brief History of *Vivandieres* and *Cantinieres* in the American Civil War," http://www.civilwarweb.com/articles/05-00/vivandieres.htm.

Hurn, Ethel Alice. *Wisconsin Women in the War between the States.* Original Papers No. 6. Wisconsin History Commission, 1911.

Ingraham, Betty. "Masquerade of Mary Owen Jenkins." *Civil War Times* (June 1959): 7.

Jaquette, Henrietta Stratton. *South After Gettysburg: Letters of Cornelia Hancock, 1863–1868.* New York: Thomas Y. Crowell, 1956.

Johnson, Whittington B. "Free African-American Women in Savannah: Affluence and Autonomy amid Adversity." *Georgia Historical Quarterly* 66 (1992): 260–283.

Jolly, Ellen Ryan. *Nuns of the Battlefield.* Providence, R.I.: Providence Visitor Press, 1927.

Jones, Gordon W. "Wartime Surgery." *Civil War Times Illustrated* 2 (1963): 7–9.

——. "Sanitation in the Civil War." *Civil War Times Illustrated* 5 (1966): 12–18.

Jones, John B. *A Rebel War Clerk's Diary.* Philadelphia: J. B. Lippincott, 1866.

Jones, Katharine M., ed. *Heroines of Dixie: Confederate Women Tell Their Story of the War.* Indianapolis: Bobbs-Merrill, 1955.

Jones, Terry L. *Lee's Tigers: The Louisiana Infantry in the Army of Northern Virginia.* Baton Rouge: Louisiana State University Press, 1987.

Joslyn, Mauriel Phillips, ed. *Confederate Women.* Gretna, La.: Pelican Publishing, 2004.

Josyph, Peter, ed. *The Wounded River: The Civil War Letters of John Vance Lauderdale, M.D.* East Lansing: Michigan State University Press, 1993.

Kane, Harnett T. *Spies for the Blue and Gray.* New York: Doubleday, 1954.

King, G. Wayne. "Death Camp at Florence." *Civil War Times Illustrated* 12, 9 (1974): 34–42.

King, Lisa Y. "In Search of Women of African Descent Who Served in the Civil War Union Navy." *The Journal of Negro History* 84 (1998): 302–309.

Kinsley, D. A. *Custer: Favor the Bold: A Soldier's Story.* New York: Promontory Press, 1988.

Kirkland, Frazar. *Pictorial Book of Anecdotes and Incidents of the War of the Rebellion.* Hartford, Conn.: Hartford Publishing, 1867.

Larson, C. Kay. "Bonny Yank and Ginny Reb." *Minerva* 8, 1 (Spring 1990): 33–48.

——. "Bonny Yank and Ginny Reb Revisited." *Minerva* 10, 2 (Summer 1992): 35–61.

Larson, Rebecca. *Blue and Gray Roses of Intrigue.* Gettysburg, Pa.: Thomas Publications, 1993.

Lauter, Don Richard. "Arabella Wharton Griffith Barlow." *Journal of Women's Civil War History* 1 (2001): 8–25.

Lee, George R. "Scene Aboard Ship Loaded with Wounded." *Civil War Times Illustrated* 5, 3 (1966): 48–49.

Leech, Margaret. *Reveille in Washington, 1860–1865.* New York: Harper & Brothers, 1941.

Leeper, Wesley Thurman. *Rebels Valiant: Second Arkansas Mounted Rifles (Dismounted).* Little Rock, Ark.: Pioneer Press, 1964.

Leonard, Elizabeth D. *All the Daring of the Soldier: Women of the Civil War Armies*. New York: W. W. Norton, 1999.

Livermore, Mary A. *My Story of the War*. Hartford, Conn.: A. D. Worthington, 1887.

Livermore, Thomas L. *Numbers and Losses in the Civil War in America, 1861–1865*. Carlisle, Pa.: John Kallmann, 1996. Reprint of 1900 edition.

Logan, Mrs. John A. *The Part Taken by Women in American History*. Wilmington, Del.: Perry-Nalle Publishing, 1912.

Longacre, Edward G. "Boots and Saddles, Part I: The Eastern Theater: A Short History of the Cavalry during the Civil War." *Civil War Times Illustrated* 31, 1 (1992): 35–40.

——. *Custer and His Wolverines: The Michigan Cavalry Brigade, 1861–1865*. Conshohocken, Pa.: Combined Publishing, 1997.

Lonn, Ella. *Foreigners in the Confederacy*. Chapel Hill: University of North Carolina Press, 2002.

Lord, Francis A. *They Fought for the Union*. New York: Bonanza Books, 1960.

Lowry, Thomas P. *The Story the Soldiers Wouldn't Tell: Sex in the Civil War*. Mechanicsburg, Pa.: Stackpole Books, 1994.

——. "The Army's Licensed Prostitutes." *Civil War Times Illustrated* 41, 4 (2002): 30–35.

Lucas, Scott J. "High Expectations: African Americans in Civil War Kentucky." *Negro History Bulletin* 1 (January 2001):19–22.

Lyman, Darryl. *Civil War Wordbook: Including Sayings, Phrases and Slang*. Conshohocken, Pa.: Combined Books, 1994.

MacCaskill, Libby, and David Novak. *Ladies on the Field: Two Civil War Nurses from Maine on the Battlefields of Virginia*. Livermore, Maine: Signal Tree Publications, 1996.

McDowell, John E. "Nathaniel Banks; Fighting Politico." *Civil War Times Illustrated* 11, 9 (1973): 4–9, 44–47.

McKay, Charlotte E. *Stories of Hospital and Camp*. Philadelphia: Claxton, Remsen & Haffelfinger, 1876.

Maher, Sister Mary Denis. *To Bind Up the Wounds: Catholic Sister Nurses in the U.S. Civil War*. Baton Rouge: Louisiana State University Press, 1989.

Markle, Donald E. *Spies and Spymasters of the Civil War*. New York: Hippocrene Books, 1994.

Mason, Philip P., and Paul J. Pentecost. *From Bull Run to Appomattox: Michigan's Role in the Civil War*. Detroit: Wayne State University, 1961.

Massey, Mary Elizabeth. *Bonnet Brigades*. New York: Alfred A. Knopf, 1966.

May, George S. *Michigan and the Civil War Years, 1860–1866: A Wartime Chronicle*. Michigan Civil War Centennial Observance Commission, 1964; 2nd edition, 1966.

Mazzula, Fred M., and William Kostka. *Mountain Charlie or the Adventures of Mrs. E. J. Guerin, Who Was Thirteen Years in Male Attire*. Norman: University of Oklahoma Press, 1968.

Mellon, Knox, Jr. "Letters of James Greenalch." *Michigan History* 44 (June 1960): 188–240.

Meriwether, Elizabeth Avery. *Recollections of 92 Years*. McLean, Va.: EPM Publications, 1994. (Original publication Nashville: Tennessee Historical Commission, 1958.)

Mescher, Virginia. "Military Laundresses in the Civil War." *Journal of Women's Civil War History* 1 (2001): 39–56.

Middleton, Lee. *Hearts of Fire: Soldier Women of the Civil War*. Torch, Ohio: privately published, 1993.

Millbrook, Minnie D. "Michigan Women Who Went to War." In Michigan Civil War Centennial Observance Commission, *Michigan Women in the Civil War* [Lansing], 1963.

Mills, H. Sinclair, Jr. *The Vivandiere: History, Tradition, Uniform and Service*. Collinswood, N.J.: C. W. Historicals, 1988.

Mogelever, Jacob. *Death to Traitors: The Story of Lafayette C. Baker, Lincoln's Forgotten Secret Service Chief*. Garden City, N.Y.: Doubleday, 1960.

Moore, Edward A. *The Story of a Cannoneer under Stonewall Jackson*. New York: Neale Publishing, 1907; reprint Time-Life Books, 1983.

Moore, Frank. *Women of the War: Their Heroism and Self-Sacrifice*. Hartford, Conn: Scranton, 1866.

——, ed. *Anecdotes, Poetry and Incidents of the War: North and South, 1860–1865*. New York: Bible House, 1867.

——. *The Civil War in Song and Story*. New York: P. F. Collier, 1889.

Morton, Joseph W., Jr., ed. *Sparks from the Camp Fire: Tales of the Old Veterans*. Philadelphia: Keystone Publishing, 1895.

Muir, Charles S. *Women: The Makers of History*. New York: Vantage Press, 1956.

O'Brien, Jean Getman. "Clara Barton Brought Mercy to Antietam." *Civil War Times Illustrated* 1, 5 (1962): 38–40.

——. "Mrs. Mary Ann (Mother) Bickerdyke: 'The Brigadier Commanding Hospitals.'" *Civil War Times Illustrated* 1, 9 (1963): 21–24.

O'Brien, Jean Getman, and Robert D. Hoffsommer. "Dorothea Dix: A Personality Profile." *Civil War Times Illustrated* 4, 5 (1965): 39–44.

Official Records of the Union and Confederate Armies. [The War of the Rebellion: A Compilation of the Official Records of the Union and Confederate Armies]. Washington, D.C.: Government Printing Office, 1884.

Parker, Sandra V. *Richmond's Civil War Prisons*. Lynchburg, Va.: H. E. Howard, 1990.

Pinkerton, Allan. *The Spy of the Rebellion: Being a True History of the Spy System of the United States Army during the Late Rebellion*. Hartford, Conn.: M. A. Winter & Hatch, 1883.

Pryor, Elizabeth Brown. *Clara Barton: Professional Angel*. Philadelphia: University of Pennsylvania Press, 1987.

Rable, George C. *Civil Wars: Women and the Crisis of Southern Nationalism*. Urbana: University of Illinois Press, 1989.

Ransom, John. *John Ransom's Andersonville Diary*. New York: Berkley Books, 1988.

Raus, Edmund J., Jr. *Ministering Angel: The Reminiscences of Harriet A. Dada, a Union Army Nurse in the Civil War*. Gettysburg, Pa.: Thomas Publications, 2004.

Rhoades, Priscilla. "The Women of Castle Thunder," *Kudzu Monthly* (ezine), August 2002 (http://www.kudzumonthly.com/kudzu/aug02/CastleThunder.html).

Richardson, Albert D. *The Secret Service, the Field, the Dungeon, and the Escape.* Hartford, Conn.: American Publishing, 1865.

Richman, Irwin. "Pauline Cushman, She Was a Heroine but Not a Lady: A Personality Profile." *Civil War Times Illustrated* 7, 10 (1969): 38–44.

Ridley, Bromfield L. *Battles and Sketches of the Army of the Tennessee.* Mexico, Mo.: Missouri Printing and Publishing, 1906.

Riggs, David F. *13th Virginia Infantry.* Lynchburg, Va.: H. E. Howard, 1988.

Robertson, James I., Jr., ed. "An Indiana Soldier in Love and War: The Civil War Letters of John V. Hadley." *Indiana Magazine of History* 59, 3 (September 1963): 237–238.

Robertson, John, comp. *Michigan in the War.* Lansing, Mich.: W. S. George, 1882.

Sauls, Diana. "The Sunset Gun: The Story of Mary Ann Bickerdyke, Civil War Nurse." *Civil War: The Magazine of the Civil War Society* 21 (1989): 28–38.

Schultz, Jane E. *Women at the Front: Hospital Workers in Civil War America.* Chapel Hill: University of North Carolina Press, 2004.

Scott, J. L. *36th Virginia Infantry.* Lynchburg, Va.: H.E. Howard, 1987.

Sears, Stephen W., ed. *On Campaign With the Army of the Potomac: The Civil War Journal of Theodore Ayrault Dodge.* New York: Cooper Square Press, 2001.

Sheridan, Philip H. *Personal Memoirs*, Vol. 1. New York: Charles L. Webster, 1888.

Sifakis, Stewart. *Who Was Who in the Confederacy.* New York: Facts on File, 1988.

——. *Who Was Who in the Union.* New York: Facts on File, 1988.

Simkins, Francis Butler, and James Welch Patton. *The Women of the Confederacy.* Richmond, Va.: Garrett and Massie, 1936.

Smith, Adelaide W. *Reminiscences of an Army Nurse during the Civil War.* New York, Greaves Publishing, 1911.

Smith, H. B. *Between the Lines: Secret Service Stories Told Fifty Years After.* New York: Booz Brothers, 1911.

Sparks, David S., ed. *Inside Lincoln's Army: The Diary of Marsena Rudolph Patrick, Provost Marshal General, Army of the Potomac.* New York: Thomas Yoseloff, 1964.

Squires, Charles W. "My Artillery Fire Was Very Destructive." *Civil War Times Illustrated* 14, 3 (1975): 18–29.

Sterkx, H. E. *Some Notable Alabama Women during the Civil War.* University: Alabama Civil War Centennial Commission, 1962.

——. "Juliet Ann Opie Hopkins–'The Angel of the South,'" http://www.mindspring.com/~redeagle/Oakwood/Hopkins.htm.

Stevens, Peter F. *Rebels in Blue: The Story of Keith and Malinda Blalock.* Dallas, Tex.: Taylor Publishing, 2000.

Straubing, Harold Elk, comp. *In Hospital and Camp: The Civil War through the Eyes of Its Doctors and Nurses.* Harrisburg, Pa.: Stackpole Books, 1993.

Stutler, Boyd B. "Nancy Hart, Lady Bushwhacker." *Civil War Times Illustrated* 1, 9 (1960): 7.

Sudlow, Lynda L. *A Vast Army of Women: Maine's Uncounted Forces in the American Civil War.* Gettysburg, Pa.: Thomas Publications, 2000.

Taylor, Charles E. *The Signal and Secret Service of the Confederate States.* Harmans, Md.: Toomey Press, 1986.

Taylor, Susie King. *A Black Woman's Civil War Memoirs: Reminiscences of My Life in Camp with the 33rd U.S. Colored Troops, Late 1st South Carolina Volunteers,* ed. Patricia W. Romero and Willie Lee Rose (originally self-published in 1902 as *Reminiscences of My Life in Camp with the 33rd U.S. Colored Troops, Late 1st South Carolina Volunteers*). Princeton, N.J.: Markus Wiener, 1997.

Tennessee Civil War Centennial Commission. *Tennesseans in the Civil War: A Military History of Confederate and Union Units with Available Rosters of Personnel,* Part 1. Nashville, Tenn., 1964.

Thomas, Martha. "Amazing Mary." *Civil War Times Illustrated* 23, 1 (1984): 37–41.

Tidwell, William A. *Come Retribution: The Confederate Secret Service and the Assassination of Lincoln.* Jackson: University Press of Mississippi, 1988.

——. *Confederate Covert Action in the American Civil War: April '65.* Kent, Ohio: Kent State University Press, 1995.

Truesdale, John. *The Blue Coats, and How They Lived, Fought, and Died for the Union.* Philadelphia: Jones Brothers, 1867.

Tucker, Phillip Thomas, ed. *Cubans in the Confederacy: José Agustín Quintero, Ambrosio José Gonzales, and Loreta Janeta Velazquez.* Jefferson, N.C.: McFarland, 2002.

Vickery, Richard. "On the Duties of a Surgeon in Action." *Civil War Times Illustrated* 17, 3 (1978): 12–23.

Wade, Richard C. *Slavery in the Cities: The South, 1820–1860.* New York: Oxford University Press, 1964.

Warner, Ezra J. *Generals in Blue: Lives of the Union Commanders.* Baton Rouge: Louisiana State University Press, 1989.

——. *Generals in Gray: Lives of the Confederate Commanders.* Baton Rouge: Louisiana State University Press, 1989.

Werlich, Robert. "Mary Walker: From Union Army Surgeon to Sideshow Freak." *Civil War Times Illustrated* 6, 3 (1967): 46–49.

Wert, Jeffry D. *From Winchester to Cedar Creek: The Shenandoah Campaign of 1864.* Carlisle, Pa.: South Mountain Press, 1987.

Wheelwright, Julie. *Amazons and Military Maids: Women Who Dressed as Men in the Pursuit of Life, Liberty and Happiness.* London: Pandora Press, 1989.

Wilbur, C. Keith, M.D. *Civil War Medicine, 1861–1865.* Old Saybrook, Conn.: Globe Pequot Press, 1998.

Wiley, Bell I. *Confederate Women.* Westport, Conn.: Greenwood Press, 1975.

——. *The Life of Johnny Reb: The Common Soldier of the Confederacy.* Baton Rouge: Louisiana State University Press, 1978.

——. *The Life of Billy Yank: The Common Soldier of the Union.* Baton Rouge: Louisiana State University Press, 1978.

Wormeley, Katharine Prescott. *The Other Side of War: On the Hospital Transports with the Army of the Potomac.* Boston: Ticknor, 1889; reprint Gansevoort, N.Y.: Corner House Historical Publications, 1998.

Worthington, C. J., ed. *The Woman in Battle.* Hartford, Conn.: T. Belknap, 1876.

Young, Agatha. *The Women and the Crisis: Women of the North in the Civil War.* New York: McDowell, Obolensky, 1959.

INDEX

BOCA RATON PUBLIC LIBRARY, FLORIDA

3 3656 0455744 7

973.7082 Hal
Hall, Richard,
Women on the Civil War
 battlefront /